The Reader's Digest Good Health Cookbooks

FISH AND MEAT

The Reader's Digest Good Health Cookbooks

FISH AND MEAT

THE READER'S DIGEST ASSOCIATION INC., PLEASANTVILLE, NEW YORK ● MONTREAL

The Reader's Digest Good Health Cookbooks—FISH AND MEAT

The acknowledgements that appear on page 192 are hereby made a part of this copyright page.

Material in this book has previously appeared in *Creative Cooking* © 1977 The Reader's Digest Association, Inc. and *The Cookery Year* © 1973 The Reader's Digest Association Ltd.

First Edition

Library of Congress Catalog Card Number 85–62336

ISBN 0–89577–222–1

THE READER'S DIGEST and are registered trademarks of the Reader's Digest Association, Inc.

Printed in Great Britain

Contents

How to use
The Good Health Cookbooks

Dieting need not be dreary. Whatever diet you may follow, you can still enjoy the classic dishes. Often, all you need are alternative ingredients that suit the recipe and suit the requirements of your diet. This book gives you the recipes for those classic dishes from *Creative Cooking*. It also gives you those vital alternatives. It has, in fact, several features unique in cookery books. In the special "Alternatives" column on each page, we identify how high each recipe is in salt, sugar, fat, cholesterol, and fiber. We also give the calorie count. We check if it is gluten-free and wholefood. Then we suggest how you could adapt the recipe to any diet you, your family, or your guests might want to follow.

We do not lay down what diet you should follow. That is your decision. The book assumes that you yourself know what you want to do and tries to help you to do it by making suggestions (not commands), some or all of which you may want to follow. Perhaps you have been told to cut down drastically on salt; perhaps you have been thinking for some time that you should eat a little less sugar; perhaps you have a friend coming to a meal who cannot eat gluten or who is avoiding food high in cholesterol. You do not have to buy a new cookbook for each diet. You do not have to produce alternative meals for every guest. With these books, you can simply adapt the existing recipes to suit your needs.

You will find that we make use of a few conventions. This is mainly in order to avoid constant repetition. **The asterisk** (★) is used as follows:

1) Salt★ indicates that this item may be omitted for those on a low-salt diet; the salt level of the recipe as given in the "Alternatives" column is calculated on the assumption that this salt has been omitted and that any ingredients that sometimes contain salt and sometimes don't (e.g. canned tomatoes) have been bought in their salt-free version.

2) Gluten-free★ indicates that the recipe is free of gluten so long as gluten-free flour (or bread or breadcrumbs) is used where appropriate.

3) Wholefood★ indicates that the recipe is wholefood if whole wheat flour (or bread or bread crumbs), brown rice and unrefined sugar are used where appropriate.

The levels of salt, **sugar**, **fat**, **cholesterol** and **fiber** for each recipe are denoted by symbols in the "Alternatives" column:

HIGH   MEDIUM   LOW   NEGLIGIBLE

For definitions of what constitutes a high threshold level of any one of these, see under the appropriate diet on the following pages. Less than half this threshold level is considered low.

Calorie counts are given, firstly for the recipe as a whole and secondly as an indication of how many calories may be avoided as a result of following particular alternative suggestions.

Calories are automatically lost when either sugar or fat is significantly reduced. The calculations for calorie-loss can be no more than approximate, and occasionally are omitted, as so many factors can vary: the fat level of fish and meat at different times of the year, the exact amount of fat trimmed off a cut of meat, or the amount of sugar that will make a dish acceptably sweet to a particular palate.

Cooking hints on when it is appropriate or helpful to use a pressure cooker, slow cooker, food processor, freezer or microwave are indicated by a tick, together with any further information required. With a microwave it is always essential that you also consult the manufacturer's instructions, as cooking times vary from oven to oven.

With practice you should find that the technique and alternatives recommended in this book will work with recipes from other books. In this way it becomes simple to adapt recipes so that they are both healthy and delicious. That is how it ought to be.

The Diets

Low-salt diet

Sodium is acknowledged to be a contributory factor in hypertension (high blood pressure) and thus in coronary heart disease and strokes; it can also be involved in some kidney disorders.

By far the most concentrated source of sodium is common salt (sodium chloride), and many processed foods contain a lot of added salt.

Diets which are very severely restricted in sodium are on occasion prescribed, but we are not concerned with them here. A certain minimum of both sodium and chloride is essential to good health, and the majority of salt-conscious people will simply want to cut out excessive consumption.

While setting an exact figure is very difficult, as the total level of salt in a meal depends on the combination of foods eaten, a target of 5 grams a day (generally considered to be not excessive) can usually be reached by cutting down on cooking or table salt as well as on monosodium glutamate. Foods such as salted or cured pork products and most cheeses should be eaten only in small quantities. Then the sodium occurring naturally in meat and fish, even in sodium-rich shellfish, need not be avoided.

It is important to check the labels on cans. Some tomatoes, for instance, are canned with added salt, others not. Egg whites and dried fruit are also relatively high in sodium and should not be overindulged in.

Salt substitutes are available but we do not specify them: they do not taste like salt and anyone suffering from heart or kidney disease should not take them without medical approval.

Many of those wishing to cut down on salt will also want to combine this with cutting down on fat. Therefore, for example, although heavy cream contains much less sodium than light cream or milk does, we do not advocate replacing milk with heavy cream.

Salt is used to to mean both common salt (sodium chloride) and sodium in general. Where the level of salt in the recipe is given, this takes into account sodium occurring naturally in the ingredients; in the list of ingredients, salt refers, as usual, to the sodium chloride commonly used for seasoning.

The salt content of a recipe is taken to be high if it contains the equivalent of more than 2 egg whites or $1\frac{1}{4}$ cups of milk per person.

Low-sugar diet

Sugar is "empty calories:" it provides no nutrients, but concentrated calories for a very little weight of food.

Sugar is the first thing to go if you are on a calorie-controlled diet. It is also known to encourage tooth decay; and high consumption, especially of refined sugar, has been correlated with certain diseases.

Refined sugar is pure sucrose, the form of sugar which is the least desirable. Sugar occurs naturally in other forms – for example, fructose in fruit, lactose in milk, dextrose (glucose) and maltose. These do not always have the same harmful effect on the body as sucrose, and are not eaten in anything like the same sort of quantity.

A low-sugar diet, therefore, usually aims at cutting out as much refined sugar as possible. This can be done simply by using less of it and deliberately cultivating a less sweet tooth, or by replacing it to some extent with other forms of sugar. Honey, for instance (which is mainly fructose and glucose, with little sucrose) is sweeter than sugar so less of it is needed. In this way you can cut down on both sucrose and the total quantity of sugar. Molasses, although a form of sucrose, has a very strong taste and again a teaspoon of it can sometimes be used instead of a tablespoon or more of sugar.

In this book, when the level of sugar in a recipe is indicated, it takes into account both the general level of sugar, including all its various forms – sucrose, fructose, glucose etc. – as well as any added sugar specified in the recipe. In the list of ingredients, sugar refers to the added sugar which is virtually pure sucrose. The suggestions for decreasing the sugar content of a recipe almost always refer to sucrose.

We are not concerned here with sugar substitutes nor with special diabetic sweeteners and jams. We do not aim to preserve an ultra-sweet taste. What we aim to do is to cut down the amount of refined sugar and to make more use of fruit and of small quantities of honey and molasses. The results will be definitely less sweet but still delicious.

The sugar content of a recipe is taken to be high if it contains the equivalent of more than 1 tablespoon of sugar per person.

Low-fat and low-cholesterol diets

One of the most common reasons for eating less fat and cholesterol is that there appears to be an undisputed link between the presence of cholesterol in the blood and liability to heart attacks.

Populations who eat less fat have lower levels of heart disease, although their consumption of oil may be high, as in many Mediterranean countries. The exact link has not yet been established, and it appears that other foods, for example garlic, onions and polyunsaturated fat, as well as fiber, have the ability to lower blood cholesterol. However, more and more people are coming to the conclusion that cutting down on fats, especially saturated fats, cannot do them any harm. Certainly it will help calorie control: fat contains twice as many calories per ounce as protein or carbohydrate.

Whether you want to lose weight or reduce the risk of a heart attack, low-fat and low-cholesterol diets are similar in many ways. Both encourage cutting down on the saturated fats which contain cholesterol.

Saturated fats are usually of animal origin but not always: coconuts, for example, have a saturated fat content of 83%. Unsaturated fats are mainly of vegetable origin and are further divided into monounsaturated and polyunsaturated fats. (These terms refer to the way in which their molecules are chemically bonded.) They are generally liquid at room temperature.

Monounsaturated fats (the most usual example is olive oil, which is 73% monounsaturated fat) have no effect on the level of cholesterol in the blood. Polyunsaturated fats can in fact, as stated above, actually lower the blood cholesterol level. There are a few foods which are very high in cholesterol relative to their fat content, notably shellfish, fish roes, and variety meats such as liver, kidney, brains and sweetbreads.

Those on a low-fat diet will want to cut down on all fats and oils. Those aiming at a low-cholesterol intake will want to eliminate as far as possible all saturated fats and will be cautious about shellfish and variety meats. This book shows you how to do either or both of these.

However the book does not purport to give a diet which actually lowers blood cholesterol. For instance, in the recipes olive oil is often specified. Those on such a diet will replace olive oil with safflower, soy or sunflower oils. Nor does this book attempt to give a fat-free diet. Such a diet should only be attempted under medical supervision, and even then it is bound to have a minimal fat content. Some fat is necessary in our diet, particularly linoleic acid, an essential fatty acid, which cannot be manufactured by the body: it is found in oils, particularly safflower oil.

Some particular foods that will be found useful in both low-fat and low-cholesterol diets are:
- skim milk, both liquid and dried
- low-fat cheese, particularly cottage cheese and low-fat curd cheese, such as quark or fromage blanc
- low-fat imitation sour cream (5–10% fat as opposed to 18% in dairy sour cream)

For low-cholesterol diets:
- safflower, soy, sunflower and walnut oils
- (for frying over high heat): corn or peanut oils. It is, however, better to avoid frying over high heat as far as possible, since this changes the composition of the oils into something resembling saturated fat
- soft margarines with a high percentage of polyunsaturated oils (all margarines labeled "all vegetable" are virtually cholesterol-free)

The fat and cholesterol content of eggs is found only in the yolks, but in many cases yolks can be decreased or omitted, sometimes with a proportionate increase in the number of whites used.

The fat content of a recipe is taken to be high if it contains the equivalent of more than any 2 of the following per person:

1 tablespoon heavy cream or oil
$\frac{1}{2}$ tablespoon butter, lard, suet or margarine
1 egg yolk
$\frac{1}{2}$ ounce ham, bacon, pork or cheese

The above applies also to the cholesterol content of a recipe, except that unsaturated oils are freely allowed, and over $\frac{1}{2}$ an egg yolk is considered to be high.

Fiber

The importance of fiber in the diet is now widely recognized, and many people pursue a high-fiber diet.

Since one of the best and easiest ways of increasing fiber intake is to eat a slice or two of whole wheat bread with your meal, the recipes themselves have not (except in one or two cases) been modified to include more fiber. The original versions of the recipes are already based on fresh ingredients, including vegetables, fruit and nuts (most of which are high in fiber), and wholefood adaptations are available for almost all the recipes, thus helping to increase the fiber level.

Gluten-free diet

As celiac sufferers are being identified more and more frequently, so the need for a gluten-free diet for them and for other gluten-sensitive patients is becoming widely recognized.

A gluten-free diet involves complete exclusion of gluten (a protein, found mainly in wheat but also, in a different form and to a lesser extent, in rye, barley and oats). Commercial gluten-free flour is available and can be used successfully for bread, and some pastry and cakes; if it is difficult to find or expensive to buy just for one recipe, there are other flours, many of which are familiar to those on wholefood diets, which are gluten-free. Chick pea flour, brown rice flour, cornstarch, potato starch and soy flour are perhaps the best known.

All labels on cans and jars must be carefully read, as wheat flour is a common ingredient not just in the obvious breads, cookies, cakes, pastries and many cereals, but in packet soups, baking powder, sausages, bouillon cubes, bottled sauces and baked beans as well as in some brands of mustard, ground white pepper, curry powder and cheap chocolate.

Gluten-free grains include rice, maize, millet and buckwheat. Cornstarch, chick pea flour and split pea flour are all suitable for making white sauces. For soufflés, cornstarch and potato starch (the latter is denser than wheat flour and half the amount given in the recipe is usually enough) can be used. Any of these will do for coating food which is to be fried. Millet flakes make a good gluten-free alternative to a breadcrumb coating.

As a gluten-free diet is often low in fiber, it is advisable to eat plenty of brown rice, other whole grains and potatoes. Pectin (available dried from specialist suppliers) can be used as a binding agent in doughs and batters; grated fresh apple can also sometimes be used.

Intolerance of gluten is often associated with an inability to digest fats, so that a low-fat diet may also need to be followed.

Wholefood diet

Since the recipes in this book are based firmly on fresh seasonal produce, they need little alteration to be acceptable to lovers of wholefood.

The main items to avoid are refined flour and sugar. Whole wheat flour and bread, and brown rice or sugar, can be used instead as desired. When buying brown sugar, look for the name of the country of origin on the packet. If this is not given, the sugar may be white sugar that has been colored brown with caramel.

In the case of sugar, it may also be necessary to follow any suggestion given for reducing the total, as a high level of even the comparatively unrefined brown sugar is not usually considered wholefood. Anything other than this will be covered in the Alternatives column. Where quantities or proportions are affected, as for instance in baking, this will also be covered.

Fish

TRADITIONAL SEAFOOD CHOWDER

A hearty fish chowder – or soup cum stew – is a perfect cold-weather dish which takes less than an hour to prepare and cook. Any type of white fish fillet may be used, and shrimp can be substituted for the crabmeat.

PREPARATION TIME: *20 min*
COOKING TIME: *20–25 min*
INGREDIENTS *(for 4–6):*
1 pound cod fillet
1 large onion
½ pound potatoes
½ cup mushrooms
3 ounces salt pork
2 tablespoons butter
4 teaspoons flour
1¼ cups milk
½ cup flaked white crabmeat
Salt★ and black pepper
Lemon juice
2 tablespoons chopped parsley
GARNISH:
Bread croûtons (page 178)

Wash the fish and cut it into three or four pieces. Peel and roughly chop the onion. Peel the potatoes and cut them into ½ in cubes; trim the mushrooms and slice them. Bring 2½ cups of water to the boil, add 1 teaspoon salt and the fish and simmer over low heat for 10 minutes. Drain the fish and set the liquid aside. Dice the salt pork. Fry the pork in a sauté pan over low heat until the fat runs. Add the butter and continue frying until the pork crisps.

Add the potatoes, onions and mushrooms to the pork and fry for a further 5 minutes.

Remove the pan from the heat and stir in the flour, then gradually add the milk. Bring the mixture to simmering point, then stir in 2 cups of the reserved fish stock. Add the fish, which will break up naturally, and the crabmeat. Simmer for 10 minutes and season to taste with salt, freshly ground pepper and lemon juice; stir in the parsley.

Serve the chowder with a bowl of crisp bread croûtons.

PESCADO A LA MARINA

The South Americans, even more than the French, are great believers in marinating meat and fish before cooking them. The marinade, which imparts an unusual flavor to any fish fillets, is used for the sauce.

PREPARATION TIME: *1 hour*
20 min
COOKING TIME: *15 min*
INGREDIENTS *(for 4–6):*
1½ pounds haddock or cod fillet
1 egg
2 cups soft breadcrumbs
Oil for frying
MARINADE:
¼ cup olive oil
2 tablespoons lemon juice
1 small onion
1 clove garlic
1–2 bay leaves
1 teaspoon salt★
Black pepper and ground nutmeg
MARINA SAUCE:
½ cup dry white wine
2 egg yolks
GARNISH:
*1 heaping tablespoon finely
    chopped parsley*

Make the marinade first, by blending together the olive oil and lemon juice; peel and finely chop the onion and garlic. Add to the oil, together with the bay leaves, salt, freshly ground pepper and a pinch of nutmeg.

Wash the fish fillets and divide into four or six portions. Place them in a shallow dish and pour over the prepared marinade. Leave for about 1 hour, turning the fish from time to time.

Lift out the fish, setting the marinade aside. Dry the fillets thoroughly on paper towels. Lightly beat the egg and brush it over the fish before coating with breadcrumbs. Press the crumbs well in, and shake off any surplus. Leave the coating to harden while making the sauce.

Bring the marinade to the boil, then strain it through a fine sieve into a bowl. Add the wine. Beat the egg yolks together in a separate bowl and gradually stir in the wine and marinade. Place the bowl over a saucepan of gently simmering water and stir continuously with a wooden spoon until the sauce thickens sufficiently to coat the back of the spoon. If the sauce shows signs of curdling, add a tablespoon of cold water and remove the bowl from the heat.

Heat the oil in a heavy-based pan and fry the fish until golden brown on both sides, turning once. Drain on paper towels.

Serve the fish hot, sprinkled with parsley. Serve the Marina sauce separately and offer creamed potatoes and buttered beans. The fillets may also be served cold with a sauce tartare (page 22) and a crisp green salad.

TRADITIONAL SEAFOOD CHOWDER

SALT   SUGAR   FAT   CHOL   FIBER

GLUTEN-FREE★   WHOLEFOOD★
TOTAL CALORIES: ABOUT 1660

The **salt** can be reduced to low if the pork is reduced or omitted and unsalted butter is used. Although crabmeat is high in sodium, the amount used is very small so that omitting it would make hardly any difference. Compensate for the lack of salt by adding extra lemon juice, parsley and pepper.
To reduce the **fat** content to low, halve or omit the pork; use half the amount of butter and use skim milk (or you could substitute fish stock). Toast the croûtons instead of frying them. (Calories lost: up to 600.)
For low **cholesterol**, adapt as for low fat, and replace the butter with vegetable margarine or sunflower oil.
You can increase the **fiber** content by using a higher proportion of potatoes to fish. As well as commercial **gluten-free** flour, cornstarch, potato starch or brown rice flour could all be used similarly for thickening the soup.

Freezing: ✓ up to 1 month.

PESCADO A LA MARINA

SALT   SUGAR   FAT   CHOL   FIBER

GLUTEN-FREE★   WHOLEFOOD★
TOTAL CALORIES: ABOUT 1800

To reduce the **salt** content to very low, replace the added salt with more lemon juice and chopped garlic.

You can reduce the **fat** level to moderate by poaching the fish, rather than frying it in the traditional way. Poach it in the marinade and the wine for about 7 minutes, then lift it out gently and use the strained liquid to make the sauce. Use a whole egg rather than two yolks for thickening the sauce. This will give medium **cholesterol**. (Calories lost: up to 500.) If you are serving cold, the fat can be reduced still further by replacing the sauce tartare with a yogurt sauce made by stirring the chopped capers and parsley into thick low-fat plain yogurt with a little lemon juice and pepper. (Further calories lost: 400.)

Instead of **gluten-free** breadcrumbs, you can use millet flakes for coating the fish.

Wholefood: instead of whole wheat breadcrumbs, oatmeal or millet flakes can be used for coating the fish.

FISH PIE WITH CHEESE CUSTARD

SALT　SUGAR　FAT　CHOL　FIBER

GLUTEN-FREE*　WHOLEFOOD*
TOTAL CALORIES: ABOUT 2050

Minimize the **salt** by halving the amount of smoked fish and increasing the fresh fish to balance; use unsalted stock and unsalted fat in the white sauce. Reduce the **fat** to low and the **cholesterol** to medium by using only 1½ tablespoons butter (or soft margarine) in the sauce; use skim milk for the custard and omit the pats of butter on the surface. (Calories lost: up to 390.) Serve with baked or boiled potatoes.

Freezing: √ up to 1 month.

FISH PIE WITH CHEESE CUSTARD

Smoked cod enhances the flavor of this fish pie, topped with a cheese and tomato custard.

PREPARATION TIME: *35 min*
COOKING TIME: *45 min*
INGREDIENTS (*for 6*):
1¼ pounds cod fillet
6 ounces smoked cod or haddock
1 quart chicken or fish stock
 (page 153)
1 onion
3 cloves
1 clove garlic
Salt* and black pepper
1 cup white sauce (pages 154–5)
1 pound tomatoes
2 eggs
1 cup milk
½ cup grated Parmesan cheese

2 tablespoons unsalted butter

Wash and skin the fresh cod, wipe the smoked cod with a cloth and cut both into 1 in wide slices. Put the fish slices in a deep sauté pan and cover with the chicken stock. Peel and finely slice the onion and add to the fish, together with the cloves and the crushed garlic. Bring slowly to the boil, and season with salt and freshly ground pepper. Simmer for 10 minutes, then remove the cod from the liquid.

Increase the heat and boil the fish liquid rapidly until it has reduced to 1 cup; strain and use for the white sauce.

Flake the fish into a deep 8 in wide pie dish, pour over the hot white sauce and coat the fish thoroughly. Skin and slice the tomatoes (page 179) in a layer over the fish, and pepper well. Beat the eggs with salt and pepper; beat in the grated cheese and milk. Pour this mixture over the tomatoes and float small pats of butter on the surface. Bake for 45 minutes or until golden brown, on the center shelf of an oven heated to 325°F (170°C, mark 3).

Sauté potatoes and Brussels sprouts or cauliflower could be served with the pie.

Fish

FISHERMAN'S PIE

Left-over cooked fish forms the basis for this savory dish, which is covered with a mustard-flavored cheese biscuit dough.

PREPARATION TIME: *25 min*
COOKING TIME: *25–30 min*
INGREDIENTS *(for 4–6):*
½ pound cooked white fish
½ pound cooked smoked haddock
Half a small green pepper
2 hard-cooked eggs
Juice of a lemon
2 tablespoons chopped parsley
2 cups white sauce (page 154)
Salt★ and black pepper
1½ cups self-rising flour
3 tablespoons butter
2 teaspoons dry mustard
½–¾ cup grated Cheddar cheese
½ cup milk

Skin and flake the fish; finely chop the green pepper and the hard-cooked eggs. Mix the fish, green pepper, eggs, lemon juice and parsley into the white sauce. Season with salt and pepper. Spoon the mixture into a 5-cup baking dish.

Sift the flour into a bowl and rub in the butter. Add the mustard and cheese and sufficient milk to make a soft pliable pastry dough. Knead this lightly on a floured surface, and roll out a circle, ¾ in thick, large enough to cover the dish. Cut the pastry into eight triangles and place over the fish so that the points meet in the center. Brush with milk and bake the dish for 25 minutes, at 425°F (220°C, mark 7), or until the top of the pastry is golden.

MATELOTE OF EELS

A *matelote* – not to be confused with *matelot* (a sailor) – is the French culinary term for a fish stew. In this recipe, eels are used for a wholesome main course for lunch or supper.

PREPARATION TIME: *20 min*
COOKING TIME: *45 min*
INGREDIENTS *(for 4–6):*
1½ pounds eels
2 small onions
6 tablespoons unsalted butter
1½ cups dry white wine
1 carrot
1 clove garlic
Bouquet garni (page 183)
½ teaspoon ground mace
Salt★ and black pepper
1 egg yolk
½ cup heavy cream
GARNISH:
12 button mushrooms
12 pearl onions
Fried bread triangles

Have the eels skinned and cleaned. Peel and thinly slice the onions and sauté half in 4 tablespoons butter for 5 minutes until golden. Wash and dry the eels; cut into 2 in pieces, add to the onion and continue frying gently, for about 10 minutes, turning the eels until lightly browned. Pour in the wine and bring to a simmer. Peel, slice and chop the carrot, peel and crush the garlic and add these to the pan, together with the remaining onion, bouquet garni, mace and seasoning. Cover with a lid and simmer for 25 minutes.

Meanwhile, wipe and trim the mushrooms, peel the pearl onions and sauté both in the remaining butter; fry the bread triangles. Remove the fish and keep warm on a serving dish.

FISHERMAN'S PIE

SALT   SUGAR   FAT   CHOL   FIBER

GLUTEN-FREE★   WHOLEFOOD★
TOTAL CALORIES: ABOUT 2695

Minimize the **salt** by halving or omitting the smoked fish, replacing it with extra fresh fish. Compensate by adding more green pepper and seasoning with cayenne.
To reduce both **fat** and **cholesterol** to low, omit one of the eggs and use skim milk. Use half the amount of Cheddar, or replace it with a reduced-fat variety. (Calories lost: up to 465.)
Instead of using commercial **gluten-free** flour, you could make the white sauce with cornstarch and cover the pie with mashed potatoes.

Microwave: ✓

MATELOTE OF EELS

SALT   SUGAR   FAT   CHOL   FIBER

GLUTEN-FREE★   WHOLEFOOD★
TOTAL CALORIES: ABOUT 3660

To reduce **salt** to almost none, substitute unsalted fish stock for the wine.
For low **fat** and **cholesterol**, sauté the eels in only 2 tablespoons butter, toast the bread triangles used to serve, and poach the vegetables in a little stock. Use very small eels. The fat content of eels is much less when they are tiny elvers. Substitute low-fat yogurt for the cream and thicken with cornstarch instead of egg yolk. (Calories lost: up to 1205.)

Freezing: ✓ up to 1 month.

SMELT WITH ALMONDS

SALT	SUGAR	FAT	CHOL	FIBER

GLUTEN-FREE*   WHOLEFOOD*
TOTAL CALORIES: ABOUT 2600

For medium **fat** and low **cholesterol** broil the smelt on a shallow baking pan containing one tablespoon each of oil and butter. Use low-fat yogurt or beaten egg white in place of the cream; and only 2 tablespoons of almonds. Broil or bake the almonds instead of frying them. (Calories lost: up to 1490.)

WHITING WITH ORANGE SAUCE

SALT	SUGAR	FAT	CHOL	FIBER

GLUTEN-FREE*   WHOLEFOOD*
TOTAL CALORIES: ABOUT 2835

To reduce **fat** to low, the sauce method needs to be completely changed. Use low-fat yogurt instead of cream and thicken with a tablespoon of arrowroot or cornstarch mixed to a smooth paste with a little of the liquid. Heat gently and let it just simmer (on no account boil) for a few minutes with the orange and lemon juice and seasoning.
Do not add any butter.
The fish could also be broiled after coating on a shallow baking pan containing 2 tablespoons hot oil or vegetable margarine. These measures reduce both fat and **cholesterol** level to low.
(Calories lost: up to 950.)
Gluten-free: cornstarch can be used for coating the fish. Serve with potatoes or rice.

Microwave: ✓ for the fish.

Beat the egg yolk and cream together and add a little of the fish liquid. Blend this into the mixture in the pan and continue gently stirring until the sauce thickens. Pour the sauce over the eels and serve garnished with the mushrooms, onions and bread triangles.

SMELT WITH ALMONDS

These small salt-water fish are at their best when caught at spawning time in late winter. Their delicate flavor is most apparent when baked or fried. If smelt are not available, young trout or sardines can be substituted.

PREPARATION TIME: *10 min*
COOKING TIME: *10 min*
INGREDIENTS *(for 6):*
18 smelt
6 tablespoons light cream
Seasoned flour (page 184)
6 tablespoons unsalted butter
1 tablespoon olive oil
1 cup sliced almonds

Lightly wash the smelt in cold water; cut off the heads and squeeze out the entrails. Dry the cleaned smelt on a cloth; dip the fish in the cream and roll in seasoned flour. Melt the butter in a heavy-based frying pan, add the olive oil and gently fry the smelt for 4 minutes on each side.
Remove the smelt from the pan and keep them warm. Increase the heat slightly and fry the almonds in the fat in which the fish has been cooked until they turn light brown. Sprinkle the smelt with the almonds and then pour over the butter.
Serve the smelt with thin slices of wholemeal bread.

WHITING WITH ORANGE SAUCE

Fish with orange was as popular in the 18th century as fish with lemon is today. Originally, sharp Seville oranges were used, but the mixture of orange and lemon in this recipe is equally good.

PREPARATION TIME: *10 min*
COOKING TIME: *40 min*
INGREDIENTS *(for 6):*
6 whiting
Salt* and black pepper
1 lemon
1 orange
¼ cup heavy cream
⅔ cup dry white wine
3 large egg yolks
Cayenne pepper
½ cup unsalted butter
Seasoned flour (page 184)
GARNISH:
1 orange
Chopped parsley

Clean and wash the whiting, and fillet each into two. Dry the fillets thoroughly on kitchen paper towels and season with salt and pepper; sprinkle over the juice of half a lemon. Set aside. Grate the rind from the orange and set aside; squeeze the juice of the orange and remaining half lemon into a bowl.
For the sauce, stir the cream, wine and egg yolks into the fruit juices and set the bowl over a pan of simmering water. Whisk the sauce mixture continuously until it has the consistency of thin cream. Season to taste with salt, pepper and cayenne, and blend in the orange rind. Cut half the butter into pieces and beat them one by one into the sauce. Keep the sauce hot, but do not allow it to boil.
Coat the whiting fillets with seasoned flour. Melt the remaining butter in a large, heavy-based pan and fry the fillets until golden brown on both sides.
Garnish the fillets with orange wedges and chopped parsley. The sauce can be served separately or poured over the fish. Offer crusty French bread with which to mop up the sauce.

Fish

SMOKED HADDOCK MOUSSE

A mousse, whether savory or sweet, should be chilled for several hours before serving. This recipe, suitable for a dinner party or a buffet, can also be made with smoked cod.

PREPARATION TIME: *45 min*
CHILLING TIME: *2–3 hours*
INGREDIENTS *(for 6–8):*

2 pounds smoked haddock fillet
1 small onion
2 cups milk
1 bay leaf
3 tablespoons unsalted butter
3 tablespoons flour
Salt* and black pepper
Cayenne pepper
1 envelope unflavored gelatin

Grated rind and juice of 1 lemon
1¼ cups heavy cream
ASPIC:
½ teaspoon unflavored gelatin
1 tablespoon lemon juice or vinegar
GARNISH:
½ cucumber

Cut the haddock fillet into 8–10 pieces and put them in a saucepan; peel and slice the onion and add, with the milk and bay leaf, to the fish. Cover the pan with a lid and simmer the fish over low heat for about 10 minutes. Strain the fish through a colander and set the milk aside. Remove all skin and bones, and flake the haddock flesh finely.

Melt the butter in a saucepan over low heat; stir in the flour and cook for a few minutes until this roux is light brown. Gradually stir in the milk, beating continuously to get a smooth sauce. Bring this to the boil and cook gently for 2–3 minutes. Season to taste with salt, freshly ground pepper and cayenne, then draw the pan off the heat. Pour the sauce into a large bowl, cover with buttered wax paper and leave to cool. Measure 4 tablespoons of water into a saucepan and sprinkle in the gelatin. Allow to soak for 5 minutes, then stir the mixture over low heat, until the gelatin has dissolved.

Remove the buttered paper and stir the sauce; blend in the fish, melted gelatin and finely grated rind and juice from the lemon. Correct seasoning if necessary. Whip the cream lightly and fold it into the fish mixture; pour this into a 1½ quart soufflé dish and leave until set.

For the aspic, measure 2 tablespoons of water into a saucepan and sprinkle over the gelatin. Soak for 5 minutes, then stir over low heat until the gelatin has dissolved. Draw the pan from the heat, add 2 tablespoons of water and the lemon juice. Pour a little aspic on top of the mousse. While this is setting slightly, wash and thinly slice the cucumber. Arrange the slices in a circular pattern on the aspic and leave to set. Spoon over the remaining aspic, and chill the mousse in the refrigerator until ready to serve.

Serve with a green salad tossed in French dressing (page 157).

COD GOURMET

This recipe for poaching cod in white wine, mushrooms and shallots is equally good with other firm-fleshed white fish.

PREPARATION TIME: *15 min*
COOKING TIME: *25 min*
INGREDIENTS *(for 4):*
4 cod fillets, about 5 ounces each
1–2 tablespoons flour
6 tablespoons unsalted butter
3 shallots
¼ pound mushrooms
Salt* and black pepper
2 tablespoons dry white wine
2 teaspoons lemon juice
GARNISH:
1 tablespoon chopped parsley

Wash and skin the cod fillets. Pat them dry on paper towels and coat with a little flour. Grease a large, shallow, ovenproof dish with 2 tablespoons of the butter and arrange the fillets in this. Peel and finely chop the shallots. Melt the remaining butter in a pan and fry the shallots over low heat for 2–3 minutes, until transparent. Wipe and trim the mushrooms, slice them thinly and add to the shallots. Cook for a further 2 minutes, then season to taste with salt and freshly ground pepper.

Spoon the shallot and mushroom mixture over the cod fillets and pour over the wine. Cover the dish with a lid or foil and bake for 25 minutes in the center of an oven pre-heated to 400°F (200°C, mark 6).

Serve the fish straight from the dish. Sprinkle with lemon juice and garnish with parsley. New potatoes and young peas go well with this dish.

SMOKED HADDOCK MOUSSE

SALT SUGAR FAT CHOL FIBER

GLUTEN-FREE* WHOLEFOOD*
TOTAL CALORIES: ABOUT 2810

For low **salt**, use fresh trout or salmon, not smoked fish.
The **fat** and **cholesterol** levels of this recipe can be reduced but this involves changing the texture. For this low-fat version, use skim milk and only 1½ tablespoons butter for the sauce, and substitute yogurt for the heavy cream, adding 3 stiffly beaten egg whites to make up the bulk as yogurt will not whip.
(Calories lost: up to 985.)
Cornstarch and potato starch are **gluten-free** flours that could be used for making the sauce.

Microwave: ✓ for cooking the haddock.

COD GOURMET

SALT SUGAR FAT CHOL FIBER

GLUTEN-FREE* WHOLEFOOD*
TOTAL CALORIES: ABOUT 1285

To reduce both **fat** and **cholesterol** to low, use only 1 teaspoon oil to grease the ovenproof dish and a further 2 teaspoons to brush the pan for sautéing the shallots and mushrooms. Serve with unbuttered vegetables.
(Calories lost: up to 500.)
Gluten-free flours: cornstarch or rice flour are both suitable for coating the fish.

Freezing: ✓ up to 1 month.
Microwave: ✓

STUFFED RED SNAPPER

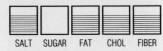

SALT	SUGAR	FAT	CHOL	FIBER

GLUTEN-FREE* WHOLEFOOD*
TOTAL CALORIES: ABOUT 5200

The **salt** can be reduced to very low by using unsalted fat and unsalted bread for the crumbs. For low **fat** and **cholesterol**, cook the onions and garlic in a pan lightly brushed with oil and halve the amount of almonds used. (Calories lost: up to 350.)

Microwave: ☑

FINNAN FILLED CRÊPES

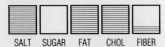

SALT	SUGAR	FAT	CHOL	FIBER

GLUTEN-FREE* WHOLEFOOD*
TOTAL CALORIES: ABOUT 2010

Reduce **salt** to low by using fresh trout or white fish in place of smoked haddock.
To reduce the **fat** and **cholesterol** to low, use skim milk in the crêpe batter and replace the butter with 2 teaspoons of oil for softening the vegetables. For cooking the crêpes, brush the pan sparingly with oil. The crêpe batter can be made using only white of egg. Omit the butter poured over the crêpes and use a reduced fat Cheddar, or Edam or thinly-sliced Mozzarella. (Calories lost: up to 870.)
Gluten-free crêpes can be made using 2 eggs beaten with 4 tablespoons gluten-free flour and 6 tablespoons skim milk.

Microwave: ☑ to finish cooking the stuffed crêpes.

STUFFED RED SNAPPER

This superb fish adapts well to baking. The stuffing is a novel combination of cucumbers, onions, and almonds. Bream, bass and gray mullet are other suitable fish.

PREPARATION TIME: *20 min*
COOKING TIME: *40–45 min*
INGREDIENTS (*for 4–5*):
1 red snapper, 4–5 pounds
Salt★ and pepper
2–4 tablespoons butter
½ cup chopped almonds
1 large onion
1 clove garlic, minced
4 cups dry breadcrumbs
½ large cucumber
1 teaspoon dried thyme
Dry sherry

Have the fish boned and prepared for stuffing. Rub the inside with salt, pepper, and butter. Toast the almonds (page 178). Sauté the sliced onion and garlic in butter until soft. Combine them with the breadcrumbs, minced cucumber, and toasted almonds. Season with salt, pepper, and thyme and moisten with a little sherry. Stuff the fish and close the opening with wooden cocktail sticks or toothpicks. Salt and pepper the fish and bake in a well-greased dish at 350°F (180°C, mark 4) for 40–45 minutes, or until the fish flakes when tested with a fork. Baste with the pan juices.

Plain boiled or steamed potatoes and a salad of tomatoes and onions go especially well with this dish.

FINNAN FILLED CRÊPES

Cured haddock from Findon in Scotland, known as finnan haddie, is cleaned and split before being smoked. Follow the recipe for crêpes on page 20, using 1 cup flour and 1¼ cups milk to 1 egg.

PREPARATION TIME: *20 min*
COOKING TIME: *30 min*
INGREDIENTS (*for 4*):
½ pound cooked smoked haddock fillet
1¼ cups crêpe batter (see above)
1 small onion
2 tablespoons chopped celery
¼ pound mushrooms
7 tablespoons unsalted butter
16-ounce can tomatoes
Salt★ and black pepper
Lemon juice
3–4 tablespoons grated Cheddar or Gruyère cheese
GARNISH:
Lemon wedges
Parsley sprigs

Make eight small thin crêpes from the batter and set them aside. Peel and finely chop the onion, and prepare the celery. Trim the mushrooms and slice them thinly.

Melt 3 tablespoons of the butter and fry the onion, celery and mushrooms until soft. Add the tomatoes, and season with salt and freshly ground pepper. Simmer the contents of the pan, uncovered, until it has reduced to a thick purée.

Meanwhile, remove the skin from the haddock, and flake the flesh. Add the haddock to the onion and tomato mixture, sharpen to taste with lemon juice and adjust seasoning.

Spoon 2 tablespoons of the filling down the center of each crêpe and fold the sides over to form an envelope. Arrange the stuffed crêpes side by side in a shallow flameproof dish. Melt the remaining butter and pour it over the crêpes. Sprinkle generously with grated cheese and set the dish under a hot, pre-heated broiler or in the oven until the cheese is bubbly brown.

Garnish the crêpes with lemon wedges and parsley sprigs and serve with buttered peas.

Fish

FLOUNDER SOUFFLÉ

Flounder is an ideal fish for pies and soufflés, served with a mousseline sauce. Any firm-fleshed white fish can be used.

PREPARATION TIME: *30 min*
COOKING TIME: *45 min*
INGREDIENTS *(for 4–6)*:
1 pound flounder fillets
Salt★ and black pepper
1 small bay leaf
Pinch of mace
½ cup milk
6 tablespoons unsalted butter
6 tablespoons flour
Nutmeg
3 large eggs
MOUSSELINE SAUCE:
Juice of ½ large lemon
2 large egg yolks
½ cup unsalted butter
Salt★ and black pepper
¼ cup heavy cream

Wash the fillets thoroughly and put them into a saucepan; cover with cold water. Add ½ teaspoon of salt, the bay leaf and mace to the fish, and cover the pan with a lid. Bring slowly to simmering point, turn off the heat and leave the pan to stand for 10 minutes. Lift out the fish, set aside 1½ cups of the liquid and make it up to 2 cups with milk.

Remove the skin and bones from the fish and flake the flesh roughly. Melt 6 tablespoons of the butter in a large saucepan and stir in the flour. Cook this roux over low heat for 2 minutes, stirring continuously, then gradually stir in the fish and milk liquid. Bring to the boil, still stirring, and cook for 2 minutes or until the mixture is thick and smooth. Season to taste with salt, freshly ground pepper and nutmeg. Carefully fold the flaked fish into the sauce. Separate the three eggs and beat the yolks into the fish mixture, one by one; beat the egg whites until stiff, then gently fold them in as well.

Spoon the mixture into a prepared 1½-quart soufflé dish; cook in the center of the oven pre-heated to 400°F (200°C, mark 6) for 45 minutes or until the soufflé is risen and golden brown on top.

For the sauce, put the lemon juice and 1 teaspoon of cold water in a basin. Beat the egg yolks lightly and stir them into the lemon juice. Stand the basin over a saucepan of gently simmering water, but do not allow the bottom of the basin to touch the water. Stir in 1 tablespoon of butter and whisk the mixture until it thickens.

Remove the basin from the heat and gradually whisk in the remaining butter, cut into small pats. Whisk until the butter is completely absorbed before adding the next pat. Season to taste with salt and pepper. Whip the cream and fold it gently into the sauce. Heat the sauce in the basin over the pan of simmering water, whisking all the time.

Serve the soufflé immediately, and offer the mousseline sauce in a sauceboat. Boiled broccoli or cauliflower, or a green salad, could be served with the soufflé.

MEDITERRANEAN FISH SOUP

On a cold winter's evening, this thick soup serves almost as a meal in itself. It can be prepared well in advance and re-heated just before serving without losing any of its delicate flavor.

PREPARATION TIME: *35 min*
COOKING TIME: *45 min*
INGREDIENTS *(for 6–8)*:
¾ pound each of fillets of sea bass,
  flounder and haddock or cod
1 large onion
6 tablespoons olive oil
1 clove garlic
16-ounce can tomatoes
2 tablespoons tomato paste
1 heaping tablespoon chopped
  parsley
4 cups fish stock (page 153) or
  water
½ cup dry white wine
1 bay leaf

FLOUNDER SOUFFLÉ

SALT	SUGAR	FAT	CHOL	FIBER

GLUTEN-FREE★   WHOLEFOOD★
TOTAL CALORIES: ABOUT 3140

You can reduce the **fat** level (but not the **cholesterol**) in the soufflé itself to medium by halving the amount of butter and flour used to make the soufflé base. However, the mousseline sauce is very high in fat, which cannot easily be reduced. Instead, try serving the soufflé with a mixture of yogurt, lemon juice and herbs, seasoned with black pepper and gently heated but *not* boiled. This gives a fairly low fat and cholesterol level. (Calories lost: up to 1255.)
For an even lower cholesterol version, use only 1 egg yolk added to 3 egg whites for the soufflé. (Further calories lost: 140.)
Commercial **gluten-free** flour can be successfully used for the soufflé; so can potato starch, in about half the quantity.

Microwave: ☑ for cooking the fish.

MEDITERRANEAN FISH SOUP

SALT	SUGAR	FAT	CHOL	FIBER

GLUTEN-FREE   WHOLEFOOD
TOTAL CALORIES: ABOUT 2675

Remember that the **salt** level will only be low if the tomatoes and tomato paste used have no added salt.
To reduce levels of both **fat** and **cholesterol** to low, use only 1 tablespoon of oil to soften the

onion, and substitute low fat yogurt for the cream. The cream can even be omitted completely and you will still have a delicious soup. (Calories lost: up to 1288).

If cholesterol content only, and not fat, is your worry, there is no need to reduce the oil so drastically, and it does contribute to the taste of the soup. The shrimp, which are rich in cholesterol, could be omitted, especially if all you can get are frozen shrimp which have little taste anyway.

Freezing: ☑ up to 1 month.
Microwave: ☑

BASS PLAKI

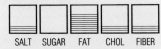

SALT	SUGAR	FAT	CHOL	FIBER

GLUTEN-FREE   WHOLEFOOD
TOTAL CALORIES: ABOUT 2025

This dish is almost ideal for whatever diet you may be following, except for the **fat**. Greek cooking tends to be generous with olive oil, and the amount given here can easily be reduced to only 1 tablespoon, making the dish low in fat. (Calories lost: up to 265.) The only **cholesterol** comes from the fish, and this type is low in cholesterol. Sunflower or safflower oil can be substituted for the olive oil if you are on a diet which aims at actually lowering the level of blood cholesterol, but the taste of good fruity olive oil is part of the character of this dish.

Freezing: ☑ up to 1 month.
Microwave: ☑

Large piece lemon peel
Salt★ and black pepper
½ cup heavy cream
GARNISH:
Shrimp
Tomato slices

Clean, fillet and skin the fish (pages 172–3); use the trimmings and bones as a base for the fish stock. Cut the fish fillets diagonally into 2 inch pieces. Peel and finely chop the onion. Heat the oil in a heavy-based pan and cook the onion in this until soft, but not browned. Crush and add the garlic, fry for a minute or two before adding the canned tomatoes with their juice, tomato paste and chopped parsley. Mix it all together and simmer slowly for 15 minutes. Add the fish, the stock, wine, bay leaf and lemon peel, bring back to the simmer, cover with a lid and cook slowly for 20 minutes. Discard the bay leaf and lemon peel. Season with salt and freshly ground pepper and leave the soup to cool slightly.

Remove one piece of fish for each serving and keep warm; liquidize the rest, along with the contents of the pan, until blended to a smooth creamy consistency.

Stir in the cream and re-heat the soup without bringing it to the boil. Place one piece of fish in each individual bowl and pour over the soup. Float slices of skinned tomatoes (page 179), garnished with a few peeled shrimp, on top of each bowl

BASS PLAKI

Large fish such as bass, trout and weakfish are well suited to being cooked by this Greek method. The fish is baked whole in the oven, and tomatoes and lemon are traditional in a plaki.

PREPARATION TIME: *15 min*
COOKING TIME: *45 min*
INGREDIENTS *(for 4–6):*
2–3 pound whole bass
1 large onion
1 large clove garlic
1 teaspoon fennel or coriander
  seeds
3 tablespoons olive oil
Salt★ and black pepper
1 large lemon
1–2 tablespoons chopped parsley
16-ounce can tomatoes
½ cup dry white wine

Peel and thinly slice the onion and peel the garlic. Crush the fennel or coriander seeds in a mortar or with a broad-bladed knife. Scale and clean the fish and place it

whole in an oiled baking dish; sprinkle generously with salt, freshly ground pepper and the juice from half the lemon.

Heat the remaining oil in a pan and fry the onion and crushed garlic over medium heat, until soft and transparent. Stir in the tomatoes, with their juice; add the parsley, crushed seeds and wine. Cook this sauce for a few minutes until well blended, then season the sauce with salt and pepper.

Pour the sauce over the fish, topping up with a little water, if the baking dish is large. Cut the remaining lemon into thin slices and lay them on top of the fish. Cover the dish with foil or a lid, and bake in the center of a pre-heated oven, at 375°F (190°C, mark 5), for about 45 minutes.

Serve the bass in the sauce, straight from the dish. Baked or boiled potatoes will go especially well with this dish.

BAKED HALIBUT STEAKS

This is a good way to cook firm fish, such as halibut, gray mullet, cod, haddock or flounder.

PREPARATION TIME: *20 min*
COOKING TIME: *10–12 min*
INGREDIENTS *(for 4):*
2–2½ pounds halibut, cut into 1 in thick slices
¼ cup olive oil
2 large onions
4 cloves garlic
16-ounce can tomatoes
Juice of ½ lemon
1 large bunch parsley
2 bay leaves
Pinch of rosemary (optional)
Pinch of thyme (optional)
Salt★ and black pepper
White wine (optional)
GARNISH:
Lemon wedges

Heat the olive oil in a heavy pan and sauté a few of the halibut slices at a time very briefly on each side to sear them. As they are seared, transfer them to an oven-proof baking dish large enough to hold the slices in one layer. Peel and slice the onion; peel and finely mince the garlic. Add these to the pan and sauté them for about 10 minutes or until they are soft and slightly colored.

Add the tomatoes, lemon juice, chopped parsley, bay leaves, and the rosemary and thyme (if used). Season generously with salt and freshly ground pepper. Stir well, then simmer very gently for about 10 minutes. If the mixture gets too thick as it cooks, add a little white wine or water.

Pour this sauce over the fish and bake in a pre-heated oven at 425°F (220°C, mark 7) for 10–12 minutes. Cover the top with a piece of cooking parchment or aluminum foil after the first 5 minutes of cooking time. Garnish with lemon wedges. This is also good served warm, rather than hot. Boiled potatoes and a green salad go well with baked fish steaks.

BAKED HALIBUT STEAKS

| SALT | SUGAR | FAT | CHOL | FIBER |

GLUTEN-FREE   WHOLEFOOD
TOTAL CALORIES: ABOUT 1855

Remember that this is only low in **salt** if the tomatoes used are unsalted.
The **fat** can be reduced to low by using only 2 teaspoons of oil to sauté the onions and garlic, and sealing the fish by placing it under a very hot broiler for 30 seconds on each side. The only **cholesterol** comes from the fish, and this type has very little. (Calories lost: up to 400.)

Freezing: ✓ up to 1 month.
Microwave: ✓

CASSEROLE OF HALIBUT

| SALT | SUGAR | FAT | CHOL | FIBER |

GLUTEN-FREE★   WHOLEFOOD★
TOTAL CALORIES: ABOUT 3080

Reduce **salt** to low by omitting the shrimp or using drained canned shrimp.
Reduce both **fat** and **cholesterol** to low by cooking the halibut in a dish that is oiled rather than buttered, and topping it with a mixture of yogurt and low-fat soft cheese, diluted to the consistency of cream with dry white wine. Omitting the shrimp will reduce the cholesterol level to low when combined with these fat-cutting changes. Serve with tiny biscuits instead of high-fat puff pastry crescents, using the biscuit dough given for the Fisherman's Pie on page 12, with the low-fat variations

suggested, and bake in a pre-heated oven at 450°F (230°C, mark 8) for 7–8 minutes. The biscuits can be made in advance, frozen if necessary, and reheated in the oven with the fish. (Calories lost: up to 1000.)
Gluten-free garnishes include piped toasted balls of mashed potato or slivers of raw carrot.

Freezing: ☑ up to 1 month.
Microwave: ☑

HALIBUT WITH CORN

SALT	SUGAR	FAT	CHOL	FIBER

GLUTEN-FREE   WHOLEFOOD
TOTAL CALORIES: ABOUT 3435

To reduce the **salt** and added **sugar** to low and none, use fresh or frozen corn.
You can reduce the **fat** and **cholesterol** to low (in the method for cooking the fish) by omitting all or most of the butter from the corn, and lightly oiling the foil for cooking the fish instead of buttering it. However, sauce Béarnaise is by nature very high in fat and cholesterol. To reduce both to medium, try replacing the egg yolks and butter with 1 whole egg blended into ½ cup of low-fat thick yogurt, then heating gently in a double boiler to thicken, and flavoring as in the main recipe with vinegar and onion. (Calories lost: up to 1160.)

Freezing: ☑ up to 1 month.
Microwave: ☑ for cooking the fish.

CASSEROLE OF HALIBUT

This is a highly nutritious, easily prepared dish. A garnish of puff pastry crescents adds a touch of sophistication.

PREPARATION TIME: *15 min*
COOKING TIME: *50 min*
INGREDIENTS *(for 6):*
2 pounds halibut or flounder
¼ cup unsalted butter
1 heaping tablespoon finely chopped onion
1¼ cups heavy cream
Juice of ½ lemon
2 heaping teaspoons paprika
¼ pound button mushrooms
¾ cup peeled shrimp
GARNISH:
Puff pastry crescents

Wipe and skin the halibut. Butter an ovenproof casserole dish, place the piece of halibut in this and cook for 15 minutes on the middle shelf of an oven pre-heated to 325°F (170°C, mark 3). Remove from the oven, sprinkle the onion over the fish, pour over the cream mixed with the lemon juice and dust with paprika.

Cover the dish with a lid or foil, return to the oven and cook for a further 20 minutes, basting twice with the cooking liquid. Trim and slice the mushrooms, and sprinkle them, with the shrimp, over the fish; cook for a further 15 minutes, again basting twice. Transfer the fish to a warm dish and pour over the liquid.

Garnish with puff pastry crescents and serve boiled new potatoes with the fish.

HALIBUT WITH CORN

In this baked fish recipe, the delicate flavor of turbot is complemented by corn and a Béarnaise sauce. The dish is also good made with flounder.

PREPARATION TIME: *15 min*
COOKING TIME: *25 min*
INGREDIENTS *(for 6):*
6 halibut steaks or fillets, 4–6 ounces each
2 teaspoons lemon juice
Black pepper
½ cup unsalted butter
16-ounce can whole kernel corn
1¼ cups Béarnaise sauce (page 156)

Wipe the fish with a damp cloth. Butter two large sheets of aluminum foil and place the fish steaks on one sheet. Sprinkle with lemon juice, grind over a little pepper and dot the fish with pats of butter. Cover with the second piece of foil and seal tightly to form a loose parcel. Bake the fish for 25 minutes on the center shelf of an oven pre-heated to 350°F (180°C, mark 4).

Heat the corn over moderate heat, then stir ¼ cup butter into it. Season with freshly ground pepper and spread the corn over the bottom of a shallow serving dish. Arrange the fish on the corn, pour over the juices from the foil parcel, and coat each steak with Béarnaise sauce.

Serve with a green vegetable such as broccoli or spinach.

HALIBUT DUGLÉRÉ

This classic French dish can be made with halibut steaks or with thick fillets of sole, which should be folded over in two. For a first course, half quantities only are necessary. The fish should be flaked, mixed with Dugléré sauce (tomato, cream and parsley), and served in small dishes.

PREPARATION TIME: *15 min*
COOKING TIME: *35 min*
INGREDIENTS *(for 4):*
4 halibut steaks
Fish bones
2 tablespoons butter
Juice of 1 lemon
Salt* and black pepper
½ cup dry white wine
SAUCE:
2–3 tomatoes
2 tablespoons butter
1½–2 tablespoons flour
1 heaping tablespoon fresh
*   chopped parsley*
5 tablespoons heavy cream
GARNISH:
Lemon twists (page 179) and
*   parsley sprigs*

Wash and trim the fish steaks and put the trimmings and fish bones in a pan of cold water to make a court bouillon (page 175).

Butter a shallow ovenproof dish thoroughly. Rub the steaks with lemon juice, place them in the dish and season with salt and freshly ground pepper. Add the wine and sufficient court bouillon to come to the top of the fish without covering it. Place a piece of buttered foil or wax paper over the fish and cook in the center of a pre-heated oven, at 375°F (190°C, mark 5), for 25 minutes, or until a white curd appears on it: this is a sign that the fish is sufficiently cooked.

Lift the halibut steaks on to a warm serving dish, and strain the cooking liquid.

While the fish is cooking, skin the tomatoes (page 179). Remove the pulp in the center of the tomatoes with a teaspoon and rub it through a sieve to remove the seeds. Set the tomato liquid aside and cut the flesh into thin strips.

Melt the butter for the sauce in a small pan, remove from the heat and stir in sufficient flour to absorb all the butter. Blend in the tomato liquid and about 1¼ cups of the reserved fish liquid. Return the pan to the heat and bring the sauce to simmering point, stirring continuously. Cook over low heat for 3–5 minutes. Add the tomato strips and the parsley, and then stir in the cream; do not let the sauce boil again. Adjust seasoning with salt, pepper and lemon juice and pour the sauce over the fish.

Garnish the fish steaks with lemon twists and sprigs of parsley. Serve with creamed potatoes or with small molds (timbales) of boiled and buttered rice.

SOLES AUX CRÊPES

The combination of buttered fillets of sole and featherlight strips of crêpe is a specialty from Bayeux in northern France.

PREPARATION TIME: *15 min*
COOKING TIME: *25 min*
INGREDIENTS *(for 6):*
12 fillets of sole
Seasoned flour (page 184)
½ cup clarified butter (page 182)
6 tablespoons unsalted butter
1 heaping tablespoon chopped
*   parsley*
BATTER:
½ cup flour
¼ teaspoon salt
1 egg
1 cup milk
GARNISH:
Lemon wedges

Begin by making the batter so that it can rest while the fillets are being fried. Sift the flour and salt into a bowl, make a well in the center and add the lightly beaten egg. Mix thoroughly and add 4 tablespoons water and the milk gradually, beating well, until the batter is free from lumps and has the consistency of light cream. Add more water to the batter if necessary.

Wipe the sole fillets on a damp cloth, coat them with seasoned flour and shake off any surplus. Melt the clarified butter in a large pan and fry the fillets until golden brown on both sides, turning once. Arrange the fillets on a serving dish and keep them warm.

Butter a clean frying pan and fry three or four crêpes from the batter. Roll the crêpes up and cut them, crosswise, into ½ in strips. Melt the remaining butter and reheat the crêpe ribbons, turning them until they are hot and golden. Blend in the chopped parsley and pile the crêpe strips over and among the sole fillets. Garnish with wedges of lemon.

A salad of endive and orange would make a good accompaniment to the pancakes.

HALIBUT DUGLÉRÉ

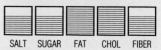

SALT   SUGAR   FAT   CHOL   FIBER

GLUTEN-FREE*   WHOLEFOOD*
TOTAL CALORIES: ABOUT 1755

To reduce both **fat** and **cholesterol** to low, oil the dish and the covering for the fish sparingly, instead of using butter. Halve the amount of butter for the sauce and replace the heavy cream with yogurt. (Calories lost: up to 400.)
For a **gluten-free** sauce, you can use cornstarch, or brown rice flour, as well as commercial gluten-free flour.

Freezing: ✓ up to 1 month.
Microwave: ✓ for cooking the fish.

SOLES AUX CRÊPES

SALT   SUGAR   FAT   CHOL   FIBER

GLUTEN-FREE*   WHOLEFOOD*
TOTAL CALORIES: ABOUT 2460

To reduce the **salt** further, and simultaneously reduce the **fat** to low, broil the sole fillets in a shallow baking dish with 1 tablespoon each of hot oil and hot butter (or use oil throughout): brush the crêpe pan sparingly with oil rather than buttering it when making the crêpe, and brush again very lightly with oil and butter to brown the crêpe strips. (Calories lost: up to 790.)
Using oil throughout and skim milk in the crêpe batter also keeps the **cholesterol** level low; to cut it even further, use only white of egg in the crêpe batter.

FILETS DE SOLE WALEWSKA

SALT	SUGAR	FAT	CHOL	FIBER

GLUTEN-FREE*   WHOLEFOOD*
TOTAL CALORIES: ABOUT 3470

The **salt** content comes mainly from the crayfish and cheese: to reduce it to low, halve the amount of each.

To reduce both **fat** and **cholesterol** content to medium, omit the crayfish or replace it with scallops or monkfish; make the sauce with only 2 tablespoons of butter or vegetable margarine; use skim milk and replace the cream with thick low-fat unflavored yogurt. Sauté the crayfish (or scallops or monkfish) in a pan lightly brushed with oil, or under a hot broiler, brushing the fish lightly with oil. (Calories lost: up to 1745.)

Microwave: ☑ for cooking the sole.

FILETS DE SOLE WALEWSKA

This classic dish is named after the beautiful Polish Countess Maria Walewska, who was so devoted to Napoleon that she begged in vain to be allowed to accompany him into exile in Elba. It is composed of sole and crayfish, garnished with slices of truffle. If truffles are too expensive, use small mushrooms.

PREPARATION TIME: *40 min*
COOKING TIME: *1¼ hours*
INGREDIENTS *(for 4):*
2 sole, 1¼ pounds each
1 bay leaf
1 large parsley sprig
1 small onion
6 peppercorns
*Salt**
Juice of 1 large lemon
½ cup dry white wine
4 cooked crayfish tails, each
  weighing 6 ounces
½ cup unsalted butter
3 tablespoons flour
½ cup milk
¾–1 cup grated Cheddar or
  Gruyère cheese
5 tablespoons heavy cream
*Salt** *and black pepper*
GARNISH:
8 thin slices of truffle or 8 small
  flat mushrooms
Lemon slices
Parsley sprigs

Have each sole skinned and filleted and cut into four. Put the bones and skin into a pan with the bay leaf, parsley, peeled onion and whole peppercorns; cover with lightly salted water. Simmer over low heat for 20–30 minutes then strain this court bouillon and set it aside.

Wash and trim the fillets. Rub

them with lemon juice to whiten them, then arrange them in a buttered shallow ovenproof dish. Pour over the wine and enough court bouillon just to cover the fillets. Cover the dish with lightly buttered wax paper, and cook in the center of a pre-heated oven, at 375°F (190°C, mark 5), for 20–25 minutes.

Meanwhile, remove the shells from the crayfish tails and take out the meat in one piece. Cut each piece in half lengthwise.

When the sole fillets are cooked, lift them out carefully with a slotted spatula and keep them warm. Pour the liquid into a pan, boil over high heat for 5 minutes to reduce it, and strain off 1 cup.

Make a roux (page 154) with half the butter and all the flour. Gradually stir in the milk and bring this sauce to simmering point. Blend in the reserved fish liquid and cook for a further 5 minutes. Stir in the grated cheese until it has melted. Gradually add the cream. Season to taste with

salt and freshly ground pepper. Cover the pan with a lid and keep the sauce warm without further cooking.

Heat the remaining butter and sauté the crayfish tails over high heat for about 3 minutes until they are just turning color.

Arrange the sole fillets in a circle on a round, warm serving dish, with the tail ends towards the center, and set the crayfish around the edge of the dish. Stir the sauce, which should now just coat a wooden spoon; otherwise thin it with a little fish liquid. Coat the fillets carefully with the sauce and put the dish under a hot broiler for a minute or two to glaze it.

Garnish each fillet with a slice of truffle – if mushrooms are used, sauté them lightly in a little butter and place them, dark side uppermost, on the fillets. Decorate the dish with lemon twists (page 179) and tiny sprigs of parsley. Serve the fish with creamed potatoes and snow or sugar peas.

Fish

GOUJONS OF SOLE WITH TARTARE SAUCE

In France, the small, smelt-like goujons or gudgeons are deep fried and served whole. This recipe is adapted to sole or flounder.

PREPARATION TIME: *20 min*
COOKING TIME: *2–3 min*
INGREDIENTS *(for 4):*
4 large fillets of sole
Seasoned flour (page 184)
1 large egg
2 teaspoons olive oil
Fine dry breadcrumbs
Oil for frying
Salt★

TARTARE SAUCE:
¼ cup mayonnaise (page 156)
1 tablespoon heavy cream
1 heaping teaspoon each, chopped parsley, gherkins, capers
2 teaspoons chopped onion

GARNISH:
Lemon wedges

Rinse the fillets of sole in cold water and pat them dry on a clean cloth. Making a slanting cut, slice each fillet in half and then cut each half lengthwise into three or four narrow strips.

Coat the fish thoroughly with seasoned flour, shaking off any surplus. Beat the egg lightly and mix in the olive oil; dip the fish pieces in this mixture before rolling them in the breadcrumbs. Set the fish aside in a cool place until required.

For the sauce mix the mayonnaise, cream, parsley, gherkins, capers and onions together. Spoon into a serving dish and chill until required.

Heat the oil in a deep fryer until a small crumb of bread sizzles. Put the fish in the basket and lower it into the hot oil; fry for 2–3 minutes until crisp and golden brown. Remove from the heat and drain the fish on crumpled paper towels. Sprinkle with salt and pile the fish on to a hot serving dish. Garnish with wedges of lemon and offer the sauce separately.

A green salad and crusty bread could be served with the fillets.

GOUJONS OF SOLE WITH TARTARE SAUCE

SALT	SUGAR	FAT	CHOL	FIBER

GLUTEN-FREE★   WHOLEFOOD★
TOTAL CALORIES: ABOUT 1650

Reduce **salt** to low by using breadcrumbs made from unsalted flour.
To reduce **fat** to low, do not deep fry the fish but broil it on a heated shallow baking dish containing 1 tablespoon of hot oil. Turn by shaking the dish once a minute for 3–4 minutes until the fish is cooked. Instead of the tartare sauce, blend the chopped parsley, gherkin, capers and onion with ¼ cup of low-fat sour cream, small curd cottage cheese or thick low-fat yogurt. (Calories lost: up to 530.) This will give low **cholesterol** if you also omit the egg for coating the fish.
For a **gluten-free** dish, use cornstarch or millet flakes for coating the fish. As an alternative to bread, try toasted baked potato skins.

Freezing: ☑ up to 1 month.

WINTER GARDEN FLOUNDER

SALT	SUGAR	FAT	CHOL	FIBER

GLUTEN-FREE   WHOLEFOOD
TOTAL CALORIES: ABOUT 1960

Reduce both **fat** and **cholesterol** to low by using only 2 teaspoons of butter and 3 tablespoons of stock in which to cook the vegetables; replace the cream with thick low-fat yogurt, taking care that the dish does not come back to the boil.

(Calories lost: up to 530.)
To cut cholesterol still further, replace all the butter with vegetable margarine or oil. Serve with unbuttered vegetables.

Freezing: ☑ up to 1 month.

Microwave: ☑ the vegetables and the fish can be cooked in a microwave, but the final reduction and thickening of the sauce must be done on the stovetop.

SOLE WITH ORANGES

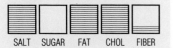

SALT	SUGAR	FAT	CHOL	FIBER

GLUTEN-FREE   WHOLEFOOD
TOTAL CALORIES: ABOUT 1675

This will be low in **salt** if the anchovies are omitted; they could be replaced by some of the strips of sweet red and green peppers. Remember to check that there is no salt in the seasoning, mayonnaise or French dressing.
Reduce the **fat** to moderate by using only half the amount of mayonnaise and mixing it with ¼ cup of low-fat small curd cottage cheese or plain yogurt (or a mixture of both). Reduce **cholesterol** by not buttering the fish before baking, and grease the dish and the wax paper or foil very lightly by brushing with a little oil instead of butter. (Calories lost: up to 500.)

Microwave: ☑ for cooking the fillets.

WINTER GARDEN FLOUNDER

The distinctive flavor of Jerusalem artichokes blended with leeks is an excellent combination with flounder or other white fish.

PREPARATION TIME: *25 min*
COOKING TIME: *50 min*
INGREDIENTS *(for 4):*
4 fillets of flounder
Fish bones
1 pound Jerusalem artichokes
½ pound leeks
¼ cup butter
½ cup hard cider or white wine
1 lemon
Salt⋆ and black pepper
5 tablespoons heavy cream

Have each fish skinned and filleted into four. Use the fish bones to make a court bouillon (page 175).
Peel and thinly slice the artichokes; wash and trim the leeks and slice them thinly. Melt the butter in a shallow flameproof casserole, add the vegetables, cover with a lid and cook gently for 5 minutes. Add the cider (or wine), the juice of half the lemon and strain in just enough court bouillon to cover the vegetables. Cover again and simmer gently for 30 minutes or until the artichokes are just tender.
Trim and wipe the fillets, season with salt, freshly ground pepper and lemon juice; fold them in half and place on top of the vegetables. Cover and cook over low heat for 15 minutes. Remove the fish to a warm plate; reduce the liquid in the pan slightly, then stir in the cream. Adjust seasoning and replace the fish; heat through.
Serve the fish in the casserole, with buttered peas.

SOLE WITH ORANGES

Cold poached sole fillets coated in mayonnaise make a quick and simple meal. The rich sauce is balanced by an orange garnish in a sharp French dressing.

PREPARATION TIME: *20 min*
COOKING TIME: *20 min*
INGREDIENTS *(for 4–6):*
12 fillets of sole
Juice of ½ lemon
3 oranges
Salt⋆ and black pepper
3 tablespoons butter
½ cup mayonnaise (page 156)
Paprika
2-ounce can anchovy fillets
2 tablespoons French dressing (page 157)

Sprinkle the fillets with the lemon juice and the juice of half an orange, then season with salt and freshly ground pepper. Finely grate the rind from one orange over the fish. Roll up the fillets; secure with wooden cocktail picks or toothpicks. Lay them in a buttered ovenproof dish.
Squeeze the juice of half an orange over the fish. Dot with small pieces of butter and cover the dish with buttered wax paper or foil. Bake in the center of a preheated oven at 350°F (180°C, mark 4) for about 20 minutes, or until the fillets are tender, but still firm. Remove from the oven and leave to cool.
Lift the cold fillets carefully on to a shallow serving dish, and remove the toothpicks. Add the juice and grated rind of half an orange, drop by drop, to the mayonnaise and coat the fillets with it. Sprinkle with paprika and decorate with halved anchovy fillets.
Peel the remaining oranges, removing all pith, and cut them into thin round slices. Dip them in the French dressing and serve as a garnish to the fillets.
Serve with a salad of blanched, sliced zucchini, strips of sweet pepper and onion rings.

Fish

HERRINGS IN OATMEAL

For brunch, herrings make a welcome change from bacon and eggs. They are equally suitable for both lunch and supper. In Scotland, small trout are often treated in the same way.

PREPARATION TIME: *15 min*
COOKING TIME: *20 min*
INGREDIENTS *(for 4):*
4 small fresh herrings
Salt★ and black pepper
3–4 tablespoons milk
4 tablespoons coarse oatmeal
½ cup unsalted butter
GARNISH:
Lemon wedges

Scale, wash and clean the herrings (page 172); cut off the heads and carefully remove the backbones. Sprinkle a little salt and freshly ground pepper over the inside of each herring. Close the fish to their original shape, dip them in milk and coat evenly and firmly with the oatmeal.

Melt the butter in a heavy-based pan; fry the herrings over gentle heat for 10 minutes on each side. Lift the fish from the pan and arrange on individual serving plates; spoon a little of the butter over each herring and garnish with lemon wedges.

MARINATED HERRINGS

In Germany and Scandinavia, fresh, smoked or salted herrings are firm favorites as a first course. Fresh herrings are usually steeped in a spicy dressing, as in this recipe.

PREPARATION TIME: *35 min*
COOKING TIME: *15–20 min*
INGREDIENTS *(for 6):*
6 large fresh herrings
2 cups cider vinegar
3 juniper berries
6 cloves
1 bay leaf
5 peppercorns
2 large onions
6 teaspoons Düsseldorf mustard
2 dill pickles

Put the vinegar, 2 cups of water, juniper berries, cloves, bay leaf and peppercorns in a saucepan and bring to the boil. Simmer this marinade for 10 minutes, then leave to cool.

Gut and clean the herrings (page 172); remove the heads and backbones but not the tails. Wash the herrings and dry them thoroughly on absorbent kitchen paper towels. Peel the onions, slice thinly and separate the slices into rings. Open the herrings out flat, and spread 1 teaspoon of mustard over the inside of each. Cut each cucumber into three slices lengthwise and place a piece of cucumber crosswise at the head end of each herring. Arrange a few of the smaller onion rings down the length of the body and roll each herring from head to tail, securing it with wooden cocktail picks or toothpicks.

Arrange the herring rolls in an ovenproof dish and pour over the strained marinade. Sprinkle with

HERRINGS IN OATMEAL

WHOLEFOOD
TOTAL CALORIES: ABOUT 2905

The **fat** and **cholesterol** inherent in the herrings cannot be reduced, but these fish provide a high level of essential fatty acids and fat-soluble vitamins as well, so are worth eating. The total levels of fat and cholesterol in the dish can be kept to low if the butter is omitted and instead the herrings are broiled on a lightly-oiled baking sheet for about 5 minutes on each side. (Calories lost: up to 900.) If trout are substituted for herrings the fat level will be lower.

The **gluten** in oatmeal is not the same as that in wheat and is sometimes tolerated by those who cannot eat wheat. If not, millet flakes make a good gluten-free substitute, as could rice flakes or ground almonds. These last go particularly well with trout.

MARINATED HERRINGS

GLUTEN-FREE   WHOLEFOOD
TOTAL CALORIES: ABOUT 2400

The low **salt** level will depend on the amount of salt previously added to dill pickles, and on the amount in the mustard. You may prefer to substitute your own prepared mustard, remembering that mustard powder contains almost no salt. The **fat** and **cholesterol** cannot be reduced as they are inherent

in herrings (see notes on the previous recipe).
Gluten-free if the mustard is gluten-free. Good Düsseldorf mustard should not contain gluten.

Microwave: ☑

SMOKED HERRING WITH HORSERADISH CREAM

| SALT | SUGAR | FAT | CHOL | FIBER |

GLUTEN-FREE   WHOLEFOOD
TOTAL CALORIES: ABOUT 1315

All smoked fish is very high in **salt**. As a low-salt alternative, use well-flavored fresh fish such as trout or monkfish, or mix smoked and fresh fish in the proportions of one part smoked to three parts fresh.
Reduce **fat** and **cholesterol** levels to medium by replacing the heavy cream with low-fat unflavored yogurt or low-fat small curd cottage cheese.
Using trout in place of herring will reduce the fat level to low. If, however, you are tempted to use sea trout, remember that it contains over twice as much natural salt as fresh-water trout. (Calories lost: up to 870.)

the remaining onion rings. Cover the dish with a lid or foil and bake the herrings for 15 minutes in the center of an oven pre-heated to 350°F (180°C, mark 4). Leave them to cool in the marinade, before setting them to marinate in the refrigerator for 2 days.

Remove the toothpicks and serve the herrings with thin slices of pumpernickel, whole wheat or coarse rye bread.

SMOKED HERRING WITH HORSERADISH CREAM

Whole smoked herrings, known as buckling, are inexpensive appetizers. Smoked trout or smoked mackerel can also be used for this recipe.

PREPARATION TIME: *15 min*
INGREDIENTS *(for 4):*
2 large smoked herring
¼ cup heavy cream
2–3 teaspoons lemon juice
2 heaping teaspoons grated horseradish
1 teaspoon tarragon vinegar
Salt★ and black pepper
½ cucumber
GARNISH:
Lemon slices

Fillet each herring into two halves, carefully removing the skin and all bones. Break the fillets up into bite-sized pieces.

Blend the cream with the lemon juice, horseradish and vinegar, and season to taste with salt and freshly ground pepper.

Cut the unpeeled cucumber into thin slices and use to line four deep scallop shells or individual shallow serving dishes. Mix the herring carefully into the dressing and pile the mixture into the center of the shells.

Top each portion with a lemon slice and serve with thin brown bread and butter.

MACKEREL WITH CUCUMBER

The cool, pale green look of young cucumber heralds summer. Its clean taste suits oily fish, such as mackerel and trout. The dish can be served hot or cold.

PREPARATION TIME: *25 min*
COOKING TIME: *35 min*
INGREDIENTS *(for 4)*:
4 mackerel, about ½ pound each
6 tablespoons butter
1 small cucumber
Salt* and black pepper
2 tablespoons white wine vinegar
  or dry white wine

Gut and clean the mackerel (page 172) and cut off the heads. Wash the fish and pat them dry on paper towels. Grease a large, shallow, ovenproof dish with 2 tablespoons of the butter. Wash and dry the cucumber and slice it thinly; put a layer of cucumber slices over the bottom of the dish. Place the mackerel on top and cover with the remaining cucumber slices. Season to taste with salt and freshly ground pepper.

Sprinkle the vinegar or wine over the fish and cucumber, and dot with 2 tablespoons of butter cut into small pieces. Cover the dish with a lid or foil and bake on the center shelf of an oven preheated to 400°F (200°C, mark 6) for 30 minutes.

Remove the dish from the oven and transfer the fish and cucumber to a serving dish. Keep it warm if the mackerel is to be served hot. Strain the juices from the fish through a fine sieve into a saucepan. Bring to the boil and continue boiling briskly, adding the remaining butter in bits and stirring occasionally. When the liquid has reduced by about half and looks thick and shiny, pour it over the mackerel and serve at once or leave to cool.

For a hot main course, serve with potatoes and young peas. Served cold, a green salad and mashed potatoes flavored with cooked garlic could complement the dish.

MACKEREL IN CIDER

It is essential to cook mackerel as soon as possible after catching it. The recipe given here comes from Somerset, England.

PREPARATION TIME: *20 min*
COOKING TIME: *35 min*
INGREDIENTS *(for 4)*:
4 mackerel
Salt* and black pepper
2 apples
1 small onion
½ pound Cheddar cheese
4–6 tablespoons butter
1 cup soft breadcrumbs
3–4 tablespoons dry hard cider
GARNISH:
Lemon wedges
Freshly chopped parsley

Prepare the mackerel as in the previous recipe and season them with salt and pepper.

Peel and coarsely grate the apples, onion and about half of the cheese. Melt the butter in a small pan over low heat. Mix the grated apple, onion, cheese and the breadcrumbs together in a bowl and bind with 1 tablespoon of the melted butter. Stuff the mackerel with this mixture and secure the opening of each with two or three wooden skewers.

Grate the remaining cheese finely. Place the mackerel side by side in an ovenproof dish and sprinkle 1 tablespoon of grated cheese over each. Pour over the remaining melted butter and enough cider to cover the bottom of the dish. Lay a piece of buttered aluminum foil or wax paper loosely over the dish and place in the center of a pre-heated oven, at 350°F (180°C, mark 4). Bake for 25–35 minutes, or until the mackerel are cooked through

MACKEREL WITH CUCUMBER

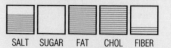

GLUTEN-FREE   WHOLEFOOD
TOTAL CALORIES: ABOUT 1665

Mackerel is fairly high in **salt**. Compensate for the lack of added salt with up to 1 teaspoon of lightly crushed dill seeds.
To reduce the **fat** and **cholesterol** to moderate, make this dish in late winter, when mackerel have least fat. Grease the baking dish with a very little oil and sprinkle the fish with a little more. The only way to reduce the fat to low is to use another kind of fish, such as trout. (Calories lost: up to 500 if mackerel is used, up to 660 if you use trout.)

Microwave: ☑ for the fish.

MACKEREL IN CIDER

GLUTEN-FREE*   WHOLEFOOD*
TOTAL CALORIES: ABOUT 2735

For medium **salt**, use only 3 ounces cheese, unsalted butter and crumbs from unsalted bread.
To reduce **fat** and **cholesterol** to moderate, use mackerel in late winter when they are least oily, halve the amount of cheese (use low-fat Cheddar if you can find it) and bind the mixture with milk instead of the butter. Omit the butter poured over the fish and brush the fish covering sparingly with a little oil. (Calories lost: up to 1100.)

Microwave: ☑

MACKEREL WITH GOOSEBERRY SAUCE

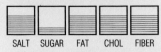

SALT	SUGAR	FAT	CHOL	FIBER

GLUTEN-FREE*   WHOLEFOOD*
TOTAL CALORIES: ABOUT 1835

To reduce **salt** in this dish, use crumbs from unsalted bread, replace mackerel with trout, or serve smaller portions.
For low **fat** use trout or make in late winter when mackerel has much less oil. Do not brush the fish with oil, but make slits in their sides and brush the broiler pan very lightly with oil. The oil from the fish will quickly provide all that is needed. For lower **cholesterol** omit butter from gooseberries. (Calories lost: up to 660.)
Wholefood: sweeten with 1 tablespoon of honey.

MACKEREL WITH TOMATOES

SALT	SUGAR	FAT	CHOL	FIBER

GLUTEN FREE*   WHOLEFOOD*
TOTAL CALORIES: ABOUT 2245

To reduce **salt** to low, use small portions, with extra garlic and parsley to compensate for the lack of added salt.
For low **fat** and **cholesterol**, reduce the portions or substitute almost any white fish or fresh water trout. Broil the mackerel. Use only 1–2 teaspoons oil to cook the onions and mushrooms, and garnish with uncooked or broiled tomatoes. (Calories lost: up to 730.)

Freezing: ☑ up to 1 month.
Microwave: ☑

and golden brown in color.
Serve the mackerel straight from the dish, garnished with lemon wedges and parsley.
Baked potatoes make a perfect addition to this dish.

MACKEREL WITH GOOSEBERRY SAUCE

The tart taste of gooseberries contrasts well with mackerel. If gooseberries are not available, rhubarb can be used instead.

PREPARATION TIME: *15 min*
COOKING TIME: *16 min*
INGREDIENTS *(for 4):*
4 mackerel
⅓ cup soft breadcrumbs
1 tablespoon chopped parsley
Grated rind of a lemon
1 egg
Grated nutmeg
Salt⋆ and black pepper
Melted butter
GOOSEBERRY SAUCE:
½ pound fresh gooseberries
2 tablespoons sugar
2 tablespoons butter
1 tablespoon fresh chopped fennel or 1 teaspoon ground fennel

Make a stuffing by mixing the breadcrumbs, parsley and lemon rind. Bind with the lightly beaten egg and season with nutmeg, salt and pepper. Secure the stuffed mackerel with wooden toothpicks. Brush lightly with melted butter and broil for about 8 minutes on each side.
To make the sauce, put the gooseberries in 6 tablespoons water with the sugar, butter and fennel. Bring to the boil and simmer until the gooseberries pop open. Serve the sauce in a bowl, with the mackerel.

MACKEREL WITH TOMATOES

Mackerel is sometimes known as the poor man's trout – unjustly so; although both are oily fish, their flavors are quite distinct. Mackerel makes an excellent and economical main course.

PREPARATION TIME: *30 min*
COOKING TIME: *20 min*
INGREDIENTS *(for 4–6):*
6 medium mackerel
Seasoned flour (page 184)
3 tablespoons vegetable or olive oil
1 onion
8 small mushrooms
1 clove garlic
¾ pound firm tomatoes
2 tablespoons butter
Salt⋆ and black pepper
1 teaspoon chopped parsley
2 teaspoons wine vinegar

Clean and fillet the mackerel (page 172). Wash the fillets, wipe them dry on a clean cloth and coat them with seasoned flour, shaking off any surplus. Heat 2 tablespoons of the oil in a heavy-based frying pan and, when hot, fry the fillets for about 10 minutes, or until golden brown, turning once.
While the mackerel is frying, peel the onion and garlic, and wipe and trim the mushrooms. Finely chop the onion and mushrooms, and crush the garlic. Skin the tomatoes (page 179) and slice them thinly. Heat the remaining oil in a clean pan and fry the onion for a few minutes over moderate heat. Add the mushrooms and garlic, and cook very gently for a further 5 minutes. Season to taste with salt and freshly ground pepper, and stir in the parsley and vinegar. Fry the tomato slices for 3 minutes in the butter, using a separate pan over gentle heat.
To serve, arrange the warm mackerel fillets on a serving dish, put the tomatoes between them and spoon a little of the onion mixture on to each fillet. Serve with new potatoes and a salad.

SALMON KEDGEREE

In the 19th century, kedgeree, of Indian origin, was an established British breakfast dish. Nowadays it is more often served for a light lunch or supper.

PREPARATION TIME: *5 min*
COOKING TIME: *30 min*
INGREDIENTS (*for 4–6*):
½ pound cooked salmon
Salt★, black pepper and cayenne
¾ cup long grain rice
1 onion
¼ cup butter
2 hard-cooked eggs
GARNISH:
Chopped parsley

Remove any skin and bones from the salmon, and flake it carefully. Bring 1½ cups of water to the boil in a large saucepan, adding a pinch each of salt, pepper and cayenne. Add the rice, cover tightly with a lid or foil, and cook over low heat for about 25 minutes, or until all the water is absorbed and the rice is fluffy.

While the rice is cooking, peel and finely chop the onion. Melt a little of the butter in a pan and fry the onion until soft and transparent. Set aside. Roughly chop the whites of the hard-cooked eggs, and press the yolks through a sieve.

Cut the remaining butter into small pieces and stir into the cooked rice, with the flaked salmon, onion and egg whites. Season to taste and heat the mixture through gently.

To serve, pile the kedgeree up on a warmed flat dish and decorate with the sieved egg yolks, arranged in a star or cross pattern. Sprinkle generously with chopped parsley. You could serve the kedgeree with hot buttered toast fingers.

SALMON IN ASPIC

This makes an excellent and attractive centerpiece for a special dinner occasion or a cold buffet. It also has the advantage that it can be prepared well in advance.

PREPARATION TIME: *30 min*
COOKING TIME: *1–1½ hours*
INGREDIENTS (*for 8*):
1 small Coho salmon,
approximately 2½–3 pounds
1 envelope unflavored gelatin
1 tablespoon white wine vinegar
6 tablespoons dry sherry
2 egg whites
STOCK:
1 carrot
1 onion
Bouquet garni (page 183)
4 peppercorns
1½ tablespoons wine vinegar
½ teaspoon salt
GARNISH:
¼ pound peeled cooked shrimp
Watercress

Begin by making the stock, putting all the ingredients, with 2½ cups of water, in a pan. Bring to the boil, cover the pan with a lid and simmer for 20 minutes. Strain the stock through cheesecloth.

Remove the fins and gills from the salmon, if not already done by the fish man, and cut a 1 in deep inverted V out of the tail to make it resemble a mermaid's tail. Wash the fish thoroughly to remove all traces of blood, and put it in a fish poacher, or large flameproof dish. Pour over the warm stock and cover with a lid or foil. Cook the fish for 25–30 minutes on top of the stove, or for 50 minutes in a pre-heated oven at

SALMON KEDGEREE

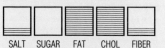

SALT · SUGAR · FAT · CHOL · FIBER

GLUTEN-FREE   WHOLEFOOD
TOTAL CALORIES: ABOUT 1690

You can reduce the **fat** level of this recipe to low by using only 1 teaspoon of butter to dress the rice. The mixture will not be dry, as salmon is an oily fish. This will give a moderate **cholesterol** level: to reduce it to low, omit the eggs or use the whites only. (Calories lost: up to 580.)

White rice provides only about 1 gram of **fiber** per person in this dish (making 4 servings). Using brown rice would provide about twice as much – still not high, but $\frac{1}{15}$th of a day's target intake. It also makes the dish **wholefood**, but will require to be cooked in about 2¼ times its own volume of water for about 40–45 minutes. In this way all the water is absorbed, recouping any minerals and vitamins leached into the water.

SALMON IN ASPIC

SALT · SUGAR · FAT · CHOL · FIBER

GLUTEN-FREE   WHOLEFOOD
TOTAL CALORIES: ABOUT 2875

The **fat** in this recipe comes almost entirely from the salmon, averaging 13% fat. However, this is still lower than much meat and is a less saturated type of fat. The **cholesterol** in salmon is medium, but high in the shrimp garnish. To avoid this, replace the shrimp with the traditional cucumber and watercress and, if liked, skinned pistachio nuts. (Calories lost: up to 120.)

Microwave: ☑ this is perfectly suitable for microwave cooking, but few microwaves are big enough to take a whole salmon, so you will probably have to cut it into chunks.

SWEET-SOUR SALMON

SALT	SUGAR	FAT	CHOL	FIBER

GLUTEN-FREE   WHOLEFOOD
TOTAL CALORIES: ABOUT 1795

The **fat** and **cholesterol** content of salmon is moderate, and the fat of a less saturated kind than in most meat. Because of the richness of the fish, the other elements pushing up the fat and cholesterol – the egg yolk and cream sauce – can be changed without spoiling the recipe. Replace with thick low-fat plain yogurt, flavored with the same cooking juices but not cooked: reduce the juice on its own. (Calories lost: up to 270.)

Microwave: ☑ for cooking the fish.

350°F (180°C, mark 4), basting with the stock.

Leave the fish to cool in the liquid. When quite cold, snip the skin near the head with a pair of scissors and peel it carefully off, leaving the head and tail intact. Split the fish along the backbone with a sharp knife and snip the bone below the head and above the tail. Ease the backbone out carefully without breaking the salmon.

Strain the fish liquid, through cheesecloth, into a saucepan. Dissolve the gelatin in ¼ cup of the liquid, and heat the remainder over moderate heat, whisking steadily until the liquid is hot. Stir in the dissolved gelatin, the vinegar, sherry and the egg whites; whisk steadily until the mixture comes to the boil. Draw the pan off the heat at once and leave the liquid to settle for 5 minutes. Bring to the boil again, draw it off the heat and leave it to settle once more. The liquid should now look clear; otherwise repeat the boiling process again. Strain the liquid through a clean cloth and set aside to cool.

Spoon a little of the cool aspic over the bottom of a serving dish and leave it to set. Lift the salmon carefully on top of the aspic. Garnish the fish with the shrimp and spoon over a little of the aspic. When the shrimp have set, spoon aspic over the whole salmon and leave to set.

Serve the salmon garnished with sprigs of watercress and the remaining chopped aspic.

SWEET-SOUR SALMON

In German cooking, a sweet-sour sauce is frequently served with fish and with braised meat. It is often served hot, but the flavor improves when chilled.

PREPARATION TIME: *10 min*
COOKING TIME: *35–40 min*
CHILLING TIME: *2–3 hours*
INGREDIENTS *(for 4):*
4 salmon steaks, 1 inch thick
Salt★ and black pepper
2 large onions
2 tablespoons white wine vinegar
2 heaping tablespoons light-brown sugar
Juice of 2 lemons
2 egg yolks
5 tablespoons heavy cream
GARNISH:
Cucumber slices

Wash and dry the salmon steaks. Season with salt and freshly ground pepper and arrange in a shallow ovenproof dish. Cover with peeled and sliced onions.

Pour boiling, lightly salted water over the fish just to cover it.

Seal the dish with foil and bake in the center of a pre-heated oven at 325°F (170°C, mark 3) for 20–25 minutes, or until cooked. Lift the steaks carefully with a slotted spatula and arrange on a serving dish.

Strain the cooking liquid through cheesecloth and measure 1¼ cups into a saucepan; add the vinegar, brown sugar and lemon juice. Simmer over low heat until the liquid has reduced slightly. Beat yolks and cream together in a bowl and stir in a tablespoon of the reduced liquid; blend thoroughly and gradually add all the liquid. Set the bowl over a pan of simmering water, and stir the sauce continuously until it thickens to a coating consistency.

Pour the sauce over the salmon and cool before chilling for at least 2 hours in the refrigerator.

Garnish the salmon steaks with thin slices of unpeeled cucumber and serve with boiled potatoes and a crisp green salad.

COULIBIAC

This traditional Russian fish pie is usually served hot, with sour cream, but also makes an exceptionally good buffet choice.

PREPARATION TIME: *2 hours*
COOKING TIME: *30 min*
INGREDIENTS *(for 8–10):*
1 cup tapioca
2 onions
¾ pound button mushrooms
¼ cup unsalted butter
Salt★ and black pepper
2 slices middle-cut salmon, each
*   1 inch thick*
1¼ cups dry white wine
3 hard-cooked eggs
6 thin crêpes (page 20: use ½–⅔
*   cup milk, leaving the other*
*   ingredients as they are)*
1 pound puff pastry
1 egg for glazing
1 cup sour cream

Bring a pan of salted water to the boil and sprinkle in the tapioca, stirring all the time. Bring to the boil and simmer gently for 30 minutes, after which the tapioca should be transparent. Drain through a fine sieve and rinse under cold water to remove excess starch. Set aside.

Meanwhile, peel and finely chop the onions; wipe, trim and finely chop the mushrooms. Melt the butter in a large frying pan and add the onions; cover with a lid and cook over low heat for 5 minutes until the onions are soft, but not brown. Increase the heat and add the mushrooms. Season with salt and freshly ground pepper and cook, stirring continuously, for 5 minutes. Remove the pan from the heat and stir in the tapioca; correct the seasoning if necessary and leave

the mixture to cool.

Wipe the salmon pieces and put them in a saucepan together with the wine and a pinch of salt and pepper. Simmer the salmon gently for about 10 minutes; draw the pan off the heat and let the salmon cool in the liquid. Drain; remove skin and bones from the salmon and flake the flesh.

When ready to assemble the coulibiac, heat the mushroom and tapioca mixture slightly to soften. If necessary warm the crêpes over a pan of boiling water to unstick them. Slice the eggs into rounds. Roll out the puff pastry to a rectangle no more than ¼ in thick and approximately 16 in long by 9 in wide. Cut the edges straight and reserve the trimmings for decoration. Brush the pastry with the lightly beaten egg to within 1 in of the edges.

Brush three of the crêpes with egg and lay them in a single line down the pastry. Spoon a quarter of the mushroom mixture in a neat strip, 2–3 in wide and to within 2 in of the shorter pastry edges, over the crêpes. Top with half the flaked salmon and then

with another layer of mushroom and all the egg slices. Spoon a further quarter of mushrooms on before the remaining salmon and then the last of the mushrooms. Top with the remaining crêpes, brush with egg and wrap the crêpes around the filling.

Fold the sides of the pastry up and over the top of the filling so that the edges overlap. Brush thoroughly with egg to seal the edges. Fold the pastry ends over the top and seal with egg. Place the coulibiac on a wet baking sheet with the sealed edges underneath. Brush the top with egg.

Roll out the pastry trimmings and use for decoration. Cut a small hole in the center of the pastry and insert a roll of wax paper.

Place the baking sheet on the center shelf of a pre-heated oven. Bake at 425°F (220°C, mark 7) for about 30 minutes or until the pastry is golden brown.

Serve the coulibiac with a separate bowl of sour cream.

COULIBIAC

SALT SUGAR FAT CHOL FIBER

GLUTEN-FREE★
TOTAL CALORIES: ABOUT 6110

The **salt** content is low only if there is no added salt in either the pastry or the crêpes.
To reduce both **fat** and **cholesterol** to low, use only 1 tablespoon of butter or oil to cook the onions and mushrooms; use only 1 yolk, with whites of other eggs if wished; make the crêpes with skim milk; and reduce the amount of sour cream (or substitute cultured buttermilk or thick low-fat plain yogurt). Puff pastry is very high in fat and usually in cholesterol, and attempts to adapt it are not really satisfactory; instead, use either purchased phyllo pastry or a yeast dough (this is in fact more traditional than puff pastry). (Calories lost: up to 1060.)
For a **wholefood** coulibiac, use whole wheat flour for the crêpes and for a yeast dough to wrap it in; substitute brown rice for the tapioca, cooking it as suggested in the alternatives to the salmon kedgeree on page 28. This will also increase the **fiber** content considerably.

GRAVAD LAX

SALT SUGAR FAT CHOL FIBER

GLUTEN-FREE* WHOLEFOOD*
TOTAL CALORIES: ABOUT 2485

The **salt** content of this recipe cannot be reduced, as it provides the pickling agent. However, you can avoid the full content of sugar in the sauce by adding a smaller amount, say half a tablespoon, of honey (which is sweeter, especially when eaten cold).

The **fat** content of salmon is moderate, but of a less saturated type than in most meat. Reduce the fat content of the total dish to moderate by making sauce with a base of sour cream or thick low-fat yogurt – both traditional to Scandinavia – rather than using oil and egg yolk. This will also reduce the **cholesterol** to low. (Calories lost: up to 650.)

Gluten-free: there will only be gluten in this dish if there is any in the mustard, and possibly in the white pepper. Check the list of ingredients.

GRAVAD LAX

This Scandinavian dish traditionally uses fresh dill, but it can also be made with dried dill. The pickling adds a subtle flavor to fresh salmon.

PREPARATION TIME: *30 min*
INGREDIENTS *(for 6):*
1½ pounds salmon tailpiece
PICKLE:
1 heaping tablespoon sea salt
1 heaping tablespoon sugar
1 teaspoon crushed black
  peppercorns
1 tablespoon brandy (optional)
1 heaping tablespoon chopped
  fresh dill or 1 tablespoon dried
  dill
SAUCE:
2 heaping tablespoons Dijon-style
  or Düsseldorf mustard
1 heaping tablespoon sugar

1 large egg yolk
7 tablespoons olive oil
2 tablespoons wine vinegar
1 heaping teaspoon chopped
  fresh dill or 1 teaspoon dried
  dill
Salt★ and white pepper

Have the salmon filleted into two triangles. Mix all the pickling ingredients together and spread a quarter of this mixture over the bottom of a flat dish. Lay the first piece of salmon, skin down, on top of the mixture and spread half of the remaining pickle over the cut side. Place the other piece of salmon, skin side up, over the first. Spread the top with the remaining mixture, rubbing it well into the skin. Cover the salmon with a piece of foil and a

board weighed down with a couple of cans.

Leave the salmon to press in a cool place or the refrigerator for anything up to 5 days, but not less than 12 hours, turning the salmon once a day.

Before serving, slice the salmon thinly, either parallel to the skin as with smoked salmon or obliquely to the skin.

For the sauce, beat the mustard with the sugar and egg yolk until smooth. Gradually add the oil and vinegar, mixing well between each addition. Season to taste with dill, salt and pepper.

Arrange the slices of salmon on individual plates, and serve buttered rye bread and the sauce separately in a bowl.

Fish

TROUT WITH BRETON SAUCE

Breton sauce is reminiscent of mayonnaise, but is easier to make and less oily, more like a Béarnaise sauce (page 156) flavored with mustard and herbs. The sharp flavor of the sauce makes it a perfect foil for fish dishes. It goes exceptionally well with cold trout, mackerel or herring as well as salmon or sea trout.

PREPARATION TIME: *25 min*
COOKING TIME: *25–30 min*
INGREDIENTS *(for 4–6):*

4 large trout
1 tablespoon olive oil
SAUCE:
2 tablespoons Dijon-style mustard
2 egg yolks
2 teaspoons wine, cider or
  tarragon vinegar
Salt★ and black pepper
6 tablespoons unsalted butter
2 tablespoons chopped fresh
  parsley and chives
GARNISH:
½ cucumber

Wash and clean the trout thoroughly; cut off the heads and dry the fish on a clean cloth. Wrap each trout in a piece of oiled aluminum foil and put them in a baking dish. Bake in the center of a pre-heated oven at 325°F (170°C, mark 3) for about 25–30 minutes or until they are cooked through.

Remove the dish from the oven and open the foil packets to allow the trout to cool slightly. Split each fish along the belly and, with a pointed knife, carefully loosen the backbone; ease it out gently so that most of the small bones come away with it (see page 173 for illustrated instructions on how to do this). Set the trout aside to cool.

To make the sauce, beat the mustard, egg yolks and vinegar together until well blended; season to taste with salt and freshly ground pepper. Put the butter in a bowl over a pan of hot water and stir until it has softened, but not melted. Gradually add the butter to the egg mixture, beating all the time, until the sauce has the consistency of thick cream. Stir in the finely chopped herbs.

Before serving, gently peel the skin from the cold trout, cut each into two fillets and arrange on a serving dish. Pour the sauce over. Peel the cucumber, cut it in half lengthwise and scrape out the seeds with a pointed teaspoon. Dice the flesh and sprinkle it over the trout.

Serve with crusty bread and butter and lightly cooked broccoli or spinach for a main course or, in small quantities and on its own or with whole wheat bread, as an appetizer for a dinner party.

SMOKED TROUT MOUSSE

This mousse, which has a creamy texture and smoky flavor, makes an attractive first course. The cottage cheese helps to counter the richness of the fish. Smoked mackerel and smoked salmon (the bits left over from slicing a whole side are ideal and not too expensive) are also suitable. It can be prepared a day in advance and kept in the refrigerator until required.

PREPARATION TIME: *15 min*
CHILLING TIME: *1 hour*
INGREDIENTS *(for 4–6):*
¾ pound smoked trout
½ cup cottage cheese
½ cup sour cream
Juice of half lemon
Salt★ and black pepper
GARNISH:
Finely chopped parsley

Remove the skin and bones from the trout, and flake the meat into a liquidizer or food processor. Sieve the cottage cheese and add, with the sour cream, to the flaked fish. Blend the mixture until smooth. Alternatively, pound the flaked fish to a smooth paste with a mortar and pestle, before mixing in the sieved cottage cheese and the sour cream. Season to taste with the lemon juice, salt and pepper.

Spoon the mousse into individual ramekin dishes and leave to chill in the refrigerator.

Sprinkle finely chopped parsley in a neat border around the edge of each dish. Serve with fingers or triangles of hot brown toast and butter. You could, if you wished, serve it with hot pita bread or French bread for a more substantial course.

TROUT WITH BRETON SAUCE

SALT   SUGAR   FAT   CHOL   FIBER

GLUTEN-FREE*   WHOLEFOOD
TOTAL CALORIES: ABOUT 1625

To keep **salt** level low, look for a mustard with little or no added salt. Mustard itself is very low in sodium.
To reduce the **fat** and **cholesterol** to low, base the sauce on thick low-fat yogurt rather than butter and egg yolks. Use about ½ cup and flavor with the mustard, vinegar, seasoning and herbs. Heat gently but do not let it boil. Chill before serving. (Calories lost: up to 750.)
Gluten-free if there is no gluten in the mustard; check the ingredients list.

Microwave: ☑ for cooking the trout.

SMOKED TROUT MOUSSE

SALT   SUGAR   FAT   CHOL   FIBER

GLUTEN-FREE   WHOLEFOOD
TOTAL CALORIES: ABOUT 700

Smoked fish is very salty. The only way to reduce the **salt** level of this dish is to mix a small amount of smoked trout with fresh, poached trout, in the proportions, say, of one part smoked trout to two parts fresh. This will give a moderate salt level.
To reduce **fat** and **cholesterol** to low, replace the sour cream with low-fat imitation sour cream or thick low-fat plain yogurt. (Calories lost: up to 200.)

Food processor: ☑ very useful for blending the mixture to a smooth paste.

TROUT WITH MUSHROOMS

SALT	SUGAR	FAT	CHOL	FIBER

GLUTEN-FREE* WHOLEFOOD*
TOTAL CALORIES: ABOUT 2615

To reduce levels of both **fat** and **cholesterol** to low, broil the trout on a baking sheet lightly brushed with butter or fat, and brush the fish itself very lightly with oil or butter before coating it with flour. Trout is a moist, slightly oily fish so it will not get dry provided it is not cooked too long. Broil the mushrooms and garlic on the same baking sheet after the fish have been removed; if necessary, add a very little more fat, shaking the sheet to coat the vegetables. Transfer the mixture to a saucepan and continue with the recipe. Reduce the sauce to the consistency of cream before stirring in thick low-fat plain yogurt (instead of cream), off the heat, just before serving. (Calories lost: up to 1225.) Alternatives for coating which are both **gluten-free** and **wholefood** include brown rice flour, potato starch and chick pea flour.

Microwave: ☑ for cooking the trout.

TROUT WITH MUSHROOMS

This recipe from the Pyrenees combines fresh river trout with button mushrooms, served in a Pernod sauce.

PREPARATION TIME: *10 min*
COOKING TIME: *15 min*
INGREDIENTS *(for 4)*:
4 trout, 6–8 ounces each
Seasoned flour (page 184)
6–8 tablespoons clarified butter
 (page 182)
½ pound button mushrooms
1 clove garlic
2–3 tablespoons Pernod or Ricard
½ cup heavy cream
Salt★
Black pepper

Wipe the trout lightly with a damp cloth, but do not remove the blue-gray outer coating. Slit the trout along the belly and remove the entrails. Coat each trout with seasoned flour, shaking off any excess. Melt the clarified butter in a large, heavy frying pan and fry the trout over moderate heat for 5 minutes on each side, or until golden brown and crisp.

Meanwhile, trim the mushrooms and slice them thinly. Peel and crush the garlic. Lift the trout on to a serving dish and keep them warm. Fry the mushrooms and garlic in the trout juices, over low heat, for 3–4 minutes. Stir in the Pernod and let the liquid bubble rapidly for a few minutes. Add the cream, stirring continuously until the sauce has reduced to the consistency of thick cream. Season to taste with salt, freshly ground pepper, and a little more Pernod if necessary. Pour the sauce over the trout.

Serve immediately, with boiled buttered potatoes and a crisp green salad or some green vegetables.

Shellfish

LOBSTER AND AVOCADO BRISTOL FASHION

Scarlet lobster and green avocados make an attractive appetizer for a special occasion. Avocados should be prepared at the last minute, otherwise the delicate green flesh turns brown. If you do have to prepare it a little bit in advance, sprinkle well with lemon juice and this will help to stop it discoloring.

PREPARATION TIME: *25 min*
INGREDIENTS *(for 4)*:
1 medium-sized cooked lobster
2 large avocados
6 tablespoons heavy cream
2 teaspoons lemon juice
Cayenne pepper
Salt★
Paprika

Have the cooked lobster split into two halves. Remove the gray sac in each half of the head and the black intestinal vein. Remove all the lobster meat from the body, tail and claws, and set the thin scarlet crawler claws aside for garnish.

Chop the lobster meat finely, put it in a basin and stir in the cream and lemon juice. Season to taste with cayenne pepper.

Cut the avocados in half lengthwise and remove the seeds. Scoop out some of the avocado flesh, leaving about ½ in lining to hold the shape of each half shell.

Dice the flesh finely and fold it into the lobster mixture. Season with salt if necessary.

Pile the lobster mixture into the avocado shells and sprinkle with a little paprika. Arrange the claws on top in a decorative pattern.

LOBSTER THERMIDOR

Lobster is the most expensive of all shellfish, but is also regarded by gourmets as the most delicious. This classic French recipe comes from the famous Café de Paris.

PREPARATION TIME: *50 min*
COOKING TIME: *1½ hours*
INGREDIENTS *(for 6)*:
3 cooked lobsters, 1¼–1½ pounds each
1¼ cups fish stock (page 153)
½ cup dry white wine
1 onion
4 peppercorns
1 bay leaf
1 sprig thyme
Salt★ and black pepper
2 cups milk
½ cup unsalted butter
6 tablespoons flour
1 teaspoon Dijon-style mustard
2 large egg yolks
½ cup light cream
1 teaspoon lemon juice
¾ cup grated Parmesan cheese
1 cup browned bread crumbs
GARNISH:
Lettuce

Pour the fish stock and white wine into a saucepan, bring to the boil and boil briskly until the liquid has reduced to ½ cup.

Peel the onion, cut it into quarters and put it in another saucepan with the peppercorns, bay leaf, thyme, a pinch of salt and the milk. Bring to the boil, remove the pan from the heat, cover with a lid and leave the milk to infuse for 30 minutes.

Meanwhile, remove the claws from the lobsters (page 176); split each body in half lengthwise, through the head and tail and along the center line of the shell.

LOBSTER AND AVOCADO BRISTOL FASHION

| SALT | SUGAR | FAT | CHOL | FIBER |

GLUTEN-FREE WHOLEFOOD
TOTAL CALORIES: ABOUT 1265

Lobster is naturally fairly high in **salt** and the exact salt level will therefore depend on the size of the lobster; if each portion has less than ¼ pound lobster, the total salt will only be about 375 mg, in other words moderate.
Lobster is also relatively high in **cholesterol**, although low in **fat**. However, the amount in ¼ pound is less than in 1 egg. To reduce fat, use thick low-fat plain yogurt or low-fat small curd cottage cheese instead of heavy cream. But the total fat in this recipe will still be at best moderate, since avocados are high in oil, ranging from 11 to 39% according to season. (Calories lost: up to 300.)

LOBSTER THERMIDOR

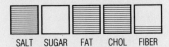

| SALT | SUGAR | FAT | CHOL | FIBER |

GLUTEN-FREE*   WHOLEFOOD*
TOTAL CALORIES: ABOUT 3350

Lobster is naturally higher than most natural foods in **salt**, while being much lower than cheese or bacon, for instance. However, the total salt content can be reduced to moderate by using less Parmesan cheese and using breadcrumbs from bread made without salt. Choose a mustard without added salt. To limit the **fat** to the low level naturally present in the lobster, use skim milk and make the sauce by blending flour and a little of the infused milk to a smooth paste, then gradually working in the remaining milk and stirring gently over a low heat. Add 1 teaspoon of butter and simmer for 5–6 minutes. Omit the egg yolks and cream from sauce, replacing with $\frac{2}{3}$ cup low-fat small curd cottage cheese, after which the sauce should not be boiled again. Use 2 teaspoons butter or oil to brush the pan in which you will sauté the lobster meat. This dish remains medium in **cholesterol**, which is fairly high in lobster. (Calories lost: up to 1330.)

Set the shells aside, with the feeler claws intact. Discard the gray sac in the head and the black intestinal vein in the body.

Rub any loose coral (or roe) through a fine sieve. Remove the meat from the shells and the claws and cut it carefully into $\frac{3}{4}$ in cubes. Melt $\frac{1}{4}$ cup of the butter in a shallow, heavy-based pan and gently fry the lobster meat, turning it frequently, for 3–4 minutes. Remove the pan from the heat and set aside.

Melt the remaining butter in a saucepan, stir in the flour and cook gently for 2 minutes; remove the pan from the heat. Strain the infused milk through a fine sieve and gradually stir this and the reduced fish stock into the roux. Bring this sauce to the boil, stirring continuously, and cook gently for 3 minutes, until the sauce thickens. Leave to cool for 2 minutes, then stir in the mustard, egg yolks, sieved coral and the cream. Season with salt and pepper, and stir in the lemon juice.

Coat the inside of the empty lobster shells with a little of the sauce. Stir half the remaining sauce into the lobster in the pan and carefully spoon the mixture into the shells. Cover with the remaining sauce. Mix the Parmesan cheese with the breadcrumbs and sprinkle over the lobsters. Place the shells under a preheated broiler and cook until the topping is golden brown.

Serve the lobster on a bed of lettuce, with crisp French bread and a tossed green salad.

Shellfish

CRAB TART

Most savory tarts or flans are baked blind – that is the pastry is partly cooked before the filling is added. They are ideal for summer fare, since they are quick to make and equally tasty served either hot or cold.

PREPARATION TIME: *20–30 min*
COOKING TIME: *30 min*
INGREDIENTS *(for 4–6):*
PASTRY:
2 cups flour
¼ teaspoon salt★
¼ teaspoon cayenne pepper
¼ cup butter
¼ cup lard
¼ cup grated Cheddar cheese
1 egg yolk
FILLING:
½–¾ pound crabmeat
3 eggs
2 teaspoons lemon juice
½ teaspoon Worcestershire sauce
½ cup heavy cream
Salt★

For the pastry, sift the flour, salt and cayenne pepper into a mixing bowl. Rub in the butter and lard, cut into pieces, until the mixture is crumbly. Mix in the cheese; bind the pastry with the egg yolk and a little cold water. Leave the pastry to rest for 30 minutes.

Roll this cheese pastry out on a lightly floured surface, and use to line a 9 in flan ring. Prick the bottom of the pastry case and bake it in the pre-heated oven at 400°F (200°C, mark 6) for 10 minutes or until golden.

Flake the crabmeat finely into a bowl. Beat the eggs lightly with the lemon juice and Worcestershire sauce and stir it into the crab meat before blending in the cream. Add salt to taste.

Spoon the crab mixture into the pastry case and bake in the oven with the temperature reduced to 375°F (190°C, mark 5) for 25–30 minutes.

Serve the tart, hot or cold, cut into wedges, and with crusty bread and a mixed salad, for a light lunch. Lemon wedges could be used to garnish.

HOT CRAB SOUFFLÉ

The French invented the soufflé, which is basically a sauce and a savory or sweet purée blended with stiffly beaten egg whites. It should emerge from the oven light, fluffy and golden.

PREPARATION TIME: *20 min*
COOKING TIME: *35–40 min*
INGREDIENTS *(for 4):*
6 ounces crabmeat, fresh, canned or frozen
2 tablespoons butter
2 tablespoons flour
1 cup milk
Salt★ and black pepper
Cayenne pepper
½ cup grated Cheddar cheese
4 eggs

Melt the butter in a saucepan; stir in the flour and cook over low heat for a few minutes. Gradually beat in the milk, stirring continuously until the sauce thickens and comes to the boil. Season to taste with salt, freshly ground pepper and cayenne. Stir in the cheese and leave the sauce to cool for 5 minutes.

Separate the eggs and beat the yolks, one at a time, into the cheese sauce. Flake the prepared crabmeat finely and blend it into the sauce. Correct seasoning if necessary. Beat the egg whites until stiff, then add to the crab mixture; fold them in gently with a metal spoon.

Pour into a buttered 1 quart soufflé dish and level the top. Bake in the center of an oven pre-heated to 375°F (190°C, mark 5), for 35–40 minutes, until well risen and golden brown. Serve immediately; a green salad could also be served.

CRAB TART

GLUTEN-FREE★ WHOLEFOOD★
TOTAL CALORIES: ABOUT 3185

It is difficult to reduce the **salt** in this dish, as most comes from the crab naturally, but you can omit the Worcestershire sauce and halve the amount of cheese. The **fat** level is also difficult to reduce unless you replace the pastry with biscuit dough (see page 12). The cream in the filling can be replaced with full cream milk or sour cream, and the number of eggs reduced to 2. (Calories lost: up to 1140.) The levels of salt, fat and **cholesterol** (from the crab and eggs) will remain medium-high.

Food processor √ for pastry.

HOT CRAB SOUFFLÉ

GLUTEN-FREE★ WHOLEFOOD★
TOTAL CALORIES: ABOUT 1330

To reduce the **salt** to medium, replace the cheese with ¼ cup grated Parmesan and mix the crabmeat half and half with flaked fresh cooked white fish. To reduce **fat** and **cholesterol**, use skim milk; use 3 yolks and 4 whites in the soufflé, and make the soufflé base with vegetable margarine instead of butter. However the levels of both will remain moderate to high. (Calories lost: up to 160.) Potato starch is a good **gluten-free** flour for soufflés, but only half the quantity given is needed.

CRAB WITH MUSHROOMS

SALT	SUGAR	FAT	CHOL	FIBER

GLUTEN-FREE   WHOLEFOOD
TOTAL CALORIES: ABOUT 1775

To reduce **salt**, replace the olives in the garnish by, for instance, slices of pepper or fennel which are lower in salt. As crab contains a substantial amount of salt, a version moderate in salt would be obtained by mixing crab half and half with poached flaked white fish or scallops.
This would also reduce the **cholesterol** level (which in crab, as in most shellfish, is fairly high) to moderate.
To reduce the **fat** level to low, substitute thick low-fat plain yogurt for the oil and heavy cream. (Calories lost: up to 900.)

CUCUMBER CUPS WITH SHRIMP

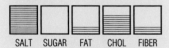

SALT	SUGAR	FAT	CHOL	FIBER

GLUTEN-FREE   WHOLEFOOD
TOTAL CALORIES: ABOUT 375

Shrimp are high in **salt** and the only way of reducing salt to a moderate level in this dish is to mix them half and half with poached flaked white fish. Monkfish is particularly good as its firm texture is not unlike that of shrimp.
The **cholesterol** also comes from the shrimp, so would be reduced to low by the same alteration. (Calories lost: up to 60.)

CRAB WITH MUSHROOMS

This combination of mushrooms and crabmeat, frozen or canned, makes a good main course. The dish can also be served as an appetizer, and shrimp can be substituted for crab.

PREPARATION TIME: *10 min*
CHILLING TIME: *1 hour*
INGREDIENTS *(for 4–6):*
½ *pound crabmeat*
½ *pound button mushrooms*
2 *cloves garlic*
Juice of half lemon
Tabasco sauce
6 *tablespoons olive oil*
¼ *teaspoon sugar*
Salt★ and black pepper
½ *cup heavy cream*
GARNISH:
¾ *cup ripe olives*
Chopped parsley

Trim and finely slice the mushrooms into a deep bowl. Crush the garlic and add to the mushrooms, together with the strained lemon juice, a few drops of Tabasco and the olive oil. Season to taste with sugar, salt and freshly ground pepper. Blend all the ingredients thoroughly; spoon them into a shallow serving dish; leave to chill for 1 hour.

Just before serving, blend the flaked crabmeat with the cream and stir this mixture into the mushrooms.

Garnish the crab and mushrooms with olives and finely chopped parsley. Serve with warm crusty bread and butter. A salad of green peppers, chicory and Florence fennel tossed in a garlic dressing would also go well with the crab.

CUCUMBER CUPS WITH SHRIMP

Few ingredients combine so well for flavor and eye-appeal as cucumber and shellfish.

PREPARATION TIME: *15 min*
CHILLING TIME: *30 min*
INGREDIENTS *(for 6–8):*
2 *large cucumbers*
1 *tablespoon finely chopped fresh mint or 1 teaspoon dried mint leaves*
2 *canned pimientos*
⅔ *cup plain yogurt*
½ *pound small cooked peeled shrimp*
Salt★ and pepper
Paprika

Chop off the stalk ends of the cucumbers and cut the remainder into eight equal pieces. Drain and chop the pimientos. Stand the cucumber sections upright on a serving dish and, with a pointed spoon, hollow out the centers to form cup shapes. Leave about ¼ in around the sides and bottom.

Add the chopped mint and pimiento to the yogurt and fold in the shrimp. Season with salt and pepper. Spoon the mixture into the cucumber cups and sprinkle with a little paprika. Chill for 30 minutes and serve with slices of whole wheat bread.

SHRIMP IN COCONUT CREAM, MALAY STYLE

It is worth making the amount of garam masala given here, as although only a little is needed in this recipe, any surplus can be stored in an airtight jar and will keep for up to a month. It is an essential ingredient of curry dishes. The Indian cook will blend spices each day according to his own choice, but the following recipe is a suitable one for most curries.

PREPARATION TIME: *10 min*
COOKING TIME: *20 min*
INGREDIENTS *(for 4)*:
2 large onions
2–3 tablespoons ghee (page 183)
*1 heaping teaspoon garam masala
   (see below)*
1 green pepper
*12–16 cooked jumbo shrimp,
   peeled and deveined*
Salt*
1¼ cups coconut cream (see below)
GARAM MASALA:
2 ounces coriander seeds
2 ounces black peppercorns
1½ ounces cumin seeds
20 peeled cardamom seeds
4 teaspoons whole cloves
2 tablespoons ground cinnamon

First make the garam masala. Grind the whole seeds, peppercorns and cloves in a coffee grinder and combine the ground mixture with the cinnamon.

Finely chop the onions and fry them over low heat in the ghee until soft and pale golden. Add the teaspoon of garam masala and cook for a further 2–3 minutes. Blend in the sliced pepper, cover and simmer for 10 minutes. Add the shrimp, season with salt and cook over low heat for 1 minute.

Keeping the heat as low as possible, stir in the coconut cream and simmer until the prawns and the sauce are heated through. Do not let the sauce boil.

Coconut cream and milk

Fresh or processed coconut yields both cream and milk which are used in many soups and sauces.

Drill two or three holes at the top of a fresh coconut and shake out the colorless liquid. Saw the coconut in half and scrape out the flesh. Shred it finely, pour over ½ cup boiling water and leave for 20 minutes. Squeeze through cheesecloth to produce cream.

For coconut milk, put the squeezed coconut and ½ cup cold water in a pan and bring to the boil. Remove from the heat, leave for 20 minutes and squeeze through cheesecloth again. Coconut cream and milk can also be made in a liquidizer.

Failing a fresh coconut, the product known as creamed coconut is very easy to grate and gives excellent results. For coconut cream, use equal quantities of grated creamed coconut and hot water; for coconut milk, double or treble the amount of water. Whether or not you use a blender, always strain before using.

Dried shredded coconut produces an acceptable milk if treated in the same way, but it does not produce a very satisfactory cream.

SHRIMP PROVENÇALE

In cooking, the term *Provençale* always implies the use of garlic and tomatoes. This recipe can be used as a first course or as a light lunch or supper dish.

PREPARATION TIME: *15 min*
COOKING TIME: *15 min*
INGREDIENTS *(for 4)*:
1 pound raw peeled jumbo shrimp
1 onion
1 clove garlic
2 tablespoons oil
16-ounce can tomatoes
3 tablespoons dry white wine
Salt* and black pepper
1 heaping teaspoon cornstarch
*1 heaping tablespoon chopped
   parsley*

Rinse the shrimp under cold running water and pat them dry on paper towels. Peel and finely chop the onion and garlic. Heat the oil in a large, heavy frying pan, add the onion and fry over low heat for about 5 minutes or until soft, but not browned. Add the garlic and shrimp and fry for a further 3 minutes, before blending in the tomatoes and the wine; season to taste with salt and freshly ground pepper. Bring to the boil and simmer for about 6 minutes.

Blend the cornstarch with 1 tablespoon of water and stir into the shrimp. Cook for a few minutes, stirring until the sauce has thickened. Remove from the heat and add the parsley.

As a first course the shrimp could be served within a ring of plain boiled rice. For a lunch or supper dish, buttered green beans would also be suitable.

SHRIMP IN COCONUT CREAM, MALAY STYLE

SALT   SUGAR   FAT   CHOL   FIBER

GLUTEN-FREE   WHOLEFOOD
TOTAL CALORIES: ABOUT 1000

The **salt** content is in the shrimp and the coconut cream. As in the previous recipe, monkfish may be substituted for some or all of the shrimp, and the coconut cream may be mixed half and half with water, which will reduce the salt level to low.
For a low **fat** level, use only 1 tablespoon of ghee (or clarified butter or oil) to fry the onions and spices. For low **cholesterol**, substitute monkfish as above, and use oil instead of ghee. Coconut cream and milk contain no cholesterol. (Calories lost: up to 300.)

Microwave: ☑

SHRIMP PROVENÇALE

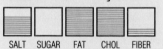

SALT   SUGAR   FAT   CHOL   FIBER

GLUTEN-FREE   WHOLEFOOD
TOTAL CALORIES: ABOUT 1000

To limit the **salt** to the amount naturally present in shrimp, choose tomatoes canned without added salt.
To reduce the **fat** level to low, cook the onions and shrimp in a pan which has been brushed lightly with oil, using a tightly fitting lid to prevent the mixture drying out. (Calories lost: up to 200.)
Shrimp naturally contain a significant amount of **cholesterol** but are lower in it

than many shellfish. For moderate to low cholesterol, replace half the shrimp with monkfish, halibut or cod. Serving with brown rice will add **fiber** as well as being **wholefood**.

Freezing: ☑ up to 1 month.

Microwave: ☑

MOULES À LA POULETTE

| SALT | SUGAR | FAT | CHOL | FIBER |

GLUTEN-FREE   WHOLEFOOD
TOTAL CALORIES: ABOUT 1400

The **salt** comes mainly from the mussels themselves, which also contain a significant amount of **cholesterol**, neither of which can therefore be substantially altered.

However, the total **fat** level can be reduced to very low, and the cholesterol to medium, if the mussel cooking liquid is thickened by blending a tablespoon of cornstarch or arrowroot with a little of the liquid to a smooth paste, then adding this back to the remaining liquid. Simmer together for at least 1 minute, then remove from the heat and stir in $\frac{1}{2}$ cup thick low-fat plain yogurt. Do not boil again. Using this method, the egg yolks and cream are omitted. (Total calories lost: up to 680.)

MOULES À LA POULETTE

In France, the mussels in this classic dish are served in their half shells and eaten with the fingers. Alternatively, remove the mussels entirely from the shells and serve them in the sauce as a soup.

PREPARATION TIME: *30 min*
COOKING TIME: *10 min*
INGREDIENTS *(for 6–8):*
4 quarts mussels
1 bay leaf
1 parsley sprig
1 shallot
6 black peppercorns
2 cups dry white wine
$\frac{1}{2}$ cup heavy cream
2 egg yolks
2 tablespoons chopped parsley
Black pepper
Lemon juice

Clean the mussels (page 176–7) thoroughly, discarding any with broken or open shells. Scrape away all grit and remove the beards. Put the mussels in a large, heavy saucepan with the bay leaf, parsley, peeled and finely chopped shallot and the peppercorns. Pour over the wine, cover the pan with a lid and cook the mussels over high heat until the shells open.

As the shells open, remove the mussels from the pan, throw away the empty top halves and place the mussels in their half shells in a warmed casserole. Cover them with a clean cloth to prevent them drying out, and to keep them warm. Strain the cooking liquid through cheesecloth.

Mix the cream and egg yolks together in a bowl and blend in a few tablespoons of the mussel liquid. Add to the remaining liquid, together with the chopped parsley. Season to taste with freshly ground pepper and lemon juice. Re-heat the liquid, without boiling, until it has thickened slightly.

Serve the mussels in individual deep soup plates, with the sauce poured over them. Set a finger bowl with a slice of lemon by each plate. Offer plenty of crusty bread to mop up the sauce and provide a spare bowl or plates for the empty mussel shells.

SCALLOPS IN THE SHELL

Scallops, with their firm white flesh, are at their best in the winter months. In this recipe, they are used for a main course, served in the deep rounded shells that can be purchased in department stores, and which afterwards make useful dishes for hors-d'oeuvre.

PREPARATION TIME: *20 min*
COOKING TIME: *35 min*
INGREDIENTS *(for 2–4):*
4 large sea scallops
¼ pound button mushrooms
½ cup dry white wine or dry hard cider
1 slice lemon
1 bay leaf
1 pound potatoes
2 tablespoons butter
SAUCE:
2 tablespoons butter
2 tablespoons flour
Salt★ and black pepper
1 egg yolk
2 tablespoons heavy cream

GARNISH:
Chopped parsley

Cut each scallop into four or six slices. Wipe and thinly slice the mushrooms. Put the scallops and mushrooms in a pan, with 1¼ cups of water, the wine (or cider), lemon slice and bay leaf. Bring to the boil, cover with a lid and simmer gently for 15–20 minutes. Strain through a colander and set aside 1¼ cups of the fish liquid for the sauce. Remove the lemon slice and bay leaf, and keep the scallops and mushrooms hot.

Meanwhile, put the peeled potatoes on to boil and make the sauce. Melt the butter in a saucepan over low heat, stir in the flour and cook gently for a few minutes. Gradually mix in the reserved fish liquid, stirring continuously until the sauce is smooth. Bring to the boil and simmer gently for 2–3 minutes. Add the mushrooms and scallops; season to taste with salt and freshly ground pepper; re-heat gently. Lightly mix the egg yolk and cream, remove the pan from the heat and stir the egg into the fish mixture.

Mash and season the potatoes. Using a large pastry bag, fitted with a rosette nozzle, pipe a border of mashed potato around the edges of the deep scallop shells. Brush the potato border with 2 tablespoons melted butter and place the shells under a hot broiler for a few minutes until the potatoes are golden brown.

Spoon the scallops into the center of each shell and sprinkle them with chopped parsley. Serve with a tossed green salad for a main course, or on their own as a first course for a dinner party.

SCALLOPS IN THE SHELL

| SALT | SUGAR | FAT | CHOL | FIBER |

GLUTEN-FREE★   WHOLEFOOD★
TOTAL CALORIES: ABOUT 1510

To reduce **fat** and **cholesterol** levels to low, mash and glaze the potatoes with milk in place of butter and enrich the fish mixture with a few tablespoons of low-fat yogurt or small curd cottage cheese in place of the egg yolk and cream.
This leaves only the cholesterol in the low-fat scallops – lower than in most mollusks – and in the butter used to make the sauce. The latter can be partly or wholly exchanged for vegetable margarine. (Calories lost: up to 150.)
Potato starch or cornstarch, both **gluten-free**, can be used for the sauce.

Freezing: ☑ up to 1 month.

Microwave: ☑ for cooking the scallops. It could be used for cooking the whole dish if you use special microwave dishes instead of the scallop shells.

SCALLOP CHOWDER

SALT	SUGAR	FAT	CHOL	FIBER

GLUTEN-FREE★ WHOLEFOOD★
TOTAL CALORIES: ABOUT 2725

Reduce the level of **salt** to the moderate amount provided by the scallops by omitting the bacon. Use 2 teaspoons of fat and a little stock in which to cook the vegetables.

To reduce **fat** to low, omit the bacon as above, use skim milk and avoid the need to thicken the chowder with flour and butter, either by simmering a little longer, or by adding 2 tablespoons rolled oats to the chowder with the milk. (Calories lost: up to 1260.)

Scallops contain a significant amount of **cholesterol**, but less than most mollusks. Replacing half the scallops with monkfish will reduce the cholesterol level to moderate.

Millet flakes can be used as an alternative to **gluten-free** flour for thickening the soup.

Freezing: ✓ up to 1 month.

SCALLOP CHOWDER

Chowder is derived from the French *chaudière*, meaning cauldron, in which this thick soup was traditionally cooked.

PREPARATION TIME: *15 min*
COOKING TIME: *1 hour*
INGREDIENTS *(for 4–6):*
12 sea scallops
Juice of 1 lemon
1¼ cups fish stock
1 large onion
6 ounces slab bacon
4 potatoes
1 carrot
1 parsnip
1 green pepper
2 stalks celery
2½ cups milk
Salt★ and black pepper
Juice of 1 orange
1 tablespoon flour

2 tablespoons butter
GARNISH:
Paprika

Sprinkle the scallops with lemon juice and allow to stand for 15 minutes. Cut each scallop into four pieces and put them in a saucepan with the fish stock. Bring to the boil, cover the pan and simmer for 10 minutes.

Peel and thinly slice the onion. Put the bacon in a saucepan and cook over low heat until the fat runs. Remove the bacon and add the onion to the pan, cooking it in the bacon fat until transparent. Peel and dice the potatoes, carrot and parsnip. Cut the pepper in half, remove the stem, seeds and white midribs, and slice the flesh. Add these vegetables, with the

cleaned and roughly chopped celery, to the onion.

Pour the milk into the pan and bring to simmering point. Season with salt and freshly ground pepper. Add the orange juice; return the bacon to the pan, and simmer, covered, until the vegetables are tender.

Lift out the bacon and dice it finely. Stir the scallops, the stock and the bacon into the chowder.

If necessary, make a beurre manié (pages 155–6) from the flour and butter and use it to thicken the chowder.

Serve the chowder in individual bowls, sprinkled with paprika.

CHICKEN AND ALMOND SOUP

Feather Fowlie is the true name of this traditional Scottish soup. By adding cream to the soup, it was given a French touch to please Mary, Queen of Scots.

PREPARATION TIME: *30 min*
COOKING TIME: *about 3½ hours*
INGREDIENTS *(for 6):*
4–5 pound stewing chicken
1 pound mixed root vegetables (onions, carrots and turnips)
3 stalks celery
10 black peppercorns
½ teaspoon salt★
Bouquet garni (page 183)
½ cup ground almonds
¼ cup soft breadcrumbs
½ cup heavy cream
GARNISH:
Chopped parsley or chives
Bread croûtons (page 178)

Peel and roughly chop the vegetables. Put the stewing chicken in a large saucepan, together with the vegetables, peppercorns, salt and bouquet garni. Cover with cold water and bring to the boil over high heat. Remove any scum from the surface, lower the heat and cover the pan with a lid. Simmer for 2–3 hours or until the chicken is sufficiently tender.

Lift the chicken from the stock; let it cool slightly before removing the skin and cutting all the meat off the carcass. Put the meat in the liquidizer, with the vegetables.

Put the purée in a large clean pan, mix in the almonds and breadcrumbs and stir in about 5 cups of the chicken stock, strained through a sieve. Bring the soup to the boil and simmer over low heat for 30 minutes, stirring frequently.

Before serving, blend half a cup of hot soup with the cream and stir this mixture back into the soup.

Correct seasoning and serve the soup garnished with finely chopped parsley or chives and with bread croûtons.

CHICKEN YOGURT SOUP

In the Middle East, yogurt is often used instead of cream. It gives a refreshing tang to a soup.

PREPARATION TIME: *15 min*
COOKING TIME: *20 min*
INGREDIENTS *(for 6):*
2 cups plain yogurt
1½ teaspoons cornstarch
4 cups chicken stock
5 egg yolks
3 tablespoons ground almonds
Salt★ and black pepper
2 tablespoons chopped fresh mint
1 tablespoon unsalted butter

Stabilize the yogurt before cooking, by blending the cornstarch with a little water, and gradually beating it into the yogurt. Pour into a saucepan and bring slowly to the boil over moderate heat, stirring continuously. Simmer gently for 10 minutes or until thickened.

Meanwhile, bring the chicken stock to the boil in another pan. Remove from the heat, let it cool slightly, while lightly beating the egg yolks. Spoon a little of the stock into the eggs and blend thoroughly, before stirring this mixture into the stock. Heat over low heat until just simmering – if brought to boiling point, the eggs will curdle – stirring all the time until the stock thickens. Gradually, stir the yogurt into the chicken stock.

Blend the ground almonds into the soup, and correct seasoning if necessary. Sauté the chopped mint for 1–2 minutes in a little butter and blend into the soup just before serving.

CHICKEN AND ALMOND SOUP

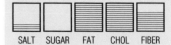

GLUTEN-FREE★ WHOLEFOOD★
TOTAL CALORIES: ABOUT 2400

To reduce both **fat** and **cholesterol** to low, skin the chicken before cooking. Cook it well ahead of time to give the stock time to cool, and remove all the fat which will have congealed on the top. Plain yogurt can be substituted for the cream and is, to some tastes, an improvement. Toast or bake the bread croûtons instead of frying them.
For very low fat, halve the amount of almonds used, or substitute chestnut flour or ground hazelnuts, both of which are less fatty than almonds and also go especially well with chicken. (Calories lost: up to 550.)
If you have no **gluten-free** bread to hand, omit the breadcrumbs and add a large potato to the other vegetables in order to thicken the soup. Omit the garnish of croûtons.

Pressure cooker: ☑
Freezing: ☑ up to 6 months.

CHICKEN YOGURT SOUP

GLUTEN-FREE WHOLEFOOD
TOTAL CALORIES: ABOUT 1020

To reduce the **fat** to fairly low and the **cholesterol** to moderate, use low-fat yogurt and substitute 2 whole eggs for the egg yolks. It is not necessary to sauté the chopped mint in butter before stirring it in. As in the previous recipe, remove all fat from the stock and, if you like, replace the almonds with hazelnuts. (Calories lost: up to 350.) This soup can also be made with no eggs at all and will then be very low in both fat and cholesterol. (Further calories lost: 400.) Without the eggs it will serve 4 people rather than 6.

COCK-A-LEEKIE SOUP

| SALT | SUGAR | FAT | CHOL | FIBER |

GLUTEN-FREE   WHOLEFOOD
TOTAL CALORIES: ABOUT 1120

Although the **salt** content is low if none is added, this is a soup that many people would find unpalatable without salt, so that omitting it simply creates other problems. Try adding the finely grated rind of half a lemon, season well with freshly ground black pepper and be generous with the chopped parsley. Dried mushrooms also add flavor; ½–1 ounce should be enough. Soak them for half an hour in a little warm water. Strain this liquid into the soup, rinse the mushrooms, chop them roughly and add them to the soup with the prunes. To ensure very low levels of both **fat** and **cholesterol**, cook the chicken ahead of time, as in the previous recipes, and scrupulously remove all fat from the surface when the stock has cooled. Make sure also that all the skin is removed.

Pressure cooker: ☑
Freezing: ☑ up to 6 months.

COCK-A-LEEKIE SOUP

Legend has it that this traditional Scottish soup originated in the days when cockfighting was a favorite sport. The loser was then thrown into the stock pot together with leeks; prunes were a later addition for extra flavor.

PREPARATION TIME: *10–15 min*
COOKING TIME: *2 hours*
INGREDIENTS (*for 6*):
1 chicken, about 3 pounds
1 tablespoon salt★
6 peppercorns
6 leeks
6 prunes
GARNISH:
Chopped parsley

Soak the prunes for 6 hours in cold water. Wipe the trussed chicken, rinse the giblets and place both in a deep saucepan. Pour over cold water to cover the chicken (if necessary, split the bird in half so that it remains submerged). Add the salt and peppercorns and bring to the boil. Remove any scum from the surface, cover with a tight-fitting lid and simmer for about 1½ hours.

Meanwhile, trim the coarse leaves off the leeks to within 2 in of the top of the white stems and cut off the roots. Split the leeks lengthwise, wash them well under running cold water, then cut them into 1 in pieces. Skim the soup again; add the leeks and the soaked prunes, which may be pitted or left whole. Simmer for another 30 minutes.

Lift the chicken and giblets from the soup; remove skin and bones from the chicken meat. Reserve the best breast pieces for another recipe, and cut the remaining meat into small pieces. Add these pieces to the soup and correct the seasoning according to taste.

Just before serving the hot soup, sprinkle finely chopped parsley over it.

GARDENER'S CHICKEN

A casserole of chicken and vegetables makes a change from roast chicken. Once in the oven, the casserole can be left to cook.

PREPARATION TIME: *40 min*
COOKING TIME: *1½ hours*
INGREDIENTS *(for 4–6):*
1 chicken, about 3 pounds
4 slices bacon
2 large onions
2 stalks celery
¼ pound mushrooms
4–6 tablespoons unsalted butter
1 pound new potatoes
½ pound turnips
16-ounce can tomatoes
1 bouquet garni (page 183)
Salt and black pepper*
GARNISH:
Fresh parsley and orange rind

Cut up the chicken (page 168) into four or six pieces, and wipe clean. Dice the bacon. Peel and thinly slice the onions; scrub and coarsely chop the celery; clean and slice the mushrooms. Melt the butter in a large, heavy-based pan and fry the bacon, onions, mushrooms and celery for 5 minutes. Tip the frying pan to drain the butter to one side, remove the vegetables with a slotted spoon and spread over the bottom of a large casserole.

Fry the chicken pieces in the butter residue, adding a little more if necessary, until they are golden brown. Remove from the pan and place on the bed of vegetables. Scrape the potatoes, peel and slice the turnips and add these, together with the tomatoes

and bouquet garni, to the casserole. Season with salt and freshly ground pepper, and cover the casserole with aluminum foil, before securing the lid so that no steam can escape. Cook on the middle shelf of the oven heated to 300°F (150°C, mark 2) for about 1½ hours or until tender.

Immediately before serving, sprinkle chopped parsley, mixed with the finely chopped rind of half an orange, over the casserole. No additional vegetables are needed.

GARDENER'S CHICKEN

| SALT | SUGAR | FAT | CHOL | FIBER |

GLUTEN-FREE   WHOLEFOOD
TOTAL CALORIES: ABOUT 2400

This is low in **salt** if the bacon is omitted and unsalted tomatoes used. You can compensate by adding a clove or two of garlic, chopped, to the onions, celery and mushrooms.
To reduce the **fat** and **cholesterol** to moderate, use Canadian bacon and use only half the quantity (or omit it entirely). Skin the chicken pieces before cooking them. There is no need to fry the skinned chicken pieces. (Calories lost: up to 700.)

Pressure cooker: ☑
Freezing: ☑ up to 4 months.

ROAST CHICKEN WITH WATERCRESS STUFFING

| SALT | SUGAR | FAT | CHOL | FIBER |

GLUTEN-FREE*   WHOLEFOOD*
TOTAL CALORIES: ABOUT 2520

Reduce both **fat** and **cholesterol** to moderate by using only 2 tablespoons butter or 2 tablespoons oil to sauté the onion and celery. Omit the bread sautéed in butter, and use instead ¼ cup brown rice, previously cooked in twice its volume of water for 30 minutes. Do not rub the chicken with butter before cooking it, and stand it on a rack so that the fat can drain. (Calories lost: up to 1200.)
Roast chicken does not really adapt to a very low-fat version

as skinning it would rather defeat the object. However, this is an ideal dish to serve if some but not all of the guests are on a low-fat diet: those who are will want to avoid the skin while the others can have double helpings. The brown rice suggested above also makes an excellent **gluten-free** and **wholefood** alternative to breadcrumbs.

CHICKEN LIVERS WITH GRAPES

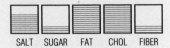

SALT	SUGAR	FAT	CHOL	FIBER

GLUTEN-FREE*   WHOLEFOOD*
TOTAL CALORIES: ABOUT 3295

The **salt** can be reduced to fairly low if the bread used contains no salt. It cannot go below this, however, as chicken livers themselves contain a fair amount of sodium.
To limit **fat** to the moderate level naturally present in chicken livers, toast, bake or broil the bread (which can be lightly brushed with melted butter if you wish) instead of frying it; or replace it with a bed of plain rice or noodles. Cook the livers in a heavy pan lightly brushed with oil and omit the remaining oil and all the butter. Cover the livers when cooking so that they do not stick and the cooking juices are retained instead of drying on the pan. (Calories lost: up to 440.)
Chicken livers, like other organ meats, are high in **cholesterol**, but could be eaten occasionally if the rest of the food that day is very low in cholesterol.
Gluten-free alternatives are rice, as above, or potato. Cut thick slices from cold baked potatoes and broil them on both sides until well heated through.

ROAST CHICKEN WITH WATERCRESS STUFFING

A combination of watercress, onions, and celery is a welcome change from the usual stuffings for poultry.

PREPARATION TIME: *40 min*
COOKING TIME: *1¼ hours*
INGREDIENTS *(for 4)*:
1 medium onion
3 stalks celery
¾ cup unsalted butter
1 bunch watercress
3–4 cups diced, day-old bread
3½-pound roaster chicken

Peel the onion, scrub the celery and dice both finely. Wash and drain the watercress, press out as much water as possible and chop it finely. Sauté the onion and celery in ¼ cup of the butter until soft. Add the watercress and cook until all the liquids have evaporated. In another pan sauté the bread in ¼ cup of the butter until lightly browned, and add to the vegetable mixture.
Stuff the chicken with this mixture. Truss the chicken (page 167), sprinkle it with salt and pepper, and rub it all over with the remaining butter. Place the chicken on its side in a roasting pan in a pre-heated oven at 425°F (220°C, mark 7) and roast for 20 minutes, basting once with the drippings. Turn the chicken on its other side and roast for another 20 minutes, basting once. Turn it on its back and continue to roast about 35 minutes more, basting about every 5 minutes. When the chicken is done, the juices will run clear at the thigh when it is pierced with the point of a knife.
Serve with baked potatoes and a green vegetable or salad.

CHICKEN LIVERS WITH GRAPES

Chicken livers are readily available, either fresh or frozen, and usually at bargain prices. They make a good lunch or supper dish, served in a wine sauce delicately flavored with grapes.

PREPARATION TIME: *25 min*
COOKING TIME: *10–12 min*
INGREDIENTS *(for 6)*:
1½ pounds chicken livers
*Salt**
¾ pound seedless green grapes
6 slices bread
¾ cup unsalted butter
2 tablespoons vegetable oil
6–8 tablespoons madeira, port or sweet sherry
Black pepper

Rinse the chicken livers in cold water and pat them dry. Cut away the white, stringy pieces and any discolored parts which may have been in contact with the gall bladder – they add a bitter flavor if left in.
Season the livers with salt and freshly ground pepper and set them aside.
Peel the grapes if desired (page 178). Remove the crusts from the bread slices. Melt ½ cup of the butter in a pan, together with the oil; when hot, fry the bread golden brown on both sides. Stand the fried bread upright on a baking sheet and keep warm in the oven.
Melt the remaining butter and cook the livers for 3–5 minutes on each side; they should be slightly pink in the center. Remove from the pan and keep warm. Stir the wine into the pan juices and reduce by rapid boiling until the sauce has thickened to a syrupy consistency. Add the grapes to the sauce and let them heat through.
To serve, arrange the hot bread on a serving dish, top with chicken livers and spoon the grapes on top. Serve immediately, before the sauce soaks into the fried bread.

CHICKEN BREASTS WITH SAGE

In Italy, where this dish originated, chicken breasts (*petti di pollo*) are usually cooked with a strong flavoring of herbs.

PREPARATION TIME: *10 min*
COOKING TIME: *45 min*
INGREDIENTS (*for 6*):
3 chicken breasts
Seasoned flour (page 184)
1 tablespoon olive oil
1 tablespoon butter
2–3 thin slices cooked ham
½ cup dry white wine
½ cup chicken stock
12 sage leaves
Salt★ and black pepper

Remove the skin from the chicken breasts and cut off the wings. Slice the breast away from the bones and cut each portion into halves, lengthwise. Coat the chicken with seasoned flour. Heat the oil and butter in a sauté pan over moderate heat and lightly brown the chicken.

Cut the ham into narrow strips and add to the chicken. When the chicken is golden brown, pour in the wine and enough stock to come about two-thirds up the chicken breasts. Add the roughly chopped sage.

Cover the pan with a lid and simmer the chicken over moderate heat for 15–20 minutes. Remove to a serving dish and keep it warm. Increase the heat and rapidly boil the liquid until it has reduced to a thin coating consistency. Season to taste with salt and freshly ground pepper.

Pour the sauce over the chicken breasts and serve at once with fresh bread and a green vegetable.

POULET À LA CRÈME

This recipe for a casserole of chicken in a rich cream and calvados sauce comes from Normandy. It loses nothing of its flavor if any leftovers are reheated later.

PREPARATION TIME: *10 min*
COOKING TIME: *1¼–1½ hours*
INGREDIENTS (*for 4–6*):
1 3–4 pound chicken
1 Spanish onion
2–3 slices cooked ham or lean bacon
Salt★ and black pepper
5 tablespoons butter
¼ cup calvados or brandy
2 teaspoons chopped celery leaves
1¼ cups dry hard cider or unsweetened apple juice
2 large egg yolks
½ cup heavy cream
GARNISH:
2 apples
2 tablespoons unsalted butter

Peel and finely chop the onion, and dice the ham or bacon after removing the rind. Wipe the trussed chicken inside and out with a clean damp cloth and set the giblets aside. Season the chicken with salt and pepper.

Melt the butter in a pan over moderate heat and cook the onion until soft and transparent. Stir in the ham or bacon and cook for another 2–3 minutes. Brown the chicken lightly all over in the butter. Warm the calvados or brandy in a small pan and set alight (calvados will produce a fair amount of flame). While the spirit is still flaming, pour it over the chicken. Shake the pan gently until the flames die out.

Add the chicken neck, gizzard and heart to the pan, but omit the liver. Sprinkle in the chopped celery leaves and pour over the cider or apple juice; let it come to the boil, then simmer for a few minutes. Turn the chicken on its side and cover the pan closely with foil and then a lid. Cook over low heat. If necessary, put the contents in a casserole and cook at 325°F (170°C, mark 3) in the center of the oven.

After 20–25 minutes cooking, turn the chicken over on the other side and cook for a similar period, still covered. Finally, turn the chicken breast upwards, cover and cook for a further 10 minutes.

Lift the chicken on to a warm serving dish and keep hot. Strain the liquid, and reduce slightly by fast boiling. Remove the pan from the heat. Beat together the egg yolks and the cream; mix in a few spoonfuls of the warm liquid, and whisk into the pan juices. Stir over low heat until the sauce has thickened.

While the chicken is cooking, peel and core the apples. Cut them into ¼ in thick rings. Fry the apple rings in butter until golden brown.

Just before serving, pour the hot sauce over the chicken and garnish with the apple slices. Little more than a green salad is needed, but boiled potatoes could also be served.

CHICKEN BREASTS WITH SAGE

SALT SUGAR FAT CHOL FIBER

GLUTEN-FREE★ WHOLEFOOD★
TOTAL CALORIES: ABOUT 1365

To reduce levels of **salt**, **fat** and **cholesterol** to low, omit the ham (or use only half a slice for flavor); omit the butter and seal the chicken on a lightly oiled baking sheet under the broiler rather than sautéing it in oil. Make sure the chicken breasts are thoroughly skinned and that all fat has been removed from the stock. (Calories lost: up to 300.)

POULET À LA CRÈME

SALT SUGAR FAT CHOL FIBER

GLUTEN-FREE WHOLEFOOD
TOTAL CALORIES: ABOUT 2910

The **salt** level can be reduced to low by using only half a slice of bacon or ham, preferably unsmoked.

To ensure low levels of both **fat** and **cholesterol**, reduce the bacon or ham as above; skin the chicken and seal it in a pan brushed lightly with oil. The butter can then be omitted. Use one whole egg instead of 2 yolks for thickening the sauce. Replace the heavy cream with plain yogurt: it may not be authentically Norman but it is very good. For the garnish, soften the apple rings by simmering them in a little cider or apple juice for a few minutes. (Calories lost: up to 1340.)

Freezing: ☑ up to 4 months.

BANGKOK CHICKEN AND RICE

SALT	SUGAR	FAT	CHOL	FIBER

GLUTEN-FREE   WHOLEFOOD*
TOTAL CALORIES: ABOUT 3560

The main sources of **salt** here are the ham and shrimp, and to some extent the peanut butter. To reduce the level to moderate, grind the peanuts without adding any salt and replace the ham with a chopped sweet green or red pepper: the shrimp can be replaced with less salty seafood, such as mussels or monkfish.

These adaptations also reduce the levels of **fat** and **cholesterol**; to reduce them still further, to low, halve the amount of peanut butter and use only 1 egg, chopped in smaller pieces. Skin the chicken before cooking and trim off any surplus fat. Cook it ahead of time and let the stock get cold enough for all the fat to be removed easily. Use only 2 tablespoons oil to fry the onion. Side dishes served with the chicken are not traditionally dressed, but served plain. Banana should be tossed in lemon juice to avoid it browning, but not fried. Coconut is very high in saturated fat and could be replaced with other oriental side dishes, such as chopped scallions. If you wish to serve a side dish of nuts, hazelnuts are lower in fat than almonds or cashews. Other alternatives include chopped cucumber with chopped mint, or slices of mango. (Calories lost: up to 300.)

Pressure cooker: ☑ for cooking the chicken.
Freezing: ☑ up to 2 months.

BANGKOK CHICKEN AND RICE

In spite of its name, this is one of the great dishes from the famous Indonesian *rijstafel*. It makes an attractive centerpiece for a buffet, surrounded by small dishes of colorful fresh vegetables and fruit to which guests can help themselves.

PREPARATION TIME: *35 min*
COOKING TIME: *2¾ hours*
INGREDIENTS *(for 6–8):*
1 small chicken, approximately 3½ pounds
1 pound onions
1 bay leaf
1 sprig parsley
Salt* and black pepper
2 cups long grain rice
3 tablespoons olive or vegetable oil
2 tablespoons peanut butter
½ teaspoon chili powder
¼ pound peeled shrimp
½ cup diced cooked ham
1 teaspoon cumin seeds
1½ teaspoons coriander seeds
1 clove garlic
Pinch ground mace
GARNISH:
Half a cucumber
2 hard-cooked eggs
8–12 cooked shrimp in shell

Put the chicken in a large pan, with one whole peeled onion, the bay leaf and parsley sprig. Add a seasoning of salt and freshly ground pepper and enough cold water to cover the chicken. Bring to the boil, remove any scum from the surface, then cover the pan with a lid and simmer over gentle heat for about 2 hours or until the chicken is tender.

Lift out the chicken and leave to cool slightly. Strain the stock through a fine sieve and use it to

cook the rice until just tender. Drain the rice through a colander and cover it with a dry cloth.

Remove the skin from the chicken and cut the meat into small pieces. Peel and thinly slice the remaining onions. Heat the oil in a large pan, and fry the onions over low heat until they begin to color. Stir in the peanut butter and chili powder. Add the peeled shrimp, diced ham and the chicken and finally the rice, which should now be dry and fluffy. Continue frying over low heat, stirring frequently until the rice is slightly brown. Crush the cumin and coriander seeds and the peeled garlic, and stir them, with the mace, into the rice. Season to taste with salt.

Pile the rice and chicken mixture on to a hot serving dish and garnish with thin slices of unpeeled cucumber, wedges of hard-cooked egg and the large cooked shrimp in shell.

Arrange a number of small side dishes or bowls around the chicken. A suitable selection might include apricot and mango chutney; sliced tomatoes, dressed with sugar and lemon juice; peeled, sliced oranges; and sliced sweet green and red pepper with raw onion rings, both in a vinaigrette dressing (page 157). Other bowls could contain small wedges of fresh pineapple; fried sliced bananas with lemon juice; and fresh shredded and toasted coconut. Shelled almonds or cashew nuts fried in a little butter are also frequently served with this dish.

CHICKEN WITH FORTY CLOVES OF GARLIC

The long cooking gives the garlic a subtle taste and in spite of the quantity it is not overpowering.

PREPARATION TIME: *15 min*
COOKING TIME: *1½ hours*
INGREDIENTS *(for 8)*:
8 chicken legs and thighs
40 cloves garlic
4 stalks celery
½ cup olive oil
6 sprigs parsley
1 tablespoon dried tarragon
½ cup dry vermouth
¼ teaspoon pepper
Dash of nutmeg
2½ teaspoons salt★

Rinse the chicken in cold water and pat dry with paper towels. Peel the garlic, leaving the cloves whole. Cut the celery into thin slices.

Pour the oil into a shallow dish or a plate and turn all the chicken pieces in the oil so that they are coated on all sides. Put the celery slices in the bottom of a heavy casserole with a tight-fitting cover. Add the parsley and tarragon. Lay the chicken pieces on top and sprinkle with the vermouth, pepper, nutmeg, and 1 teaspoon of the salt.

Pour the remaining oil in the plate into the casserole. Add the garlic cloves; sprinkle with the remaining salt. Over the top of the casserole lay a piece of aluminum foil large enough to extend 1 inch over the edge all around. Cover with the lid of the casserole to make a tight seal. Alternatively, make a thick flour and water paste and spread it with the fingers all around the edge of the casserole where the cover and casserole

meet, to make an airtight seal. Put a layer of foil around the lid to cover the circle of flour paste.

Bake at 375°F (190°C, mark 5) for 1½ hours. Do not remove the lid during the cooking period. Serve from the casserole, with hot toast or thin slices of pumpernickel on which to spread the softened garlic cloves.

CHICKEN LIVER PÂTÉ

Frozen chicken livers are readily available and are excellent for pâtés and terrines.

PREPARATION TIME: *15 min*
COOKING TIME: *10 min*
CHILLING TIME: *2–3 hours*
INGREDIENTS *(for 6)*:
1 pound chicken livers
¼ cup butter
1 small onion
2 bay leaves
Dried thyme
Salt★ and black pepper
2 tablespoons brandy

Melt the butter and fry the peeled and finely chopped onion, the bay leaves and a good pinch of thyme for 2–3 minutes. Trim away any green bits of gall bladder, and cut the chicken livers into small pieces; add to the pan. Cook over low heat for 5 minutes or until the livers are cooked. Discard the bay leaves and put the liver mixture in a liquidizer until smooth, or grind the liver twice.

Season to taste with salt and freshly ground pepper and stir in the brandy. Pour the pâté into a jar and leave to chill in the refrigerator for several hours.

CHICKEN MARYLAND

A favorite dish on the American dinner table, chicken Maryland is traditionally accompanied by corn fritters. These batter cakes are, like all the other ingredients in this dish, fried until golden.

PREPARATION TIME: *25 min*
COOKING TIME: *45 min*
INGREDIENTS *(for 6)*:
1 3-pound chicken, cut into 8 pieces, or 6 chicken pieces
Seasoned flour (page 184)
1 egg
1½–2 cups soft breadcrumbs
½–⅔ cup unsalted butter
8 lean bacon slices
3 bananas
1 tablespoon olive or corn oil
CORN FRITTERS:
1 cup flour
1 egg
¾–1 cup milk
12-oz can cream-style corn
Salt★ and black pepper
GARNISH:
Watercress

Remove the skin from the chicken pieces and coat them with seasoned flour. Lightly beat the egg and dip the chicken portions in this before coating them with breadcrumbs. Shake off any loose crumbs. Melt about ¼ cup of the butter in a large frying pan and fry the chicken pieces for about 10 minutes, until brown on both sides. Turn down the heat, cover the pan with a lid or tight-fitting foil and cook gently, turning the chicken once, for 25–30 minutes. If cooked in the oven, allow 40 minutes at 400°F (200°C, mark 6).

Cut each bacon slice in half crosswise, roll them up and thread them on two skewers. Peel

SALT SUGAR FAT CHOL FIBER

GLUTEN-FREE   WHOLEFOOD
TOTAL CALORIES: ABOUT 3255

The **salt** content is very high, but omitting it will alter the taste of the dish. This is one occasion when a salt substitute might be worth considering, if your diet allows it.
To reduce the **fat** to moderate, first skin the chicken pieces. This also reduces the **cholesterol** to low. 4–6 tablespoons of oil will be enough to cook the chicken. (Calories lost: up to 600.) If you can use good olive oil it is well worth it as the taste will come through, but if you are actually on a cholesterol-lowering diet use sunflower oil instead.

CHICKEN LIVER PÂTÉ

SALT SUGAR FAT CHOL FIBER

GLUTEN-FREE   WHOLEFOOD
TOTAL CALORIES: ABOUT 1110

The **salt** level cannot be less than moderate, even if unsalted butter is used, as chicken livers are high in sodium, but this should not be a problem as pâté is not normally eaten in vast quantities.
The **fat** content becomes moderate if only half the quantity of butter is used. It could be reduced still further, to about a quarter, if you do not mind losing a certain softness and richness of texture. (Calories lost: up to 340.) Substituting sunflower oil or other vegetable fat for the

butter will help to lower the **cholesterol**, but as the livers are high in it anyway this remains something to be eaten only on occasion.

Food processor: ☑ for blending to a smooth purée.

Freezing: ☑ up to 2 months.

Microwave: ☑ Very suitable for this recipe, as the livers can be cooked in a covered container using less fat.

CHICKEN MARYLAND

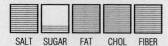

SALT	SUGAR	FAT	CHOL	FIBER

GLUTEN-FREE*　WHOLEFOOD*
TOTAL CALORIES: ABOUT 4680

The high level of **salt** in this dish comes mainly from the bacon, followed by the breadcrumbs, with possibly some in the corn. To reduce it to low, omit the bacon. Use fresh or frozen whole kernel corn, or buy unsalted corn and purée it yourself.

The **fat** level can be reduced, and the **cholesterol** limited to the low amount in the chicken itself, by cooking the chicken in the oven with $\frac{1}{4}$ cup olive or peanut oil instead of butter. The bananas and corn fritters can also be cooked in a pan lightly brushed with oil and well heated, rather than using butter. Use skim milk and egg white only in the fritters, and serve with plain rice. (Calories lost: up to 720.)

Gluten-free alternatives are cornstarch or millet flakes for coating the chicken, and corn fritters made with fine cornmeal (or a mixture of cornmeal and potato starch) instead of flour.

and halve the bananas lengthwise; coat them evenly in seasoned flour, ready for frying.

Sift the flour for the fritters into a mixing bowl, make a well in the center and add the egg and milk. Using a wooden spoon, mix from the center, gradually drawing in the flour from around the sides of the bowl. Beat to make a smooth batter. Stir in the corn and season to taste with salt and freshly ground pepper.

When the chicken pieces are tender, transfer them to a serving dish and keep them warm. Melt 2 tablespoons of butter in the pan, add the bananas and fry over low heat.

Heat the remaining butter and the oil in a second frying pan. When hot, add tablespoons of the corn fritter batter, cook until golden brown on the underside, then turn each fritter and fry on the other side. Fry the fritters a few at a time – they take 1–2 minutes to cook; keep the fritters warm in the oven while frying the next batch.

While the last fritters are cooking, put the skewers with bacon rolls under a pre-heated broiler for about 2 minutes.

Serve the chicken pieces garnished with the corn fritters, bacon rolls and fried bananas and sprigs of watercress. A tossed green salad also goes well with this dish.

CHICKEN IN MUSHROOM SAUCE

This method of cooking chicken produces a light, easily digestible meal, particularly suitable for invalids. Any remains of the chicken and mushroom sauce can be made into soup.

PREPARATION TIME: *25 min*
COOKING TIME: *1½ hours*
INGREDIENTS *(for 6)*:
1 chicken, approx. 3½ pounds
2 onions
2 stalks celery
3 tablespoons unsalted butter
Salt⋆ and black pepper
1 bay leaf
12–16 button mushrooms
Worcestershire sauce
1 tablespoon flour
5 tablespoons heavy cream
GARNISH:
1 tablespoon finely chopped
parsley

Peel and finely chop the onions; scrub the celery and chop finely. Melt 2 tablespoons of the butter in a large, heavy-based pan over low heat; cook the onion and celery until soft and just beginning to color.

Meanwhile, wash and wipe the chicken, inside and out; clean the giblets and liver. Put the chicken, giblets and liver in the pan with the onion and celery, with enough water to cover the chicken. Bring to the boil, remove any scum and add salt, freshly ground pepper and the bay leaf. Cover the pan with a lid and simmer gently for about 1½ hours, or until the chicken is tender. Lift the chicken on to a warm dish and keep it hot. Strain the cooking liquid and set aside.

Trim and thinly slice the mushrooms. Melt the remaining butter in a small pan and cook the mushrooms over low heat for 2–3 minutes. Add a few drops of Worcestershire sauce and sprinkle the flour over the mushrooms. Cook, stirring continuously, until all the fat has been absorbed into the flour. Gradually blend in about ½ cup of the strained chicken liquid, to make a smooth sauce. Correct seasoning if necessary. Stir in the cream and heat the sauce through.

Carve the chicken and arrange the pieces in a deep serving dish. Pour the mushroom sauce over it and garnish with chopped parsley. Serve with broccoli spears and plain boiled potatoes, or with buttered rice.

COQ AU VIN

Burgundy is the home of this classic method of cooking a cockerel (or chicken), and wine from the same region is the obvious choice to cook it in, although any reasonably good red wine can be used.

PREPARATION TIME: *40 min*
COOKING TIME: *about 1¼ hours*
INGREDIENTS *(for 4)*:
1 chicken, 3–3½ pounds
Bouquet garni (page 183)
Salt⋆ and black pepper
¼ pound salt pork or slab bacon
¼ pound pearl onions
1 large clove garlic
¼ pound button mushrooms
¼ cup unsalted butter
1 tablespoon olive oil
2 tablespoons brandy
2½ cups red wine
1¼ cups chicken stock
Beurre manié (pages 155–6)
GARNISH:
¼ pound pearl onions

⅔ cup button mushrooms
1 tablespoon chopped parsley

Clean and truss the bird. Use the giblets with the bouquet garni, a little salt and freshly ground pepper to make stock. Dice the salt pork or bacon. Peel the onions and garlic and trim and slice the mushrooms.

Heat the butter and oil in a flameproof casserole dish or pan and fry the pork or bacon until the fat runs. Remove from the casserole. Brown the bird all over in the hot fat, then spoon off any surplus fat. Warm the brandy in a spoon or small pan, set it alight and pour it flaming over the bird. As soon as the flames subside, pour in the wine and add the pork, onions, mushrooms and crushed garlic. Pour over enough stock to make the liquid come halfway up the bird. Cover with a lid and cook over low heat on top of the stove or in the oven, at 300°F (150°C, mark 2), for 1 hour or until the bird is tender, turning it from time to time.

Remove the bird and divide it into pieces; keep these warm on a serving dish. Lift out the onions, bacon and mushrooms with a slotted spoon and arrange them over the chicken. Reduce the cooking liquid by brisk boiling, then lower the heat and gradually whisk in pieces of beurre manié until the sauce has thickened. Correct seasoning and pour the sauce over the chicken.

Serve garnished with glazed pearl onions, fried or broiled button mushrooms and freshly chopped parsley.

CHICKEN IN MUSHROOM SAUCE

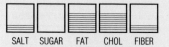

GLUTEN-FREE⋆   WHOLEFOOD⋆
TOTAL CALORIES: ABOUT 1905

To reduce the **fat** and **cholesterol** to low, first of all skin the chicken. This is most easily done after it has been simmered. Try to do this a little ahead of time so that the stock will have time to cool and the fat to solidify on top of it. Remove all the fat before using the stock to make the sauce. Use yogurt instead of the heavy cream, and do not boil the sauce after working it in. Soften the vegetables in a heavy pan lightly brushed with oil instead of butter and do the same for the mushrooms. (Calories lost: up to 400.)
Use cornstarch or potato starch as **gluten-free** alternatives in the mushroom sauce.

Pressure cooker: ☑ for cooking the chicken.
Freezing: ☑ up to 4 months.

COQ AU VIN

GLUTEN-FREE   WHOLEFOOD
TOTAL CALORIES: ABOUT 2985

To reduce the **salt** to moderate, use sweet cured bacon and only half the amount; to reduce it to low, the pork or bacon can be omitted completely. Compensate by adding an extra clove or two of garlic and ½ ounce dried mushrooms, soaked for half an hour in a little warm water. (Their soaking juice, strained, can be added to the stock.)

For low to moderate **fat** and **cholesterol**, skin the chicken, preferably before cooking, although it is easier to do so after it is cooked. Use only half the amount of pork or bacon in its own fat, omitting the butter. Skim as much fat as possible off the stock. Instead of the beurre manié, thicken with ½ tablespoon of cornstarch or arrowroot (see page 155). (Calories lost: up to 1050.)

Freezing: ☑ up to 4 months.

CHICKEN CHAUD-FROID

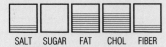

SALT	SUGAR	FAT	CHOL	FIBER

GLUTEN-FREE★   WHOLEFOOD★
TOTAL CALORIES: ABOUT 1700

The **fat** in this recipe can be reduced to low if the milk is replaced with skim milk, chicken stock or a mixture of the two. If you are using chicken stock make sure it has cooled enough for the fat to rise to the surface so that it can be skimmed off easily. (Calories lost: up to 80.)

Cholesterol can be reduced to very low by using vegetable oil or margarine in place of butter, and skim milk or stock as above.

Use cornstarch or potato starch as a **gluten-free** alternative to flour.

Potato starch is also **wholefood**. You can make a wholefood aspic by using 2 teaspoons gelatin or 1 teaspoon kanten to set 1 cup chicken or vegetable stock.

Pressure cooker: ☑ for cooking the chicken pieces.

CHICKEN CHAUD-FROID

This is a classic French dish of whole cooked chicken, coated with aspic sauce (chaud-froid sauce) and elaborately garnished. Individual chicken pieces are however easier to coat than a whole chicken.

PREPARATION TIME: *1 hour*
COOKING TIME: *1½–1¾ hours*
INGREDIENTS *(for 6)*:
6 chicken portions
1 large onion
1 sprig thyme
1 small bay leaf
1 small carrot
6 parsley stalks
6 peppercorns
¼ teaspoon salt★
1¼ cups milk
2 tablespoons unsalted butter
2 tablespoons flour
Salt★ and black pepper
1¼ cups liquid aspic
2 teaspoons unflavored gelatin
GARNISH:
Cucumber peel
1 large tomato
1 small green pepper
Peel of a small lemon

Wipe the chicken portions and put them in a large saucepan. Peel the onion, cut off a 1 in slice and add the larger piece to the pan together with the thyme, bay leaf and enough cold water to cover the chicken. Bring slowly to the boil, remove the scum and cover the pan with a lid. Simmer for 1–1¼ hours or until tender. Lift out the chicken portions and drain.

Scrape the carrot, leaving it whole, and put it in a saucepan with the onion slice, parsley stalks, peppercorns, salt and milk. Bring slowly to the boil, then turn off the heat and leave the

milk to infuse for 30 minutes.

Melt the butter in a saucepan, stir in the flour and cook for 2 minutes; strain the infused milk and gradually stir into the butter and flour mixture. Bring the sauce to the boil over low heat, stirring continuously, and cook gently for 2 minutes. Season to taste with salt and freshly ground pepper.

Warm the aspic, then add the gelatin and stir until it has dissolved. Allow the aspic to stand until almost set, then gradually add half to the white sauce, stirring until thick but not set.

Remove the skin carefully from the chicken portions, pat them dry and place on a wire rack. Coat each portion carefully with the aspic sauce, allowing any excess to run off. Leave for 15 minutes to set.

Cut a 1 in piece of cucumber peel, the tomato, pepper and lemon peel into narrow strips, dip them in the remaining aspic and arrange them in decorative patterns on the chicken pieces. Allow the decorations to set before spooning over the remaining aspic; leave the chicken in a cool place to set completely.

Salads, crusty bread or new potatoes could be served as side dishes with the chicken.

DUCK BREASTS EN CROÛTE

A little duck goes a long way and still constitutes a festive dish for a special occasion. The preparation of this dish can be done well in advance.

PREPARATION TIME: *1½ hours*
COOKING TIME: *25 min*
INGREDIENTS (*for 12*):
3 ducks
¼ cup chopped lean bacon
2 duck livers, chopped
¼ cup finely chopped onion
Grated rind of 1 orange
2 tablespoons butter
3 tablespoons chopped green olives
1 tablespoon brandy
1½ pounds puff pastry
1 large egg, beaten

Roast the ducks in the center of the oven for 45–60 minutes, at 400°F (200°C, mark 6). Set aside to cool.

Sauté the bacon, duck livers, onions and orange rind in the butter. Add the olives moistened with the brandy and cook this mixture over moderate heat for about 5 minutes.

Skin the ducks and carve the breasts off each in two whole slices; cut each breast into two equal portions (set the duck carcasses aside for a pâté to be made the following day). Roll out the puff pastry, ¼ in thick, and divide into 12 pieces. Lay a portion of duck breast on each pastry square, spread a little of the bacon and onion mixture over the duck and wrap the pastry around each to form an envelope.

Seal the joins with egg and place the envelopes, seams up, on a moist, floured baking sheet. Brush with egg and bake in a pre-heated oven at 400°F (200°C, mark 6) for about 25 minutes.

Serve with croquette potatoes and mushroom caps filled with green peas.

DUCK PÂTÉ

The rest of the duck meat and liver from the preceding recipe can be used to make a savory pâté.

PREPARATION TIME: *15 min*
COOKING TIME: *1¼ hours*
INGREDIENTS (*for 8–10*):
3 duck carcasses (see above)
1 duck liver
½ pound ground veal
1 cup soft breadcrumbs
2 tablespoons finely chopped onion
1 tablespoon chopped chervil
3 tablespoons chopped parsley
Salt* and pepper
Grated rind of an orange
2 tablespoons brandy or dry sherry
2 eggs
¼ pound bacon slices

Cut the meat from the duck carcasses and grind it coarsely, together with the remaining duck liver. Mix with the ground veal, breadcrumbs, finely chopped onion, chervil and parsley. Season to taste. Stir in the grated orange rind and the brandy or dry sherry. Beat the eggs lightly and mix them in to bind the pâté.

Spoon into a buttered terrine and cover with the bacon. Put into a roasting pan half filled with boiling water and bake in the center of an oven pre-heated to 325°F (170°C, mark 3) for 1¼ hours.

When cool, cover and store in the refrigerator for a day or two before serving.

DUCK BREASTS EN CROÛTE

SALT SUGAR FAT CHOL FIBER

TOTAL CALORIES: ABOUT 6330

For a **low-salt** version, replace the bacon and olives in the stuffing with chunks of apple and pieces of cooked dried apricot, mango or fennel; or use the stuffing suggested below. The **fat** and **cholesterol** cannot be reduced to less than moderate, unless you can substitute wild duck (which is much leaner) or pheasant. To reduce them as much as possible, roast the birds on a rack, first pricking them all over so that as much fat as possible drains off. Skinning the birds before cooking will also help. Yeast pastry, or bought phyllo pastry, are both good low-fat alternatives to puff pastry. (Calories lost: up to 800.) Serve with baked potatoes, scooped out and mashed with a little skim milk and the grated rind of an orange.
Neither **gluten-free** nor **whole wheat** puff pastry is very successful. Try a yeast dough instead, made if necessary with a special gluten-free mix.

ALTERNATIVE STUFFING:
Use only 1 tablespoon bacon and add ½ ounce dried mushrooms (soaked in warm water for half an hour and drained), and 4 tablespoons very finely chopped celery; omit the duck livers. This is low in both salt and cholesterol.

DUCK PÂTÉ

SALT	SUGAR	FAT	CHOL	FIBER

GLUTEN-FREE* WHOLEFOOD*
TOTAL CALORIES: ABOUT 2415

To reduce the **salt** even further, use breadcrumbs from a loaf made without added salt, and use spinach leaves to wrap the pâté in instead of the terrine lining of bacon. The spinach leaves also help to lower **cholesterol** content although this will still be high.
To reduce the **fat** content, the duck should be cooked as in the notes on previous recipe and the ground veal should be lean: to be certain of this, buy lean meat and grind it yourself at home. Use spinach leaves instead of bacon as above. Even so the fat content will be between low and moderate. (Calories lost: up to 1000.)

Food processor: ☑ for grinding and chopping.

Freezing: ☑ up to 1 month.

DUCKLING WITH ORANGE

SALT	SUGAR	FAT	CHOL	FIBER

GLUTEN-FREE WHOLEFOOD
TOTAL CALORIES: ABOUT 2030

To reduce **fat** and **cholesterol**, skin the ducks before roasting; roast on a rack so that the fat can drain off, and do not baste. Even so the levels of both fat and cholesterol will be moderate, the meat alone averages 10% fat when cooked: with the skin, this can be 29%!

DUCKLING WITH ORANGE

This classic dish is easy to cook and a good choice for a dinner party. It can be made in advance and kept hot over low heat.

PREPARATION TIME: *45 min*
COOKING TIME: *1¾ hours*
INGREDIENTS *(for 4–6):*
2 ducks, each 4–5 pounds
4 oranges
1 tablespoon sugar
½ cup red wine vinegar
1¼ cups giblet stock
Juice of half lemon
1 tablespoon arrowroot
3 tablespoons Curaçao

Peel the oranges over a plate to catch the juice. Remove all pith and divide the oranges into segments. Cut the rind into strips and boil them for 10 minutes in a little water. Drain them and set aside, with the orange segments, for garnishing.

Pre-heat the oven to 400°F (200°C, mark 6) and place the trussed ducks on their sides in a greased roasting pan. Cook for 40 minutes, then turn the ducks on to the other side and cook for 30 minutes. Finally place the ducks on their backs and cook for 30

minutes more. Baste frequently.
Boil the sugar and vinegar until reduced to a light caramel. Add the stock, reserved orange and the lemon juice and boil for 5 minutes. Thicken the sauce with diluted arrowroot and stir until shiny. Strain the sauce, then stir in the Curaçao and pour over the duck.

Serve with new potatoes, green peas and perhaps an endive and watercress salad.

Poultry and Game

DUCK PAPRIKA

The Hungarians traditionally flavor many of their poultry and meat dishes with paprika. This recipe makes a change from plain roast duck and is a good main course for a dinner party.

PREPARATION TIME: *15 min*
COOKING TIME: *1¼–1½ hours*
INGREDIENTS (*for 4–6*):
1 5–6 pound duck
2 onions
1 clove garlic
3 tablespoons unsalted butter
2 tablespoons flour
2 teaspoons paprika
1 cup red wine
Salt★ and black pepper
4–5 tomatoes
Chicken or duck stock (page 153)
1 teaspoon arrowroot

Wipe the duck inside and out with a damp cloth, pat it thoroughly dry and truss it neatly (page 167). Peel and finely chop the onions and garlic. Melt the butter in a large flameproof casserole or sauté dish, and cook the onions and garlic for a few minutes until transparent. Add the duck, and brown on all sides. Lift the duck from the pan, sprinkle in the flour and paprika and cook for a few minutes. Pour in the wine and stir until this is a smooth sauce. Season to taste with salt and freshly ground pepper. Return the duck to the pan.

Skin and roughly chop the tomatoes (page 179) and add them to the duck, thinning with a little stock if necessary.

Cover the dish with a lid and simmer over low heat for about 1¼ hours or until the duck is tender. If necessary add more stock.

Remove the duck and carve it into six to eight portions; arrange these on a serving dish and keep hot. Skim any fat off the sauce; if necessary, blend a little arrowroot with cold water and stir into the sauce to thicken it. Spoon the sauce over the duck and serve with boiled rice.

WILD DUCK WITH TANGERINES

The largest wild duck is the mallard, which usually provides three or four servings; teal and widgeon are even smaller. As the meat is tough, wild duck are best roasted continental style with liquid in the roasting pan, and should be served with a fruit-flavored sauce. The recipe is also successful for domestic duck.

PREPARATION TIME: *35–40 min*
COOKING TIME: *1 hour*
INGREDIENTS (*for 3–4*):
1 large wild duck
Bouquet garni (page 183)
1 cup cooked noodles
1 onion
2 teaspoons fresh chopped parsley
½ teaspoon dried thyme
Pinch nutmeg
2½ tablespoons honey
2 tablespoons beer
2 egg yolks
5 tablespoons heavy cream
3 tangerines
¼ cup port
Lemon juice
Salt★ and black pepper
GARNISH:
Tangerine slices and watercress

Clean the duck giblets and put them in a saucepan with water to cover; add salt, freshly ground pepper and the bouquet garni. Cover the pan with a lid and cook for about 25 minutes or until the giblets are tender. Strain and set the cooking liquid aside. Skin the gizzard and chop this, the heart and the liver finely.

Chop the drained noodles roughly and mix in the giblets, chopped onion, herbs and nutmeg. Mix half the honey and half the beer with the egg yolks and

DUCK PAPRIKA

| SALT | SUGAR | FAT | CHOL | FIBER |

GLUTEN-FREE★   WHOLEFOOD★
TOTAL CALORIES: ABOUT 2360

The **fat** and **cholesterol** can be reduced to medium if the duck is skinned before cooking and if it is then browned with the onions in the fat which it produces itself, without adding any butter. Skim the fat from the cooking juices; one way of doing this is to put the juices in a narrow jug and add a few ice cubes. The fat will solidify quickly on the ice, which can then be lifted out. (Calories lost: up to 500.)

Freezing: ☑ up to 2 months.

WILD DUCK WITH TANGERINES

| SALT | SUGAR | FAT | CHOL | FIBER |

GLUTEN-FREE   WHOLEFOOD
TOTAL CALORIES: ABOUT 2920

Wild duck has much less **fat** than duck bred for the table. Removing the skin will reduce the fat level to some extent, but is not really necessary unless you need a very low-fat diet. The fat in the rest of the recipe can be reduced by omitting the egg yolks and cream from the noodle stuffing and stirring in 4 tablespoons of low-fat small curd cottage cheese or yogurt instead. Roast the duck on a rack throughout, and skim the pan juices before adding the oranges and other flavorings. Doing all this will result in low fat and medium **cholesterol**. (Calories lost: up to 375.)

This recipe is very sweet, and you may prefer to use half the amount of honey.
A **gluten-free** alternative to the noodles would be rice. Brown rice will also be **wholefood**. Use about 3 tablespoons uncooked brown rice if you have none ready cooked.

Pressure cooker: ☑ for stock.

SALMI OF WILD DUCK

SALT SUGAR FAT CHOL FIBER

GLUTEN-FREE* WHOLEFOOD*
TOTAL CALORIES: ABOUT 3370

To reduce the **salt** to low, omit the bacon slices and olives. If you are substituting a domestic, or bred, duck, you will not need the bacon anyway. Make sure the stock is made without salt, and omit the ketchup unless it is salt-free.
For low **fat** and medium **cholesterol**, omit the bacon. Even wild duck has enough fat to keep it moist while cooking. If you fear it is getting dry, cover with foil or a lid. Make sure both the stock and the pan juices are well skimmed of fat, and thicken the sauce without using butter. This can be done by adding a tablespoon of arrowroot, blended with water to a smooth consistency, and boiling for a few minutes; or simply by puréeing the onions and carrots in a blender and adding the purée back to the mixture. (Calories lost: up to 680.) Either of these methods of thickening the sauce will make the recipe **gluten-free**, if there is no gluten in the ketchup.

Pressure cooker: ☑ for stock.
Freezing: ☑ up to 2 months.

cream and stir this into the noodle mixture. Open the vent and remove any pieces of fat from the duck, spoon in the stuffing and close the opening.

Put the duck in a roasting pan, breast downwards, and pour water into the pan to a depth of ½ in. Roast in the center of a pre-heated oven, at 375°F (190°C, mark 5), for 20 minutes, basting occasionally. Remove the duck from the roasting pan, put in a wire rack and replace the duck, breast upwards. Pour the remaining honey and beer over the duck and continue roasting for a further 30 minutes, or until the duck is crisp and golden and the legs are tender when tested with a skewer.

Meanwhile grate the rind from the tangerines and set aside. Remove the pith and seeds and put the fruit in the liquidizer.

When the duck is ready, lift it on to a warm serving dish. Add the tangerine pulp and rind to the pan, together with the port and 1¼ cups of the reserved giblet stock. Boil on top of the stove over high heat until the gravy has reduced and thickened slightly. Sharpen with lemon juice and adjust seasoning. Strain the gravy into a warm sauce boat.

Garnish the duck with water-cress sprigs and thin slices of unpeeled tangerine. Serve with mashed potatoes and buttered green beans.

SALMI OF WILD DUCK

Salmi – a French cooking term – means a rich brown stew or casserole of game. It is a suitable method for making a party dish out of wild duck towards the end of their season.

PREPARATION TIME: *1 hour*
COOKING TIME: 40–45 min
INGREDIENTS (*for 6*):

2 wild ducks	*3 tablespoons flour*
Coarse salt	*1 tablespoon mushroom ketchup*
3 carrots	*(optional)*
2 large onions	*3–4 tablespoons medium dry*
4 slices bacon	*sherry or port*
1 bay leaf	*Salt**
SAUCE:	*Squeeze lemon juice*
2½ cups duck stock	*6–8 pitted green olives*
¼ cup butter	*Black pepper*

Wipe the ducks inside and out, and rub the skin with coarse salt. Peel and thinly slice a carrot and an onion and put them in a saucepan, together with the duck giblets. Pour over about 1 quart of cold water, cover with a lid, bring to the boil and simmer for 30 minutes to make the stock.

Meanwhile, cover the breast of the ducks with the slices. Peel and slice the remaining carrots and onion and use them to cover the bottom of a lightly greased roasting pan. Add the bay leaf, place the birds on the bed of vegetables and roast for 30 minutes only, in the center of the oven pre-heated to 375°F (190°C, mark 5). Remove the birds, discarding the bacon; carve each duck into four portions and put in a casserole.

Strain the fat from the roasting pan, but retain the vegetables. Pour 2½ cups of strained duck stock into the pan and stir over moderate heat until boiling.

Simmer gently until it has reduced by about one-third. Meanwhile, melt the butter in a saucepan over low heat. Stir in the flour and cook gently for 5–10 minutes, stirring occasionally until the mixture is nutty brown. Remove from the heat and stir in the hot reduced duck stock. Return the pan to the heat; stir until boiling, then add the mush-room ketchup (if used), sherry or port, a squeeze of lemon and salt and pepper to taste. Strain the sauce over the ducks in the casserole, cover with a lid and place in the center of the oven pre-heated to 350°F (180°C, mark 4). Cook for 40–50 minutes or until the ducks are tender (if the juices that come out, when a meat skewer is gently pushed into the thigh, are clear, the ducks are cooked). Add the olives and allow to heat through for a few moments.

Serve creamed potatoes and broccoli with the salmi.

ROAST GOOSE WITH GERMAN-STYLE SWEET STUFFING

Goose is a much-neglected bird, yet it has endless possibilities. It is not only an excellent choice for holidays but makes a festive dinner any time of the year.

PREPARATION TIME: *30 min*
COOKING TIME: *2½–3 hours*
INGREDIENTS *(for 6–8):*
1 goose, fresh or frozen, 8–10 pounds
STUFFING:
6 cups day-old bread cut into cubes
4 apples
1 cup raisins
½ cup sugar
1 teaspoon salt★
1 teaspoon cinnamon
½ teaspoon allspice
½ cup water
¼ cup melted butter

If the goose is frozen, place it, still in its original wrap, on a tray in the refrigerator for 1–1½ days to thaw. The goose may be thawed in 4 or 5 hours if it is placed, unwrapped, in a sink with cool or cold water. Change the water often to hasten thawing. To thaw at room temperature in 6–10 hours, leave the goose in its original wrap and place it in a brown paper bag, or wrap in 2 or 3 layers of newspaper and place on a tray.

Cook immediately after thawing, or refrigerate until ready to cook. Remove the neck and giblets from the body cavity; cook them immediately in enough salted water to cover and reserve for another use. Remove the excess fat from the body cavity and neck skin. Reserve this fat and render it (page 184) for use in

other cooking. Rinse the bird inside and out, and drain well.

The wings may be removed at the second joint or tied flat against the body with a cord around each wing and across the back. If two end pieces of wings are removed, cook them with the neck and giblets.

To make the stuffing, chop the apples and combine them with the bread cubes and raisins in a large bowl. Mix the sugar with the salt, cinnamon, and allspice; sprinkle this over the bread mixture and toss well. Stir in the water and butter. Fill the neck and the body cavity loosely with the stuffing. Fasten the neck skin to the back of the goose with a skewer. Tie the legs together with string, or tuck the legs in the band of skin at the tail, if it is present. It is not necessary to truss the bird.

Place the goose, breast side up, on a rack in a roasting pan. Insert a meat thermometer deep into the inside thigh muscle without touching the bone. Roast, uncovered, for 1 hour in a pre-heated oven at 400°F (200°C, mark 6). Do not baste. During roasting, spoon or siphon off accumulated fat and reserve it for use in other cooking. This should be done at half-hour intervals to stop the fat browning excessively.

After roasting for 1 hour, reduce the oven temperature to 325°F (170°C, mark 3) and continue cooking for 1½–2 hours, or until the thermometer registers 180°–185°F (82°–85°C). Stuffing temperature should also be checked and should register 165°F (75°C). If a thermometer is not used, press the meaty part of

the leg between protected fingers. It should feel very soft. Also, prick the thigh with a fork. The juices running out should be beige in color, not pink.

Serve with braised red cabbage or with Brussels sprouts.

GOOSE IN CIDER

This recipe adapts well for wild goose, should you ever have to cope with one. As wild goose is very lean, it will need plenty of butter added to the stuffing and should be rubbed with more butter and barded with strips of bacon.

PREPARATION TIME: *15 min*
COOKING TIME: *3¼ hours*
INGREDIENTS *(for 4–6):*
1 8-pound goose
2 cups stock (page 153)
1 onion
6 cloves
½ orange
Salt★ and black pepper
2½ cups dry hard cider or white wine
2 tablespoons calvados or brandy (optional)
GARNISH:
Saratoga chips (potato chips)
Thick slices of bacon
Watercress
Oranges

Wipe the goose thoroughly inside and out with a damp cloth. Use the giblets to make stock.

Put the peeled onion, stuck with the cloves, and half an orange inside the goose. Sew up the vent or secure it with small skewers. Rub the skin with salt and freshly ground pepper and prick the breast with a fork so that the fat can drain out.

Place the goose, breast side up,

ROAST GOOSE WITH GERMAN-STYLE SWEET STUFFING

| SALT | SUGAR | FAT | CHOL | FIBER |

GLUTEN-FREE★   WHOLEFOOD★
TOTAL CALORIES: ABOUT 5910

Reduce the **salt** to low by using crumbs from bread made without added salt.
Goose is naturally a fatty bird (about 22% fat when roasted) and the levels of both **fat** and **cholesterol** will be high, unless you can acquire a wild goose, which is much leaner. Reduce both fat and cholesterol as far as possible (if you have managed to find a wild goose, the fat will be much lower anyway) by omitting the butter in the stuffing and being meticulous in removing as much of the goose fat as possible. (Calories lost: up to 450.)
Rice is a good **gluten-free** alternative to breadcrumbs in the stuffing. If you use white rice, wash about 2 cups well to remove the starch. Measure the same volume of water as rice into a pan and bring it to the boil. Add the rice, cover tightly, turn down the heat and let it just simmer for 20 minutes. All the water should be absorbed. If it looks like drying out while cooking, add a little more cold water, up to half as much again.
This method of cooking rice ensures that all the vitamins and minerals stay in it and do not leach out into the cooking water to be thrown away.
The same method can be used for brown rice, which makes an excellent stuffing and is of course **wholefood**. It needs more water, about 2¼ times the volume of the rice, and a longer cooking time, about 35–40

minutes (although this is not crucial, as it will continue to cook in the oven with the goose).

GOOSE IN CIDER

SALT SUGAR FAT CHOL FIBER

GLUTEN-FREE   WHOLEFOOD
TOTAL CALORIES: ABOUT 3930

For **fat** and **cholesterol** levels, see the notes on the previous recipe. To avoid any extra fat, skim the pan juices and stock meticulously, and garnish with plain potatoes, rice or toast snippets, omitting the potato chips and bacon.
This recipe is particularly good for wild duck, with its gamey taste. Wild duck needs constant basting while cooking.

Pressure cooker: √ The result will be more like a casserole, but is good, and time is saved. Be sure to skim off all the fat.

in a large roasting pan. Pour in half the cider and all the stock and roast the goose in the lower half of a pre-heated oven at 450°F (230°C, mark 8) for 15 minutes. Baste with more cider and reduce the heat to 350°F (180°C, mark 4). Continue roasting for about 3 hours, removing fat as it accumulates in the pan. Baste occasionally with cider.

Remove the roasting pan from the oven and skim as much fat as possible from the pan juices. Pour the warmed calvados over the goose and set it alight. As soon as the flames die down, transfer the goose to a serving dish and keep it warm while making the gravy.
Pour the pan juices into a saucepan and boil them briskly

until they have reduced to a thin gravy.
Serve the goose garnished with Saratoga chips, thick slices of bacon cooked crisp, sprigs of watercress, and small halved oranges.
Red cabbage cooked with apple and vinegar is an excellent accompaniment. Serve the gravy separately.

Poultry and Game

GOOSE WITH BLOOD SAUSAGE

In France, the main Christmas meal, the *réveillon*, is served after Midnight Mass on Christmas Eve. Whatever other glories it may include, there is always a dish of blood sausage. This Norman recipe combines traditional ingredients: goose and blood sausage, garnished with small red apples.

PREPARATION TIME: *25 min*
COOKING TIME: *2¾ hours*
INGREDIENTS *(for 6–8):*
1 goose, about 10 pounds
1 pound blood sausage
1 clove garlic
2 large apples
5 tablespoons port
Salt★ and black pepper

Peel and grate the apples; crush the garlic. Skin the blood sausage and pound it smooth with the goose liver and garlic. Blend in the apples and bind the stuffing with the wine. Stuff the goose with this mixture. Prick the skin all over with a skewer, and rub it thoroughly with salt and pepper.

Place the goose in a roasting pan and cover with foil. Roast on the lowest shelf of an oven, preheated to 400°F (200°C, mark 6), and allow 15 minutes to the pound, plus 15 minutes. After 1 hour, drain the fat from the pan and pour ½ cup cold water over the goose. Remove the foil 30 minutes before cooking is complete, and baste the goose every 10 minutes with the pan juices.

Serve the goose on a thick bed of unsweetened apple purée and garnish with polished apples set on cocktail picks.

BLANQUETTE OF TURKEY

After Christmas, cold turkey tends to lose its charms; even so, the last left-overs may be turned into a savory main course, and an excellent stock can be made from the carcass.

PREPARATION TIME: *20 min*
COOKING TIME: *30 min*
INGREDIENTS *(for 4–6):*
1½ pounds cooked turkey meat
1 large onion
6 tablespoons unsalted butter
¼ cup flour
2½ cups turkey or chicken stock
1 small can pimientos
⅔ cup button mushrooms
1 clove garlic
Pinch each of ground mace and nutmeg
2 egg yolks
¼ cup heavy cream
1 tablespoon lemon juice
Salt★ and black pepper

Cut the turkey meat into small pieces and peel and thinly slice the onion. Melt the butter in a large frying pan and cook the onion over low heat until soft and transparent. Mix in the flour and cook this roux for 3 minutes. Gradually stir in the stock, and simmer the sauce for a few minutes until the sauce thickens.

Meanwhile, slice the drained pimientos thinly, trim and slice the mushrooms and peel and crush the garlic. Add these ingredients to the sauce, with the turkey; season to taste with salt, freshly ground pepper, mace and nutmeg. Heat the mixture through and then remove from the heat. Beat the egg yolks, cream and lemon juice until the mixture has the consistency of thin cream. Blend this slowly into the turkey mixture and return the pan to the heat. Heat through over low heat, but do not let the mixture boil.

Spoon the turkey into a warm serving dish, and serve with Brussels sprouts tossed in a little butter, soft brown sugar and allspice.

TURKEY OR CHICKEN TOASTS

This quick recipe provides another solution to the problem of what to do with Christmas leftovers from turkey, and cooked vegetables such as cauliflower, carrots, or broccoli.

PREPARATION TIME: *15 min*
COOKING TIME: *5 min*
INGREDIENTS *(for 4):*
8 thin slices turkey or chicken (skinned)
½ cup thick white sauce (page 154)
Salt★
Dried tarragon
4 slices bread
Butter
2 cups cooked, chopped vegetables
½ cup grated Cheddar cheese
Black pepper

Make the white sauce and season with salt, freshly ground pepper and tarragon. Toast the bread, trim off the crusts and spread with butter. Arrange the turkey on the toast, cover with the vegetables and spoon over the sauce.

Sprinkle the toasts with the cheese and brown them under a broiler until the cheese has melted and is golden brown on top. Serve at once.

GOOSE WITH BLOOD SAUSAGE

SALT SUGAR FAT CHOL FIBER

GLUTEN-FREE* WHOLEFOOD
TOTAL CALORIES: ABOUT 5800

The only reduction in **salt** possible for this dish is using less blood sausage.
This will also limit the fat to some extent, but levels of both **fat** and **cholesterol** will remain high unless you can use wild goose (see notes on the two preceding recipes). Use a roasting rack and do not baste. This recipe is **gluten-free** if there is no gluten in the blood sausage. Some blood sausages contain wheat, but most contain oatmeal, which can be tolerated by some but not all people on gluten-free diets.

Food processor: √ for making the stuffing.

BLANQUETTE OF TURKEY

SALT SUGAR FAT CHOL FIBER

GLUTEN-FREE* WHOLEFOOD*
TOTAL CALORIES: ABOUT 2780

To reduce **fat** and **cholesterol** to low, make a sauce which is predominantly onion rather than an enriched white sauce. Soften 2 large onions in only 2 tablespoons oil. Thinly slice a potato, add this to the onions and cook for 2 or 3 more minutes before stirring in the stock. Omit the egg yolks and use yogurt instead of cream; omit the lemon juice. (Calories lost: up to 970.)
This method omits the flour, so it is **gluten-free**.

TURKEY OR CHICKEN TOASTS

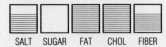

SALT	SUGAR	FAT	CHOL	FIBER

GLUTEN-FREE*   WHOLEFOOD*
TOTAL CALORIES: ABOUT 3100

Reduce the **salt** to low by using bread made without salt and only ¼ cup Cheddar (or Parmesan) cheese, finely grated.
Reduce **fat** and **cholesterol** to low by using skim milk and only 2 teaspoons butter (or vegetable margarine) in the sauce. Do not butter the toast and use only half the cheese (as above). (Calories lost: up to 700.)

TURKEY SCALLOPS CORDON BLEU

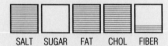

SALT	SUGAR	FAT	CHOL	FIBER

GLUTEN-FREE*   WHOLEFOOD*
TOTAL CALORIES: ABOUT 2760

It is impossible to reduce the **salt** in this recipe unless you omit the ham and cheese, which give it its character. However, you can reduce the **fat** and **cholesterol**: check that the ham you use is very lean; soften the mushrooms in a pan lightly brushed with oil in place of butter; cook the scallops also in a pan lightly brushed with oil and cover it tightly. Thin slices of cheese plus the small amount of oil for cooking will add up to a low-to-medium fat and cholesterol level. (Calories lost: up to 680.) Do not butter the noodles or add an oily salad dressing.

TURKEY SCALLOPS CORDON BLEU

Fresh turkey makes a good main course for a dinner party, especially as scallops can now be bought ready-cut.

PREPARATION TIME: *20 min*
COOKING TIME: *25 min*
INGREDIENTS *(for 4):*
4 turkey breast tenderloin slices
4 slices lean cooked ham
4 thin slices Fontina, Bel Paese,
*   or Gruyère cheese*
4–6 ounces button mushrooms
6 tablespoons unsalted butter
Seasoned flour (page 184)
1 tablespoon olive oil
Black pepper
1–2 tablespoons chopped parsley
4–6 tablespoons stock (page 153)
GARNISH (OPTIONAL):
Watercress

Buy the turkey scallops ready-cut, or cut them from a large uncooked bird which is intended for a casserole, risotto or for deep-freezing in portions. The white breast meat should give 5 slices from each side. Before slicing the breast, cut down slantwise behind the wishbone and remove this to give another scallop. Store the surplus scallops in the freezer.

Cut the ham and cheese slices to fit the scallops. Trim the mushrooms and slice them thinly; cook until soft in 1 table-spoon of the butter and set them aside. Coat the turkey scallops evenly, but not too thickly, with the seasoned flour.

Melt the remaining butter and the oil in a large frying pan over moderate heat. Fry the scallops for about 5 minutes on each side. Place a slice of ham on each scallop, spoon over a thin layer of mushrooms and season lightly with freshly ground pepper. Sprinkle some of the parsley over the mushrooms and cover with a slice of cheese. Pour the hot stock over the scallops. Cover the pan closely with a lid or foil and cook over low heat for about 10 minutes or until the cheese has melted.

Lift out the scallops and arrange on a hot serving dish; sprinkle over the remaining parsley or garnish with sprigs of watercress. The richness of the scallops is best offset by a dish of buttered ribbon noodles and a tossed green salad.

GUINEA HEN
WITH GRAPES

In this French recipe, guinea hen is cooked with white grapes. This domesticated game bird has a flavor reminiscent of pheasant, which may be cooked in the same way. A small guinea hen will provide two servings and a fully grown bird three. They are usually sold ready trussed and barded with pork fat.

PREPARATION TIME: *30 min*
COOKING TIME: *55 min*
INGREDIENTS *(for 3):*
1 guinea hen
1 onion
1 bouquet garni (page 183)
Salt★ and black pepper
½ pound seedless green grapes
Juice of a lemon
2 tablespoons butter
4 slices bacon (optional)
½ cup dry white wine
2 egg yolks
5 tablespoons heavy cream
GARNISH:
Lemon wedges and vine leaves or
    additional seedless green grapes

Clean the giblets thoroughly and put them in a saucepan with 2½ cups of cold water. Peel and quarter the onion, add it to the giblets with the bouquet garni and a good seasoning of salt and freshly ground pepper. Bring to the boil, remove any scum and simmer the stock, covered, for 20 minutes. Strain and set aside.

Meanwhile, peel the grapes (page 178) if they are thick-skinned. Sprinkle them with a little lemon juice and salt before stuffing them into the guinea hen. Sew up the vent. Melt the butter and brush it all over the bird. Tie the bacon slices over the breast of the guinea hen if not already barded.

Roast the guinea hen in the center of a pre-heated oven, at 400°F (200°C, mark 6), for 30 minutes. Remove the bacon or fat and continue cooking the guinea hen for a further 15 minutes or until golden brown and tender. Place on a serving dish and keep it warm in the oven.

Pour the wine into the roasting pan and bring to the boil on top of the stove, scraping up all the residue. Pour it into a measuring jug, making it up to ½ cup with the giblet stock. Beat the egg yolks with the cream in a bowl and gradually stir in the wine and stock mixture. Place the bowl over a saucepan containing ½ in of gently simmering water. Stir this sauce continuously until it has thickened enough to coat thinly the back of a wooden spoon. Do not let the sauce reach boiling point or it will curdle. Correct seasoning and sharpen to taste with lemon juice.

Garnish the guinea hen with lemon wedges arranged on fresh vine leaves, or with small bunches of seedless green grapes. Pour the sauce into a warm sauce boat and serve with, for example, new potatoes and cauliflower or broccoli over which the crisp bacon has been crumbled as a garnish.

GUINEA HEN
IN RED WINE

The somewhat dry flesh of guinea hen is made tender by cooking it in wine, using a method similar to that for the classic French *coq au vin*. Chicken may be cooked in the same way.

PREPARATION TIME: *20 min*
COOKING TIME: *1 hour*
INGREDIENTS *(for 4–6):*
1 or 2 guinea hen, cut up
3 ounces slab bacon
4 tablespoons unsalted butter
Salt★ and black pepper
16 pearl onions
6 tablespoons brandy
1 bottle Beaujolais
½ cup chicken stock
1 bouquet garni (page 183)
2 cloves garlic
¼ pound mushrooms
SAUCE:
2 tablespoons flour
2 tablespoons unsalted butter
GARNISH:
Parsley sprigs

Cut the bacon into small cubes and fry in half of the butter in a deep sauté pan. Wipe and season the poultry pieces with salt and freshly ground pepper. Remove the bacon from the pan and slowly brown the guinea hen in the butter over gentle heat.

Peel the onions and add to the pan, together with the fried bacon; turn the onions until they are glazed. Warm the brandy, pour over the guinea hen and set alight. As soon as the flames have died down, pour over the wine and stock, add the bouquet garni and the crushed garlic. Increase the heat to bring the contents of the pan slowly to boiling point. Check the seasoning, cover the

GUINEA HEN WITH GRAPES

| SALT | SUGAR | FAT | CHOL | FIBER |

GLUTEN-FREE   WHOLEFOOD
TOTAL CALORIES: ABOUT 2360

The low **salt** level assumes that the bacon is not used: if it is, the level of salt will be high. To reduce **fat** and **cholesterol** to low, omit the bacon; omit brushing the bird with butter; and replace the egg yolks and cream in the sauce with ¼ cup low-fat small curd cottage cheese or plain yogurt. After blending this in do not let the sauce come back to the boil or the mixture will curdle. (Calories lost: up to 940.)

Pressure cooker: ✓ for the stock.

GUINEA HEN IN RED WINE

SALT	SUGAR	FAT	CHOL	FIBER

GLUTEN-FREE   WHOLEFOOD
TOTAL CALORIES: ABOUT 3740

The **salt** content is high because of the bacon: if this is omitted the salt will be low.
To reduce **fat** and **cholesterol** to the low level natural in guinea hen, brown the bird in a heavy pan lightly brushed with oil; omit the butter. Do the same with the mushrooms. To thicken the sauce, liquidize the mushrooms in the stock. If you would like the sauce to be still thicker, blend 1 tablespoon cornstarch, rice flour (both **gluten-free**) or arrowroot with enough water to make a smooth paste. Work in a little hot stock, return to the pan and simmer for at least 4 minutes for it to thicken up. (Calories lost: up to 750.) Do not butter the side vegetables.

Freezing: ✓ up to 2 months.

pan with a lid and simmer for 30 minutes.

Meanwhile, trim and clean the mushrooms, sauté them in the remaining butter, drain and add to the guinea hen after this has simmered for 30 minutes. Cover and cook for a further 10 minutes or until the guinea hen is tender.

Transfer the contents of the pan to a heated serving dish and keep it warm.

Turn up the heat and boil the liquid in the pan rapidly until it is reduced to about 2 cups. Work the flour and butter together to form a paste; remove the pan from the heat and beat in bits of the

paste until the sauce thickens. Return to the heat and bring slowly to the boil. Pour the sauce over the guinea hen and garnish with parsley.

Boiled new potatoes and young blanched broccoli spears, cooked in butter, could be served as well.

SQUAB WITH OLIVES

Squab, or young domestic pigeons, can be roasted or broiled like other game birds. But since the meat is rather dry, they are more suitable for braising or a casserole. Partridges may be cooked in the same way.

PREPARATION TIME: *1 hour*
COOKING TIME: *2 hours*
INGREDIENTS *(for 4)*:

4 squab
3 onions
1 carrot
¼ pound slab bacon
2 cloves garlic
Seasoned flour (page 184)
2–3 tablespoons brandy

½ cup dry white wine or vermouth
½ cup squab stock
1 cup green stuffed olives
1 bouquet garni (page 183)
4 large slices bread
1 tablespoon olive oil

Skin the squab carefully. Cut along and down each side of the breastbone on each squab so that each breast, leg and wing comes away in one piece.

Wash the squab halves thoroughly in cold water and dry them on a clean cloth. Clean the carcasses and giblets thoroughly.

Peel and finely slice one onion, scrape and roughly chop the carrot. Put the carcasses, giblets, onion and carrot in a saucepan and cover with cold water. Bring to the boil and simmer, covered with a lid, until all the meat has come off the bones. Strain the stock and set aside.

Meanwhile, cut the bacon into ½ in wide strips, crosswise. Put the strips in a large flameproof casserole over a moderate heat and cook until the fat runs. Peel and finely chop the remaining onions, and peel and crush the garlic. Add these to the bacon and cook until soft.

Coat the squab thickly with the seasoned flour. Add them to the onion mixture and brown them well on both sides. Warm the brandy, set it alight and pour over the squab, shaking the casserole until the flames die down. Add the wine and ½ cup of the stock. Put in the olives and bouquet garni and bring to the boil. Remove the casserole from the heat and cover closely with foil and a lid. Cook in the center of a pre-heated oven at 300°F (150°C, mark 2), for 1½–2 hours or until tender.

Fry the bread golden in the oil and arrange two squab halves on each slice. Top with the bacon and olives and pour over the strained gravy. Serve with mashed potatoes or boiled rice.

SQUAB WITH FORCEMEAT BALLS

These inexpensive little game birds can be ordered cleaned and trussed, ready for cooking. Young, tender squab can be roasted or broiled, but when older they are best used for a casserole.

PREPARATION TIME: *1 hour*
COOKING TIME: *1¼ hours*
INGREDIENTS *(for 6)*:
3 squab
¼ pound bacon
2 tablespoons unsalted butter
1 tablespoon flour
2 cups hot chicken stock (page 153) or water
1 teaspoon salt★
Black pepper
1 bouquet garni (page 183)
12 pearl onions
½ pound button mushrooms
FORCEMEAT BALLS:
2 cups soft breadcrumbs
¼ cup shredded beef suet
1 heaping tablespoon finely chopped parsley
Finely grated rind of half lemon
Salt★ and black pepper
1–2 eggs
GARNISH:
Chopped parsley

Dice the bacon; heat the butter in a deep, heavy-based pan. Fry the bacon in the butter over moderate heat until the fat runs and the bacon pieces are crisp. Remove the bacon from the pan with a slotted spoon and leave to drain on crumpled paper towels. Put the squab in the pan to brown them, turning several times. Lift out the squab carefully and put them in a casserole.

Pour away all but one tablespoon of the hot fat from the pan;

SQUAB WITH OLIVES

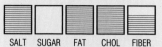

SALT　SUGAR　FAT　CHOL　FIBER

GLUTEN-FREE★　WHOLEFOOD★
TOTAL CALORIES: ABOUT 2280

Reduce the **salt** to low by omitting the bacon and the olives, and using bread made without salt. The olives could be replaced with large chunks of apple, very lightly poached (and the dish re-named).
For moderate **fat** and **cholesterol** brown the onions and squab in a heavy pan brushed with oil and serve on toast rather than fried bread. Although lower in fat than much red meat, squab contain about 13%, more than most game, so the overall fat content cannot be less than moderate. (Calories lost: up to 500.)
As a **gluten-free** alternative to the fried bread (and a way of compensating for the dryness of the squab), serve them on a bed of lightly cooked vegetables, such as braised celery, fennel or Chinese cabbage.

Pressure cooker: ☑ for the stock.

Freezing: ☑ up to 4 months (the casserole only, not the fried bread).

SQUAB WITH FORCEMEAT BALLS

SALT	SUGAR	FAT	CHOL	FIBER

GLUTEN-FREE*   WHOLEFOOD*
TOTAL CALORIES: ABOUT 3180

To reduce **salt** to low, omit the bacon and use breadcrumbs made without salt.

Limit **fat** and **cholesterol** to the moderate level naturally present in squab as follows: omit the bacon; brown the squab in a heavy pan brushed lightly with oil; do not add any extra fat before stirring in the flour. Make the forcemeat balls with 1 tablespoon butter or vegetable margarine instead of suet and use only one (small) egg to bind the mixture. (Calories lost: up to 1000.) Cornstarch or rice flour can be used for a **gluten-free** sauce, but the forcemeat balls are best made with crumbs from a gluten-free loaf.

Freezing: ☑ up to 4 months (the squabs and the forcemeat balls should be frozen separately).

Microwave: ☑

stir in the flour and cook gently for a few minutes until browned. Gradually blend in the hot stock and bring the sauce slowly to the boil. Simmer for a few minutes, then strain the sauce over the squab in the casserole. Add the bacon pieces, the salt, a few twists of pepper and the bouquet garni. Peel the onions and add them whole to the squab. Cover the casserole with a lid and cook in the center of a pre-heated oven for 1 hour at 350°F (180°C, mark 4).

Meanwhile, trim and finely slice the mushrooms. For the forcemeat balls, measure the breadcrumbs, shredded suet, chopped parsley and lemon rind into a mixing bowl; season with salt and freshly ground pepper. Beat the eggs lightly and stir them into the mixture with a fork until the forcemeat has a moist, but not too wet, consistency. Using the tips of the fingers, shape the forcemeat into 8–12 round balls and put these, together with the

mushrooms, in the casserole. Replace the lid and continue cooking for 15–20 minutes.

Lift the squab from the casserole, cut them in half and arrange them on a hot serving dish. Surround them with the mushrooms, onions and forcemeat balls. Remove the bouquet garni from the sauce before pouring it over the squab.

Garnish with chopped parsley and serve the squab with new potatoes.

Poultry and Game

PARTRIDGE WITH CABBAGE

Partridge with cabbage is a classic French farmhouse method of cooking older game birds. Gourmets maintain that the casserole should be cooked with older partridges, which are replaced with young, oven-roasted partridges just before serving.

PREPARATION TIME: *30 min*
COOKING TIME: *2 hours*
INGREDIENTS *(for 4)*:
2 plump partridges
4 slices bacon
2 tablespoons flour
2 tablespoons lard or bacon fat
4 pork link sausages
¼ pound salt pork
1 large onion
1 small head white cabbage
Salt★ and black pepper
½ cup red wine

Truss the partridges neatly, bard (page 168) the breasts with the bacon slices and secure with string. Peel and thinly slice the onion. Roll the birds in the flour and pat off the surplus.

Heat the lard or fat in a flameproof casserole or large pan and brown the birds and the sausages all over, then remove from the pan. Cut the salt pork into ½ in chunks, then put into the casserole together with the sliced onion; fry until both are just turning color. Pour off any remaining fat. Remove any coarse outer leaves from the cabbage, wash it and blanch for 5 minutes in boiling salted water. Cut into quarters, remove the tough center stalk and shred the cabbage coarsely.

Put half the shredded cabbage in the pan and mix with the pork and onion. Add a few twists of pepper–the pork is already salty–put in the partridges and cover with the remaining cabbage.

Pour over the wine, cover the casserole tightly and cook over low heat on top of the stove, or in the center of a pre-heated oven at 325°F (170°C, mark 3), for about 2 hours or until tender, depending on the age of the birds. If necessary add more wine or a little chicken stock.

To serve, lift out the partridge, remove the string and cut each bird in half. Arrange the partridge and sausages on the cabbage. Serve with baked potatoes.

POACHED PARTRIDGES IN VINE LEAVES

Vine leaves impart an unusual flavor to these succulent game birds. Order the partridges ready for cooking and have the giblets included with the order.

PREPARATION TIME: *25 min*
COOKING TIME: *1½ hours*
INGREDIENTS *(for 4)*:
2 young partridges
Salt★ and black pepper
6 lemon slices
4 teaspoons quince, red currant or cranberry jelly
16-ounce jar of vine leaves
¾ pound bacon slices
1¼ cups dry white wine
4 cups chicken stock
GARNISH:
Watercress, lemon wedges

Wipe the partridges inside and out and season with salt and black pepper. Put 3 lemon slices and half the quince jelly inside each bird. Wrap the drained vine leaves around the birds, cover with the bacon slices and tie firmly with fine string.

Bring the wine and stock to the boil in a large saucepan, together with the giblets. Add the partridges and simmer for 1¼ hours.

Chill the partridges quickly by immersing them in a bowl of iced water until quite cold. Remove from the water, unwrap the bacon and vine leaves; dry the partridges with paper towels.

Serve the partridges whole, on a bed of watercress, garnished with lemon wedges and Cumberland sauce. A lettuce and celery salad would be a good side dish.

CUMBERLAND SAUCE

PREPARATION TIME: *15 min*
COOKING TIME: *10 min*
STANDING TIME: *24 hours*
INGREDIENTS *(about 2½ cups)*
2 oranges
2 lemons
1 pound redcurrant jelly
1 cup port or red wine
2 heaping teaspoons arrowroot

Thinly peel one orange and one lemon. Remove pith and shred the peel finely. Boil the shreds for 3 minutes. Drain and cover with cold water for 1 minute; drain again and set aside. Squeeze and strain all the fruit juices into a pan, add the jelly and bring slowly to the boil. Simmer for 5 minutes, then add the port and bring the sauce back to the boil. Remove from the heat and stir in the arrowroot, mixed to a paste with a little cold water. Cook for 1 minute more. Add the blanched peel and leave the sauce in a cool place for 24 hours.

PARTRIDGE WITH CABBAGE

| SALT | SUGAR | FAT | CHOL | FIBER |

TOTAL CALORIES: ABOUT 2900

The high **salt** level of this dish comes from the bacon, sausages and pork; if the quantities of these are halved, or if the bacon and pork are omitted, the level will be reduced to moderate. Omitting the pork and bacon and all (or all but one) of the sausages will also reduce the **fat** and **cholesterol** content to low. (Calories lost: up to 1120.)
Apart from the flour (for which cornstarch, potato starch or rice flour all make good **gluten-free** substitutes), there is generally gluten in sausages (in the form of breadcrumbs), but local butchers can often make up gluten-free sausages on request.

Freezing: ☑ up to 2 months.
Microwave: ☑

POACHED PARTRIDGES IN VINE LEAVES WITH CUMBERLAND SAUCE

| SALT | SUGAR | FAT | CHOL | FIBER |

GLUTEN-FREE★   WHOLEFOOD★
TOTAL CALORIES: ABOUT 3690

To achieve a low **salt** level, use fresh vine leaves (or cabbage leaves), blanched in simmering water for 5 minutes, and omit the bacon.
The only way to reduce the **sugar** content of the sauce is to use fresh red currants or cranberries – about 4 cups – and simmer them gently with

the fruit juices and arrowroot before sweetening to taste. Add honey a little at a time, tasting as you go, to avoid over-sweetening. Liquidize if you like. (Calories lost: up to 100.) Without the bacon this dish also becomes low in both **fat** and **cholesterol**, especially if the chicken stock has been carefully skimmed of all fat. (Calories lost: up to 2000.)

GROUSE À LA GRAND-MÈRE

SALT	SUGAR	FAT	CHOL	FIBER

GLUTEN-FREE*   WHOLEFOOD*
TOTAL CALORIES: ABOUT 3280

The **salt** level can be reduced to very low by using bread made without salt, or by serving the grouse on a bed of plain rice, mashed potato or lightly cooked vegetables instead of bread. Replacing the bread also avoids the **fat** in fried bread. To reduce the fat further (to low), and the **cholesterol** also to low, brown the grouse and the onions in a heavy pan brushed lightly with oil, omitting the butter; add flour to the pan to make the sauce without adding any more fat. Replace the cream with low-fat small curd cottage cheese or thick plain yogurt into which you have stirred 1 teaspoon cornstarch before heating (this will prevent it separating and curdling when heated). (Total calories lost: up to 1250.)
The alternatives to bread given above are all **gluten-free**.

Freezing: ✓ up to 2 months (as a casserole, not on the bread slices).
Microwave: ✓ for cooking the casserole.

GROUSE À LA GRAND-MÈRE

Mature grouse which have escaped the guns for some years are not tender enough for plain roasting. They can, however, be made into a tasty casserole, flavored with herbs and brandy. Quail can be treated in the same way.

PREPARATION TIME: *30 min*
COOKING TIME: *1½ hours*
INGREDIENTS *(for 4):*
4 mature grouse
8–12 pearl onions
1 stalk celery
½ pound mushrooms
½ cup butter
1–1½ tablespoons flour
2½ cups stock
Fresh thyme, marjoram and
*   rosemary*
Salt★ and black pepper
3–4 tablespoons heavy cream
2 tablespoons brandy
Lemon juice
4 small slices crustless bread
GARNISH:
1 tablespoon chopped parsley

Peel the onions, leaving them whole. Scrub the celery, trim the mushrooms and chop both roughly. Melt half the butter in a flameproof casserole and, when hot, brown the neatly trussed grouse all over, together with the onions.
   Lift out the grouse and onions, and fry the celery and mushrooms in the butter until soft. Remove the pan from the heat, stir in sufficient flour to absorb all the fat, and return the pan to the heat. Cook this roux until brown, then gradually blend in the stock. Bring the mixture to simmering point and season to taste with the herbs, salt and some freshly ground pepper.
   Return the grouse and onions to the casserole, cover with a lid and cook over low heat on top of the stove for about 1½ hours or until the grouse are tender. Mix the cream and brandy together, blend in 2 or 3 tablespoons of the sauce from the grouse, and stir it back into the casserole. Sharpen to taste with lemon juice and adjust seasoning.
   In a clean pan, fry the bread in the remaining butter until crisp and golden. Drain the bread on crumpled paper towels, then arrange it on a hot serving dish. Place one grouse on each bread slice, pour over a little sauce and sprinkle with parsley. Pour the remaining sauce into a sauce boat. Serve the grouse with fluffy creamed potatoes and cauliflower or broccoli.

PHEASANT STEWED WITH APPLES

This is an excellent Normandy method of cooking older or slightly tough cock pheasants with apples. Frozen whole or cut up pheasants and guinea hen are also suitable.

PREPARATION TIME: *40 min*
COOKING TIME: *45 min*
INGREDIENTS *(for 4)*:
1 pheasant
1 bay leaf
1 sprig parsley
Salt* and black pepper
1 onion
2 stalks celery
2 tart apples
2–3 tablespoons flour
3 tablespoons butter
½ cup hard cider
2 tablespoons calvados (optional)
5 tablespoons heavy cream
GARNISH:
2 apples
Celery leaves

Cut up the pheasant by first removing the legs, then cut away the two breast sections down and along the backbone. Leave the flesh on the bone, so that it will not shrink during cooking, and cut off the lower part of the wings.

Put the pheasant carcass, the neck and the cleaned giblets into a pan, together with the bay leaf, parsley, and a seasoning of salt and freshly ground pepper. Cover the carcass with cold water, put the lid on the pan and simmer this stock over low heat for about 20 minutes.

Peel and thinly slice the onion. Cut the leafy tops off the celery and set aside for garnish. Scrub the celery stalks and chop them finely. Peel, core and roughly chop both the apples.

Coat the pheasant pieces lightly with a little flour, and heat the butter in a flameproof casserole or heavy-based pan. Fry the pheasant over high heat until golden brown all over, then remove from the casserole. Lower the heat and fry the onion and celery for 5 minutes. Add the apples and fry for a further 5 minutes. Draw the casserole from the heat and stir in sufficient of the remaining flour to absorb all the fat. Gradually blend in the cider (and calvados if used) and 1¼ cups of strained pheasant stock. Bring this sauce to simmering point over low heat.

Put the pheasant back into the casserole, and if necessary add more stock to the sauce until it almost covers the pieces.

Season to taste with salt and freshly ground pepper, and cover the casserole with a lid.

Cook the casserole in the center of a pre-heated oven, at 325°F (170°C, mark 3), for 45 minutes or until tender. Remove the pheasant and keep warm in the oven. Boil the sauce briskly on top of the stove, stir into the cream and pour this mixture back into the pan; adjust seasoning.

Return the pheasant pieces to the sauce and serve straight from the casserole. Alternatively, arrange the pieces on a warm deep serving dish and spoon the sauce over them. Surround with the cored, but unpeeled apples, cut into thick slices and fried in a little butter until golden. Push a small tuft of celery leaves through the center of each apple slice.

Boiled or mashed potatoes could also be served.

PHEASANT STEWED WITH APPLES

SALT	SUGAR	FAT	CHOL	FIBER

GLUTEN-FREE*   WHOLEFOOD*
TOTAL CALORIES: ABOUT 2025

Pheasant has a low to medium fat content of under 10%. To reduce both **fat** and **cholesterol** to this level, brown the bird in a casserole lightly brushed with oil, omitting the butter. To soften the vegetables, add them to the pan with 2 tablespoons stock and cover tightly. No extra fat will be needed. Replace the cream with 3 tablespoons low-fat small curd cottage cheese or thick plain yogurt; after blending in, do not let the dish boil again. Apple rings for the garnish can be cut from a baked apple instead of being fried. (Calories lost: up to 500.)

Pressure cooker: ☑ for the stock.

Freezing: ☑ up to 2 months.

Microwave: ☑ for cooking the casserole once it has been assembled.

PHEASANT WITH CABBAGE

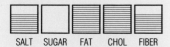

SALT   SUGAR   FAT   CHOL   FIBER

GLUTEN-FREE   WHOLEFOOD
TOTAL CALORIES: ABOUT 3690

The **salt** comes mainly from the bacon and bacon fat. To reduce the level to low, halve the amount of bacon used (or omit it); omit the bacon fat and brown the pheasant in a casserole lightly brushed with oil.
These measures will also reduce the **fat** and **cholesterol** levels. To reduce them further (to low-medium), replace the cream with cultured buttermilk, low-fat small curd cottage cheese or low-fat plain yogurt. In each case, blend in $1\frac{1}{2}$ teaspoons of cornstarch before heating, and heat over low heat for only just long enough to warm through. (Calories lost: up to 1750.)

PHEASANT WITH CABBAGE

This has long been a favorite of pheasant lovers and makes a satisfying meal on a cool autumn evening. However, if pheasant is unavailable or too expensive, the dish may be prepared with chicken.

PREPARATION TIME: *15 min*
COOKING TIME: *about 1 hour*
INGREDIENTS *(for 4)*:
2 young pheasants
Salt*
6 tablespoons bacon fat or butter
4 slices bacon
1 medium head green cabbage
1¼ cups heavy cream
12 juniper berries
Paprika
Pepper

Sprinkle the pheasants inside and out with salt and pepper. Brown the pheasants in hot bacon fat or butter on all sides in a large casserole. Top the breasts with bacon slices and secure the bacon with wooden cocktail picks or toothpicks. Reduce the heat, cover, and cook gently for 1 hour until almost tender. Remove the pheasants and set aside.

While the pheasants are cooking, shred the cabbage and parboil it in salted water for 10 minutes. Drain.

Put the cabbage in a casserole, cover, and cook slowly for 10 minutes. Season with salt and freshly ground pepper. Add the pheasants to the cabbage, pour the cream over them, and add the juniper berries. Simmer, covered, for 5 minutes. Before serving, sprinkle the birds and cabbage with a little paprika.

Serve on a heated dish with boiled new potatoes.

Poultry and Game

MUSTARD RABBIT

Wild rabbit traditionally went into this French farmhouse stew, perfect for a chilly late summer day when autumn seems near. Today, most rabbits available are bred for the table.

PREPARATION TIME: *15 min*
COOKING TIME: *1½–2 hours*
INGREDIENTS *(for 4–6):*
1 2½–3 pound rabbit or 6 rabbit
  pieces
⅓ cup Dijon-style mustard
Seasoned flour (page 184)
¼ cup unsalted butter
4 slices bacon
1 onion
1 clove garlic
1¼ cups heavy cream
GARNISH:
Chopped chervil or parsley
Bread croûtons (page 178)

Wash and dry the rabbit thoroughly. Cut it into six or eight neat pieces and put them in a large bowl. Cover with cold salted water and leave to soak for 1–2 hours. Then drain and dry thoroughly. Coat the rabbit pieces evenly with mustard and leave them in a cool place overnight, covered with cheesecloth.

The following day dust the rabbit lightly with seasoned flour, shaking off any surplus. Melt the butter in a flameproof casserole and lightly brown the pieces on both sides; lift them out and set aside. Roughly chop the bacon. Peel and finely chop the onion and garlic. Fry the bacon for 2–3 minutes in the butter, then add the onion and garlic and continue cooking over low heat until the onion is soft.

Return the rabbit pieces to the casserole, cover closely with a lid or foil and simmer over low heat for 30 minutes. Remove the casserole from the heat and stir in the cream. Cover again and cook over low heat on top of the stove, or in an oven pre-heated to 325°F

(170°C, mark 3) for about 45 minutes, or until the rabbit is tender. Stir once or twice.

Serve the rabbit straight from the casserole, sprinkled with the fresh herbs and garnished with bread croûtons. Buttered rice or boiled potatoes can be served with the rabbit, together with a green vegetable.

RABBIT WITH PRUNES

Rabbit, which can be bought frozen in supermarkets the year round, makes a pleasant change from chicken. The delicate flesh is enhanced by a well-flavored marinade and the fruity contrast of the prunes.

PREPARATION TIME: *45 min*
MARINATING TIME: *1 hour*
COOKING TIME: *1½ hours*
INGREDIENTS *(for 4–6):*
2 rabbits, cut up
1 large onion
4 peppercorns, crushed
4 bay leaves
½ cup wine vinegar
Seasoned flour (page 184)
¼ cup unsalted butter
2 onions
2½ cups light beer
Juice of 1 lemon
1 sprig thyme
1 teaspoon Dijon-style mustard
1 tablespoon tarragon vinegar
2–3 tablespoons sugar
Salt and black pepper*
8 ready-to-eat pitted prunes
2 teaspoons cornstarch

Peel and slice the large onion and add it, with the crushed peppercorns and 2 of the bay leaves, to the rabbit. Mix the wine vinegar with 2½ cups of water and pour over the rabbit, covering the pieces completely. Leave the

MUSTARD RABBIT

SALT	SUGAR	FAT	CHOL	FIBER

GLUTEN-FREE*   WHOLEFOOD*
TOTAL CALORIES: ABOUT 4230

The **salt** content will be low if the bacon is omitted. This will also reduce the **fat** level; to limit both this and **cholesterol** to low, you should also brown the rabbit in a heavy pan lightly brushed with oil, omit the bacon, and replace the cream with the same amount of low-fat small curd cottage cheese or thick low-fat plain yogurt, into which you have thoroughly blended 1½ teaspoons cornstarch to help it keep stable when heated. With this method the cooking of the rabbit should be completed first, as once your chosen cream substitute is added the mixture should only be reheated gently for a few minutes, not brought back to the boil or cooked. (Calories lost: up to 1200.)

Freezing: ✓ up to 2 months.

RABBIT WITH PRUNES

SALT	SUGAR	FAT	CHOL	FIBER

GLUTEN-FREE*   WHOLEFOOD*
TOTAL CALORIES: ABOUT 3300

The **sugar** content can be reduced to medium simply by adding less: the recipe as it stands is very sweet, and ½ tablespoon would suit many people's palates, since sweet prunes and beer are also included.
Rabbit is one of the leanest meats with around 4% fat, despite its rich flavor. If it is

browned in a heavy pan lightly brushed with oil, omitting the butter, this dish will be very low in both **fat** and **cholesterol**. (Calories lost: up to 570.)

Pressure cooker: ☑ for the rabbit (not the prunes; they must be cooked separately).

Freezing: ☑ up to 2 months.

Microwave: ☑

CIVET DE LIÈVRE

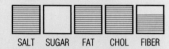

SALT	SUGAR	FAT	CHOL	FIBER

GLUTEN-FREE* WHOLEFOOD*
TOTAL CALORIES: ABOUT 3780

The high **salt** level comes mainly from the bacon. Omitting this brings the level down to low, and also helps reduce the fat content.
To reduce the **fat** further, to the low 8% naturally present in hare plus a very little oil (and also reduce the **cholesterol** to low), brown the meat in a heavy pan lightly brushed with oil. Do the same with the mushrooms, and omit the butter and the 3 tablespoons of the oil from the marinade. Do not use beurre manié to thicken the sauce. (Calories lost: up to 1180.)

Pressure cooker: ☑
Freezing: ☑ up to 2 months.
Microwave: ☑

bowl in a cool place to marinate for about 1 hour, turning the meat occasionally.

Lift the rabbit from the marinade and dry the pieces thoroughly; coat them with seasoned flour. Melt the butter in a large frying pan, add the rabbit, and cook until evenly brown all over. Put the pieces of rabbit in a large flameproof casserole. Strain the marinade and pour ½ cup of it over the meat. Peel and finely chop the onions and add to the rabbit, together with the beer, the lemon juice, the other 2 bay leaves, thyme, mustard, vinegar, and sugar. Season to taste with salt and freshly ground pepper. Bring the mixture to a boil; cover the pan with a lid and leave to simmer gently for 1½ hours, or until rabbit is tender. About 20 minutes before the end of cooking time add the soaked prunes.

When the rabbit is cooked, blend the cornstarch with a little water to a smooth paste. Add some of the hot liquid from the pan and blend thoroughly before stirring it into the liquid. Bring the mixture back to the boil, stirring gently until the sauce has thickened.

Remove the pan from the heat and transfer the pieces of rabbit and the prunes to a hot serving dish. Correct seasoning, if necessary, and pour the sauce over the rabbit. Serve with creamed potatoes and a green vegetable.

CIVET DE LIÈVRE

Literally, hare stew, this is a classic recipe from French farmhouse cooking, reminiscent of traditional English jugged hare.

The ingredients can be either a whole cut up hare or the legs and rib pieces after the saddle has been roasted whole.

PREPARATION TIME: *45 min*
COOKING TIME: *about 3 hours*
INGREDIENTS *(for 6):*

2½–3 pounds hare pieces	1 bottle red wine
2–3 carrots	¼ cup butter
2 onions	2 liqueur glasses brandy
1 clove garlic	2 tablespoons flour
1 shallot	1 cup chicken stock
3 bay leaves	¼ pound bacon
3 sprigs thyme	¼ pound button mushrooms
6 parsley stalks	1 pound pearl onions
Black pepper	GARNISH:
3 tablespoons olive oil	Freshly chopped parsley

Wipe the hare pieces and put them in a large basin. Peel and finely slice the carrots and the onions. Skin and finely chop the garlic and shallot. Add these vegetables, with the bay leaves, thyme, the parsley stalks and freshly ground pepper, to the hare. Pour over the oil and wine and marinate for 24 hours.

Remove the meat from the marinade and pat it dry on paper towels. Melt the butter in a large saucepan and fry the meat gently for about 15 minutes, until browned on all sides. Pour the brandy over the meat and, when hot, set it alight. As soon as the flames have died down, sprinkle in the flour, stirring to blend it well with the butter. Add the marinade ingredients and sufficient stock just to cover the meat. Bring to the boil, cover and simmer for 2–3 hours.

Cut the bacon into strips 1 in long. Place in a saucepan, cover with cold water and bring to the boil. Simmer for 1 minute, then drain. Put the bacon strips in a dry frying pan and sauté gently until the fat runs. Wipe and trim the mushrooms, cut each in half and add to the pan. Sauté gently for a few minutes before seasoning, then remove from the pan and set aside. Peel the onions, leaving them whole; put them in a saucepan and cover with cold water. Bring to the boil and simmer gently for 10–15 minutes. Drain and set aside. Lift the hare pieces from the pan and keep them hot. Strain off the liquid and return it to the saucepan. Add more salt and pepper if necessary; if the sauce appears too thin, thicken with a little beurre manié (pages 155–6). Put the hare into the pan, with the bacon, mushrooms and onions. Re-heat gently.

Arrange on a hot serving dish, pour over the sauce and sprinkle with parsley. Croquette potatoes and braised celery could also be served.

GAME SOUP WITH PORT WINE

This is a rich, sustaining soup for cold autumn days. It can be made from neck of venison or from any game bird, such as pheasant, partridge or grouse, that is too tough for roasting or broiling.

PREPARATION TIME: *55 min*
COOKING TIME: *2½–3 hours*
INGREDIENTS *(for 6):*
1 pound boneless venison or a 2-pound game bird
1 large onion
1 parsnip or turnip
1 carrot
1 leek
3 stalks celery
½ pound mushrooms
½ cup butter
1 bay leaf
Thyme, marjoram and basil
Salt* and black pepper
1–2 cloves garlic
¼ cup flour
½ cup port or red wine
GARNISH:
Bread croûtons (page 178)

Cut the venison into 2–3 in chunks, trimming off any gristle. If a game bird is being used, chop it, through the bone, into small portions; clean thoroughly. Peel and roughly chop the onion, parsnip and carrot. Wash all dirt off the leek and celery under cold running water and chop them roughly as well. Trim and thinly slice the mushrooms.

Melt half the butter in a large pan over moderate heat and fry the meat, turning it frequently, until it begins to color. Add the onion, leek and celery to the pan and brown it evenly. Put the parsnip, carrot and bay leaf, together with a pinch of thyme,

marjoram and basil into the pan. Season with salt, freshly ground pepper and the crushed garlic. Pour in about 7–8 cups of water, or enough to cover the contents in the pan; bring to the boil over high heat.

Remove any scum which rises on the surface, then add the mushrooms. Cover the pan with a lid and simmer over low heat for about 2 hours or until the meat is perfectly tender.

Strain the stock through a fine sieve and leave to cool slightly. Remove the bay leaf and all bones, then put the meat and vegetables in the liquidizer with a little of the soup, to make a thick purée.

Melt the remaining butter in a large, clean pan over moderate heat; blend in the flour and cook, stirring continuously, until this roux is caramel colored. Take the pan off the heat and gradually blend in the port and about 1¼ cups of stock. Return the pan to the heat, bring to simmering point, stirring all the time, then blend in the meat and vegetable purée and about 4 cups of stock to make a thick soup. Heat the soup through over low heat for about 15 minutes and correct seasoning if necessary.

Serve the soup in individual bowls, garnished with small bread croûtons.

SADDLE OF VENISON

For a special dinner occasion, venison in port is an excellent choice. The saddle should have been hung for at least three weeks to ensure a truly succulent roast. A saddle will serve eight people handsomely, and the recipe is also suitable for a smaller roast.

PREPARATION TIME: *25 min*
COOKING TIME: *2¾ hours*
INGREDIENTS *(for 8–10):*
1 saddle of venison, 6–7 pounds
2 carrots
1 Spanish onion
2 stalks celery
Salt* and black pepper
½ cup unsalted butter
½ cup olive oil
2 cloves garlic
2 bay leaves
1 sprig fresh or ½ teaspoon dried thyme
1¼ cups chicken stock
½ bottle port
1 heaping tablespoon flour
4 tablespoons unsalted butter
1 heaping tablespoon red currant jelly

Peel and chop the carrots, onion and celery. Trim any gristle from the venison, wipe well with a cloth and season with salt and pepper. Melt the butter and combine with the olive oil in a large roasting or sauté pan; quickly brown the venison, then remove. Reduce the heat. Peel and crush the garlic, and add to the pan together with the bay leaves, thyme and chopped vegetables; cook for 5 minutes without coloring. Return the venison to the pan and cover with foil, making sure it is tightly sealed. Cook for 45 minutes on the bottom shelf of an oven pre-heated to 375°F (190°C,

GAME SOUP WITH PORT WINE

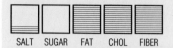

GLUTEN-FREE* WHOLEFOOD*
TOTAL CALORIES: ABOUT 2230

The high level of fat comes almost entirely from the butter, since venison is very lean at around 6.4% fat. To reduce both **fat** and **cholesterol** to low, brown the meat and soften the vegetables in 1 tablespoon of oil in a large casserole, adding a little stock if the mixture shows signs of sticking, and keeping it tightly covered over very low heat. (Calories lost: up to 770.) As **gluten-free** alternatives to flour and bread, thicken the soup by a technique that adds no fat instead of by the roux method: to do this, either add ½ cup split red lentils to the mixture and simmer for 25 minutes before liquidizing to a smooth texture, or increase the amount of vegetables used so that, when puréed, they produce a thick soup. Instead of croûtons, sprinkle with a little finely chopped carrot and parsley; or cut some firm tofu into dice and heat this up gently in the soup just before serving.

Pressure cooker: ✓
Freezing: ✓ up to 3 months.
Microwave: ✓

SADDLE OF VENISON

SALT   SUGAR   FAT   CHOL   FIBER

GLUTEN-FREE*   WHOLEFOOD*
TOTAL CALORIES: ABOUT 8975

Although there is a certain amount of **sugar** in the port and red currant jelly, it should not cause too much worry among 8–10 people. If you do want to cut it down (perhaps because you are having something sweet to follow) you could replace the port with a sound red wine and use a purée of dried apricots instead of the jelly.

Venison itself is very lean and to avoid dryness in cooking it must be kept moist. This can be done however without adding the amount of butter and oil given, and the **fat** and **cholesterol** reduced to low. To achieve this, brown the meat in a heavy pan lightly brushed with oil and keep it moist by sealing it in with stock, as in the recipe. If wished, a cup of the port can be added at this stage, as it helps to tenderize the meat, thus shortening the cooking time and so reducing the risk of dryness.

To thicken the sauce without using the flour and butter paste, add some fresh red currants (or cranberries), say 1 cup, and when they burst after simmering, liquidize the mixture in a blender with 1 tablespoon arrowroot which has been blended with water to a smooth paste. Re-boil the mixture for 2–3 minutes and allow to cool slightly before serving. (Calories lost: up to 2000.) Instead of serving with fried mushrooms, simmer them in 2–3 tablespoons of stock for 5 minutes. Small boiled potatoes make a **gluten-free** alternative to croûtons.

mark 5), then pour in the boiling stock, re-seal and cook for 1 hour.

Remove the pan to the top of the stove; pour the port over the venison and heat until the juices are simmering, then return to the oven. Do not re-seal, but cook for another hour, basting every 15 minutes. If the roast appears to be cooking too quickly, turn the heat down slightly for the last 30 minutes. Transfer the venison to a dish and keep it hot in the oven while making the sauce.

Strain the liquid from the roasting pan into a saucepan and keep at a fast boil until reduced by half. Meanwhile, combine the flour and butter to make a paste and use bits of this to thicken the reduced sauce, stirring continuously. Finally mix in the red currant jelly, and as soon as this has dissolved, season the sauce with salt and pepper if necessary.

Carve the roast and arrange the slices on a serving dish. Pour some of the sauce over the meat and decorate it with glazed onions, mushroom caps fried in butter, and bread croûtons (page 178).

Serve the remainder of the sauce in a separate bowl.

White Fish

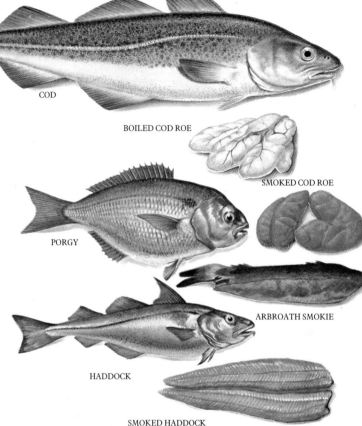

COD

BOILED COD ROE

SMOKED COD ROE

PORGY

ARBROATH SMOKIE

HADDOCK

SMOKED HADDOCK

When buying fish make sure that they have a fresh, clean smell. Take a careful look at the eyes; they should be bright and bulging. If they have a sunken or cloudy look, the fish is not fresh. The gills should be bright red and free from slime. As the fish becomes stale, the color of the gills gradually fades to light pink, then gray, then to a greenish or brownish color. The skin of fresh fish has a shiny, iridescent look, and the scales will adhere firmly to the flesh. The flesh is elastic and springs back to its original shape when pressed.

To judge the freshness of steaks and fillets, look for a fresh-cut appearance–firm-textured flesh with no traces of browning around the edges or signs of drying out. The fish will have a fresh, mild smell. Wrapped steaks and fillets are packaged in moistureproof material, with little or no air between the fish and the wrapping. Frozen fish should be frozen solid, with no brownish tinge or other discoloration.

It is an advantage to have a neighborhood fish dealer. Even though supermarkets sell fish–usually a limited selection–a merchant whose business is fish will know much more and will help the customer to understand how to buy and cook fish.

Small white fish, whether flat or round, are sold whole or filleted. Large fish, such as bass, halibut, haddock, hake and cod, may be purchased whole or as fillets, cutlets and steaks. These basic cuts of fish are shown below. The fillet from a large round fish, such as cod (top), is longer and thicker than a fillet from a flat fish such as flounder and sole (below). The steak, also cut from a round fish, is taken from between the middle part of the body and the tail. The cutlet comes from between the head and the middle part of the body.

THE FOUR BASIC CUTS OF FISH

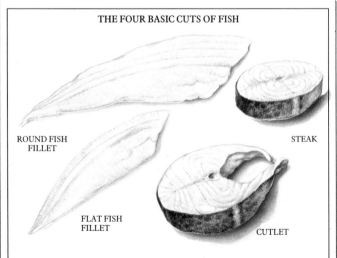

ROUND FISH
FILLET

STEAK

FLAT FISH
FILLET

CUTLET

Bass There are several varieties of this popular fish. The delicate flesh should be uniformly creamy-pink and sweet-smelling. Sold whole, or as steaks or fillets. Bake, broil, poach or fry.

Cod Large round fish which weighs up to 80 pounds. It has an olive-brown back with yellow and brown spots, small soft gray scales which should look bright, and white underside. The firm white flesh is sold whole, as fillets (fresh, salted or smoked) or steaks, often sold frozen. Avoid any fish with pink or gray discoloration. Can be poached, baked or broiled. Scrod, young cod, weighs 1½–2½ pounds.

Cod roe The pinkish hard female roe and the soft male roe are sold boiled or uncooked. The hard roe is also smoked.

Flounder Flat fish, creamy-white on the underside, dark gray black on the upper side. Included in the flounder family are gray sole, lemon sole, fluke (summer flounder), winter flounder, yellowtail and dab. Sold whole or as fillets. Broil, poach, bake or fry.

Haddock A round fish of the cod family, with gray skin. A dark line runs along both flanks and there is a dark smudge behind the gills. The white flesh, which should be very firm, is sold whole or as

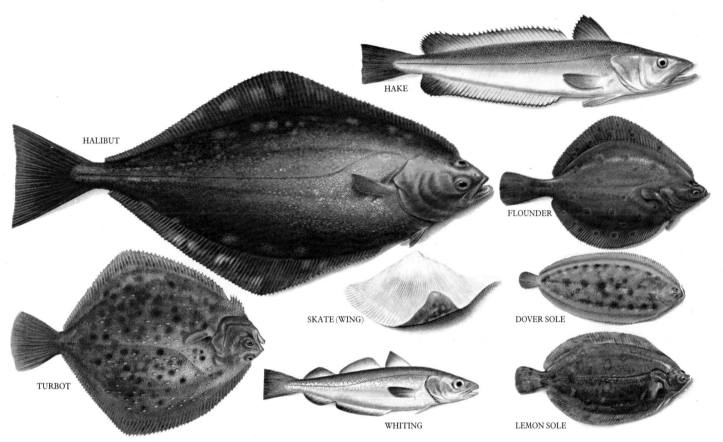

HAKE

HALIBUT

FLOUNDER

SKATE (WING)

DOVER SOLE

TURBOT

WHITING

LEMON SOLE

steaks and fillets. Suitable for poaching, baking, broiling and frying. Available all year round. **Smoked haddock** is smoked until pale yellow. Very yellow smoked haddock has probably been artificially colored. It loses flavor quickly. **Arbroath smokies** are small whole haddock hot smoked to a brown color.

Hake A round, long and slender fish with scaly silver-gray skin and tender, white, flaky flesh. Practically boneless. Sold whole or as fillets. Poach or bake.

Halibut This flat fish usually weighs from 5–75 pounds, or up to 600 pounds. It has dark olive skin, marbled with lighter olive. The white dry flesh should be quite firm. Chicken halibut is smaller, 1–9 pounds in weight. Halibut is available fresh, frozen, smoked or in cans. It is sold whole or as steaks or fillets.

Porgy (scup or sea bream) This fish from the Atlantic coast averages 12 inches in length and weighs $\frac{1}{2}$–$1\frac{1}{2}$ pounds. It is usually sold fresh and whole. Bake, poach, broil or fry.

Skate This flat, ray-shaped fish has slightly moist and slimy skin, with pink flesh. Only the wings, with prominent bones, are sold. Poach, broil or fry.

Sole The true sole is not found in American waters; but it is imported from England, the Netherlands, Belgium and Denmark and commands a high price. The best is the Channel (English or Dover) sole. The elongated to oval body is almost completely surrounded by fins and is covered with tiny hard scales, firmly attached to the skin. The color is usually olive-brown with irregular black markings on the upper side. The underside is white. The flesh is finely textured and delicate in flavor. Fresh sole is covered with slime and the skin is difficult to peel off. Sold whole or in fillets, for poaching, broiling and frying. Most so-called sole

available in the markets is a variety of flounder.

Turbot A flat fish of the flounder family, with black skin and raised growths on its back. Creamy-white on the underside with firm white flesh. Similar to halibut but less dry and more delicately flavored. Suitable for poaching, baking and broiling.

Whiting (silver hake) A round fish belonging to the cod family. Gray-olive-green on the back, with pale yellow shading to silvery on the underside. When fresh the soft flesh is flaky, but deteriorates rapidly. Poach, bake or fry.

Oily Fish

Oily fish are so called because the oil content is found throughout the flesh, while in white fish the oil is present only in the liver. Oily fish come from the sea and some are also caught in freshwater lakes, rivers and streams or produced in fish farms.

When buying oily fish, look for fresh fish with firm, even-textured flesh, clear, full and shiny eyes, bright red gills and a clean, fresh smell.

The herring is the most common oily fish; it is delicious when cooked fresh, but is perhaps more popular salted and smoked. It is probable that more people eat kippers – the most famous smoked variety – than fresh herring, or any other kind of fish.

Generally speaking, there are two methods of smoking fish: hot-smoking in which the temperature in the smoking kiln is raised sufficiently to cook the fish which then requires no cooking prior to eating; and cold-smoking in which the finished product is normally cooked in the kitchen before consumption. Hot-smoked fish must be eaten soon after curing; cold-smoked fish will keep longer if lightly wrapped in plastic film and stored in the refrigerator.

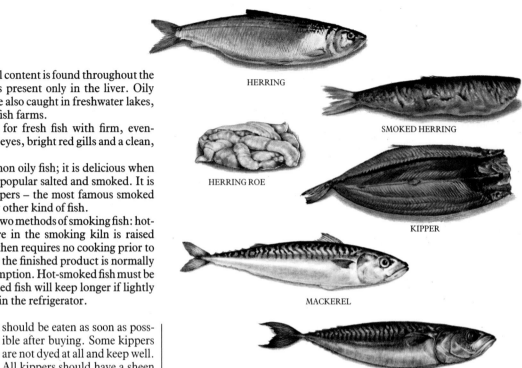

HERRING

SMOKED HERRING

HERRING ROE

KIPPER

MACKEREL

SMOKED MACKEREL

Eel, common A richly flavored freshwater fish up to 3 feet in length. It has shiny gray-black skin and firm, white flesh. It is always sold alive and should be cooked as soon as possible after killing. The fish man will kill and skin an eel whole. Steam, braise or deep fry.

Herring A small, delicately flavored and bony saltwater fish, usually weighing about 5 ounces to 1 pound. It has silvery-blue scales on the back, silvery flanks and underside, and firm brownish flesh. Sold whole; suitable for frying and broiling.
Lake herring (cisco) A freshwater fish, not a true herring.
Herring roes Both hard and soft roes are in short supply.
Kipper The most common smoked herring. It is split and put in brine before being smoked. Some kippers look dark because artificial coloring is added. These

should be eaten as soon as possible after buying. Some kippers are not dyed at all and keep well. All kippers should have a sheen and the flesh should be soft to the touch. Kippers are sold whole, usually in pairs or as fillets.

Mackerel A long, slender, saltwater fish with striped blue and green back, silvery underside and firm flesh. It deteriorates quickly and must be used on the day of purchase. Sold whole, for broiling, frying and baking. On fresh mackerel, the skin should be shiny and the flesh quite stiff.
Smoked mackerel Hot-smoked and ready for eating.

Salmon The king of fish is caught in cool, fast-running rivers. It is a saltwater fish which travels up rivers to spawn. A fresh salmon has bright silvery scales, red gills and pink-red, close-textured flesh. Sold fresh or frozen whole,

weighing 5 to 30 pounds, or as steaks or fillets. Avoid fish with watery, gray-looking flesh. Also available in cans or salted.
Smoked salmon Scotch smoked salmon is considered the finest. Smoked Canadian, Norwegian and Pacific salmon is less expensive but drier.

Sardine, Pacific (or pilchard) A small and immature member of the herring family. It is usually sold canned, in oil or with tomatoes, although fresh sardines are available in some areas.

Shad A member of the herring family, this fish lives in saltwater as well as fresh. It is extremely

bony, with delicately-flavored, light, creamy flesh. The roe is a delicacy. Bake or fry.

Smelt Tiny fresh or saltwater fish which, like salmon, spawns and is caught in rivers or along the Atlantic and Pacific coasts. It has bright silvery scales and pure white flesh when quite fresh. It has a strong aroma which has been compared to that of violets and cucumbers, and a delicate flavor. Clean by pressing the entrails out through a cut just below the gills, and serve smelt shallow or deep-fried.

Sprat Small, silvery-skinned saltwater fish of the herring

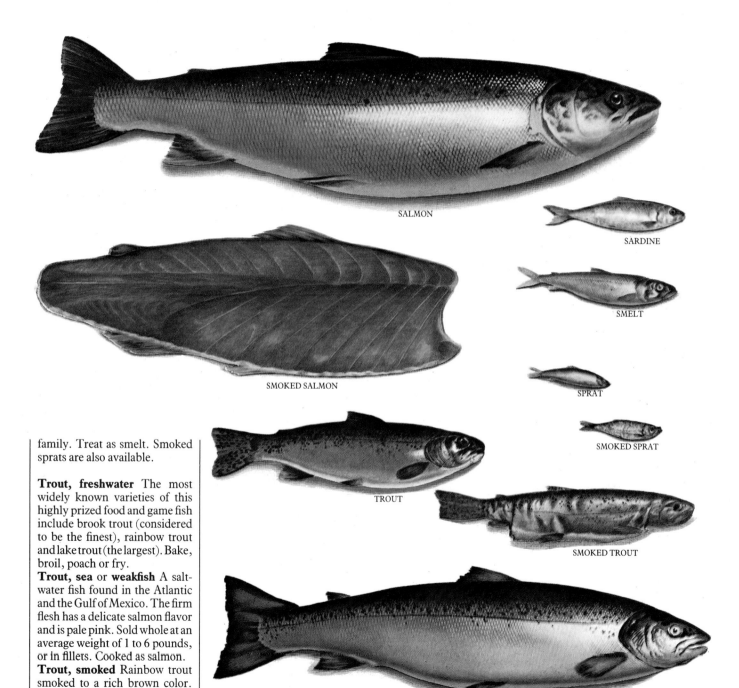

SALMON

SARDINE

SMELT

SMOKED SALMON

SPRAT

SMOKED SPRAT

TROUT

SMOKED TROUT

SEA TROUT

family. Treat as smelt. Smoked sprats are also available.

Trout, freshwater The most widely known varieties of this highly prized food and game fish include brook trout (considered to be the finest), rainbow trout and lake trout (the largest). Bake, broil, poach or fry.

Trout, sea or **weakfish** A saltwater fish found in the Atlantic and the Gulf of Mexico. The firm flesh has a delicate salmon flavor and is pale pink. Sold whole at an average weight of 1 to 6 pounds, or in fillets. Cooked as salmon.

Trout, smoked Rainbow trout smoked to a rich brown color. Requires no cooking.

Shellfish

Shellfish are divided into two groups: crustaceans, such as crabs, lobsters and shrimp, which have jointed shells; and mollusks, such as mussels, oysters and scallops. Shellfish are usually expensive, but they are very nutritious and low in calories. When sold already shelled, they are even more expensive, but there is no waste.

Clams Soft-shell clams abound in the waters off Cape Cod and northern New England. The smaller sizes are called steamers, the larger ones are called in-shells. Steam, deep-fry, or use in chowders.

Hard-shell clams, sometimes called quahogs, are found on the East Coast south of Cape Cod and also from Florida to Texas. The small clams are known as littlenecks, and the medium ones as cherrystones. Broil, bake, or eat raw. The larger hard-shell clams are usually made into chowders.

The numerous varieties of clams on the West Coast include the hard-shell butter, littleneck (different from the Atlantic Coast variety), mud, Pismo, the giant goeduck clam, and the popular soft-shell razor clam.

Clams are available fresh, frozen, and canned.

Crabs The blue, or common, hard-shell crabs are found in the North and South Atlantic and Gulf of Mexico. They weigh approximately 5 ounces. Available live in the shell, cooked in the shell, cooked and frozen, fresh-cooked meat, and canned meat. Bake, steam, or boil.

Soft-shell crabs are blue crabs that have shed their old shells; they are not a distinct species. They are caught by fishermen before new, hard shells have

formed. Available live or frozen. Deep-fry or sauté. Season: May through September.

The Dungeness crabs from the Pacific Coast and Alaska are larger than the blue crabs, weighing from $1\frac{3}{4}$ to $3\frac{1}{2}$ pounds. They are usually available live in the shell, frozen, cooked, and canned. These crabs are cooked in the same way as blue crabs. Season: all year.

Alaskan King crabs are the largest edible variety, weighing 6–20 pounds. Available as frozen cooked meat, frozen cooked in the shell, or canned. Broil. Season: all year.

Lobster, Northern or Maine Crustacean, dark blue when alive and scarlet when boiled. The male lobster is brighter in color, smaller than the female, but with larger claws. Best at a weight of 1–2 pounds. The female has a broader tail and more tender flesh. The female also contains the coral, or eggs, used for lobster butter. Sold live or cooked. When buying, choose a medium-sized one which feels heavy for its size. The tail should spring back when straightened out. Avoid lobsters with white shells on their backs as this is a sign of age.

Lobster, Rock or Spiny These lobsters, from the Caribbean, Mediterranean, New Zealand and South Africa, have smaller

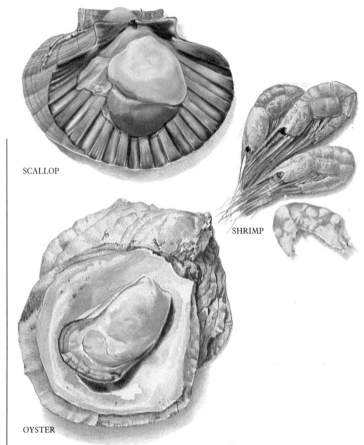

SCALLOP

SHRIMP

OYSTER

claws than the American lobster. Available as frozen tails and canned meat.

Mussels These mollusks with blue-black shells and orange-pink flesh are boiled and served in a sauce. Before cooking, discard any with broken shells and any which do not close when tapped. Mussels are sold by the pint; allow $1\frac{1}{2}$ pints per person.

Oysters These highly priced mollusks are usually eaten raw, but may also be cooked. Shells should be closed, or else they should shut when tapped. Oysters must be absolutely fresh and should be opened just before serving. Allow six per person.

Scallops Sea scallops come from the deep waters of the North Atlantic; the smaller bay scallops are found in shallower waters from the Bay of Fundy to the Gulf of Mexico. Bay scallops are tenderer, more delicately flavored, and command a higher price. Sea scallops are more readily available and can be bought

DUNGENESS CRAB

MUSSELS

LOBSTER

fresh, frozen, and frozen breaded precooked. Broil, deep-fry, or sauté. Season: all year.

Shrimp These small ten-legged crustaceans are found in the Gulf of Mexico and the South Atlantic and Pacific oceans. Their colors are gray, pale pink, and brown, depending on the variety. It will take 40–50 very small shrimp to make a pound, but only 10–15 large ones. Available fresh, frozen in the shell, frozen shelled, and canned. Broil, boil, sauté, or deep-fry. Season: all year.

DUBLIN BAY PRAWN
(LANGOUSTINE)

BAY SHRIMP

Poultry

Poultry, or domestic birds bred specially for the table, includes chicken, turkey, duck, and goose. In the United States, dressed birds that have been inspected and graded by the U.S. Department of Agriculture (including all poultry sold across state lines) often carry the official grade mark, although such labeling is not compulsory. Grade A birds are fully fleshed and meaty; Grade B and C birds are less meaty and less attractive in appearance. Grades B and C are seldom printed on poultry labels in the U.S. In Canada all poultry sold must be inspected and graded by Agriculture Canada and must carry A, B, Utility, C, or Canner grade marks.

Grades do not indicate tenderness: the age of the bird determines this. Young birds are tenderer than old ones, and are best for barbecuing, frying, sautéing, broiling, or roasting. Older birds are more suitable for soups, stews, and other slow-cooked dishes. When buying fresh poultry, check for age by touching the breastbone. In young poultry the tip of the breastbone is soft and flexible; as the bird ages, the breastbone becomes harder and more rigid.

Poultry is also sold frozen or deep-chilled, although these birds may be slightly inferior to fresh poultry in flavor and texture. Frozen birds are quick-frozen at the processing plant and are rock-hard to the touch. Deep-chilled birds are rapidly cooled at the processing plants but not frozen; the flesh can be depressed with the fingers.

Chicken Available throughout the year, fresh or frozen, and usually sold oven-ready – that is plucked, drawn and trussed. A fresh chicken should have a plump, white breast, smooth and pliable legs and a pliable beak and breastbone. Chickens are usually sold under different names, according to their age and weight, and can be cooked in numerous ways. Whole chickens may be roasted, spit-roasted, pot-roasted and braised. They can be boiled or cooked in a casserole. They can be boned and made into galantines; and cut up they are broiled, fried or stewed.

Broiler-fryers About 9 weeks old, weighing 1½–3½ pounds. Cut up, they are excellent for frying, sautéing, and baking; whole they can be roasted or barbecued.

Roasters The most popular size for a family. They are about 12 weeks old and weigh 3½–5 pounds, enough for 4–6 people. Whole or cut up, they are ideal for roasting, barbecuing or frying.

Stewing chicken An older bird, usually a hen after the laying season and about eight months old, weighing 2½–5 pounds. A meatier mature chicken is the **Bro-Hen**, which weighs 4½–6 pounds. These birds are meaty but also fatty, and are suitable for stews or casseroles.

Capon A young, desexed male chicken, specially bred to give a high proportion of white, flavorful flesh. Capons, weighing 4–8 pounds, are larger than most chickens. They are exceptionally tender and are most often roasted.

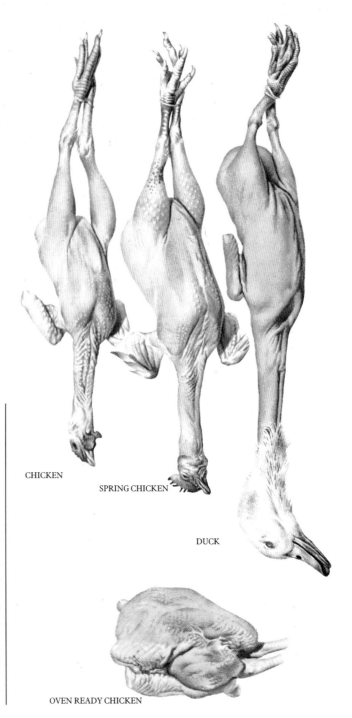

CHICKEN

SPRING CHICKEN

DUCK

OVEN READY CHICKEN

78

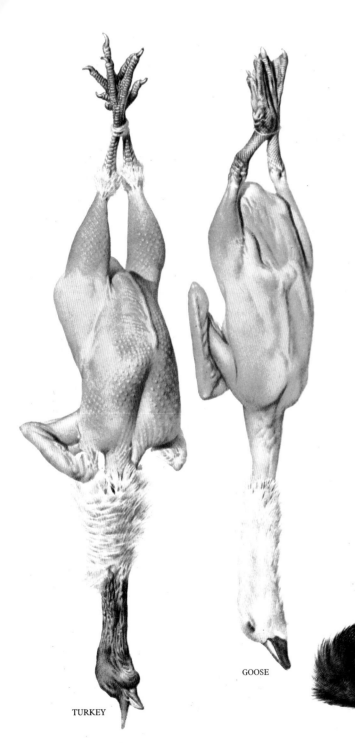

Rock Cornish Game Hen This smallest member of the chicken family, produced by crossing Cornish and White Rock chickens, usually weighs 1½ pounds or less. It is tender and has a meaty, plump breast. Suitable for roasting, baking, broiling, or sautéing. Allow a whole bird for each serving.

Frozen chickens These are drawn and trussed, ready for roasting, and are sold whole or cut up. They must be completely thawed in the wrapping before being cooked. Never put a frozen chicken in hot water to thaw – the only effect this has is to toughen the flesh. A bird can be thawed quickly under cold, slow-running water. The giblets are usually wrapped separately and put inside the chicken.

Duck Most duck is sold frozen, and ready to cook when thawed. It usually weighs 3½–5½ pounds, but a duck does not serve as many as a chicken of similar weight. A 5½ pound duck is only enough for four people. Duck is a fatty bird that is best roasted, although it may also be broiled or barbecued. Available whole or cut up.

Duckling A young duck 7–8 weeks old. It is usually roasted and will serve only two persons.

Goose This is considered by many gourmets the best of all poultry and is becoming increasingly popular. It is a fatty bird with creamy-white flesh which cooks to a light brown, and has a slightly gamey flavor. Average weight is 6–12 pounds, but again it serves less per pound than chicken. Allow 1–1½ pounds per person. Usually sold frozen or deep-chilled, but fresh goose is sometimes available during the Christmas season.

Guinea hen Originally a game bird, but now bred for the table, guinea hen should be hung for several days. It has gray plumage, tinged with purple and spotted with white. The flesh is firm and creamy-white with a flavor slightly reminiscent of pheasant. Suitable for roasting, braising and casseroles. Available all the year round.

Turkey The weight of a turkey ranges from about 4 pounds to 25 pounds, the average weight being 10–14 pounds. Allow 10–12 ounces per serving. Young birds, labeled as Young Hen, Young Tom or Fryer-Roasters, are the best buy at seven to nine months old. Older turkeys, for use in stews, soups and salads, are labeled Yearling or Old Turkey.

GUINEA HEN

GOOSE

TURKEY

Game

The term game is applied to wild animals and birds which are hunted and eaten. For roasting and grilling, all game should be young – a condition that is easiest recognised on unplucked game. The beak and feet should be pliable, the plumage or fur soft, and the breast plump.

If not bought already prepared for cooking, game must be hung in order to tenderize the flesh and develop the gamey flavor. Hanging time depends on the weather – game matures more quickly in warm humid weather – and on individual taste. Game birds are hung, unplucked and undrawn, by their beaks in a cool airy place and are ready for cooking when the tail feathers can be pulled out easily. Furred game is hung by the feet for one or two weeks.

Although many types of game are commercially frozen and therefore available throughout the year, the flavor is at its best in freshly killed and well-hung game.

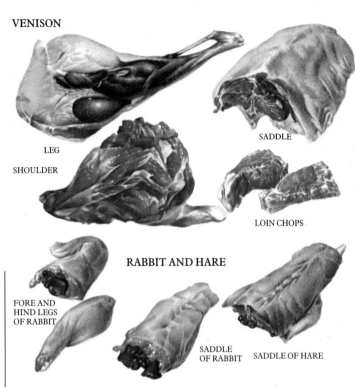

VENISON

LEG

SHOULDER

SADDLE

LOIN CHOPS

RABBIT AND HARE

FORE AND HIND LEGS OF RABBIT

SADDLE OF RABBIT

SADDLE OF HARE

GAME BIRDS

Grouse Young birds, with soft downy breast feathers and pointed flight wings, are roasted and served one per person. Older birds, with rounded tips to the wings, are better casseroled. Hang for about three days.

Mallard The largest wild duck with lean, dry flesh. The flight feathers are pointed and the breast is downy in young birds. Hang for one day only. Serve roasted. One bird serves two to three.

Partridge There are two varieties of partridge in North America, the Gray which has the better flavor, and the Chukar. Young birds have yellow-brown pliable feet and light-colored plump flesh. Hang for three or four days before roasting or broiling; serve one per person.

Pheasant Young birds of both sexes have pliable beaks and feet, soft and pointed feathers; on cocks the short spurs are rounded. A hen pheasant, which is considered the tenderer and better-tasting of the two, will serve three people, and a cock pheasant four people.

Pigeon Wild or wood pigeons are inexpensive game birds, often tough and best suited for casseroles and other slow-cooked dishes. Very young birds, called squabs, are now specially bred for the table. They are tender and flavorful, and can be roasted, sautéed or broiled. Allow one bird per person.

Quail Quail has a less gamey flavor than other birds and should not be hung. On young birds, the feathers are pointed and the feet soft with rounded spurs. Roast or broil, serving at least one bird per person.

Wild goose Canada goose is the variety most usually available. On young birds, with lean dark flesh, the flight feathers are pointed and the long dark feet pliable. Hang for four or five days. One goose, average weight 7 pounds, will serve six persons. Brant geese are smaller.

FURRED GAME

Hare Hare, also known as jackrabbit, is a relative of the rabbit but is larger and has a gamier flavor. A young hare (weighing 6–7 pounds), can be recognized by its small, sharp, white teeth; smooth fur and hidden claws; the soft ears tear easily. Hang for about one week. Young hares may be roasted whole, to serve four to six persons; older animals are better casseroled although the saddle can be roasted.

Rabbit The flesh of the wild rabbit often has a gamey flavor. Smaller than the hare (serves three persons), a young rabbit can be recognised by the same signs. It is prepared and cooked in the same way, but is skinned at once after killing and should not be hung. Rabbits on sale in the shops are domesticated, with a flavor like chicken. They are available cut up and frozen.

Venison The best meat comes from the young male deer (buck), at an age of $1\frac{1}{2}$–2 years. The lean meat is dark red and close-grained, with firm white fat. Hang for at least one week. Venison is sold in roasts, the leg and saddle being the choicest cuts. Loin chops, neck cutlets and shoulder may be braised.

MEAT
DISHES

Beef

CHILLED MULLIGATAWNY SOUP

Mulligatawny soup – a favorite among the British in India, and brought home by them – is a rich meat stock strongly flavored with curry. This version transforms the traditional soup into a cool summer appetizer.

PREPARATION TIME: *20 min*
COOKING TIME: *30 min*
CHILLING TIME: *1½–2 hours*
INGREDIENTS *(for 6):*
1 onion
1 carrot
¼ cup unsalted butter
1½ tablespoons flour
2 teaspoons curry powder
1½ quarts beef stock
2 tablespoons syrup drained from mango chutney
GARNISH:
Cauliflower florets

Peel and finely chop the onion and carrot. Melt the butter in a large pan over moderate heat and cook the vegetables until the onion is transparent. Sift the flour and curry powder together and stir into the vegetables. Continue cooking over moderate heat, stirring constantly, until the mixture is a deep brown color. Gradually stir in the hot stock and bring the soup to the boil. Simmer over low heat for 30 minutes, then set aside to cool slightly.

Put the soup through a coarse sieve, or liquidize it for 1–2 minutes, then stir in the mango syrup. Chill for at least 1½ hours.

Before serving, remove any fat from the surface of the soup. Pour into bowls and garnish with tiny florets of raw cauliflower.

BEEF AND SHRIMP SOUP

A soup from Malaysia, where it can be served either before the main curry course or as an accompaniment to it.

PREPARATION TIME: *30 min*
COOKING TIME: *2 hours*
INGREDIENTS *(for 4–6):*
1 pound boneless lean beef
3 onions
2 cloves garlic
Piece ginger root
¾ teaspoon ground turmeric
1 teaspoon ground coriander
½ pound shelled shrimp
3 tablespoons ghee (page 183) or melted butter
Salt★
1 tablespoon fresh lime or lemon juice

Put the beef in a pan with 1½ quarts cold water, 1 peeled and quartered onion, and 1 flattened clove of garlic. Bring to the boil, cover and simmer for 1 hour.

Peel and mince one onion and pound it with the remaining garlic, ginger, turmeric and coriander. Chop the shrimp roughly and fry them in 2 tablespoons butter for 2 minutes. Add the pounded onion mixture and fry for 3–4 minutes.

Using a slotted spoon, lift out the onion and garlic from the soup. Add the shrimp and onion mixture and continue simmering the soup until the beef is quite tender. Take out the beef, slice it thinly and return it to the soup. Season to taste with salt. Cut the remaining onion into thin rings and fry in the rest of the butter until crisp.

Stir the lime juice into the soup and sprinkle with the fried onion rings.

BEEF SATAY

These delicious little skewers with their peanut-flavored sauce can be made with beef or chicken. In Malaysia and Indonesia they are sold from roadside stalls, but they are also simple to make at home.

PREPARATION TIME: *20 min*
STANDING TIME: *2 hours*
COOKING TIME: *20 min*
INGREDIENTS *(for 4–6):*
1½ pounds boneless lean beef
1 tablespoon blanched almonds (page 179)
1 tablespoon sliced ginger root
1 teaspoon ground coriander
1 teaspoon ground turmeric
1¼ cups coconut milk (see below)
Salt★ and black pepper
1 teaspoon brown sugar
SATAY SAUCE:
PREPARATION TIME: *15 min*
COOKING TIME: *15 min*
INGREDIENTS:
2 onions
1–2 tablespoons peanut oil
¾ cup roasted peanuts
½ teaspoon chili powder or cayenne
1 teaspoon light brown sugar
Salt★
1 tablespoon soy sauce
Juice of ½ lime

Pound the almonds, ginger, coriander and turmeric to a paste in a mortar and gradually dilute it with coconut milk. Cut the meat into bite-size pieces and sprinkle them with salt and ground pepper. Marinate the meat in the spiced coconut milk for 2 hours.

Peel and thinly slice one onion and fry in the hot peanut oil. Peel and finely chop the second onion and pound with the peanuts and

CHILLED MULLIGATAWNY SOUP

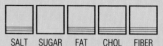

SALT SUGAR FAT CHOL FIBER

GLUTEN-FREE*   WHOLEFOOD*
TOTAL CALORIES: ABOUT 660

To reduce the **fat** level even further, the vegetables should be cooked in only 3 tablespoons butter. Make sure the beef stock has been thoroughly skimmed of fat.

For minimal **cholesterol** level, replace the butter with vegetable margarine or oil; again, be sure to skim the stock thoroughly before using. (Calories lost: up to 230.)

A good **gluten-free** flour to use is potato starch: use only about 2 tablespoons. Check the label on your curry powder to make certain that it does not contain gluten.

Freezing: ☑ up to 3 months.
Microwave: ☑

BEEF AND SHRIMP SOUP

SALT SUGAR FAT CHOL FIBER

GLUTEN-FREE   WHOLEFOOD
TOTAL CALORIES: ABOUT 1830

The **salt** comes mainly from the shrimp; to reduce the level, use a smaller proportion of shrimp, or substitute monkfish. (Monkfish gives an interesting, if less authentic, flavor to the dish.)

The **fat** can be reduced to low by using only 2 teaspoons oil in which to cook the shrimp. The **cholesterol**, like the salt, comes mainly from the shrimp, which can be reduced or replaced as above. If this is done and if the butter is replaced with vegetable margarine (or peanut oil, which would be authentic for this region's cuisine), the cholesterol level will be low. (Calories lost: up to 160.)

Pressure cooker: ☑

Microwave: ☑

BEEF SATAY

SALT SUGAR FAT CHOL FIBER

GLUTEN FREE   WHOLEFOOD
TOTAL CALORIES: ABOUT 2980

Provided that the beef used is really lean, the method of cooking the beef itself is very healthy. The satay sauce adds some **salt**, mainly in the soy sauce. For a low-salt version reduce the soy sauce to 1 teaspoon or omit it entirely. The sauce also contributes a high **fat** level. To reduce this to medium, use only 2 teaspoons oil to soften the onions, adding a spoonful or two of stock if the mixture looks dry; cover tightly while cooking; and use only half the amount of peanuts. (Calories lost: up to 370.)

chili powder in a mortar or liquidizer. Add this paste to the pan and fry for a further 3 minutes, stirring continuously. Gradually dilute the mixture with ½ cup warm water and stir in the sugar. Cook for a few minutes until the sauce has the consistency of light cream. Season to taste with salt, soy sauce and lime juice. Keep hot.

Remove the meat from the marinade and thread on to one end of bamboo skewers; sprinkle them with sugar and broil, turning and basting frequently with the marinade. Allow two skewers per person and serve with satay sauce.

Coconut cream and milk
Fresh or processed coconut yields both cream and milk which are used in many soups and sauces.

Drill two or three holes at the top of the coconut and shake out the colorless liquid. Saw the coconut in half and scrape out the flesh. Shred it finely, pour over ½ cup boiling water and leave for 20 minutes. Squeeze through cheesecloth to produce cream.

For coconut milk, put the squeezed coconut and ½ cup cold water in a pan, and bring to the boil. Remove from the heat, leave for 20 minutes, then squeeze through cheesecloth again. Coconut cream and milk can also be made in a liquidizer (see also page 38).

Beef

DAUBE DE BOEUF

The French culinary term "daube" describes a braising method of slowly cooking tougher cuts of meat, usually beef, in red wine stock. This cooking method, in a covered casserole, prevents the meat from shrinking.

PREPARATION TIME: *45 min*
COOKING TIME: *3 hours*
INGREDIENTS *(for 6):*
2 pounds round or chuck steak
¼ pound salt pork
½ bottle red wine
1 pound carrots
1 pound onions
6 tablespoons butter
1–2 cloves garlic
Bouquet garni (page 183)
2 cups beef stock
2 heaping tablespoons tomato paste
1 heaping tablespoon chopped parsley
Salt★ and black pepper

Trim the fat from the beef and cut the meat into 1 in pieces. Dice the salt pork. Put the meat and pork in a large mixing bowl, pour over the red wine and leave to marinate for 3–4 hours.

Lift the meat from the marinade (the liquid will be used later). Peel or scrape the carrots and cut them into ¼ in slices; peel and finely slice the onions. Using half the butter, fry the beef and the pork in a heavy frying pan until they are evenly brown. Lift out the beef and pork, then fry the vegetables in the remainder of the butter. Peel and chop the garlic and add to the vegetables during frying.

Cover the bottom of a large casserole dish with half the vegetables, then add the beef and pork and top with the remaining vegetables. Pour the marinade into the casserole and add the bouquet garni.

Rinse out the frying pan with the stock. Stir with a wooden spatula to loosen all sediment, and bring the stock to the boil. Stir in the tomato paste and pour this liquid over the contents in the casserole. Add the chopped parsley, cover with a lid and cook for 3 hours in the center of an oven pre-heated to 300°F (160°C, mark 2). Check and if necessary correct the seasoning and remove the bouquet garni. Skim off as much fat as possible – this is more easily done if the casserole is allowed to cool and then re-heated.

Traditionally, this dish is served with creamed potatoes.

BEEF STEW WITH OLIVES

Shank of beef is an inexpensive cut and excellent for stewing. The gelatinous part holding the nuggets of meat together adds a good texture to the sauce and prevents the meat becoming stringy during cooking.

PREPARATION TIME: *20 min*
COOKING TIME: *3¼ hours*
INGREDIENTS *(for 4–6):*
2½–3 pounds beef shank
Seasoned flour (page 184)
1 large onion
1 large carrot
2 cloves garlic
Vegetable oil
½ cup red wine
2½ cups beef stock
Bouquet garni (page 183)
½ teaspoon anchovy paste
Salt★ and black pepper
1–1½ cups ripe or green olives

GARNISH:
Chopped parsley

Remove any large lumps of fat from the beef. Cut the meat into 1–1½ in chunks and coat with seasoned flour. Peel and finely slice the onion, carrot and garlic. Pour a thin layer of oil into a large frying pan; when hot, fry the meat and vegetables until brown. Transfer the contents of the pan to a casserole dish.

Pour the wine and a little stock into the frying pan. Boil these juices rapidly, scraping in all the residue. Pour into the casserole, adding enough stock to cover the meat. Tuck in the bouquet garni, stir in the anchovy paste and plenty of freshly ground pepper. Cover with a lid or foil. Simmer the casserole in the center of an oven, pre-heated to 300°F (160°C, mark 2), for 2–3 hours or until the meat is tender.

Remove the cooked meat and vegetables to a shallow warm serving dish and sprinkle with a little salt. Boil the liquid in the casserole rapidly until it has reduced and thickened to a rich sauce. Remove the bouquet garni. Add the olives and simmer for 5 minutes. Correct seasoning if necessary. Pour some of the sauce over the meat and serve the remainder in a sauce boat.

Garnish the meat with parsley and surround with triangles of toast or boiled potatoes.

DAUBE DE BOEUF

SALT SUGAR FAT CHOL FIBER

GLUTEN-FREE WHOLEFOOD
TOTAL CALORIES: ABOUT 4000

To reduce the **salt**, halve or omit the salt pork. This brings the level down to medium-high, allowing for the amount of salt in the wine, the tomato paste and the beef itself.
For low **fat** and **cholesterol**, choose very lean beef, omit the pork and brown the meat in a heavy pan lightly brushed with oil instead of butter. Ensure that the beef stock is well skimmed of fat. (Total calories lost: up to 1200.)

Pressure cooker: ☑
Slow cooker: ☑
Freezing: ☑ up to 2 months.

BEEF STEW WITH OLIVES

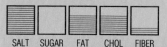

SALT SUGAR FAT CHOL FIBER

GLUTEN-FREE★ WHOLEFOOD★
TOTAL CALORIES: ABOUT 4980

Most of the **salt** comes from the olives, the rest from the anchovy paste and wine. To reduce the level of salt to medium, halve the amount of olives used.
This will also reduce the **fat** as olives average 11% oil. If, as well, the meat is browned in a heavy pan brushed lightly with oil, rather than in a thin layer of oil, and provided the beef is very lean, the dish will be low fat. (Calories lost: up to 200.)
The medium **cholesterol** level results from the generous portions. If smaller helpings are

served, with more vegetables, the cholesterol level (which comes entirely from the meat) will be low.

Pressure cooker: ✓
Slow cooker: ✓
Freezing: ✓ up to 4 months

MOUSSAKA

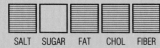

| SALT | SUGAR | FAT | CHOL | FIBER |

GLUTEN-FREE*   WHOLEFOOD*
TOTAL CALORIES: ABOUT 2730

The high **salt** level is mainly due to the salting of the eggplants. This step can perfectly well be omitted and the salt level thus reduced to low. Eggplants nowadays do not seem to have particularly bitter juices. Where salting does help is in reducing the need for so much oil, but this can be dealt with in another way (see below).

To reduce the **fat** level to low, choose very lean beef and instead of frying the eggplant slices, broil them for about 3 minutes on each side on a baking pan lightly brushed with oil. The onion can be softened in 2 teaspoons of oil, provided the pan is tightly covered and 1 tablespoon of stock or water is added after a minute or two. Use skim milk for the sauce, blending the flour, milk and egg instead of using the usual roux method, and omit the butter. The **cholesterol** level will now be moderate. (Calories lost: up to 1020.) Fat and cholesterol can be further reduced by having smaller helpings with plenty of salad.

Freezing: ✓ up to 4 months.
Microwave: ✓ for the mince.

MOUSSAKA

The eggplant is the staple vegetable of the Middle East. It is the basic ingredient in moussaka, meaning eggplant casserole; the dish may also include ground beef or lamb.

PREPARATION TIME: *45 min*
COOKING TIME: *35–40 min*
INGREDIENTS *(for 4):*
4 eggplants
1 large onion
4–6 tablespoons olive oil
1 pound ground round
*1 teaspoon salt**
2 heaping teaspoons tomato paste
½ cup beef stock or water
Salt and black pepper
2 tablespoons unsalted butter
2 tablespoons plain flour
1¼ cups milk
1 egg

Peel and finely chop the onion; heat 1 tablespoon of the oil in a heavy-based pan and gently fry the onions for about 5 minutes, covering the pan with a lid. Add the ground beef and fry until brown and thoroughly sealed. Stir in the salt, tomato paste and stock; season to taste with freshly ground pepper. Bring this mixture to the boil, cover the pan with a lid and simmer gently for 30 minutes or until the meat is tender and the liquid is almost absorbed.

Meanwhile, peel and thinly slice the eggplants, arrange them in a layer on a plate and sprinkle generously with salt; let the eggplants stand for 30 minutes to draw out the bitter juices. Drain, rinse in cold water and pat thoroughly dry on kitchen paper towels. Fry the eggplant slices in the remaining oil until golden, then drain on paper

towels. Arrange a layer of eggplant in the bottom of a large buttered dish or casserole. Cover with a layer of the meat, another layer of eggplant and so on, until all is used up; finish with a layer of eggplant.

Melt the butter in a saucepan over low heat and stir in the flour. Cook gently for 1 minute, then gradually blend in the milk, stirring continuously. Bring this sauce to the boil, season with salt and freshly ground pepper and simmer for 1–2 minutes. Draw the pan off the heat and beat in the egg. Spoon this sauce over the moussaka; place in the center of a pre-heated oven and bake at 350°F (180°C, mark 4) for 35–40 minutes or until bubbling hot and browned.

This is a rich and substantial meal, best served straight from the casserole. A tomato and onion salad could be served with it.

Beef

BEEF PAUPIETTES

Paupiettes are thin slices of meat, usually beef, which are stuffed with forcemeat and rolled into cork shapes which the French call *alouettes sans têtes* (larks without heads). The meat should be cut very thinly: ask the butcher to cut it on the meat slicer.

PREPARATION TIME: *45 min*
COOKING TIME: *1½ hours*
INGREDIENTS *(for 4)*:
1½ pounds top round of beef, cut in thin slices
2 heaping teaspoons Dijon-style mustard
Salt* and black pepper
STUFFING:
3 ounces bacon
1 cup diced cooked chicken or pork
1 shallot
1 large clove garlic
3 tablespoons butter
1 cup fine soft breadcrumbs
1 egg
1 tablespoon chopped parsley
½ teaspoon chopped thyme
5 tablespoons brandy
SAUCE:
1 pound mixed vegetables (onions, carrots, turnips, peas, green beans, parsnips)
3 tablespoons beef drippings or lard
1¼ cups beef stock
½ cup red wine
Beurre manié (page 155) made from 2 tablespoons each butter and flour

Beat the beef slices wafer-thin between two pieces of waxed paper; each slice should measure about 4 in square. Spread a little mustard over each slice; season with salt and ground pepper.

Chop the bacon finely, together with the chicken or pork. Peel and finely chop the shallot and garlic. Melt the butter in a small frying pan over moderate heat and cook the shallot and garlic until soft and transparent.

In a mixing bowl, blend together the bacon, chicken, shallot and garlic. Add the breadcrumbs and the lightly beaten egg. Stir in the thyme and parsley, and season the stuffing with salt and pepper; add the brandy.

Spoon the stuffing equally on the beef slices; roll up each slice and tuck the ends over to keep the stuffing in place. Tie each paupiette securely with fine string. Set the meat aside.

To make the sauce, peel and finely chop the onion, then brown it lightly over moderate heat in the lard or drippings. Wash and prepare the vegetables used, then chop them finely. Add these to the onion and cook for a few minutes to brown slightly. Spoon the vegetables into a large shallow casserole and put the paupiettes on top in a single layer. Pour the stock and wine into the pan in which the vegetables were fried, scraping up all the residue.

Pour the pan juices over the meat, cover the casserole with a lid and cook in the center of the oven, pre-heated to 325°F (170°C, mark 3), for 1½ hours. Remove the lid after 20 minutes. Turn the meat over once during cooking.

Lift the paupiettes from the casserole, remove the string and arrange the meat on a warm serving dish. Surround them with the vegetables. Pour the cooking liquid into a small saucepan and boil rapidly to reduce the sauce by a third. Thicken the sauce with beurre manié, and heat it through. Spoon a little of the sauce over the meat and serve the rest in a sauce boat.

Serve with buttered noodles or creamed potatoes.

HUNGARIAN GOULASH

This internationally famous stew is usually made from beef, though pork, veal and chicken may also be used. Different regions of Hungary have their own favorite goulash recipes. Some use fresh tomatoes, others caraway seeds, garlic or marjoram. But whatever else goes into a goulash, it always contains paprika.

PREPARATION TIME: *35 min*
COOKING TIME: *about 2 hours*
INGREDIENTS *(for 4)*:
1¼ pounds chuck steak
1 pound onions
¼ cup lard
4 cups beef stock or water
Salt*
¼ cup tomato paste
3–4 teaspoons paprika
2 teaspoons sugar
2 tablespoons flour
5 tablespoons sour cream

Wipe the meat and trim off any fat and gristle. Cut it into 1½ in cubes. Peel and thinly slice the onions. Melt the lard in a deep, heavy-based sauté pan and fry the meat and onions over moderate heat until the onions are golden and the meat is sealed. Pour over the hot stock, season with salt and bring to simmering point.

Meanwhile, blend the tomato paste, paprika, sugar and flour in a small bowl until smooth. Stir in a few tablespoons of the simmering liquid from the stew.

SALT   SUGAR   FAT   CHOL   FIBER

GLUTEN-FREE*   WHOLEFOOD*
TOTAL CALORIES: ABOUT 4200

For low **salt**, omit the bacon and use crumbs from bread made without salt.
To reduce **fat** and **cholesterol** to low, choose very lean meat; omit the bacon and soften the shallot and garlic in a pan lightly brushed with oil instead of butter. Soften the sauce vegetables in the same way, and thicken the dish by making a purée of some of them, rather than using beurre manié. (Calories lost: up to 1400.)
Serve with plain rice or potatoes rather than buttered noodles. These steps will make the dish **gluten-free**, if there is no gluten in the mustard. Cooked millet makes a good substitute for breadcrumbs in the stuffing.

Pressure cooker: ☑
Slow cooker: ☑
Food processor: ☑ for the stuffing.
Freezing: ☑ up to 2 months.
Microwave: ☑

HUNGARIAN GOULASH

SALT   SUGAR   FAT   CHOL   FIBER

GLUTEN-FREE*   WHOLEFOOD*
TOTAL CALORIES: ABOUT 2870

The **salt** level is taken as low on the assumption that you have used unsalted tomato paste.
To reduce the levels of **fat** and **cholesterol** to low, choose very lean meat and brown it in a heavy pan lightly brushed with

oil, thus avoiding the lard. Replace the sour cream with plain yogurt or cultured buttermilk. (Calories lost: up to 560.)

Pressure cooker: ✓
Slow cooker: ✓
Freezing: ✓ up to 4 months.
Microwave: ✓

STEAK AU POIVRE

SALT	SUGAR	FAT	CHOL	FIBER

GLUTEN-FREE   WHOLEFOOD
TOTAL CALORIES: ABOUT 3640

To compensate for the lack of added **salt**, crumble a little dried tarragon or marjoram over the steak.

The lavish use of butter, oil and cream in this recipe makes it very rich indeed. To keep the peppery character but reduce **fat** and **cholesterol** to moderate (low if the steak is extremely lean), brush the steaks lightly with butter or oil before pressing in the peppercorns, then broil instead of frying for the same cooking time.

Transfer the steaks to a heated metal serving dish; warm the brandy and pour it over, set it alight immediately and pour over warmed low-fat plain yogurt (or fromage blanc thinned with a little skim milk). Be careful not to boil. (Calories lost: up to 960.)

Instead of the traditional brandy sauce, this is also good with a purée of watercress made by softening watercress for about 10 minutes in a little stock and then liquidizing. It could be mixed with a little yogurt or fromage blanc if you like.

Draw the pan with the onions and meat from the heat and stir in the tomato mixture, blending thoroughly. Return to the heat and bring back to a simmer. Cover and leave the stew to cook over gentle heat for about 2 hours or until the meat is quite tender. Stir occasionally.

Just before serving, stir in the sour cream and adjust seasoning. Ribbon noodles are traditional with goulash, but boiled floury potatoes could be served instead.

STEAK AU POIVRE

A classic peppered steak is always prepared with whole, crushed peppercorns. It is traditionally served with brandy sauce and is ideal for cooking in a chafing dish at the table.

PREPARATION TIME: *15 min*
COOKING TIME: *15–20 min*
INGREDIENTS *(for 4):*
4 boneless or shell steaks
2 tablespoons whole black
    peppercorns
¼ cup unsalted butter
1 tablespoon olive oil
2 tablespoons brandy
½ cup heavy cream
Salt★

Wipe the steaks and trim off any fat and gristle. Crush the peppercorns coarsely in a mortar or on a wooden board with a rolling pin. With the fingers, press the crushed peppercorns into the surface of the meat on both sides.

Heat the butter and oil in a heavy-based pan; cook the steaks over high heat for 2 minutes, turning them once. This initial hot frying seals the juices and peppercorns in the meat; lower the heat and cook the steaks for 5 minutes for rare steaks, 8–10 minutes for medium-rare and 12 minutes for well-done steaks.

Lift the steaks from the pan on to a hot serving dish; add the brandy to the butter in the pan and set it alight when hot. Draw the pan off the heat and as soon as the flames have died down, gradually stir in the cream. Season the sauce with salt and pour it over the steaks. Freshly cooked broccoli and croquette potatoes, or a green salad, go well with these steaks.

Beef

BOEUF À LA JARDINIÈRE

Cuts of beef, such as top round, bottom round and brisket, are not tender enough to oven-roast successfully. They do, however, make excellent pot roasts, cooked with fresh vegetables (*à la jardin-ière*). Top and bottom round are lean cuts, but brisket usually needs some of the fat trimmed off before being rolled and tied.

PREPARATION TIME: *25 min*
COOKING TIME: *2½–3 hours*
INGREDIENTS *(for 6)*:

3 pounds rolled top or bottom
   round or brisket of beef
8 pearl onions
½ pound small carrots
2 young turnips
¼ cup beef drippings
½ cup dry red wine

2 bay leaves
½ teaspoon mixed herbs
6 peppercorns
1 teaspoon salt*
½ pound young green beans or
   fresh peas
1 pound potatoes (optional)

Peel the onions, leaving them whole. Scrape or peel the carrots, and peel and quarter the turnips. Melt the drippings over high heat in a large heavy-based pan or flameproof casserole. Brown the meat quickly on all sides in the fat to seal in the juices. Add the onions and fry until golden. Put the carrots, turnips and wine into the pan, together with the bay leaves, mixed herbs, pepper-corns and salt.

Cover the pan with a close-fitting lid or foil and simmer over low heat or in the center of an oven pre-heated to 300°F (160°C, mark 2) for 2½–3 hours or until the meat is tender. If the liquid evaporates during cooking, add a little beef stock or water.

Trim the beans and cut them into 1 in pieces. Alternatively, shell the peas. Cook them in lightly salted boiling water for 10 minutes or until just tender.

Remove the meat from the pan, carve it and arrange the slices on a hot serving dish. Surround the meat with the vegetables and garnish with the beans. Remove the bay leaves from the pan juices; skim off the fat or soak it off the surface with kitchen paper towels. Season the gravy to taste with salt and freshly ground pepper and pour into a warm sauce boat.

Potatoes may be added to the meat for the last hour of cooking, or served separately.

STEAK DIANE

This famous dish originated in Australia where tender beef fillet is obligatory, but sirloin steak is equally suitable.

PREPARATION TIME: *20 min*
COOKING TIME: *10 min*
INGREDIENTS *(for 6)*:
1½ pounds boneless sirloin or shell
   steak
1 small onion
2 teaspoons sugar
1 large lemon
¾ cup unsalted butter
Worcestershire sauce
1 tablespoon chopped parsley
4 tablespoons brandy

Trim the steak and cut it into six equal pieces; beat them flat with a rolling pin until they are no more than ¼ in thick. Peel and finely chop the onion. Grate the lemon rind finely, squeeze out the juice and strain.

Melt ¼ cup of the butter in a large, heavy-based pan and fry the onion for about 5 minutes or until soft and transparent. Lift the onion on to a plate with a slotted spoon and keep warm. Fry two steaks at a time, over high heat for 1 minute only on each side. Lift out and keep hot.

Melt another ¼ cup of butter until foaming and fry two more steaks; repeat with the remaining meat. Return the onions to the pan, stir in the sugar, lemon rind and juice, add a few drops of Worcestershire sauce and the parsley. Cook lightly, then put in the steaks. Flame the steaks with warm brandy.

Serve the steaks with the onion and brandy poured over them. New potatoes and braised celery are suitable vegetables.

BOEUF À LA JARDINIÈRE

SALT   SUGAR   FAT   CHOL   FIBER

GLUTEN-FREE   WHOLEFOOD
TOTAL CALORIES: ABOUT 5570

The **salt** is only low if fresh beef is used.
The exact **fat** content depends on the cut of meat. For low fat and **cholesterol** choose a lean cut, trim off all the visible fat carefully, and brown the meat in a heavy pan lightly brushed with oil; omit the drippings. (Calories lost: up to 550.)

Pressure cooker: ☑ (but you might need a little more liquid).

Freezing: ☑ up to 4 months.

STEAK DIANE

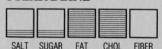

SALT   SUGAR   FAT   CHOL   FIBER

GLUTEN-FREE   WHOLEFOOD
TOTAL CALORIES: ABOUT 3680

To reduce both the **fat** and **cholesterol** levels of this recipe to low, soften the onions in a heavy pan, using only 2 teaspoons butter or oil. Choose very lean meat and either broil it, brushing it first with a little of the butter or oil from the pan in which the onions have been softened, or cook it in the same pan. Special pans for frying meat are available which need virtually no fat and give an attractive criss-cross pattern, as if the meat had been broiled. (Calories lost: up to 1200.)

TOURNEDOS EN CROÛTE

SALT	SUGAR	FAT	CHOL	FIBER

TOTAL CALORIES: ABOUT 4580

The moderate **salt** level assumes that you have been able to buy (or make) a low-salt pâté. (See the recipe for liver pâté on page 139.)
To reduce **fat** and **cholesterol** to moderate, the puff pastry must be replaced by a dough much less rich in butter. Bought phyllo pastry makes a very good wrapping; yeast pastry and strudel pastry can also be used. Halve the amount of butter used for sealing, and fry the onion for the sauce in a pan very lightly brushed with butter or oil. Make your own pâté (see page 139) using a minimum of fat. (Calories lost: up to 850.)
Wholefood: strong whole wheat flour is very successful in both strudel and yeast pastry.

TOURNEDOS EN CROÛTE

The small, thick, round slices, or tournedos, cut from the fillet of beef are among the most expensive cuts of meat. But for a special occasion, tournedos can be encased in puff pastry, and a $\frac{1}{4}$ pound portion of meat will then be sufficient for each person.

PREPARATION TIME: *30 min*
COOKING TIME: *40 min*
INGREDIENTS *(for 6)*:
6 tournedos (or filet mignon)
$\frac{1}{4}$ cup unsalted butter
12–13 ounces puff pastry
$\frac{1}{4}$ pound pâté with mushrooms or truffles
1 egg
1 onion
$\frac{1}{2}$ cup red wine
$1\frac{1}{4}$ cups beef stock
Salt★ and black pepper
GARNISH:
Watercress

Trim any excess fat off the tournedos and wipe them with a damp cloth. Heat the butter in a heavy-based pan and brown the meat quickly on both sides to seal in the juices. Set aside to cool.

Roll out the puff pastry on a floured surface, to a rectangle, $\frac{1}{8}$ in thick. Divide the pastry into six equal squares, each large enough to wrap around a tournedos. Spread one side of each tournedos with pâté and place it, pâté side down, on a pastry square. Brush the edges of the pastry with cold water and draw them together over the meat to form a neat package. Seal the edges carefully.

Place the pastry packages, with the seams underneath, on a wet baking sheet. Lightly beat the egg and brush over the pastry.

Make two or three slits in each package for the steam to escape, and decorate with leaves cut from the pastry trimmings. Brush with beaten egg.

Bake the tournedos in the center of a pre-heated oven at 425°F (220°C, mark 7) for 15–20 minutes. At this point, the pastry should be well risen and golden brown and the meat will be rosy-pink in the middle. For well-done steaks, lower the heat to 350°F (180°C, mark 4) and cook for a further 10 minutes.

Make the sauce while the tournedos are cooking. Peel and finely chop the onion and fry until just colored in the butter left in the pan. Add the wine and let it bubble over moderate heat for 2–3 minutes, stirring up the residue from the pan. Blend in the stock and simmer for a further 5 minutes. Season with salt and freshly-ground pepper.

Arrange the tournedos on a warm serving dish garnished with sprigs of watercress. Pour the sauce into a sauce boat and serve with potatoes and perhaps carrots or a salad.

Beef

SAUERBRATEN

This German farmhouse dish of spiced braised beef is marinated for 4–6 days to flavor and tenderize the meat. It is tradition- ally served with potato dumplings, but noodles or macaroni are less heavy alternatives and also go well.

PREPARATION TIME: *15 min*
COOKING TIME: *1½ hours*
INGREDIENTS *(for 4):*

2 pounds top round of beef	*1 teaspoon sugar*
1 onion	*1¼ cups wine vinegar*
4 peppercorns	*¼ cup unsalted butter*
1 clove	*1 piece bread crust*
1 small bay leaf	*2 heaping teaspoons cornstarch*
Salt★ and black pepper	

Wipe the meat with a clean cloth and trim off any fat. Tie the meat with thin string to maintain its round shape and put it in a large earthenware bowl. Peel and slice the onion, and add it to the meat, together with the peppercorns, clove, bay leaf, salt, freshly ground pepper and the sugar. Pour the vinegar mixed with 2 cups of water over the meat and leave it to stand, covered, in a cold place for 4–6 days, turning it once a day in the marinade.

Lift the meat from the marinade and pat it thoroughly dry on paper towels. Melt the butter in a deep, heavy-based pan, add the meat and brown it quickly all over. Season to taste with salt and pour 1¼ cups of the strained marinade over the meat. Add the crust of bread (or, as in Germany, a piece of honey cake or gingerbread as well to give extra flavor). Cover the pan with a lid and simmer over low heat for 1½ hours or until the meat is tender. Add extra marinade if it becomes necessary.

Lift out the meat and keep it warm. Strain the gravy through a fine sieve, measure 1¼ cups and add more marinade if necessary. Blend the cornstarch with a little water and stir into the gravy; bring to the boil, stirring until smooth. Check and correct flavor and seasoning – the gravy should taste slightly sweet and sour.

Serve the meat cut into slices, with boiled noodles or macaroni; pass the gravy separately. Glazed carrots or a green vegetable such as broccoli would also be suitable.

CARBONNADES À LA FLAMANDE

This is an adaptation of a Belgian recipe for beef in beer. The beer gives the meat a distinctly nutty flavor, heightened by the garlic crust. The dish is best prepared in advance and later re-heated.

PREPARATION TIME: *55 min*
COOKING TIME: *2¾ hours*
INGREDIENTS *(for 6):*
3 pounds lean beef round or chuck
½ cup beef drippings or unsalted butter
1 tablespoon olive oil
3 large onions
4 cloves garlic (optional)
Salt★ and black pepper
2 tablespoons flour
1 tablespoon dark brown sugar
1¼ cups strong beef stock
2 cups dark beer
1 tablespoon wine vinegar
1 bouquet garni (page 183)
2 bay leaves
GARLIC CRUST:
1 cup unsalted butter
3 cloves garlic
1 French loaf

Melt the drippings or butter, together with the oil, in a large sauté pan on top of the stove. Cut the beef into ½ in thick slices, about 3 in long and 1½ in wide. Peel and finely slice the onions and crush the four cloves of garlic. Quickly brown the beef slices or carbonnades in the fat, drain and put to one side. Lower the heat and in the remaining fat cook the onions until golden, then add the garlic. Layer the onions and beef in a deep casserole, beginning with the onions and finishing with meat; salt and pepper each layer lightly.

Scrape up the juices in the pan

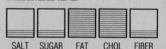

Wholefood: whole wheat French bread is quite good for this, but if it is unobtainable try the potato topping. A whole wheat biscuit dough, giving a cobbler topping, is also good.

Pressure cooker: ☑ but not the crust – this should be done in the oven.

Slow cooker: ☑ but not the crust – see above.

Freezing: ☑ up to 4 months (without the crust. Add this when reheating).

Microwave: ☑ but not the crust – see above.

STEAK TARTARE

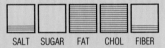

SALT	SUGAR	FAT	CHOL	FIBER

GLUTEN-FREE   WHOLEFOOD
TOTAL CALORIES: ABOUT 2110

The high **fat** content comes mainly from the tartare sauce or mayonnaise, plus the egg yolks which also give a very high level of **cholesterol**. The meat itself can be as low as 5% fat if very lean, or as much as 20% or more. Instead of the high-fat sauce or mayonnaise, flavor plain yogurt or fromage blanc in the same way, with chopped tarragon, lemon juice and Tabasco, and mix it in with the meat. Instead of putting 1 egg yolk on each portion, 2 yolks can be beaten together and a little poured into the center of a small onion ring on top of the meat. This will reduce both fat and cholesterol to low if the meat is really lean. (Calories lost: up to 400.)
If you are using purchased tartare sauce or mayonnaise, check the ingredients to make sure it is **gluten-free** – wheat stabilizers, for instance, are often used.

in which the beef and onions were cooked, stir in the flour and sugar and increase the heat until the mixture forms a roux (page 154). Stir in a little of the stock until the mixture is smooth; bring to the boil. Add the remainder of the stock, the beer and the vinegar; bring back to the boil and simmer for a few minutes. Put the bouquet garni and bay leaves in the casserole and pour over the sauce to just cover the meat. Cover the casserole with a lid, and cook on a shelf low in the oven for 2½ hours, at 325°F (170°C, mark 3).
The flavor of the carbonnades is improved if the casserole is put aside at this stage and re-heated the next day, before making the garlic crust.
For the garlic crust, melt the butter in a frying pan over low heat. Crush the three cloves of garlic and stir into the butter. Cut the French bread into ½ in thick slices and soak in the garlic butter, until this is completely absorbed. Put the bread on top of the carbonnades and cook the casserole in an oven pre-heated to 325°F (170°C, mark 3) for 30 minutes. The meat should then be thoroughly heated and the garlic crust should be crisp with a golden tinge.
Serve direct from the casserole. Cauliflower sprinkled with fried or toasted almonds could also be served.

STEAK TARTARE

This dish of raw steak, garnished with raw onions and egg yolk, is becoming increasingly popular. It is served with a number of finely chopped vegetables to which guests help themselves.

PREPARATION TIME: *15–20 min*
INGREDIENTS *(for 4):*
1 pound top sirloin or round steak
2 onions
1 cooked beet
4 tablespoons capers
1 large sweet green or red pepper
2 tablespoons finely chopped
  parsley
½ cup tartare sauce or mayonnaise
  (page 156)
1–2 teaspoons Dijon-style
  mustard
Salt★ and black pepper
Tabasco sauce
4 egg yolks
GARNISH:
Grated horseradish

Peel and thinly slice the onions. Set four onion rings aside and chop the remainder finely. Peel and finely dice the beet. Chop the capers. Remove the stalk end and the seeds from the pepper and dice the flesh.

Make the tartare sauce or the mayonnaise (flavor the latter with mustard and a few drops of Tabasco sauce). Chill the sauce while assembling the dish.

Scrape the steak into fine thin shreds with a sharp knife or put it through the fine blade of a grinder. Season to taste with salt and freshly ground pepper, and shape the mixture into four flat rounds. Arrange them in the center of a serving dish. Make a shallow hollow in the center of each steak, put an onion ring around the depression and slip an egg yolk inside (the egg yolk may also be set in a half shell within the onion ring).

Arrange the chopped vegetables in small mounds around the steaks, and sprinkle the steaks and vegetables with finely grated horseradish. Serve the chilled sauce separately, with a tossed green salad and slices of buttered rye bread.

Beef

BOILED BEEF AND CARROTS

This is one of the classic dishes from the English kitchen. Carrots and onions are always cooked with the beef, which should, according to tradition, also be served with dumplings.

PREPARATION TIME: *30 min*
COOKING TIME: *3–3½ hours*
INGREDIENTS *(for 6):*

4 pound piece corned beef
1 large onion
4 cloves
Bouquet garni (page 183)
6 peppercorns
2 bay leaves
1 slice bacon
10 small carrots
12 pearl onions
2 small turnips
½ cup dry hard cider
½ teaspoon dry mustard
½ teaspoon ground cinnamon

DUMPLINGS:
PREPARATION TIME: *5 min*
COOKING TIME: *15 min*
INGREDIENTS *(8 dumplings):*
*Prepared suet crust pastry (half
    the quantity given for the steak
    and kidney pudding on page
    94)*
Salt★ and black pepper
*Mixed herbs or chopped parsley or
    ¼ cup grated cheese*

Put the beef in a large saucepan; peel the large onion, stud it with the cloves and add to the beef, together with the bouquet garni, peppercorns, bay leaves and bacon. Cover with cold water, bring to the boil and after a few minutes remove the scum; keep the meat on the boil and continue skimming for about 10 minutes. Cover the pan with a lid and reduce the heat, then simmer for 1¾ hours. Remove from the heat and lift out the meat; strain the liquid into a basin.

When the liquid has cooled, remove the congealed fat from the surface. Peel the carrots and onions, and peel and coarsely slice the turnips. Arrange the vegetables in a deep pan, with the beef on top. Pour over enough strained liquid and the cider to cover. Sprinkle in the mustard and cinnamon, and cover the pan with a lid. Bring to the boil, then reduce the heat and simmer for 1 hour.

Make the pastry for the dumplings as described on page 94, adding the herbs or cheese to the dry mix. Divide the pastry into eight equal pieces and shape these into balls. Add them to the simmering beef for the last 20 minutes of cooking. Winter cabbage, cut into chunks, may also be added with the dumplings.

Arrange the piece of beef in the center of a serving dish and surround with the vegetables; serve the liquid separately in a sauceboat. Serve with plain boiled potatoes.

MINCED COLLOPS

In Britain, Collop Monday, the Monday before Lent, was the day on which all meats in the house had to be used up before fasting began. There are numerous recipes for collops. This one, from Scotland, uses beef.

PREPARATION TIME: *5 min*
COOKING TIME: *45–60 min*
INGREDIENTS *(for 4):*
1 pound ground beef
2 onions
2 tablespoons beef drippings
Salt★ and black pepper
1¼ cups water or beef stock
4 eggs

Peel and finely chop the onions. Melt the drippings in a heavy-based saucepan and fry the onions over low heat for about 5 minutes or until soft. Add the ground beef, cover with a lid and fry until the beef is browned and has separated into grains. Season to taste with salt and freshly ground pepper; pour over the water or stock until the meat is almost covered. Then put the lid on the pan and simmer the contents for 45 minutes. Stir occasionally and take the lid off the pan towards the end of the cooking time. When the meat is cooked, the liquid should have almost evaporated.

Poach the eggs in simmering salted water until just set. Spoon the meat on to slices of hot toast and top each portion with a poached egg. The minced collops could also be served with creamed potatoes instead of toast.

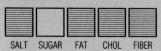
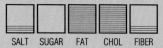

and cook it in its own fat, omitting the drippings; if you are using beef stock ensure it is well skimmed of fat; and omit the poached eggs, topping each serving instead with a whole mushroom, lightly poached for about 5 minutes in a little stock. (Calories lost: up to 1260.)

Pressure cooker: ☑ for the beef.

Freezing: ☑ up to 4 months for the beef (not the eggs).

Microwave: ☑

CHILI CON CARNE

SALT SUGAR FAT CHOL FIBER

GLUTEN-FREE WHOLEFOOD
TOTAL CALORIES: ABOUT 2120

The low **salt** content assumes that the kidney beans and tomatoes have not had salt added. Check the labels on the cans, or use fresh tomatoes and dried beans.
For low **fat** choose really lean meat, and cook it in its own fat (see notes on the previous recipe). Soften the onions after the meat in the same fat, omitting the oil.
(Calories lost: up to 265.)
Cholesterol is already low, assuming that the meat is really lean.

Pressure cooker: ☑
Slow cooker: ☑
Freezing: ☑ up to 4 months
Microwave: ☑

CHILI CON CARNE

The Mexican national dish of beef and bean stew with chili is ideal on a cold winter's night. For an even spicier dish, a few cumin seeds may be added.

PREPARATION TIME: *30 min*
COOKING TIME: *2–2½ hours*
INGREDIENTS (*for 6*):
1 pound ground round
2 cups dried or 2 16-ounce cans red kidney beans
2 onions
2 tablespoons olive oil
16-ounce can of tomatoes
2 teaspoons chili powder or 1 finely chopped chili pepper
Salt★
Cumin seeds (optional)

Soak dried beans in cold water overnight. Drain them and put in pan with plenty of fresh water (no salt). Bring to boil and keep boiling for 10 minutes. Lower heat, cover pan with lid and simmer for 1 hour. Peel and thinly slice onions.

Heat the oil in a flameproof dish over low heat and fry the onions until soft. Stir in the meat and continue frying, stirring occasionally, until the meat has browned. Blend in the drained kidney beans, add the tomatoes with their juice, and season to taste with chili, salt and crushed cumin seeds.

Cover the pan with a lid and cook on top of the stove or in the center of a pre-heated oven, at 300°F (160°C, mark 2), for 1–1½ hours. Add a little water if the stew dries out during cooking.

Serve the stew straight from the dish, with crusty bread and a tossed green salad.

Beef

ROLLATINE DI MANZO AL FORNO

The name of this Italian dish means little beef rolls cooked in the oven. Wafer-thin slices of beef and ham are rolled around a savory and sweet stuffing and cooked in wine.

PREPARATION TIME: *45 min*
COOKING TIME: *1 hour*
INGREDIENTS *(for 6)*:
12 thin slices top round of beef, each 4 in by 3 in by ¼ in
12 wafer-thin slices cooked ham
3 cloves garlic
12 thin slices salami
4 hard-cooked eggs
1 cup raisins
½ cup grated Parmesan cheese
½ cup finely chopped parsley
½ teaspoon grated nutmeg
½ teaspoon oregano
Salt★ and black pepper
2 tablespoons unsalted butter
1¼ cups beef stock
1¼ cups dry white wine
4 bay leaves
6 cloves
2 tablespoons Marsala wine

Place each slice of beef between sheets of wax paper and flatten it with a rolling pin. Cover the beef slices with ham, trimmed to fit, and spread with peeled and crushed garlic.

Finely chop the skinned salami, the hard-cooked eggs and raisins, and put them in a bowl. Blend in the cheese, parsley, nutmeg and oregano, and season with salt and freshly ground pepper.

Divide this mixture equally over the beef and ham slices. Fold over the long sides to keep the stuffing in place and roll the slices up. Tie the packages with fine string.

Place the rolls in a buttered ovenproof dish. Pour over the stock and wine and cook for 30 minutes in the center of the oven, pre-heated to 375°F (190°C, mark 5). Add the bay leaves, cloves and Marsala, and cook for a further 30 minutes.

Serve the beef rolls with plainly boiled new potatoes and lightly cooked cauliflower or broccoli. Remove the bay leaves before serving.

STEAK AND KIDNEY PUDDING

The traditional English beef-steak and kidney pudding is always served from the mold in which it was steamed. Have ready a white folded napkin or cloth to tie around the hot steaming mold before serving.

PREPARATION TIME: *30 min*
COOKING TIME: *3–4 hours*
INGREDIENTS *(for 4)*:
1½ pounds lean chuck steak
¼ pound beef kidney
1 onion
2 tablespoons seasoned flour (page 184)
2 tablespoons butter
Salt★ and black pepper

Suet crust pastry:
PREPARATION TIME: *15 min*
RESTING TIME: *15 min*
INGREDIENTS:
2 cups self-rising flour or 2 cups all-purpose flour and 1 tablespoon baking powder
½ teaspoon salt★
½ cup shredded beef suet
¾–1 cup cold water

To make the suet crust pastry, sift the flour and salt into a bowl (together with baking powder if all-purpose flour is used). Add the suet – remove the skin from fresh suet, then grate or chop it finely with a little of the flour to prevent sticking – and mix thoroughly. Using a round-bladed knife, stir in the water to form a light, elastic dough. Turn the dough on to a lightly floured surface, and sprinkle it with a little flour. Knead the dough lightly with the fingertips and shape it into a ball. Put the dough on a plate and cover with an

ROLLATINE DI MANZO AL FORNO

| SALT | SUGAR | FAT | CHOL | FIBER |

GLUTEN-FREE   WHOLEFOOD
TOTAL CALORIES: ABOUT 6210

The **salt** in this recipe comes mainly from the ham, salami and Parmesan and so is difficult to reduce, but using half quantities of salami and Parmesan would give a moderate to high salt level. Since salami average over 40% fat these measures would also help reduce **fat** and **cholesterol** levels. To keep these no more than moderate, also reduce the number of eggs to two (you can compensate by using double the amount of parsley) and choose lean ham. Make sure you buy very lean beef, which can have only a quarter of the fat of a less lean piece, and instead of buttering the oven dish, brush it lightly with oil. (Calories lost: up to 1000.)

Freezing: ✓ up to 2 months.
Microwave: ✓

STEAK AND KIDNEY PUDDING

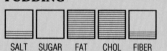

| SALT | SUGAR | FAT | CHOL | FIBER |

WHOLEFOOD★
TOTAL CALORIES: ABOUT 4490

Most of the **fat** in this recipe comes from the suet crust, and there is no way of reducing this without losing the traditional character of the dish. However, the fat can be reduced slightly by choosing very lean meat and using 3 onions in place of one: if you make a larger pudding the ratio of pastry to lean filling will fall.

Kidney, like most organ meats, is very high in **cholesterol** although not in fat. To reduce the level of cholesterol to moderate, use only half the amount the kidney and increase the steak proportionately.

Pressure cooker: ☑

Freezing: ☑ up to 3 months.

Microwave: ☑

HAMBURGERS WITH PIZZAIOLA SAUCE

SALT	SUGAR	FAT	CHOL	FIBER

GLUTEN-FREE WHOLEFOOD
TOTAL CALORIES: ABOUT 3720

To reduce **fat** and **cholesterol** levels to low, choose very lean meat. Broil the hamburgers instead of cooking them in butter, using a baking sheet lightly brushed with oil (broiling them on a rack may result in the hamburgers breaking up slightly).

Freezing: ☑ up to 4 months.

Microwave: ☑ for the sauce. The hamburgers could be cooked in the microwave, but they will not brown.

inverted bowl; leave to rest for 10–15 minutes while the filling is prepared.

Trim away any fat or gristle from the beef, then cut it into $\frac{1}{2}$ in pieces. Remove the core from the kidney (page 163) and cut it into $\frac{1}{2}$ in pieces. Peel and finely chop the onion. Coat the steak and kidney with seasoned flour and mix with the onion.

Cut off a quarter of the prepared suet crust pastry and set it aside for the pudding top. Roll out the remainder to a circle, $\frac{1}{2}$ in thick. Grease a 1-quart steaming mold well, and fit the pastry to the bottom and sides, allowing it to overhang the edge of the mold by about $\frac{1}{2}$ in. Spoon the meat and onion mixture, with a seasoning of salt and freshly ground pepper, into the mold; pour over enough cold water to come three-quarters up the sides of the mold.

Roll out the remaining pastry to a circle to fit the top of the mold. Dampen the edges of the suet crust lining, cover with the pastry top and pinch the edges of the lining and the lid tightly together to seal. Cover the top of the mold with double thickness of buttered wax paper, folding in a wide pleat across the center, to allow the pudding to rise; secure the paper tightly with string.

Put the mold in a saucepan and pour boiling water around it until it reaches one-third up the sides. Steam briskly for 3–4 hours, replenishing with boiling water.

Serve the pudding hot, usually accompanied by boiled potatoes and Brussels sprouts.

HAMBURGERS WITH PIZZAIOLA SAUCE

One of the classics of the American kitchen – hamburgers – is here combined with a classic Italian tomato sauce.

PREPARATION TIME:
*Hamburgers 15 min;
sauce 20 min*
COOKING TIME:
*Hamburgers 6–10 min;
sauce 35 min*
INGREDIENTS *(for 4–6)*:
*2 pounds ground sirloin or top
round*
2 tablespoons unsalted butter
Salt* and black pepper
SAUCE:
2 onions
2 cloves garlic
2 green peppers
2 teaspoons olive oil
$\frac{1}{2}$ cup mushroom caps
16-ounce can of tomatoes
*2 teaspoons oregano (or
marjoram)*
Chili sauce
Salt* and black pepper

Divide the ground beef into six or eight portions, and shape each into a patty about $1\frac{1}{2}$ in thick. Avoid overhandling as this makes the hamburgers tough. Leave the hamburgers to rest while preparing the sauce.

Peel and mince the onions and garlic. Remove the stalks and seeds from the peppers and cut them crosswise into thin slices. Heat the oil in a deep, heavy-based frying pan and, over a gentle heat, cook the onions and garlic until they are pale golden. Add the pepper slices and cook for a further 15 minutes. Wash or peel the mushrooms, chop them roughly and add to the pan together with the tomatoes and the oregano or marjoram. Cover and continue cooking for another 10 minutes. Season to taste with chili sauce, salt and freshly ground pepper. Keep warm while cooking the hamburgers.

Melt the butter in a heavy-based frying pan; fry rare hamburgers for 3 minutes on each side; for pink-rare hamburgers, add another minute each side; for medium, add 2 minutes. Sprinkle with salt and pepper.

Put the hamburgers on a hot serving dish and pour the sauce over them. Serve with coleslaw.

Beef

BEEF DIABLE

Deviled sauces (strong and spicy) are popular and add a different taste to leftover meat.

PREPARATION TIME: *5 min*
COOKING TIME: *35 min*
INGREDIENTS *(for 4)*:
8–10 slices roast or boiled beef
1 tablespoon olive oil
2 onions
1 clove garlic
2 teaspoons flour
1 tablespoon Dijon-style mustard
1 tablespoon white wine vinegar
1 cup beef stock
2 teaspoons dark brown sugar
¼ teaspoon Worcestershire sauce
1 teaspoon chopped capers
1 bay leaf
Salt★ and black pepper
3–4 tablespoons browned breadcrumbs
3 tablespoons unsalted melted butter

Heat the oil over medium heat, and cook the finely chopped onions and garlic until golden brown. Blend in the flour. Add mustard and vinegar, and gradually stir in the stock. Bring this sauce to boiling point and stir until thick and smooth. Add the sugar, Worcestershire sauce, capers and bay leaf and season with salt and pepper. Simmer for some 5–10 minutes, stirring frequently.

Put the sliced beef in a lightly buttered ovenproof dish. Pour over the sauce (first removing the bay leaf), sprinkle with the breadcrumbs and pour over the melted butter. Bake in the center of a pre-heated oven at 375°F (190°C, mark 5) for about 20 minutes or until golden brown. Serve hot, with buttered rice.

BOEUF BOURGUIGNONNE

A hearty and satisfying stew, perfect for a dinner party on a winter evening. Bottom round of beef can also be used.

PREPARATION TIME: *30 min*
COOKING TIME: *3 hours*
INGREDIENTS:
2 pounds top round of beef, cut into 2 in cubes
6 tablespoons unsalted butter
1 tablespoon olive oil
1 onion
1 tablespoon flour
3 tablespoons brandy
2 cloves garlic
Bouquet garni (page 183)
Salt★ and black pepper
1 bottle red wine
6 ounces slab bacon
20 pearl onions
6 ounces mushrooms
Finely chopped parsley

Melt the butter in a large, flame-proof casserole dish, add the oil and then the meat. Cook over high heat until the meat is browned, then add the sliced onion. Cook until transparent, sprinkle over the flour and continue cooking for a few minutes. Pour over the warmed brandy and set it alight.

When the flames have died down, add the crushed garlic, the bouquet garni, salt and plenty of pepper. Pour over enough wine to cover the meat. Bring to simmering point, cover the casserole with a lid and cook in the center of a pre-heated oven, at 300°F (160°C, mark 2), for 2 hours. The casserole can be cooked ahead of time to this stage, left to cool, and the fat skimmed off.

Meanwhile, fry the diced bacon until crisp, add the pearl onions and cook until golden. Stir the contents of the pan into the casserole and continue cooking for a further 30 minutes. Add the sliced mushrooms and cook for another 15 minutes.

Remove the bouquet garni, sprinkle the casserole generously with parsley and serve straight from the pan. Plain boiled potatoes are all that are necessary with it.

SPICED BRISKET OF BEEF

This Irish dish is part of the traditional cold Christmas buffet. It also makes a perfect dish for summer, ideal for a buffet or a large dinner party. The beef should be left to steep in spices for 8 days before being cooked and pressed.

PREPARATION TIME: *20 min*
COOKING TIME: *4–5 hours*
INGREDIENTS *(for 8–10)*:
4 pounds lean boned brisket of beef
2 cups kitchen salt
2 shallots
3 bay leaves
1 teaspoon potassium nitrate (saltpeter)
1 teaspoon allspice
4 heaping tablespoons brown sugar
1 teaspoon powdered cloves
1 teaspoon powdered mace
½ teaspoon crushed black peppercorns
½ teaspoon chopped thyme

Wipe the boned, but not rolled, meat with a clean damp cloth and put it in a large bowl. Rub the meat well on all sides with 1½ cups of the salt. Cover the bowl with cheesecloth and leave for 24

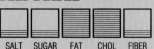
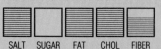

the meat sticking. Instead of frying the onions, add them directly to the pan, followed by the mushrooms. (Calories lost: up to 1000.)

Potato starch and cornstarch, both **gluten-free**, can be used for thickening the stew. If you are using potato starch you will probably need only half a tablespoon.

Pressure cooker: ☑
Slow cooker: ☑
Freezing: ☑ up to 2 months.
Microwave: ☑

SPICED BRISKET OF BEEF

SALT SUGAR FAT CHOL FIBER

GLUTEN-FREE
TOTAL CALORIES: ABOUT 6640

The **salt** and **sugar** content of this dish cannot really be reduced: both are necessary parts of the curing mixture. As it stands, the **fat** and **cholesterol** content is also high, since brisket is naturally about 20% fat (including all its visible fat). A dish with moderate levels of both can be achieved if lean bottom round, which has less fat than brisket, is used. Trim the roast of all visible fat before cooking: there will be enough unseen fat left within the meat to keep it moist. (Calories lost: up to 900.)

Pressure cooker: ☑

hours in the lower part of the refrigerator or in a cool place.

Peel and finely chop the shallots and the bay leaves. Put these in a bowl with the remainder of the salt and the rest of the ingredients and mix together. Each day, rub this mixture well into the salted meat, pouring off any liquid that may have formed. All the spicing mixture should have been absorbed after 7 days.

Roll the spiced meat neatly and tie it securely with fine string. Put it in a heavy-based pan and cover with warm water. Simmer, covered, over low heat for 4–5 hours or until tender when stuck

with a fork. Let the meat cool in the liquid, then lift it out. Place it between two plates with a heavy weight on top and leave it to press for 8 hours.

Serve the spiced brisket cold, sliced and accompanied by baked potatoes, a selection of salads and pickled beet and gherkins.

Beef

CHATEAUBRIAND

This famous dish is named after the 18th-century French writer, Chateaubriand. It cannot be served for less than two persons, as it is a double steak cut from the thick end of the beef fillet.

PREPARATION TIME: *5 min*
COOKING TIME: *8–10 min*
INGREDIENTS *(for 2)*:
12–14 ounce chateaubriand
1 tablespoon melted butter
Salt★ and black pepper
GARNISH:
Watercress
Maître d'hôtel butter (page 182)

Trim the steak and if necessary flatten it slightly. It should be 1½–2 in thick. Brush one side with melted butter and season with freshly ground pepper. Do not add salt as this will extract the juices.

Put the steak, buttered and seasoned side up, under a hot broiler and cook close to the heat to brown the surface and seal in the juices. Turn the steak over, brush with the remaining melted butter and season with pepper. Move further away from the heat and broil the steak for a further 4–5 minutes, turning it once only. The steak should be cooked through, but remain rosy-pink inside.

Lift the steak on to a board and carve it, at a slight angle, into six even slices. Remove the sliced steak, in one movement, on to a warm serving dish and garnish with sprigs of watercress and slices of maître d'hôtel butter.

Traditionally, a chateaubriand is served with a sauce Béarnaise (page 156) and with château potatoes (peeled potatoes shaped into small ovals, coated with melted butter and cooked, covered, for 30–35 minutes, shaking occasionally). A tossed green salad makes an excellent side dish.

BEEF WITH GREEN PEAS

Top round of beef is rather tough and is usually stewed or braised. It can, however, be made into a succulent dish by pot-roasting it slowly in a casserole with a tightly fitting lid.

PREPARATION TIME: *10 min*
COOKING TIME: *2–2½ hours*
INGREDIENTS *(for 6)*:
2½–3 pounds lean top round of beef
Salt★ and black pepper
¼ cup unsalted butter
1½ pounds fresh green peas

Wipe the meat with a damp cloth and season with freshly ground pepper. Melt the butter in a heavy-based frying pan over high heat and brown the beef in it on all sides to seal in the juices.

Put the meat in an ovenproof casserole into which it will fit fairly closely. Shell the peas and put them around the sides of the beef, and pour the butter from the pan over the meat. Cover the casserole with a lid and cook in the center of a pre-heated oven at 325°F (170°C, mark 3) for 2 hours. At this stage the meat will be rare; allow another 30 minutes for well-done meat.

Lift out the beef, carve into thin slices and arrange them on a warmed serving dish, surrounded by the peas. Boiled new potatoes sprinkled generously with chopped mint or parsley are ideal for this dish.

BOEUF À LA MODE EN GELÉE

Most classic recipes for cold jellied beef use the expensive fillet, but top round, poached slowly until very tender, makes an excellent alternative. The dish, ideal for buffet entertaining, should be prepared a day in advance.

PREPARATION TIME: *30 min*
COOKING TIME: *4½–5 hours*
INGREDIENTS *(for 6–8)*:
3 pounds top round or rump of beef
¼ pound pork fatback
1 calf's foot
1¼ cups dry red wine
2 cloves garlic
Salt★ and black pepper
1–2 tablespoons beef drippings
2 tablespoons brandy
2 shallots
2 bay leaves
1¼ cups beef stock or water
15 pearl onions
10 young carrots

Ask your meat man to lard the beef with the pork fatback. Also have the calf's foot chopped into pieces. If the meat is not larded, cut the pork fat into strips, narrow enough to go through the eye of a larding needle, and long enough to be threaded through the meat. Pull the fat strips through the meat and trim them off at each end.

Put the meat in a deep bowl, pour over the wine and marinate for about 4 hours, turning the meat frequently.

Peel the garlic, cut it into small strips and push them into the meat with the point of a knife. Season with salt and pepper.

Bring a large pan of salted

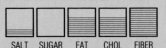

BOEUF À LA MODE EN GELÉE

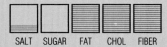

| SALT | SUGAR | FAT | CHOL | FIBER |

GLUTEN-FREE   WHOLEFOOD
TOTAL CALORIES: ABOUT 5740

The **fat** and **cholesterol** levels of this recipe can be reduced to low simply by choosing a very lean piece of meat and omitting the larding with pork fat. The meat can also be browned in a heavy pan lightly brushed with oil, using less fat than the beef drippings specified. Be careful to skim all possible fat from the chilled cooked meat and jelly. (Calories lost: up to 1000.)

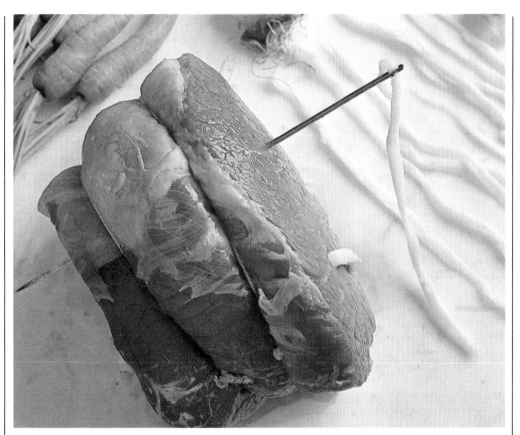

water to the boil and blanch the calf's foot pieces for 10 minutes. Drain and set aside.

Melt half the drippings in a heavy deep pan or flameproof casserole over high heat, and brown the meat all over to seal in the juices. Reduce the heat. Pour the brandy over the meat, let it warm through slightly, then set it alight. When the flames have died down, add the calf's foot pieces.

Peel and finely chop the shallots and add them, with the bay leaves, to the pan. Heat the stock or water in a separate pan, blend in the wine and pour it over the meat. Bring to boiling point and

cover the pan tightly with foil and the lid. Cook in the center of a preheated oven, at 300°F (160°C, mark 2), for 3 hours.

Meanwhile, peel the onions, leaving them whole. Wash and scrape the carrots and split them in half lengthwise. Heat the remaining drippings in a small pan and lightly brown the vegetables. Add them to the meat after 3 hours' cooking and simmer for a further 1–1½ hours.

Lift the meat on to a dish and remove the vegetables with a slotted spoon. Let the liquid cool, then strain it through cheesecloth into a bowl. Leave the liquid

in the refrigerator overnight to set to a jelly.

The next day, carefully scrape the surface fat from the jelly with a spoon dipped in hot water. Cut the meat into neat thin slices and arrange them in a deep serving dish together with the carrots and onions. Melt the jelly in a saucepan over low heat, then pour it carefully over the meat and vegetables. Leave the dish in a cool place to allow the jelly to re-set.

Serve the jellied beef with a selection of salads, such as a crisp green salad tossed in a French dressing (page 157), a tomato salad and a cold potato salad.

Veal

OSSO BUCO

Italy is the homeland of this appetizing, inexpensive stew of veal with marrow. The traditional Milanese garnish – known as *gremolata* – adds a colorful look to the finished dish.

PREPARATION TIME: *30 min*
COOKING TIME: *1¾–2 hours*
INGREDIENTS *(for 6)*:
2½ pounds veal shank
Seasoned flour (page 184)
3 carrots
2 stalks celery
1 onion
2 cloves garlic
¼ cup butter
1 cup dry white wine
1 cup chicken or veal stock
16-ounce can of tomatoes
Salt* and black pepper
Sugar
1 sprig fresh or ½ teaspoon dried rosemary

GARNISH:
¼ cup finely chopped parsley
Finely grated rind of 2 large lemons
2–3 cloves finely chopped garlic

Ask the butcher to saw the veal into pieces, about 1½ in thick. Wash and dry the meat and remove any chips of bone. Coat the veal pieces with seasoned flour. Clean the vegetables and chop them finely.

Melt the butter in a heavy-based pan, large enough to take all the meat in one layer. Brown the meat and the vegetables. When the meat has taken color, stand each piece upright to prevent the marrow falling out during cooking. Pour over the wine and stock and add the tomatoes with their juice. Season to taste with salt, freshly ground pepper and sugar. Then add the rosemary. Simmer, covered, over low heat for 1½

hours, or until the meat is tender.

While the veal is cooking, mix together the ingredients for the garnish.

Pour the sauce over the meat and sprinkle with the garnish. The marrow is usually left in the bones, but it can also be extracted and spread on toast. In Italy, osso buco is traditionally served with a saffron-flavored risotto (risotto alla milanese), but plain boiled rice also makes an appropriate accompaniment.

VITELLO TONNATO

In Italy, this cold terrine of veal in tuna fish sauce is a stand-by for hot summer days. The classic version uses boiled veal, but in some regions the meat is roasted instead. It should be made the day before and left to chill overnight.

PREPARATION TIME: *30 min*
COOKING TIME: *1¾ hours*
INGREDIENTS *(for 6)*:
2½ pounds leg or loin of veal
1 carrot
1 onion
1 stalk celery
4 peppercorns
1 teaspoon salt*
3½-ounce can tuna fish
4 anchovy fillets
½ cup olive oil
2 egg yolks
Black pepper
1½ tablespoons lemon juice
GARNISH:
Capers
Gherkins
Fresh tarragon (if available)

Ask the butcher to bone the meat, tie it in a neat roll and give you the bones.

Scrape and wash the carrot and peel the onion; quarter both.

OSSO BUCO

SALT SUGAR FAT CHOL FIBER

GLUTEN-FREE* WHOLEFOOD*
TOTAL CALORIES: ABOUT 3710

The low **salt** level assumes that there is no added salt in the tomatoes or the stock. Veal is a little higher in sodium than some meat, but the total level can still be under 200 mg per portion in this dish.
To reduce the **fat** and **cholesterol** content to low, brown the meat in a heavy pan brushed lightly with oil; omit the butter. (Calories lost: up to 450.)

Pressure cooker: ☑
Slow cooker: ☑
Freezing: ☑ up to 4 months.

VITELLO TONNATO

SALT SUGAR FAT CHOL FIBER

GLUTEN-FREE WHOLEFOOD
TOTAL CALORIES: ABOUT 4585

The high **salt** content comes partly from the tuna, partly from the anchovies. Both can be rinsed in a sieve under running water to remove some of the salt, but will still remain permeated with it. You could use only half the amount of each, which will reduce the salt level to moderate, but it will take away some of the character of the dish.
The high level of **fat** is largely due to the oil. Again, it is characteristic of the dish, but you could reduce the oil to only 2 teaspoons (just enough to keep a little of the olive oil

flavor – use a strong virgin oil if you can) mashed with the fish, and complete the sauce using about ½ cup of low-fat sour cream, fromage blanc or thick plain yogurt. If you choose tuna canned in brine rather than oil the total fat content will then be low. (Calories lost: up to 1300.) To reduce the **cholesterol** level to low, use one whole egg instead of the two yolks. (Calories lost: up to 90.)

Pressure cooker: ☑ for the veal (not the tuna sauce).

Slow cooker: ☑ for the veal (not the tuna sauce).

VEAL SCALLOPS WITH GINGER WINE

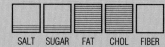

SALT	SUGAR	FAT	CHOL	FIBER

GLUTEN-FREE*   WHOLEFOOD*
TOTAL CALORIES: ABOUT 1300

Veal is naturally very low in **fat** provided any visible fat is trimmed off. To minimize added fat and **cholesterol**, cook the scallops in a non-stick pan lightly brushed with olive oil and omit the butter. Replace the heavy cream with 3 tablespoons of low-fat small curd cottage cheese or low-fat plain yogurt, but do not add until just about to serve and only heat gently; if it boils it will curdle.
With these changes, the fat and cholesterol content will be low. (Calories lost: up to 560.)

Scrub and chop the celery. Put the meat into a large saucepan together with the bones. Add the vegetables, peppercorns, salt and enough water to cover the meat. Bring the water quickly to the boil, turn down the heat, cover the pan with a lid and simmer for about 1¾ hours, or until the meat is tender. Lift the meat carefully out of the pan and set aside to cool. Reduce the cooking liquid by fast boiling, strain through cheesecloth and set aside.

To make the sauce, drain the tuna and anchovy and put in a bowl with 1 tablespoon of the oil. Mash with a fork until thoroughly mixed. Blend in the egg yolks and season with pepper. Rub this paste through a sieve into a small bowl. Stir in half the lemon juice, then add the remaining oil, little by little, beating well after each addition. When the sauce has become thick and shiny, add more lemon juice to taste. Stir in about 2 tablespoons of the veal liquid to give the sauce the consistency of thin cream.

Cut the cold meat into thin slices and arrange them in a terrine. Cover the meat completely with the sauce, then wrap the dish closely in foil and leave overnight to marinate.

Before serving, garnish the dish with capers, a few sliced gherkins or with a sprig of tarragon. A cold rice salad or a tossed green salad could complement the meat.

VEAL SCALLOPS WITH GINGER WINE

These thin cuts from the veal leg are usually served with a creamy sauce. This is frequently made from white wine or Marsala – the ginger wine in this recipe adds an unusual, slightly spicy flavor.

PREPARATION TIME: *10 min*
COOKING TIME: *15 min*
INGREDIENTS *(for 4):*
4 veal scallops, each ¼ in thick and
    weighing about 3 ounces
Seasoned flour (page 184)
¼ cup unsalted butter
1 teaspoon olive oil
6 tablespoons ginger wine
2 teaspoons lemon juice
3 tablespoons heavy cream
Salt* and black pepper
GARNISH:
4 lemon twists (page 179)
1 tablespoon chopped parsley

Cut off any fat from the scallops and trim them into neat shapes. Dust them lightly with the seasoned flour. Heat the butter and oil in a heavy-based pan over moderate heat and fry the veal for 5–6 minutes, until golden brown on both sides. Lift the slices on to a serving dish and keep them warm while you are making the ginger wine sauce.

Add the ginger wine to the pan and bring it gently to the boil, scraping up the pan juices with a rubber spatula. Reduce the heat and simmer slowly for 5 minutes, or until the wine is syrupy. Stir in the lemon juice and the cream, and simmer for a further 2–3 minutes, or until the sauce has a pale coffee color. Season to taste with salt and freshly ground pepper. Pour the sauce over the meat and garnish each scallop with a lemon twist sprinkled with chopped parsley.

Serve the scallops with plain boiled potatoes and green beans. A plain green salad would also go well with them.

Veal

VEAL ROLLS WITH FRITTATA FILLING

A frittata is an Italian cross between an omelette and a crêpe. It is a traditional filling for rolled veal and is first fried like thin crêpes and then spread over the meat. The frittatas can also be served as a garnish with veal scallops.

PREPARATION TIME: *30 min*
COOKING TIME: *1½ hours*
INGREDIENTS *(for 4):*

8 veal scallops, about 3 ounces
    each
2 eggs
½ cup chopped mortadella sausage
    or lean ham
1 heaping tablespoon chopped
    fresh parsley
1½–2 tablespoons grated
    Parmesan cheese
6 tablespoons butter
4–6 ounces button mushrooms
1 onion
1–1½ tablespoons flour
½ cup milk
½–1 cup veal or chicken stock
Salt* and black pepper
Lemon juice
Dried mixed herbs

Beat the scallops thin between sheets of wax paper. Trim them neatly and set aside. Beat the eggs lightly and stir in the chopped sausage, the parsley and grated cheese.

Melt a little butter in a small omelette pan and, when hot, spoon in enough of the egg mixture to cover the bottom of the pan thinly. Cook the frittata until golden brown, then turn it and cook the other side. Cook the remaining mixture, to make eight frittatas in all.

Cover each scallop with a frittata, trimming these to the shape of the meat. Roll up each scallop and tie at intervals with fine string.

Trim the mushrooms and cut them in half if large. Peel the onion and slice it thinly. Melt the remaining butter in a heavy-based pan and fry the veal rolls over high heat until golden brown. Lift the rolls from the pan. Fry the mushrooms and onion in the remaining butter in the pan until soft, then draw the pan off the heat. Blend in enough flour to absorb all the fat, and gradually stir in the milk and ½ cup of stock. Lower the heat and bring the sauce to simmering point, stirring continuously. Cook for about 5 minutes, then season with salt, pepper, lemon juice and dried herbs.

Add the veal rolls to the sauce, thinning it with a little more stock if necessary – the sauce should cover the rolls completely. Put a lid on the pan and simmer over low heat for about 1 hour or until the meat is tender.

Lift out the veal rolls, remove the string, and arrange them on a hot serving dish. Spoon a little of the sauce over the meat and serve the remainder in a sauce boat. Creamed potatoes and buttered broccoli or beans would be good vegetable dishes.

TERRINE DE CAMPAGNE

The French word "terrine" originally meant an earthenware dish, but by extension it now also refers to the contents of the dish, whether fish, meat or poultry. This farmhouse-style terrine of calf liver and veal is a good choice for a picnic, lunch or supper. It should, like all other terrines, be served cold.

PREPARATION TIME: *20 min*
COOKING TIME: *2 hours*
INGREDIENTS *(for 6–8):*

¾ pound thin slices bacon
¾ pound calf liver
1½ pounds ground veal
1 large onion
2 cloves garlic
1 heaping tablespoon tomato paste
¼ teaspoon summer savory or sage
¼ teaspoon oregano
½ cup butter
½ cup dry red wine
Salt* and black pepper
4 bay leaves

Stretch the bacon slices with the flat blade of a knife. Line a 1-quart terrine or soufflé dish with the bacon, allowing the slices to hang over the edges.

Clean the liver, removing any gristle, and put the meat through the coarse disk of a grinder. Peel the onion and chop it finely. Mix together the liver, onion and veal in a large bowl. Peel the garlic and crush it over the meat mixture. Stir in the tomato paste, savory and oregano. Melt the butter and stir into the terrine mixture together with enough wine to give a moist but not wet consistency. Season to taste with salt and freshly ground pepper.

Spoon the mixture into the dish, over the bacon slices.

VEAL ROLLS WITH FRITTATA FILLING

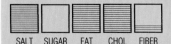

SALT   SUGAR   FAT   CHOL   FIBER

GLUTEN-FREE*   WHOLEFOOD*
TOTAL CALORIES: ABOUT 2215

The high **salt** is a result of the combination of natural sodium from veal, the high salt level of cured meats like ham and mortadella, and the cheese. The best way of cutting down in this recipe is simply to use a little less of each of these three ingredients, as the portions are very generous. If you use only half quantities, and assuming there is no salt in the stock, the salt level will be moderate.

To reduce **fat** and **cholesterol** to moderate, choose lean ham instead of mortadella; cook the frittata in a pan lightly brushed with oil, rather than in butter; use the same method for cooking the veal rolls, mushrooms and onions; and use skim milk in the sauce. (Calories lost: up to 920.)

Freezing: ✓ up to 2 months.

102

TERRINE DE CAMPAGNE

SALT   SUGAR   FAT   CHOL   FIBER

GLUTEN-FREE   WHOLEFOOD
TOTAL CALORIES: ABOUT 4170

To avoid the high **salt** content of the large amount of bacon, line the terrine dish with a double thickness of spinach leaves, previously dipped in simmering water for 30 seconds to soften them. If you also use unsalted tomato paste the overall salt level will be low. Leaving out the bacon will help to lower the **fat** level. You can also omit the butter, and although the resulting terrine will be far less rich, it will taste fresher. Make sure the terrine is very well sealed while cooking to prevent it drying out. (Calories lost: up to 2125.) These measures will reduce the fat level to low, but the **cholesterol** will still be high, since liver, like other organ meats, is very rich in cholesterol. Its other nutrients, such as iron, B vitamins and zinc, make it worth eating regularly, but not every day, especially if you are worried about the build-up of antibiotics and hormones, which do accumulate in the liver.

Food processor: ☑ for grinding the meat.

Freezing: ☑ up to 1 month.

Microwave: ☑

Arrange the bay leaves on top and fold over the bacon slices. Cover the dish with a lid or tight-fitting foil. Cook the terrine for 2 hours on the middle shelf of an oven pre-heated to 350°F (180°C, mark 4).

When cooked, remove the lid from the dish, cover with fresh foil and a flat board which will fit neatly inside the terrine. Place a heavy weight on the board and leave overnight.

Serve straight from the terrine or turn out on to a serving dish and cut into wedges. Crusty bread and a tossed green salad make this terrine a substantial main course for lunch, or serve in smaller portions as a first course.

Veal

VEAL SCALOPPINE

Italian scaloppine are similar to French escalopes, but they are cut against the grain of the meat. Ask the butcher to beat the scaloppine flat and thin.

PREPARATION TIME: *15 min*
COOKING TIME: *30 min*
INGREDIENTS *(for 4):*
4 veal scallops
Seasoned flour (page 184)
¾ cup unsalted butter
1 tablespoon olive oil
½ pound button mushrooms
½ cup Marsala or cream sherry
1¼ cups chicken stock

Trim any fat and gristle from the scallops and coat them thoroughly with seasoned flour. Heat ¼ cup of the butter and the oil in a heavy-based pan and fry the meat over low heat for 3–4 minutes on each side, turning once. Lift the meat from the pan and keep it hot.

Pour all but one tablespoon of the hot fat from the pan. Trim and slice the mushrooms and add to the pan; cook over low heat, tossing the mushrooms until coated in the butter, then stir in the wine and stock. Bring this sauce to the boil and return the scallops to the pan. Cover with a lid, lower the heat and simmer gently for 15–20 minutes. Turn the meat once or twice so that it cooks evenly. Arrange the scallops and mushrooms on a serving dish and keep it hot. Boil the sauce rapidly until it has reduced by about one-third and has thickened slightly. Whisk in the remaining butter, remove the pan from the heat and pour the sauce over the veal.

Boiled rice or buttered pasta, and green beans or broccoli can be served with the scaloppine.

VEAL WITH TOMATOES

Shoulder of veal, used in this recipe, is cut from the top of the fore leg and boned. It is best cooked in a casserole.

PREPARATION TIME: *20 min*
COOKING TIME: *1½–2 hours*
INGREDIENTS *(for 6):*
2½-pound boned shoulder of veal
Salt*
¼ cup unsalted butter
1½ pounds tomatoes
2 onions
6–8 black peppercorns
Sprig tarragon (fresh or dried)

Wipe the meat with a damp cloth and tie it neatly with string to keep its shape during cooking. Season lightly with salt. Melt half the butter in a flameproof casserole over moderate heat, and brown the meat on all sides to seal in the juices.

Skin and roughly chop the tomatoes. Peel and finely chop the onions. Melt the remaining butter in a pan and fry the tomatoes and onions over moderate heat for 3–4 minutes. Grind the pepper into the tomato mixture, add the tarragon and pour it all over the meat in the casserole. Cover with a lid or foil and bake in the center of a pre-heated oven at 300°F (160°C, mark 2) for 1½–2 hours.

Remove the string and serve the veal hot, cut into thick slices, with the tomato sauce spooned over. Plain boiled potatoes and a green vegetable would make this a substantial meal.

VEAL WITH ORANGE

This veal roast is prepared with a fruity stuffing and sauce which add extra flavor to the meat.

PREPARATION TIME: *20 min*
COOKING TIME: *2½ hours*
INGREDIENTS *(for 6):*
4–5 pound breast of veal, boned
2 cups soft breadcrumbs
⅓ cup raisins
⅓ cup currants
¼ cup shredded beef suet
Salt* and black pepper
Nutmeg
2 large oranges
1 large egg yolk (or 2 small ones)
¼ cup lard
¼ cup cornstarch
Sugar
6 tablespoons red wine

Prepare the stuffing first by mixing the breadcrumbs, raisins, currants, suet and a pinch of salt, pepper and nutmeg together in a bowl. Finely grate the rind from the oranges and add to the stuffing, together with the lightly beaten egg yolk. Stir in enough cold water to bind the mixture.

Spread the stuffing over the boned veal, roll it up and tie with thin string at 1 in intervals. Put the meat in a roasting pan, add the lard and roast the meat for 2½ hours in the center of an oven, pre-heated to 400°F (200°C, mark 6). Baste occasionally and cover the meat with foil if it browns too quickly.

Put the meat on a serving dish and keep it hot in the oven. Skim all the fat from the juices in the roasting pan and heat them in a small saucepan. Blend the cornstarch with 1 tablespoon of cold water and add to the juices, stirring continuously until the

VEAL SCALOPPINE

SALT SUGAR FAT CHOL FIBER

GLUTEN-FREE*   WHOLEFOOD*
TOTAL CALORIES: ABOUT 2370

The very high **fat** content is mainly due to the thickening method used for the sauce. If instead of butter you use low-fat imitation sour cream, fromage blanc or thick low-fat plain yogurt, and if the veal is cooked in only 1 tablespoon olive oil, this recipe becomes low fat and low **cholesterol**, since veal is basically lean. (Calories lost: up to 800.)

Alternatively, omit the butter for thickening the sauce. Use less liquid – about 1 cup of Marsala and stock mixed. (This will also reduce the **sugar** level to low.) There is no need to simmer the veal for more than 5 minutes. (Calories lost: up to 100.)

Pasta, buttered or otherwise, is not an Italian accompaniment to meat. Serve the veal with a few plainly boiled potatoes and a side salad of lightly cooked spinach, well drained and allowed to cool, dressed with a good squeeze of lemon juice and (if your diet permits) a generous trickle of good olive oil.

VEAL WITH TOMATOES

SALT SUGAR FAT CHOL FIBER

GLUTEN-FREE   WHOLEFOOD
TOTAL CALORIES: ABOUT 3000

This is a very easy recipe to adapt. For low **fat** and **cholesterol**, simply brown the meat in a heavy pan brushed lightly with oil and omit the butter. Be sure to trim any visible fat from the veal, although it is generally low in fat. (Calories lost: up to 450.)

Pressure cooker: ☑

Freezing: ☑ up to 4 months.

VEAL WITH ORANGE

SALT SUGAR FAT CHOL FIBER

GLUTEN-FREE* WHOLEFOOD*
TOTAL CALORIES: ABOUT 7290

The high **salt** level is due not to any particularly salty ingredients, although bread has a substantial salt content; here, the intake is raised simply by the very generous amounts of meat per portion. A smaller helping, say not more than 5 ounces meat per person, and the use of unsalted bread, will give a moderate salt level.
The low **sugar** level assumes that only a teaspoon or two of sugar is added to the sauce.
As veal is basically lean, the **fat** and **cholesterol** content of this dish will be low if the suet is omitted from the stuffing and the meat roasted without adding fat. To avoid dryness, cover the roasting dish tightly throughout, removing the cover only 20 minutes before the end of cooking to allow the meat to brown. Again, a smaller portion will produce a drop in fat intake without being ungenerous. (Calories lost: up to 1040.)
Suet and lard are both disliked by **wholefood** lovers for their high saturated fat content; omitting them will make this dish wholefood.

Pressure cooker: ☑

Freezing: ☑ up to 4 months.

sauce has thickened. Bring to the boil and season to taste with salt, freshly ground pepper, sugar and nutmeg. Stir in the wine and simmer the sauce gently. Remove the pith from the oranges and cut the flesh into small sections. Add these to the sauce and heat it through.

Cut the veal into thick slices and arrange them on a warmed serving dish; offer the sauce separately. An orange and endive salad, sauté potatoes and pearl onions would go well with this roast.

Veal

SCALOPPINE WITH ARTICHOKES AND LEMON SAUCE

For this easily prepared dish, choose small veal scallops (*scaloppine*), ¼ in thick. Veal chops may be used instead but will require longer cooking. Be sure to buy *fonds* (bottoms) of artichokes, not the hearts.

PREPARATION TIME: *15 min*
COOKING TIME: *25 min*
INGREDIENTS (*for 4*):
8 veal scallops, each about 2–3 ounces
Seasoned flour (page 184)
¼ cup butter
1 tablespoon finely chopped shallot or onion
14-ounce jar or can artichoke bottoms
½ cup dry white wine
1¼ cups chicken stock
2 small lemons
½ cup heavy cream
Salt★ and black pepper

Trim any fat from the scallops and coat them in seasoned flour. Heat the butter in a heavy-based pan over medium heat and fry the scallops for a few minutes, until golden brown, turning once. Add the shallots and artichoke bottoms, and pour over the wine. Bring the mixture to simmering point, and reduce the heat. Add sufficient stock to cover the veal completely. Grate the rind from the lemons and set aside, and add the squeezed lemon juice to the sauce. Cover the pan with a lid and cook over low heat for 20 minutes or until the veal is tender.

Stir in the cream and simmer the sauce for 5–6 minutes more, uncovered, until the sauce has a creamy texture. Adjust seasoning with salt and freshly ground pepper.

Arrange the scallops in the center of a warmed serving dish and surround with a border of buttered noodles or fluffy rice. Pour the sauce over the meat and top with a scattering of grated lemon rind.

VEAL CHOPS MAGYAR

Paprika is the most usual spicing in Hungarian dishes. It varies considerably in strength according to its origin, and the sauce should be tasted after being cooked for a while.

PREPARATION TIME: *20 min*
COOKING TIME: *1¼ hours*
INGREDIENTS (*for 4*):
4 large veal chops
Seasoned flour (page 184)
½ pound mushrooms
1 onion
2 tablespoons butter
1 tablespoon oil
2 tablespoons flour
1¼ cups milk
1¼ cups veal or chicken stock
Salt★
Juice of a small lemon
¼ cup tomato paste
3–4 teaspoons paprika
2 teaspoons sugar
½ cup light cream
GARNISH:
Rice
6–8 mushroom caps
Paprika
1 tablespoon chopped parsley

Trim the fat off the chops and coat them with seasoned flour. Trim the mushrooms and, if large, cut them into quarters or halves. Peel and thinly slice the onion. Heat the butter and oil in a flameproof casserole, pat the loose flour off the chops and fry them over high heat until golden brown, turning

The low **salt** level will depend on the canned artichoke bottoms not having had salt added. If they have, the salt content is likely to be medium. To restrict the **fat** and **cholesterol** count to the low level naturally present in lean veal, broil the scallops on a baking sheet brushed with oil and omit the butter; then enrich the sauce by stirring in ½ cup low-fat imitation sour cream, fromage blanc or thick low-fat yogurt in place of the cream. However, do not do this until after you have reduced the sauce, as it should only warm through and not boil once a cultured milk product has been added or it will curdle.
As an alternative to using a milk product, thicken the mixture by puréeing a few of the artichoke bottoms with a little of the stock and then stirring this back into the main pan. (Calories lost: up to 1000.)

To restrict **fat** and **cholesterol** to the low level present in veal which has been carefully trimmed of visible fat, brush the chops with oil very lightly before dipping in flour and broil on a lightly oiled baking sheet

instead of frying; this avoids using butter. Cook the mushrooms and onions in a lightly greased heavy pan and use skim milk in the sauce. Replace the cream with low-fat small curd cottage cheese or plain yogurt, adding this only at the end of cooking (see notes on the previous recipe). (Calories lost: up to 550.)
A **gluten-free** flour such as brown rice flour, potato starch or split pea flour can be used in the sauce.

BAKED STUFFED SHOULDER OF VEAL

SALT	SUGAR	FAT	CHOL	FIBER

GLUTEN-FREE   WHOLEFOOD*
TOTAL CALORIES: ABOUT 4290

The high **salt** comes mainly from the bacon; omitting this will give the dish a low salt level provided the stock is unsalted and the butter is either unsalted or omitted.
Leaving out the bacon will also substantially reduce the **fat** content, which can be limited to low by omitting the butter used to brown the veal before roasting and using only half the amount of walnuts. This will also give low **cholesterol**, providing portions are not more than about 5 ounces. (Calories lost: up to 850.)
Use brown rice to make this **wholefood:** it will need to cook for 20–25 minutes, even though it will continue to cook with the roast.

Pressure cooker: ☑ both for the stock and, later, for the meat.
Freezing: ☑ up to 2 months.

once. Remove the chops from the pan and fry the mushrooms and onion for a few minutes, until they are soft.

Remove the casserole from the heat and stir in sufficient flour to absorb the fat. Gradually blend in the milk and then the stock, stirring continuously. Bring to simmering point and cook for 3 minutes until the sauce has thickened. Season to taste with salt and lemon juice. Mix the tomato paste, paprika, sugar and cream together in a small bowl. Blend in 2 or 3 tablespoons of the hot sauce and pour the mixture back into the sauce, stirring thoroughly.

Return the veal chops to the casserole. They should be completely covered by the sauce, so add a little more stock if necessary. Cover the casserole with a lid and cook over low heat for 45 minutes or until the veal is tender, stirring from time to time to prevent sticking. Do not allow to reach boiling point or the sauce will separate.

Adjust seasoning and arrange the chops in the center of a serving dish with the sauce spooned over them. Surround with a border of fluffy rice, garnished with the whole mushroom caps fried in a little butter. Set the mushrooms, dark side uppermost, on the rice and dust the center of each with paprika. Sprinkle chopped parsley between the mushrooms.

BAKED STUFFED SHOULDER OF VEAL

This is one of the less expensive cuts of veal. It is braised rather than roasted, to preserve the juices. Make the stock the day before if possible, since it takes 3–4 hours to cook.

PREPARATION TIME: *35 min*
COOKING TIME: *1¾ hours*
INGREDIENTS *(for 6):*

3-pound boned shoulder of veal	*½ cup long grain rice*
3 tablespoons butter	*Pinch saffron*
½ cup dry white wine	*¼ pound bacon*
½–1 cup stock	*1 bunch watercress*
STOCK:	*½ cup walnut meats*
1 large onion	*1 lemon*
2 carrots	*Salt★ and freshly ground black*
1 stalk celery	*pepper*
Bouquet garni (page 183)	*1 egg*
STUFFING:	GARNISH:
2 cups stock	*Watercress*

Ask the butcher to bone the shoulder of veal and to give you the chopped bones. Put the bones, together with the cleaned and chopped stock vegetables, in a saucepan and cover with cold water. Add the bouquet garni and a good seasoning of salt and black pepper. Cook this stock for about 3 hours, strain and set aside.

With a sharp knife, open the cavities in the meat to make pockets for the stuffing. Cook the rice, with the saffron, in 2 cups of the reserved stock for 12–14 minutes or until tender.

Meanwhile, wash and chop the watercress, chop the walnuts finely and grate the rind from the lemon. Fry the bacon, over low heat, until crisp. Remove the bacon from the pan, drain and crumble it.

Put the drained rice in a mixing bowl, and add the bacon fat from the pan, the bacon, watercress, walnuts and lemon rind. Season to taste. Bind the stuffing with the lightly beaten egg.

Spread the stuffing evenly into the pockets of the veal, roll up the roast and tie with string.

Brown the veal briskly in the butter in a roasting pan. Pour over the wine and roast the veal in the center of a pre-heated oven at 350°F (180°C, mark 4) for about 1½ hours. Baste frequently with the wine, adding a little stock if necessary.

Put the roast on a warm serving dish and remove the string. Add ½ cup of stock to the roasting pan. Boil over high heat until the liquid is light brown and has reduced by about half. Pour the gravy into a warm sauce boat.

Serve the sliced veal garnished with sprigs of watercress. Baked potatoes go well with the meat; so do zucchini, plain or au gratin.

Veal

VEAL STUFFED WITH KIDNEYS

This makes an excellent and substantial main course dish for a formal picnic party.

PREPARATION TIME: *25 min*
COOKING TIME: *3 hours*
INGREDIENTS *(for 8–10):*
5-pound loin of veal
½ pound veal kidneys
Salt and black pepper*
2 cloves garlic
2–3 sprigs marjoram or thyme
1 small onion
2 carrots
½ cup dry white wine
GARNISH:
Watercress

Ask the butcher to bone the loin and to give you the bone. Trim the fat off the kidneys and remove the outer skin; snip out the cores with scissors. Lay the boned meat flat on a board and spread the kidneys over the cut side. Season with salt and freshly ground pepper. Peel and finely chop the garlic and herbs; sprinkle them over the kidneys. Carefully roll up the meat and tie it securely with string at 1–2 in intervals.

Rub the outside of the meat thoroughly with salt and pepper, place it in a roasting pan, and surround with the veal bones. Peel and roughly chop the onion; scrape and finely chop the carrots. Arrange the vegetables around the meat. Heat the wine, with ½ cup of water, in a small pan and pour over the meat. Cover the pan with foil or a lid and cook in the center of the oven, preheated to 350°F (180°C, mark 4) for 2¼ hours. Turn the meat over halfway through cooking, and add more liquid if needed. Remove the covering for the last 30 minutes to brown the meat.

Lift the meat from the pan and set it aside to cool. Pour the pan juices, bones and vegetables into a pan and simmer over low heat for 45 minutes. Strain the liquid into a bowl and leave until cool. Let it set in the refrigerator and remove any fat on the top.

Serve the stuffed veal with the cold chopped jelly, romaine lettuce, sliced tomatoes, cucumber in sour cream, and new potatoes dressed in mayonnaise.

VEAL STUFFED WITH KIDNEYS

SALT SUGAR FAT CHOL FIBER

GLUTEN-FREE   WHOLEFOOD
TOTAL CALORIES: ABOUT 4400

The medium **salt** level is due to the generous portions of meat, plus the higher level naturally present in kidneys, so it cannot be reduced except by using only 6 ounces kidneys in the recipe, and serving smaller helpings.

The high **cholesterol** comes from the kidneys. You could replace them with a completely different stuffing, combining the herbs with, for instance, chopped mushrooms or leeks, or with boiled chestnuts. This would provide a dish low in both fat and cholesterol, assuming the veal is lean and all visible fat trimmed off it. (Calories lost: up to 200.)

Pressure cooker: ☑

NOISETTES OF LAMB SHREWSBURY

SALT	SUGAR	FAT	CHOL	FIBER

GLUTEN-FREE*   WHOLEFOOD*
TOTAL CALORIES: ABOUT 4170

The **sugar** content is due to the red currant jelly; to reduce it to very low, use only 1 tablespoon, or substitute jelly made with no added sugar, if you can find it.

The **fat** and **cholesterol** content will vary hugely depending on how lean the lamb is. Fatty lamb can have as much as 30% fat if both lean and fat are eaten; lean cuts can have as little as 9% – not extremely low, but acceptably so. Choose lean lamb and trim off all visible fat. Soften the sauce vegetables in a pan lightly brushed with oil, omitting the butter. Cover tightly, adding a few tablespoons of stock if necessary to prevent sticking. Cook the noisettes by broiling instead of frying, for the same length of time. All these changes will produce low fat and cholesterol levels. (Calories lost: up to 1000.)

Pressure cooker: ☑ for the sauce.
Freezing: ☑ up to 4 months.

NOISETTES OF LAMB SHREWSBURY

These little round medallions, or noisettes, are cut from the loin or rib of lamb. They are excellent as the main course for a dinner party, especially as the time-consuming sauce can be made well in advance.

PREPARATION TIME: *15–25 min*
COOKING TIME: *2 hours for the sauce; 30 min for the noisettes*
INGREDIENTS *(for 4–6):*
8–12 noisettes of lamb
5 tablespoons unsalted butter
1 tablespoon olive oil
SAUCE:
1 small carrot
1 small onion
2 stalks celery
2 slices lean bacon
3 tablespoons butter
Lamb trimmings
2 tablespoons flour
2½ cups brown stock (page 153)
1¼ cups dry white or red wine
2 heaping teaspoons tomato paste
Bouquet garni (page 183)
1 sprig fresh or ½ teaspoon dried rosemary
Salt and black pepper*
2–3 tablespoons red currant jelly

The noisettes, weighing 2–3 ounces each, can be cut from chops from the loin or from the rib; the latter are smaller, but have a more delicate flavor. Most butchers will prepare the noisettes on request, but ask for the trimmings to be included with the order.

Alternatively, cut the piece of meat into single chops, remove the bone from each, and shape the meat into a neat round, about 2 in across. Tie firmly with string.

Prepare the sauce first: scrape the carrot, peel the onion and scrub the celery; dice these vegetables. Cut the bacon into small dice; blanch in boiling water for a few minutes. Melt the butter in a heavy pan over moderate heat. Fry the diced vegetables, chopped lamb trimmings and bacon in this for 10 minutes. Remove the pan from the heat and stir in the flour; return the pan to a low heat and cook for a further 10 minutes, stirring continuously, until the mixture is light brown. Take the pan off the heat.

Bring the stock and wine to the boil in a separate pan; whisk this into the vegetable mixture. Stir in the tomato paste and add the bouquet garni (with fresh rosemary if used). Simmer the sauce, partly covered, over gentle heat for at least 2 hours, stirring occasionally to prevent sticking.

Remove any scum from time to time. When the sauce is thick enough to coat the back of a spoon, remove it from the heat. Strain the sauce through a coarse sieve and remove any fat which rises to the top.

About 30 minutes before serving, reheat the sauce gently, stir in the red currant jelly and dried rosemary (if used); simmer until the jelly has melted. Season to taste and keep warm.

Heat the butter and oil in a heavy-based pan and cook the prepared noisettes over moderate heat for 4–6 minutes on each side, depending on the size. They should be well browned, and slightly pink inside.

Serve the noisettes with the thick, dark brown sauce poured over them. Boiled new potatoes and zucchini or green beans are suitable vegetables.

Lamb

LAMB AND LEMON SOUP

This Greek soup is a thick and meaty broth, and almost a meal in itself.

PREPARATION TIME: *15 min*
COOKING TIME: *3¼ hours*
INGREDIENTS *(for 6)*:
2 pounds neck of lamb, chopped
2 carrots
1–2 turnips
2 onions
2 leeks
1 stalk celery
1 sprig parsley
2 bay leaves
½ teaspoon dried oregano or
  marjoram
½ teaspoon dried thyme
¼ cup barley or rice
Salt★ and black pepper
Juice of a lemon
2 egg yolks
GARNISH:
1 lettuce heart

Trim as much fat as possible off the lamb, put the meat into a large saucepan with 5 cups of water and bring to the boil. Meanwhile, wash and scrape the carrots and turnips and chop them roughly; peel and roughly chop the onions. Trim the leeks and wash them under cold running water. Scrub the celery and chop this and the leeks roughly.

Remove any scum from the broth. Add the vegetables to the lamb, together with the herbs and barley (if using rice, add this 1 hour later). Season to taste with salt and freshly ground pepper. Cover the pan and simmer the broth for 2–2½ hours, or until the meat comes away from the bones.

Remove the bay leaves and parsley and lift out the meat. Leave the soup to simmer while picking the meat off the bones. Chop up the lamb and return it to the pan.

Remove the broth from the heat and allow it to get cold (if possible leave overnight). Lift off the fat which has solidified in a layer on top of the broth. Bring the soup back to the boil and, just before serving, beat the lemon juice and the egg yolks together in a small bowl. Mix in 3 or 4 tablespoons of the hot broth and add this mixture to the pan; heat the broth through without allowing it to boil.

Serve the soup sprinkled with finely shredded lettuce heart.

CARRÉ D'AGNEAU DORDONNAISE

Walnuts and liver pâté are an integral part of many dishes from the Dordogne region of France. They are both used in this recipe, which transforms rack of lamb into a party dish.

PREPARATION TIME: *30 min*
COOKING TIME: *1¼ hours*
INGREDIENTS *(for 4–6)*:
2 racks of lamb
½ cup shelled walnuts
½ small onion
4 ounces pâté de foie truffé
¼ cup soft breadcrumbs
2 tablespoons finely chopped
  parsley
Salt★ and black pepper
Lemon juice
2 tablespoons cooking oil
½ cup dry white wine
1 teaspoon powdered rosemary

Have the racks skinned and boned and ask the butcher to give you the bones. Trim any excess fat off the meat before wiping it with a damp cloth. Chop the walnuts finely or put them through an electric grinder. Peel and grate the onion. Stir the pâté smooth, and beat in the walnuts and onion. Mix the breadcrumbs and parsley into the stuffing and season with salt, pepper and lemon juice.

Spread the underside of each rack with the stuffing. Roll the meat neatly and tie with string at 2 in intervals. Put the two meat rolls in an oiled roasting pan and brush them with oil. Cook in the center of the oven pre-heated to 400°F (200°C, mark 6) for about 20 minutes, or until golden brown. Reduce the heat to 375°F (190°C, mark 5) and cook for a further 40–50 minutes, or until tender.

Meanwhile, put the lamb bones in a saucepan with salt and pepper. Cover with cold water, bring to the boil and simmer the stock for 30–40 minutes.

Remove the meat from the roasting pan and leave to cool and set slightly before removing the string. Put the meat back in the oven to keep warm. Carefully pour off the fat in the roasting pan and add the wine to the meat juices. Bring to the boil on top of the stove, add about 1 cup of strained stock and the rosemary. Cook this gravy over high heat until it has reduced slightly. Correct seasoning and strain the gravy into a warm sauce boat, preferably of the kind which separates the fat from the gravy.

Serve the lamb, cut into thick slices, on a warm serving dish. Sauté potatoes, Brussels sprouts and broiled tomatoes could be arranged around the lamb.

LAMB AND LEMON SOUP

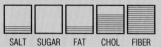

SALT SUGAR FAT CHOL FIBER

GLUTEN-FREE★   WHOLEFOOD★
TOTAL CALORIES: ABOUT 3310

To ensure the low **fat** level, buy lean lamb and skim off all the fat after the soup has cooled. The **cholesterol** level is raised by the eggs: the egg and lemon mixture is very typical of Greek cooking, but you can perfectly well use 1 whole egg instead of the yolks. If the lamb is lean and the stock de-fatted as above, the cholesterol will be fairly low. To reduce it even further, leave out the eggs altogether, add a potato to the vegetables, and liquidize some of the cooked vegetables, stirring them back into the soup to give it a thicker consistency. (Calories lost: up to 500.)
Rice is **gluten-free**, but barley does contain some gluten.
For a **wholefood** dish, buy pot barley and brown rice. Short-grain rice is the kind typically used for this soup.

Pressure cooker: ☑
Freezing: ☑ up to 3 months.

CARRÉ D'AGNEAU DORDONNAISE

SALT SUGAR FAT CHOL FIBER

GLUTEN-FREE★   WHOLEFOOD★
TOTAL CALORIES: ABOUT 3410

The **fat** level will vary widely depending on the lamb (see notes on the previous recipes); but even if it is very lean, the dish will have a high fat content because of the pâté de foie and the walnuts. You can reduce

this level to medium by halving the amount of walnuts and using the low-fat version of the pâté on page 139. Also, avoid brushing the meat with oil before roasting, and cook it on a rack so that the fat drains off. Then pour the pan juices off (ideally into a fat-separating gravy boat with a lower spout for pouring off juice after the fat has risen to the surface) and allow to cool so that the fat separates, before adding the stock (also carefully skimmed of fat) to make the gravy. (Calories lost: up to 570.) The **cholesterol** level will remain high because it is naturally high in liver.
Gluten-free: check the ingredients on the label if you buy a pâté. The same applies to **wholefood**.

Pressure cooker: ☑ for the stock.
Food processor: ☑ for the stuffing.

DURHAM LAMB SQUAB PIE

SALT	SUGAR	FAT	CHOL	FIBER

GLUTEN-FREE   WHOLEFOOD
TOTAL CALORIES: ABOUT 4250

To reduce the **fat** and **cholesterol** levels to low, choose lean meat and brown it in a non-stick or heavy pan brushed lightly with oil, omitting the butter. Replace the remaining butter for greasing the pie dish with a bare smear of oil. Do not brush the potato layer with butter, but cover the casserole while it cooks so that it does not dry out. (Calories lost: up to 680.)

Freezing: ☑ up to 4 months.

DURHAM LAMB SQUAB PIE

Originally, this recipe probably contained squabs – or young pigeons – but, in the course of time, meat became the chief constituent of the pie. There are several variations of this English farmhouse dish; the following comes from Durham.

PREPARATION TIME: *30 min*
COOKING TIME: *1–1¼ hours*
INGREDIENTS *(for 4–6):*
8 lamb chops
2 pounds potatoes
1 large onion
3 tart apples
6 tablespoons unsalted butter
1 heaping teaspoon brown sugar
Salt* and black pepper
1 cup chicken stock

Peel and thinly slice the potatoes and cover with cold water. Trim excess fat from the lamb chops. Peel and finely chop the onion, and peel, core and chop the apples. Melt ¼ cup of the butter in a pan and fry the chops lightly on both sides. Remove them as soon as the blood starts to run. Fry the apples and onion in the fat for about 5 minutes.

Use half the remaining butter to grease the inside of a pie dish. Dry the sliced potatoes and line the bottom of the dish with half of them. Arrange the chops on the potato bed and spoon the apple and onion mixture over them. Sprinkle over the sugar, a little salt and a couple of twists of

pepper from the mill. Cover with the rest of the potatoes and pour over the chicken stock. Melt the remaining butter and brush it over the potato layer. Put the dish on the middle shelf of an oven preheated to 350°F (180°C, mark 4) and cook for 1 hour or until the potatoes are tender and golden brown.

Serve straight from the casserole. Brussels sprouts tossed in brown sugar and allspice could be served with it.

Lamb

LAMB IN RED WINE

A leg of lamb makes a good choice for a large gathering. Spices and wine give a fresh summer taste to succulent young lamb.

PREPARATION TIME: *15 min*
COOKING TIME: *1¾–2 hours*
INGREDIENTS *(for 6–8)*:
4–5 pound leg of lamb
2 cloves garlic
½ tablespoon lard
Salt★ and black pepper
Ground ginger
2 onions
2 carrots
¼ cup unsalted butter
3–4 sprigs of thyme
1¼ cups dry red wine

Wipe the lamb thoroughly with a damp cloth. Peel the garlic and cut each clove into three or four slivers. With the point of a sharp knife, make small incisions in the meat and press the garlic into these. Rub the skin with the lard, a little salt, freshly ground pepper and dust with ginger. Peel the onions and carrots and chop them roughly.

Melt the butter in a roasting pan, and quickly brown the meat over moderate heat to seal in the juices. Remove the meat from the pan and cook the onions and carrots for a few minutes in the butter until golden. Spoon the pan mixture into a large oven-proof dish, add the thyme and place the meat on top; cover with a lid or foil.

Roast the meat in the center of an oven pre-heated to 425°F (220°C, mark 7) for 25 minutes, then pour over the wine and reduce the heat to 350°F (180°C, mark 4) for a further 1–1¼ hours. Baste two or three times with the wine.

Remove the roast and keep it warm on a serving dish in the oven. Strain the cooking juices and boil them briskly until they have reduced by about one-third. Remove any fat by drawing kitchen paper towels over the surface of this gravy. Heat through and correct seasoning.

Serve potatoes and young carrots, tossed in parsley, with the lamb. Pour the gravy into a sauceboat and serve separately.

LAMB KEBABS

Skewered chunks of meat, or kebabs, may also be broiled over a charcoal fire.

PREPARATION TIME: *20 min*
COOKING TIME: *10 min*
INGREDIENTS *(for 4)*:
1½ pounds boned shoulder of lamb
¼ teaspoon minced green chili pepper
1 in piece ginger root
½ cup plain yogurt
¼ teaspoon ground coriander
¼ teaspoon ground cumin
1 clove garlic
Juice of ½ lemon
1 teaspoon salt★
GARNISH:
Lemon wedges
Mint

Trim any excess fat from the lamb, wipe with a damp cloth and cut it into 1 in cubes. Peel the ginger until the green part just shows, and chop it roughly. Put the yogurt in a large bowl and stir in the coriander, cumin, chili pepper and ginger. Peel the garlic and crush it into the yogurt before adding the lemon juice and salt. Mix the lamb into the yogurt and leave to marinate for at least 30 minutes.

Remove the lamb chunks from the marinade and thread them on to four steel skewers, 8–10 in long, packing the pieces closely together. Put the skewers under a broiler or on a barbecue and cook, turning from time to time, for 8–10 minutes, or until they are browned on the outside and pink in the center.

Arrange the lamb kebabs, on their skewers, on a bed of rice garnished with lemon wedges and sprigs of mint.

LAMB IN RED WINE

SALT   SUGAR   FAT   CHOL   FIBER

GLUTEN-FREE   WHOLEFOOD
TOTAL CALORIES: ABOUT 7550

To reduce the **fat** and **cholesterol** level of this dish to low, choose the leanest possible piece of lamb and trim off any visible fat. Omit rubbing with lard and bake the meat and vegetables without sealing them first, thus omitting the butter. To reduce the fat level further, pour the pan juices into a fat-separating gravy boat, which will have a spout set low down on one side. When the fat separates after cooling a little, the juice alone can be poured off via this spout to make the gravy. It is easier to do this before reducing the gravy by boiling. (Calories lost: up to 550.)

LAMB KEBABS

SALT   SUGAR   FAT   CHOL   FIBER

GLUTEN-FREE   WHOLEFOOD
TOTAL CALORIES: ABOUT 2115

This recipe needs no alteration to suit healthier eating, provided the lamb chosen is lean and is trimmed as the recipe suggests.

ORANGE-GLAZED LAMB ROAST

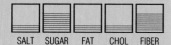

| SALT | SUGAR | FAT | CHOL | FIBER |

GLUTEN-FREE*   WHOLEFOOD*
TOTAL CALORIES: ABOUT 7380

To reduce the amount of added **sugar** to low, mix the glaze ingredients with 1 tablespoon clear honey and smear this over the meat.

The low **fat** and **cholesterol** levels (and the calorie count) assume that you choose a very lean leg of lamb, trim off any visible fat and, after cooking, allow the pan juices to cool slightly so that you can pour off any fat before using them to make the gravy. Serve with unbuttered vegetables.

ORANGE-GLAZED LAMB ROAST

A fruit-flavored glaze and stuffing transform a leg of lamb into a dish fit for a special occasion. Ask the butcher to bone the lamb, but not to roll it.

PREPARATION TIME: *20 min*
COOKING TIME: *2¼ hours*
INGREDIENTS *(for 6–8)*:
4–4½ pound leg of lamb (boned)
1 large onion
Grated rind of 2 oranges
2 tablespoons butter
1½ cups soft breadcrumbs
⅔ cup raisins
⅓ cup currants
½ teaspoon dried rosemary
½ teaspoon dried thyme
Salt★ and black pepper
Juice of an orange
GLAZE:
⅓ cup finely packed dark brown sugar
Juice of ½ lemon
Juice of an orange

2 tablespoons Worcestershire sauce
SAUCE:
½ cup red wine
1¼ cups beef stock
GARNISH:
Orange slices and watercress

Prepare the stuffing for the lamb first. Peel and finely chop the onion and grate the rind from two oranges. Melt the butter in a pan over medium heat and fry the onion for 3 minutes. Mix together in a bowl the breadcrumbs, raisins, currants and the fried onion. Blend in the orange rind, rosemary and thyme and season to taste with salt and pepper. Bind the stuffing with the juice of one orange.

Wipe the meat with a damp cloth, and pack the stuffing into the lamb. Tie the roast into a neat shape, securing it with string. Put

it in a greased baking pan.

Place the glaze ingredients in a small pan and cook over low heat for 1 minute, then spoon the glaze over the meat. Roast in the center of a pre-heated oven, at 375°F (190°C, mark 5), for 2 hours, basting frequently.

Remove the roast to a warm serving dish and keep it hot. Stir into the pan the wine and stock for the sauce, and boil over high heat, scraping up all the residue from the glaze. Continue boiling briskly until the sauce has reduced and thickened slightly. Correct seasoning if necessary.

Serve the roast, having first removed the string, and garnish with thin orange twists (page 179) and with sprigs of watercress. Potatoes and buttered baby Brussels sprouts or salsify would go well with the roast.

Lamb

DOLMAS

In Turkey, one of the most popular main course dishes is fresh vine leaves stuffed with rice and ground lamb. Bottled vine leaves or young cabbage leaves make good substitutes.

PREPARATION TIME: *40 min*
COOKING TIME: *1 hour*
INGREDIENTS *(for 4–6):*
12 fresh vine or cabbage leaves or imported bottled vine leaves
1 onion
½ cup long grain rice
6 tablespoons butter
4 cups white stock or water
1 pound lean ground lamb
2 teaspoons chopped fresh mint or parsley
1 teaspoon powdered rosemary
Salt★ and black pepper
Juice of ½ lemon
½ cup plain yogurt

Peel the onion and chop it finely.
Melt 2 tablespoons of the butter in a large heavy-based pan and fry the onion and rice until lightly colored. Add enough stock to cover the rice and cook over low heat until tender. Stir frequently and add more stock if necessary.

Leave the rice and onion to cool and set. Stir in the ground lamb, the mint or parsley and rosemary and mix thoroughly. Season to taste with salt and freshly ground pepper. Blanch the fresh vine or cabbage leaves for a few minutes in boiling water, then remove the coarse stalks. If using bottled vine leaves, unravel them carefully without breaking them.

Spread out the leaves and put a spoonful of the lamb and rice filling on each; fold the leaves over to make small, neat parcels. Pack them closely in layers in a flameproof casserole or sauté pan. Add enough stock to cover, and sprinkle with the lemon juice; dot with the remaining butter. Put a plate on top of the stuffed vine parcels to keep them under the liquid.

Cover the dish with a lid or foil and simmer over low heat for about 1 hour. Lift out the vine parcels with a slotted spoon and arrange them on a warm serving dish. Serve the yogurt in a separate bowl.

HARICOT LAMB CASSEROLE

This French country-style casserole is made from one of the least expensive cuts of meat, but has great appeal to both eye and palate.

PREPARATION TIME: *35 min*
COOKING TIME: *1¾ hours*
INGREDIENTS *(for 4–6):*
3 pounds lamb shoulder blade chops
3 leeks
6 fresh or 16-ounce can tomatoes
½ pound carrots
2 cloves garlic
2 tablespoons oil
1 tablespoon sugar
Salt★ and black pepper
1 heaping tablespoon flour
2 cups stock
1 bay leaf
½ teaspoon powdered thyme
½ pound green beans

Pre-heat the oven to 450°F (230°C, mark 8). Trim the roots and coarse outer leaves off the leeks, wash them thoroughly and chop them roughly. Skin the tomatoes. Peel or scrape the carrots, but leave them whole, and peel the garlic cloves.

Heat the oil in a flameproof casserole on top of the stove and quickly brown the lamb chops on

DOLMAS

| SALT | SUGAR | FAT | CHOL | FIBER |

GLUTEN-FREE   WHOLEFOOD★
TOTAL CALORIES: ABOUT 2530

The **salt** level is only low if fresh leaves are used.
The **fat** level of this recipe will depend largely on the meat used. Buy lean lamb and grind it yourself. The amount of butter can be reduced by cooking the onion and rice in a heavy pan lightly brushed with oil rather than in melted butter, and by omitting the butter dotted on top of the casserole. Butter is not a traditional part of Middle Eastern recipes. Assuming the yogurt is low-fat, making these changes will produce a dish low in both fat and **cholesterol**. (Calories lost: up to 700.)

Freezing: ☑ up to 4 months.
Microwave: ☑

HARICOT LAMB CASSEROLE

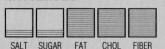

| SALT | SUGAR | FAT | CHOL | FIBER |

GLUTEN-FREE★   WHOLEFOOD★
TOTAL CALORIES: ABOUT 5570

The high **fat** level can be somewhat reduced by browning the meat in a non-stick pan or in a large heavy pan lightly brushed with oil. Blade chops are a fatty cut of lamb in most cases, and will quickly melt out enough to lubricate their own cooking. The remaining fat comes from the meat itself. As well as searching out the leanest piece you can and trimming off the visible fat, cook the meat on a roasting rack so that the fat can drain off, and remove as much of the fat as possible before adding the leeks and other vegetables. This will give a low-fat dish. (Calories lost: up to 300.) The high **cholesterol** level relates to the generous helpings: for low cholesterol, use not more than 6 ounces meat per person.

Pressure cooker: ✓
Slow cooker: ✓
Freezing: ✓ up to 4 months.
Microwave: ✓

LAMB ARGENTEUIL

SALT	SUGAR	FAT	CHOL	FIBER

GLUTEN-FREE*   WHOLEFOOD*
TOTAL CALORIES: ABOUT 4310

The **fat** and **cholesterol** levels can be reduced to low by the following measures: choose lean lamb, perhaps substituting leg for shoulder, which always has more fat; brown the meat in a non-stick pan brushed lightly with oil instead of using butter; replace the cream with low-fat small curd cottage cheese or thick yogurt, or with cultured buttermilk, making sure the dish does not boil after adding any of these or it will curdle. (Calories lost: up to 1000.) This low cholesterol level assumes that each portion of meat (boned weight) does not exceed 5–6 ounces.

Pressure cooker: ✓
Freezing: ✓ up to 4 months.
Microwave: ✓

both sides. Sprinkle with sugar, lower the heat and toss the contents until the sugar caramelizes slightly. Season with salt and freshly ground pepper, and sprinkle in half the flour.

Place the casserole, uncovered, in the hot oven for 5 minutes. Turn the meat over, season again and sprinkle with the remaining flour. Bake for a further 5 minutes. Reduce the oven heat to 325°F (170°C, mark 3). Remove the casserole, lift out the meat, and lightly fry the leeks in the casserole on top of the stove. Add the stock and bring to the boil, scraping up any residue on the bottom of the casserole. Put in the meat; add the tomatoes, carrots, bay leaf, thyme and crushed garlic. Cover the casserole with a lid and bring to simmering point. The sauce should almost cover the meat; add a little more stock if you think it is necessary.

Return the casserole to the center of the oven and cook for 1½ hours or until the meat is tender. Trim the beans, and string them if necessary. Cut them into ½ in pieces and cook in boiling salted water for 10 minutes, or until just tender. Drain, and add to the casserole and cook them in the sauce for a further 5 minutes.

Serve the lamb straight from the casserole, with baked potatoes. No other vegetables are needed, but a green salad would go well with it.

LAMB ARGENTEUIL

In its classic form, this recipe uses asparagus from the district of Argenteuil in France.

PREPARATION TIME: *30 min*
COOKING TIME: *1 hour*
INGREDIENTS *(for 6):*
2 pounds asparagus
2 pounds boned shoulder of lamb
4 small onions
¼ cup butter
1 heaping tablespoon seasoned flour (page 184)
½ cup heavy cream
Salt★ and black pepper
Lemon juice

Wash and scrape the asparagus, but do not trim; tie in three or four bundles with soft tape and cook in a large pan of lightly salted water. When the asparagus is tender, after 15–20 minutes, drain well and set the cooking liquid aside. Cut off the asparagus tips about 3 in down the stems. Put the tips aside and first blend, then sieve the stems to make a purée, discarding any tough or stringy parts left in the sieve.

Trim as much fat as possible off the lamb and cut the meat into 2 in pieces. Toss them in the seasoned flour to coat evenly. Peel and roughly chop the onions. Melt the butter in a deep frying or sauté pan, and cook the meat and onions until brown. Gradually blend in about 1¼ cups of the asparagus liquid, stirring continuously until the sauce is smooth and creamy. Simmer until the meat is tender (about 50 minutes), stirring occasionally and removing any fat which rises to the surface of the sauce. If the liquid evaporates too quickly, cover the pan with a lid.

When the meat is cooked, stir the asparagus purée and cream into the sauce. Season to taste with salt, freshly ground pepper and lemon juice. The sauce should be fairly thick.

Arrange the asparagus tips around the edge of a warm serving dish and spoon the meat and sauce into the center. Boiled new potatoes are all that is needed with the meat.

Lamb

LANCASHIRE HOT POT

In Northern England, the "hot pot" was a tall earthenware pot. Mutton chops were stood upright around the inside and the center was filled with vegetables. It was usual, too, in the days when they were cheap, to put a layer of oysters beneath the potato crust.

PREPARATION TIME: *30 min*
COOKING TIME: *2–2½ hours*
INGREDIENTS *(for 4–6):*

2 pounds lamb shoulder
Seasoned flour (page 184)
2 tablespoons drippings
1½ pounds potatoes
2 onions
6–8 carrots
2 stalks celery
1 leek
Salt* and black pepper
¼ teaspoon mixed herbs
GARNISH:
Chopped parsley

Wipe and bone the lamb. Put the bones in a saucepan and cover with cold water. Bring to the boil, and after a few minutes remove the scum; cover with a lid and let the bones simmer while the vegetables and meat are being prepared.

Trim away any fat and gristle, and cut the meat into small, even pieces. Roll them in seasoned flour, before frying in hot drippings until browned and sealed on all sides. Peel the potatoes and cut them into ¼ in thick slices. Put aside half the slices for the top and place the remainder in the bottom of a deep buttered casserole dish.

Peel and coarsely chop the onions. Scrape or peel the carrots and slice them thinly. Scrub the celery and chop it finely. Remove the outer coarse leaves and the root of the leek, wash it well and cut it across into thin slices. Mix all the vegetables together in a deep bowl, season with salt and pepper and sprinkle the herbs over them. Arrange layers of seasoned vegetables and meat in the casserole, beginning and ending with a layer of vegetables. Top with the remaining potato slices, arranging them neatly in overlapping circles. Strain the liquid from the bones and pour about 2 cups of it into the casserole until it just reaches the upper potato layer. Cover with buttered wax paper and a tight-fitting lid. Place in the center of an oven preheated to 350°F (180°C, mark 4) and cook for 2–2½ hours.

About 30 minutes before serving, remove the lid and paper from the casserole. Brush the potatoes with a little melted drippings and sprinkle with coarse salt. Raise the oven heat to 400°F (200°C, mark 6) and return the uncovered casserole to the oven, placing it above the center so that the potatoes will crisp and brown slightly.

Sprinkle with finely chopped parsley immediately before serving. The hot pot is a meal on its own, but is traditionally served with pickled red cabbage.

SUFFOLK STEW

This is one of those hearty, satisfying stews that requires nothing before it, and very little afterwards. Have the rack of lamb chined (page 161), and begin the preparations a day in advance.

PREPARATION TIME: *30 min*
COOKING TIME: *3 hours*
INGREDIENTS *(for 4–6):*
1 rack lamb
⅓ cup dried lentils
3 tablespoons dried navy beans
3 tablespoons barley
2 large potatoes
1 large turnip
4 carrots
4 onions
2 bay leaves
½ teaspoon salt*
½ teaspoon black pepper
1 clove garlic
1 teaspoon mixed herbs

Soak the lentils, navy beans and barley in cold water overnight. The following day, peel and roughly chop all the vegetables; put them in a large saucepan. Trim any excess fat from the lamb and cut the meat into single chops. Add these, together with the bay leaves, salt, pepper, crushed garlic and herbs to the vegetables.

Drain the lentils, navy beans and barley, before adding them to the pan. Pour over 4 pints of water, cover the pan with a lid and bring to the boil. Simmer gently for 3 hours.

Spoon the stew into a warm serving dish. No other vegetables are necessary, but buttered hot muffins would make an unusual accompaniment to the stew.

LANCASHIRE HOT POT

SALT SUGAR FAT CHOL FIBER

GLUTEN-FREE*   WHOLEFOOD*
TOTAL CALORIES: ABOUT 4340

The exact **fat** level depends on the cut of meat. Choose lean meat and trim off the fat carefully. In addition, for low fat and **cholesterol**, brown the meat in a non-stick pan in its own fat, which will soon melt out (if necessary, brush the pan lightly with oil). This avoids the need for drippings; do not, naturally, brush the potatoes with drippings near the end of cooking. (Calories lost: up to 300.)

Freezing: ☑ up to 4 months.

SUFFOLK STEW

SALT SUGAR FAT CHOL FIBER

WHOLEFOOD*
TOTAL CALORIES: ABOUT 3890

The exact **fat** and **cholesterol** levels depend on the meat chosen. To ensure this dish is low in both, buy the leanest piece of meat available and trim off any visible fat. Instead of serving with buttered muffins, try adding dumplings (see the recipe on page 92) to the top of the stew, or serve with lightly cooked sprouts.
For a completely **gluten-free** dish, replace the barley, which does contain some gluten, with rice, lentils or pre-soaked chick peas.
For a **wholefood** dish, use pot barley, or replace the barley with brown rice, lentils or chick peas as above.

Pressure cooker: ☑
Slow cooker: ☑
Freezing: ☑ up to 4 months.

CROWN ROAST OF LAMB

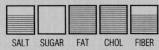

SALT	SUGAR	FAT	CHOL	FIBER

GLUTEN-FREE★   WHOLEFOOD★
TOTAL CALORIES: ABOUT 5330

The **salt** level can be reduced to low by using breadcrumbs from bread made without added salt, and using fresh pork sides instead of bacon.

To reduce the **fat** and **cholesterol** levels, omit the bacon from the stuffing and brown the stuffing ingredients in a heavy pan brushed lightly with oil, not butter. No drippings need be used as even lean lamb carries plenty of fat. For an overall low fat and cholesterol dish, use very lean lamb, trim off all visible fat and skim the pan juices thoroughly before making gravy. (Calories lost: up to 1550.)

If wished, the loss of bulk in the stuffing due to leaving out the bacon can be made up by including two extra onions and a chopped apple.

Food processor: ☑ for the stuffing.

CROWN ROAST OF LAMB

The crown is formed by joining two racks of lamb, and the hollow between them is stuffed with a savory filling. The chop bones are frequently decorated with paper frills, but glazed onions make an unusual, and edible, garnish for this meat dish.

PREPARATION TIME: *45 min*
COOKING TIME: *2 hours*
INGREDIENTS *(for 6):*
2 racks of lamb (6 chops each)
¼ cup beef drippings
STUFFING:
½ pound cranberries
½ cup chicken stock
2 tablespoons sugar
1 onion
¼ pound mushrooms
½ pound bacon
2 tablespoons butter
1 clove garlic
¼ cup chopped parsley
1½ teaspoons ground thyme
2 cups soft breadcrumbs
1 egg
Salt★ and black pepper
GARNISH:
Glazed onions

Ask the butcher to trim off any excess fat and to shape the racks of lamb into a crown (page 161).

For the stuffing, put the cranberries, stock and sugar in a saucepan; if necessary, top up the stock with enough water to cover the fruit. Bring the cranberries to the boil and cook over high heat until they burst open, and the liquid has reduced to a thick sauce.

Peel and finely chop the onion, trim and coarsely chop the mushrooms, and grind the bacon. Melt the butter in a pan and fry the onion until soft but not colored.

Add the peeled and crushed garlic and cook for 1 minute. Add the mushrooms, turning them in the butter until they are lightly colored. In a bowl, combine the cranberries and the onion and mushroom mixture with the ground bacon. Mix in the parsley, thyme and breadcrumbs. Beat the egg lightly and use to bind the stuffing. Season to taste with salt and freshly ground pepper.

Spoon the stuffing into the hollow crown. Wrap foil around the chop bones to protect them during roasting. Melt the drippings in a roasting pan and place the stuffed crown in it. Roast on a shelf low in a pre-heated oven at 375°F (190°C, mark 5), for 10 minutes. Reduce the heat to 350°F (180°C, mark 4) and continue roasting. Allow 30 minutes to the pound, and baste frequently.

Remove the crown roast and keep it warm. Skim off as much fat as possible and boil the pan juices to make a gravy. Sweeten with red currant jelly or a tablespoon of cranberry sauce, and pour into a warm sauce boat.

Serve the crown roast with garlic potatoes and an endive and orange salad. Spike a glazed onion on each chop bone.

Lamb

NAVARIN OF LAMB

Navarin is a French cooking term applied exclusively to a casserole of lamb, or mutton, and young root vegetables.

PREPARATION TIME: *30 min*
COOKING TIME: *1¾ hours*
INGREDIENTS *(for 4):*
2 pounds lamb rib chops
Seasoned flour (page 184)
3 tablespoons drippings or
 vegetable oil
1 pound young carrots
1 onion
2 cups chicken or beef stock
1 tablespoon tomato paste
Salt★ and black pepper
Bouquet garni (page 183)
8 small pearl onions
8 small new potatoes
GARNISH:
Chopped parsley

Trim fat from the meat and coat the pieces with the seasoned flour. Melt the fat in a large frying pan and add the meat. Fry as many chops as possible at one time, turning them to brown evenly on both sides. Remove from the pan and put them in a large casserole. Scrape and thinly slice the carrots, and peel and roughly chop the onion. Add these to the casserole. Drain off most of the fat from the frying pan. Stir in 1 tablespoon of the seasoned flour; cook over low heat for a few minutes to brown, then gradually stir in the hot stock. Add the tomato paste and bring the sauce to the boil.

Draw the pan off the heat and strain the sauce into the casserole; season with salt and freshly ground pepper. Add the bouquet

garni. Cover the casserole with a lid and place in the center of a preheated oven at 325°F (170°C, mark 3); cook for 1¼ hours.

Peel the pearl onions, leaving them whole. Put them in a saucepan and cover with cold water. Bring this to the boil, then drain the onions at once. Scrape the new potatoes and add, with the onions, to the casserole, placing them on top of the meat. Replace the lid and cook the casserole for a further 30 minutes or until the vegetables are tender.

Remove the bouquet garni from the casserole, sprinkle with chopped parsley and serve the lamb straight from the casserole.

NAVARIN OF LAMB

SALT	SUGAR	FAT	CHOL	FIBER

GLUTEN-FREE* WHOLEFOOD*
TOTAL CALORIES: ABOUT 4315

Moderate **fat** and **cholesterol** levels can be achieved by choosing lean meat, carefully trimming it of fat, and browning it in a heavy or non-stick pan, brushed lightly with oil rather than drippings. (Calories lost: up to 360.) If wished, the casserole can be made 24 hours before it is wanted, and chilled. Any fat that solidifies on the top can then be removed before reheating and serving.

Pressure cooker: ☑
Slow cooker: ☑
Freezing: ☑ up to 4 months.
Microwave: ☑

CORDERO A LA CHILINDRÓN

SALT	SUGAR	FAT	CHOL	FIBER

GLUTEN-FREE WHOLEFOOD
TOTAL CALORIES: ABOUT 3640

The medium **salt** level assumes the tomatoes have no added salt. The only way to reduce it to low is to use less ham, say half the quantity.
Usually both leg and shoulder of lamb are high in **fat** – 20% or over – but if you choose a very fat-free piece, trim it carefully, also trim the edge fat off the ham, and use only 1 tablespoon oil to brown the ingredients (quite possible if you use a heavy or non-stick pan), the total fat content can be reduced

to medium, especially if the dish is served with unbuttered vegetables. (Calories lost: up to 600.) The **cholesterol** will be moderate if the portions are reduced – the quantities given are generous.

Freezing: ✓ up to 4 months.
Microwave: ✓

ÉPIGRAMMES D'AGNEAU

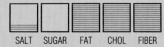

| SALT | SUGAR | FAT | CHOL | FIBER |

GLUTEN-FREE★   WHOLEFOOD★
TOTAL CALORIES: ABOUT 6710

Breast of lamb is one of the fattiest meat cuts. Even if all visible fat is trimmed, the lean meat contains enough marbling to make it about 16% fat. However, this recipe allows you to remove more fat later. If you choose the leanest breast possible, trim it carefully both before and after cooking, the **fat** content will be medium – provided you broil, rather than fry, the breadcrumb-coated épigrammes at the last stage of cooking. This is in fact the more usual way of cooking épigrammes. Broil for about 10 minutes each side under a medium heat, thus eliminating the butter and oil. For a low **cholesterol** level, use only the egg white for coating the meat. (Calories lost: up to 600.)

Pressure cooker: ✓ for the first stage of cooking.

CORDERO A LA CHILINDRÓN

The mountain districts of Spain favor lamb as a festive dish: this version with red pepper and tomatoes comes from Navarre.

PREPARATION TIME: *20 min*
COOKING TIME: *50 min*
INGREDIENTS *(for 6)*:
2 pounds boned leg or shoulder of lamb
1 sweet red pepper
Salt★ and black pepper
2 tablespoons olive oil
2 cloves garlic
1 onion
¼ pound cured ham
16-ounce can tomatoes

Put the pepper under a preheated broiler. Turn it frequently until charred all over, then rub the skin off under cold water. Remove the stalk and the seeds, and cut the flesh into narrow strips.

Finely chop the onion and garlic. Dice the ham. In Spain the ham used is mountain ham, chewy and full of taste.

Cut the lamb into 1½–2 in cubes, removing excess fat. Season to taste with salt and freshly ground black pepper. Heat the oil in a large, heavy-based pan and fry the garlic until golden. Add the onion, lamb and ham and cook over moderate heat for about 10 minutes or until the lamb is browned. Stir the chopped pepper and tomatoes, with their juice, into the pan.

Simmer the lamb, covered, over low heat for about 40 minutes or until tender.

Serve with buttered rice, crusty French bread and a tossed green side salad.

ÉPIGRAMMES D'AGNEAU

This is an unusual way of cooking breast of lamb. It is also an economical dish, for the stock can be used as the basis for the soup on page 110.

PREPARATION TIME: *30 min*
COOKING TIME: *2 hours*
STANDING TIME: *3 hours*
INGREDIENTS *(for 4–6)*:
2 breasts of lamb, unboned and weighing about 3 pounds
1 onion
2 leeks
1–2 stalks celery
3–4 carrots
Bouquet garni (page 183)
2 teaspoons salt★
6 peppercorns
1 large egg
⅔–1 cup dry breadcrumbs
¼ cup unsalted butter
2 tablespoons corn oil
GARNISH:
Watercress sprigs
Lemon wedges

Peel and slice the onion. Cut the roots and coarse outer leaves from the leeks, wash them thoroughly under cold running water and chop them roughly. Scrub the celery and scrape or peel the carrots; chop both roughly.

Trim as much fat as possible from the breasts of lamb, and put them in a large pan, with the prepared vegetables, the bouquet garni, salt and peppercorns. Cover with cold water and bring to the boil. Remove any scum from the surface, then cover the pan with a lid and simmer gently for 1½ hours. Remove the meat from the pan, leave to cool slightly, then carefully pull out all the bones.

Lay the meat flat between two boards and place a heavy weight on top. Leave until quite cold, then trim off any remaining fat and cut the meat into 2 in squares. Dip the meat in the lightly beaten egg and coat evenly with the breadcrumbs. Set aside until the coating has hardened.

Heat the butter and oil in a heavy-based pan and fry the meat squares until crisp and golden on both sides, after about 20 minutes. Drain on crumpled kitchen paper towels.

Serve the épigrammes garnished with watercress and lemon wedges. Sauté potatoes and broccoli spears would go well with the épigrammes.

Lamb

LAMB À LA GRECQUE

Greek cooking is characterized by its use of spices and eggplant. Lamb is the meat most commonly used in Greece, but it is often lean and stringy and more suitable for casserole dishes than for roasting.

PREPARATION TIME: *1–1½ hours*
COOKING TIME: *1¼ hours*
INGREDIENTS (*for 6*):
3 pounds boned shoulder of lamb
½ pound eggplants
Salt and black pepper
¼ cup olive oil
½ cup sugar
1 pound apricots
2 large onions
16-ounce can tomatoes
¾ cup tomato paste
4 bay leaves
¼ teaspoon crushed coriander seeds
¼ teaspoon grated nutmeg
1 tablespoon chopped parsley
Juice of a lemon
6 tablespoons unsalted butter
5 cups chicken stock

1 cup long grain rice
GARNISH:
1 cup pitted ripe olives
Orange peel

Remove the stalk ends and wipe the eggplants; cut them lengthwise into ¼ in thick slices. Place the eggplant slices in a bowl and sprinkle them with 2 teaspoons salt, to draw out the excess water. Mix thoroughly, cover with a cloth and leave for 45 minutes. Wipe them dry.

Heat the olive oil in a heavy-based pan and fry the eggplant slices for just 1 minute until golden, then drain on kitchen paper towels.

Dissolve the sugar in a pan containing 1 cup cold water. Boil this syrup for 10 minutes, and meanwhile halve and pit the apricots. Add the apricots to the syrup and poach for 5–15 minutes until tender.

Trim any excess fat from the lamb, cut the meat into 1 in cubes and fry it over low heat in a dry sauté pan, turning it frequently, until the fat runs and the meat turns a light brown.

Peel and finely chop the onions, add them to the lamb and continue cooking until the onions are transparent. Add the chopped tomatoes with their juice, the tomato paste, bay leaves, coriander seeds, nutmeg, parsley, salt, pepper and lemon juice. Top up the apricot syrup with water to make 1¼ cups, pour it over the lamb and bring to the boil.

Line the bottom of a large buttered casserole with the eggplant slices and spoon over the lamb mixture. Cover the casserole tightly with foil and the lid. Cook for 1 hour in the center of an oven pre-heated to 350°F (180°C, mark 4). Remove the covering from the casserole, lay the apricots over the lamb and return the casserole to the oven.

Bring the stock and 3½ quarts of water to the boil in a large saucepan. Add 2 teaspoons salt and the rice, stirring until the water returns to the boil. Cover the pan with a lid and boil the rice for 12–14 minutes or until just tender. Drain the rice in a sieve and rinse under hot water.

Melt the remaining butter in a saucepan and stir in the rice. Spoon the rice in a ring on to a warm serving dish and fill the center with the lamb and eggplants. Garnish the rice with ripe olives, the apricots, and narrow strips of orange peel.

Serve with a lettuce and tomato salad tossed in an oil and orange juice dressing.

LAMB À LA GRECQUE

SALT   SUGAR   FAT   CHOL   FIBER

GLUTEN-FREE   WHOLEFOOD
TOTAL CALORIES: ABOUT 7430

To reduce the **salt** level to low, do not salt the eggplants. The main advantage of salting them is that they then absorb less fat when fried, but if they are cooked as suggested below this does not arise. Ensure the canned tomatoes and tomato paste have no added salt.
To eliminate added **sugar**, using fresh apricots (or apricots canned in unsweetened juice), bake them, covered, in a medium oven with a few tablespoons of water or juice for about 30 minutes, until just tender. Halve, pit and use as garnish as suggested. (Calories lost: up to 440.)
Alternatively, for a sweeter taste (but still eliminating added sugar), use dried apricots, about half the quantity or a little less; soak them in water for an hour or two and then bake them as above.
For low **fat** and **cholesterol**, buy lean meat (leg is leaner than shoulder of lamb) and trim off all visible fat. Instead of frying the eggplant slices, broil them on a baking sheet lightly brushed with oil for about 4 minutes on each side. (Calories lost: up to 1000.)
Do not butter the cooked rice, but stir in a few tablespoons of chopped fresh herbs.

Freezing: ☑ up to 4 months (the lamb stew only, not the rice or apricots).

RILLETTES OF PORK

| SALT | SUGAR | FAT | CHOL | FIBER |

GLUTEN-FREE   WHOLEFOOD
TOTAL CALORIES: ABOUT 5045

The high **fat** and **cholesterol** levels are of course due to the amount of pork fat needed. A lot of this drains out anyway through the sieve; to ensure as much as possible is lost, reheat the mixture very gently to melt any fat that may have cooled and solidified and let this drip through. The purpose of adding the fat back to the rillettes is to preserve them. Nowadays, with refrigeration, this is not necessary, so simply cover them when chilling. The fat and cholesterol will now be moderately, rather than astronomically, high.

Pressure cooker: ☑

Food processor: ☑ if you wish, but remember that rillettes should not have too smooth a texture.

Freezing: ☑ up to 1 month.

RILLETTES OF PORK

In France, most country towns have their own versions of rillettes – a coarse-textured terrine of pork and pork fat. It makes a change from smooth pâtés and is simple to make.

PREPARATION TIME: *30 min*
COOKING TIME: *4 hours*
INGREDIENTS *(for 6):*
2 pounds fresh pork sides or
    shoulder
¾ pound pork kidney fat
Salt★ and black pepper
1 clove garlic
1 bay leaf
1 sprig parsley
1 sprig thyme or rosemary

Have the pork sides or shoulder boned. Wipe the meat with a damp cloth and cut it into narrow strips. Dice the pork fat finely and season the meat and fat with salt, freshly ground pepper and the peeled crushed garlic. Pack the meat and fat into a casserole or terrine. Push the herbs down into the center of the meat and pour over about ½ cup of water. Cover the casserole with a lid or foil.

Bake for 4 hours in the center of the oven pre-heated to 275°F (140°C, mark 1). Stir the contents of the casserole occasionally to prevent a crusty top forming. When the meat is tender, turn the contents of the casserole into a sieve placed over a mixing bowl; leave until the fat has dripped through the sieve and into the bowl. Remove the herbs and shred the meat with two forks or put it in a liquidizer for a few moments to make a coarse purée. Adjust seasoning if necessary.

Pack the meat into one large earthenware pot, or several small ones. Pour enough liquid fat over the jar to cover the meat by ¼ in and chill until the fat on the surface has set solid.

Serve the terrine with crusty French bread for a first course or with a watercress salad for a cold snack.

Pork

BARBECUED SPARERIBS

This is a substantial first course, prepared in the Chinese style – in this case, baked in a sauce. The racks of pork spareribs should be cut into 12 individual ribs for easy eating with the fingers.

PREPARATION TIME: *15 min*
COOKING TIME: *45 min*
INGREDIENTS *(for 4)*:
12 single pork spareribs
¼ cup clear honey
3 tablespoons soy sauce
3 tablespoons tomato ketchup
Tabasco sauce
1 small clove garlic
Dry mustard
Paprika
Salt★ and black pepper
Juice of 1 small orange
¼ cup wine vinegar

Broil the ribs for 10–15 minutes under a pre-heated broiler until they are brown, turning them several times. Arrange them in a single layer in a large roasting pan and pour in the pan juices.

Put the honey, soy sauce, tomato ketchup and a few drops of Tabasco sauce into a bowl; peel the garlic; crush it with the side of a knife and add it to the bowl. Season to taste with the dry mustard, paprika, salt and freshly ground pepper, then add the orange juice and wine vinegar. Mix, then pour over the spareribs.

Cook, uncovered, in the center of a pre-heated oven at 350°F (180°C, mark 4) for 30 minutes. Serve the ribs piping hot in the sauce. Provide a finger bowl for each guest.

SWEET AND SOUR PORK

Served the Chinese way, with three or four other dishes, this would be enough for six or eight people. On its own, with rice, it will serve four.

PREPARATION TIME: *5–6 min*
COOKING TIME: *8 min*
INGREDIENTS *(for 4)*:
2 pounds boneless lean pork
2 tablespoons cornstarch
½ cup vegetable oil
2½ tablespoons soy sauce
1 green pepper
SAUCE:
1 tablespoon cornstarch
2 tablespoons sugar
2 tablespoons white wine vinegar
2 tablespoons fresh orange juice
1½ tablespoons soy sauce
1½ tablespoons tomato paste
1½ tablespoons dry sherry

Mix all the sauce ingredients, with 6 tablespoons of water, in a bowl. Blend until smooth. Cut the pork into ½–¾ in cubes and toss them in cornstarch.

Heat 6 tablespoons of oil in a frying pan, and fry the pork cubes over high heat for 4–5 minutes, turning them often until nearly brown. Pour off all the oil, add the soy sauce and mix with the pork, over low heat, for 1 minute.

Heat the remaining oil in a separate pan, and add the green pepper, cut into strips, 1 in long by ½ in wide. Stir-fry in the oil for 1½ minutes, over moderate heat. Reduce the heat, stir the sauce and pour it over the pepper. Stir continuously until the sauce thickens and becomes smooth and translucent.

Add the pork cubes and turn them in the sauce for 1 minute. Serve with plain boiled rice.

SPARERIBS IN MARSALA

To many people, spareribs of pork are synonymous with Chinese cooking. This recipe, however, imparts a different flavor to spareribs.

PREPARATION TIME: *40 min*
COOKING TIME: *45 min*
INGREDIENTS *(for 6)*:
6 large country-style pork spareribs
3 tablespoons olive oil
2 cloves garlic
2 heaping tablespoons chopped parsley
1 teaspoon ground fennel
Salt★ and black pepper
½ cup fresh orange juice
½ cup chicken stock
3 tablespoons Marsala wine
GARNISH:
Orange and watercress

Trim away as much fat from the ribs as possible, and heat the oil in a heavy-based pan. Peel and crush the cloves of garlic and rub over the ribs; chop the parsley finely and mix with the fennel; rub into the ribs. Put the ribs in the pan, pepper each well, and cook on both sides until pale brown. Pour over the orange juice and stock, add the Marsala, and correct seasoning.

Cook the spareribs on the middle shelf of an oven pre-heated to 350°F (180°C, mark 4) for 45 minutes.

Lift out the ribs and arrange them on a bed of noodles or rice. Skim the fat off the juices and pour these over the meat. Garnish with slices of orange and small bunches of watercress. Broccoli spears or cauliflower au gratin could also be served.

BARBECUED SPARERIBS

SALT   SUGAR   FAT   CHOL   FIBER

GLUTEN-FREE★   WHOLEFOOD★
TOTAL CALORIES: ABOUT 2270

Soy sauce and tomato ketchup are both very high in **salt**. To reduce the level to low, use only 2 teaspoons of each, or replace the ketchup with tomato paste (canned without added salt). The high level of added **sugar** comes partly from the honey and partly from the ketchup, with its typical 23% sugar level. Using tomato paste instead will eliminate the added sugar, and the honey can be reduced to about 1 tablespoon. If you omit the ketchup, you may like to add a little extra lemon juice and vinegar to the flavoring. (Calories lost: up to 200.)
For low **fat** and **cholesterol** levels, choose very lean ribs and trim off visible fat. (Calories lost: up to 900.)
This dish is **gluten-free** and **wholefood** if there is no wheat or additives in the soy sauce or ketchup; check the labels.

SWEET AND SOUR PORK

SALT   SUGAR   FAT   CHOL   FIBER

GLUTEN-FREE★   WHOLEFOOD★
TOTAL CALORIES: ABOUT 3770

To reduce the **salt** level to low, omit the soy sauce and use salt-free tomato paste.
As the amount of **sugar** added in this recipe is generous, adding only 2 teaspoons will give enough sweetness for most tastes and reduces the sugar level to medium. (Calories lost: up to 50.)

To reduce **fat** to low choose very lean pork and sauté it in a non-stick pan merely brushed with oil, tossing constantly. (Calories lost: up to 500.)
This is **gluten-free** and **wholefood** on the assumption that the soy sauce contains no wheat or additives. Tamari is a Japanese soy product and should contain no wheat.

Freezing: ☑ up to 1 month.

SPARERIBS IN MARSALA

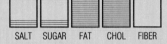

SALT	SUGAR	FAT	CHOL	FIBER

GLUTEN-FREE   WHOLEFOOD
TOTAL CALORIES: ABOUT 3615

For low **fat** and **cholesterol**, choose lean spareribs and trim the fat carefully; omit the olive oil and brown the meat in a heavy or non-stick pan, heating it gently to allow its own fat to run. (Calories lost: up to 400.)

PORK WITH PISTACHIO NUTS

SALT	SUGAR	FAT	CHOL	FIBER

GLUTEN-FREE
TOTAL CALORIES: ABOUT 5510

There is no way to reduce the high **salt** level which is inherent in the method of curing.
The **fat** and **cholesterol** levels are not very malleable either. About all you can do is avoid eating the fat and jelly, which would give a medium fat and cholesterol intake.

PORK WITH PISTACHIO NUTS

A loin of pork is particularly suitable as a main dish for a cold buffet. Leave it to season for two or three days in saltpeter, which gives a pink glow to cold pork. If saltpeter is unobtainable, slices of salt pork placed down the middle of the roast can be used to impart a similar flavor and color.

PREPARATION TIME: *20 min*
COOKING TIME: *2½ hours*
INGREDIENTS *(for 8–10):*
4–5 pound loin of pork
¼ teaspoon saltpeter
1 heaping tablespoon salt
1 tablespoon brown sugar
2 tablespoons shelled pistachio nuts
Black pepper
½ cup dry white wine

Buy the pork two or three days before it is wanted and ask the butcher to bone the roast, and to give you the bones. Mix together the saltpeter, salt and brown sugar; run it into the pork,

particularly on the boned side. Place the pork, boned side down, in a deep dish and leave in the refrigerator for two days.

Before cooking, pat the meat dry with a clean cloth. Make small incisions with a sharp knife in the fat and press in the shelled pistachio nuts. Sprinkle the meat with plenty of freshly ground black pepper; roll it neatly and tie securely with string.

For the cooking, use a deep, ovenproof .pot into which the meat fits snugly with the bones tucked around the sides. Pour the wine and 2 cups of water over it. Add a little more water if the meat does not fit tightly into the dish. Cook, uncovered, in an oven preheated to 350°F (180°C, mark 4) for 30 minutes until the fat has colored. Then cover with a double layer of foil; reduce the temperature to 300°F (160°C, mark 2) and continue cooking in the oven for a further 2 hours.

When the pork is cooked,

remove the bones and leave the meat to cool in the juice, which will set to a jelly. Remove the jelly when set and chop it up finely. Scrape the fat from the top of the meat and put into a serving jar. Carve the cold pork into ¼ in thick slices and arrange them on a dish garnished with the chopped jelly.

Serve with whole wheat bread and the jar of pork fat. The pistachio nuts give the pork a distinctive flavor and an attractive appearance – green and purple against the pink and white of the pork. A green salad, tossed in a French dressing (page 157), would go well with the cold pork.

Pork

PORK BLADE CHOPS IN CIDER

With the onset of cool autumn weather, casseroles give a warm and welcoming glow to the evening meal. Lean blade chops of pork are ideal for this easily prepared dish; veal chops may also be cooked in the same way.

PREPARATION TIME: *30 min*
COOKING TIME: *45 min*
INGREDIENTS *(for 6):*
6 pork blade chops
½ pound mushrooms
1 large onion
6 tablespoons butter
1 teaspoon dried savory
Salt★ and black pepper
½–1¼ cups dry hard cider
1–1½ cups grated Cheddar cheese
6 tablespoons toasted breadcrumbs
GARNISH:
Parsley sprigs

Wipe and trim the mushrooms, set six or seven caps aside and slice the remainder thinly. Peel the onion and chop it finely. Grease a shallow ovenproof dish with a little of the butter and arrange the sliced mushrooms over the bottom. Scatter the onion and savory over the mushrooms, and season with salt and pepper.

Trim most of the fat off the chops and lay them on top of the vegetables. Pour over enough cider to come just level with the meat, and push the mushroom caps, dark side uppermost, between the chops.

Grate the cheese and mix it with the breadcrumbs. Spread this mixture evenly over the chops and the mushroom caps, and dot with the remaining butter. Bake in the center of a pre-heated oven at 400°F (200°C, mark 6) for 45 minutes, or until the chops are tender and the topping crisp and brown.

Serve the chops straight from the dish and garnish each mushroom cap with a small sprig of parsley. Green beans and baked potatoes dressed with sour cream and chopped chives go well with this dish.

ROAST LOIN OF PORK

The Scandinavians celebrate Christmas joyously. From December 13th, St. Lucia's Day, until well into the New Year, the tables are laden with traditional Christmas fare, including this popular loin of pork which has a crisp crackling.

PREPARATION TIME: *15 min*
COOKING TIME: *3¼ hours*
INGREDIENTS *(for 8):*
6-pound loin of pork, with skin
¼ cup drippings or butter
Coarse salt
6 cloves
12 small bay leaves

Have the loin deeply scored into ½ in wide strips. For a really crisp crackling place the roast, skin side down, in a roasting pan and pour in boiling water to a depth of 1 in. Set the pan just below center of an oven pre-heated to 450°F (230°C, mark 8). Cook for 15 minutes. Remove the pan, pour off the liquid and set aside for basting.

Grease the pan with drippings and rub the skin of the loin with salt. Insert the cloves and bay leaves in the score marks. Roast the pork, skin side up, at 350°F (180°C, mark 4), at 30 minutes to the pound (450 g). Baste every 30 minutes.

Serve the loin of pork garnished with roasted half apples filled with red currant jelly. Traditionally, the Christmas roast is served with roast potatoes and long-cooked red cabbage.

HAM WITH CIDER AND RAISINS

Ham, cooked with dried peas or beans, is one of the oldest known English dishes, dating back to the 14th century. The following is a 20th-century version of the medieval recipe.

PREPARATION TIME: *20 min*
COOKING TIME: *2½ hours*
INGREDIENTS *(for 6):*
2–2½ pound smoked ham, shank end, or smoked arm picnic
1 cup dried split peas, lentils or chick peas
1 small onion
2 tablespoons chopped celery
3 tablespoons butter
3 tablespoons flour
1¼ cups dry hard cider
⅓ cup raisins
½ cup ham or chicken stock
2 teaspoons light brown sugar
2 tablespoons chopped parsley

Put the peas or lentils in a large bowl. Cover with cold water and leave to soak for 8 hours or overnight. Drain the peas, put them in a large heavy-based pan, add the ham and cover with fresh cold water. Bring to the boil, then lower the heat and cover the pan with a lid. Simmer for 1½ hours or until the ham is tender.

Lift the meat from the pan and set it aside to cool slightly. Leave the peas to cook for a further 30–40 minutes or until quite tender. Skin the ham carefully while still

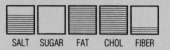

a bit of trouble, but you can remove the skin alone from the roast, trim off all the fat layer underneath, then lay the skin back over the top and fasten it on with skewers, scoring it as in the recipe. Do not baste while cooking. This should reduce fat and cholesterol to medium. (Calories lost: up to 520.)

HAM WITH CIDER AND RAISINS

SALT	SUGAR	FAT	CHOL	FIBER

GLUTEN-FREE*
TOTAL CALORIES: ABOUT 4700

The high **salt** level is inherent in the ham, which is cured with a high salt mixture. Soaking before cooking could remove some salt, but the level will remain high.

The **fat** content of ham can be very low if you choose a lean cut and remove all visible fat. For low levels in the dish itself, omit the sauce-making stage of the recipe and add the celery, onion and cider to the empty pan. Cook them together gently to make a thin sauce, without adding the ham stock which will be extremely salty. You can then thicken the sauce, either by stirring in some low-fat yogurt or fromage blanc just before serving, or by liquidizing the sauce with enough of the dried legumes to make a smooth, thick texture (or you can combine the two methods). The **cholesterol** will also be low. (Calories lost: up to 500.)

This method is **gluten-free**. Cured ham dishes are not **wholefood** because of the nitrates used. However this recipe, and the ones that follow, could be adapted to other meats if you choose something less salty.

warm, and cut the meat into 1 in cubes, discarding the fat.

Peel and finely chop the onion, and prepare the celery. Melt the butter in a heavy-based pan over moderate heat, and fry the onion and celery for a few minutes until soft. Remove the pan from the heat and stir in the flour until it has absorbed all the butter. Gradually stir in the cider to make a smooth sauce. Return the pan to the heat and bring the sauce to simmering point, stirring continuously. Mix in the raisins, and add enough stock to make a creamy sauce. Blend in the sugar and continue cooking and stirring over low heat for a further 10 minutes.

Add the cubed ham to the cider sauce, heating it through thoroughly and stirring occasionally. Drain the peas or lentils thoroughly and toss them in a little butter and parsley. Spoon the meat and sauce into the center of a warmed serving dish and surround with a border of the peas or lentils.

Pork

HAM SLICES IN MADEIRA SAUCE

This easily made appetizing dish uses convenient ham slices.

PREPARATION TIME: *20 min*
COOKING TIME: *20–25 min*
INGREDIENTS *(for 4)*:
4 ham slices, each ½–¾ in thick
4–6 ounces mushrooms
1 large onion
4 large tomatoes
¼ cup butter or lard
¼ teaspoon dried basil
¼ teaspoon dried marjoram
¼ cup Madeira or cream sherry
½ cup ham or chicken stock
Salt★ and black pepper
1 teaspoon sugar
Lemon juice

Slash the fat on the ham slices to prevent them curling while cooking. Wipe the mushrooms, remove the stalks and chop them roughly, leaving the caps whole. Peel and thinly slice the onion; skin the tomatoes and chop them roughly.

Heat the butter or lard in a heavy-based pan over moderate heat until it stops bubbling. Fry the ham slices until golden on both sides, after about 8 minutes, turning once only. Remove the ham from the pan and keep hot in the oven.

Fry the onion, mushroom caps and stalks lightly in the pan juices until softened; add the tomatoes, the basil and marjoram. Cover the pan with a lid or kitchen foil and simmer for about 5 minutes, shaking the pan occasionally.

Return the ham slices to the pan and add the Madeira or sherry, with enough stock to almost cover the meat. Season to taste with salt, freshly ground pepper, sugar and lemon juice. Cover the pan again and continue cooking over low heat for 10 minutes or until the ham is tender.

Arrange the steaks on a hot serving dish with the sauce poured over them. Baby sprouts, tossed in butter, and creamed potatoes or fluffy boiled rice, to mop up the sauce, would be suitable with the ham.

BAKED SMOKED PORK SHOULDER

Shoulder is one of the most economical pork cuts, ideal for a family meal and providing plenty of left-over meat to serve cold or in sandwiches. The roast here is served with peaches; for a dinner party, a smoked ham rump portion could replace the shoulder.

PREPARATION TIME: *20 min*
COOKING TIME: *2–2¼ hours*
INGREDIENTS *(for 8)*:
4-pound smoked pork shoulder roll
8 peppercorns
3 cloves
Bouquet garni (page 183)
½ cup light brown sugar
½ cup dry hard cider or unsweetened apple juice
4 peaches
6 tablespoons unsalted butter
1½ tablespoons honey or ⅓ cup dark brown sugar
Cinnamon

Put the pork in a large pan with enough cold water to cover it completely. Add the peppercorns, cloves and bouquet garni. Bring to the boil over moderate heat, remove any scum from the surface, and cover the pan with a lid. Reduce the heat, and simmer the pork for 1¼ hours.

Lift the meat from the pan, leave it to cool and set, then remove all the string. Cut away any rind with a sharp knife, score the fat in a diamond pattern at ½ in intervals, and press the light brown sugar firmly all over the fat. Put the meat in a roasting pan, heat the cider or apple juice and pour it over the meat, basting it without disturbing the sugar.

Skin the peaches (the skins will slip off easily if the peaches are covered with boiling water and left for 1 minute), cut them in half and remove the pits, and enlarge the cavities slightly with a pointed teaspoon. Blend the butter, honey (or sugar) and a pinch of cinnamon until creamy. Spoon this mixture into the peach halves.

Bake the pork in the center of a pre-heated oven, set at 350°F (180°C, mark 4), for ½ hour, basting frequently with the juice. Place the peaches around the roast and raise the temperature to 400°F (200°C, mark 6) and bake for a further 15 minutes, or until the top of the roast is golden and shiny.

Serve the roast whole or sliced, garnished with the peaches. Plain boiled potatoes and a tossed green salad, or carrots, would make good vegetable dishes to accompany the pork.

HAM SLICES IN MADEIRA SAUCE

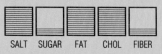

SALT   SUGAR   FAT   CHOL   FIBER

GLUTEN-FREE
TOTAL CALORIES: ABOUT 2810

All ham is high in **salt**, even after soaking (see notes on the previous recipe).
As ham can be very lean, this recipe will be low in both **fat** and **cholesterol** if you remove all visible fat; broil rather than fry the steaks, omitting the butter or lard; and cook the vegetables in a few spoonfuls of unsalted stock in a heavy pan for about 10 minutes. (Calories lost: up to 450.)

Freezing: ☑ up to 1 month.

BAKED SMOKED PORK SHOULDER

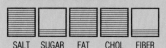

SALT   SUGAR   FAT   CHOL   FIBER

GLUTEN-FREE
TOTAL CALORIES: ABOUT 6500

As in the previous recipes, the **salt** level is inherently high, even after soaking, and cannot be reduced (except by serving smaller portions).
This cut of smoked pork is also high in **fat** and **cholesterol**; to reduce it to medium, trim away all fat before cooking or use a leaner cut such as a ham, also well trimmed of fat. Roast the meat on a rack, so that the fat can drain, and do not baste. (Calories lost: up to 450.)

Pressure cooker: ☑ for boiling the pork.

HAM IN PUFF PASTRY

SALT	SUGAR	FAT	CHOL	FIBER

TOTAL CALORIES: ABOUT 7150

As with the previous recipes, the **salt** level of ham is inherently high.
The **fat** and **cholesterol** content is mainly in the puff pastry. Minimize the fat in the meat by choosing a lean cut and trimming the skin and fat thoroughly. If you like, although it is fiddly, remove first the skin and then the fat; then replace the skin before cooking, keeping it in place with skewers. For low fat and cholesterol, replace the puff pastry with yeast pastry or phyllo pastry; use egg white only for sealing and glazing the pastry. This last step reduces the cholesterol but has little effect on the overall fat. To keep the fat level low, if you are using phyllo pastry do not brush each layer with oil as is generally done. (Calories lost: up to 1000.)

HAM IN PUFF PASTRY

A shank end of ham looks impressive and serves more people when encased in puff pastry which keeps the meat moist. It makes a good lunch or supper dish, but preparations should begin the day before.

PREPARATION TIME: *30 min*
COOKING TIME: *2¾ hours*
INGREDIENTS *(for 6)*:
4-pound smoked ham, shank end
1 large bay leaf
12 peppercorns
Pinch mace
4–6 parsley stalks
2 sprigs thyme
1 small onion
1 pound puff pastry
1 egg

Ask the butcher to bone part of the ham, leaving the end bone in to make carving easier.

Put the ham in a large saucepan. Cover with fresh cold water and add the bay leaf, peppercorns, mace, parsley stalks, thyme and onion. Bring to the boil, turn down the heat, then cover the pan with a lid and simmer for 20 minutes to each 1 pound. Remove the pan from the heat and let the ham cool overnight in the cooking liquid.

Remove the ham from the liquid and carefully pull off the skin. Roll out the puff pastry to an oblong shape, ⅛ in thick, and put the ham in the center. Brush the pastry edges with some of the lightly beaten egg; wrap the pastry over the ham, and press the edges together to enclose the meat. Seal the edges, pleating the pastry around the bone. Brush with egg.

Cover the bone with a piece of foil to keep it white while cooking. Use the pastry trimmings to decorate the casing, and carefully lift the ham on to a wet baking sheet; brush the pastry with the remaining egg.

Bake the ham for 20 minutes in the center of an oven pre-heated to 450°F (230°C, mark 8); lower the heat to 350°F (180°C, mark 4) and continue cooking for a further 30 minutes. Cover the roast with buttered wax paper as soon as the pastry is golden.

Serve the roast hot or cold. A savory rice salad, new potatoes and lettuce with green peas are appropriate side dishes for the ham.

Pork

GRATIN OF HAM

The Morvan district of Burgundy is famous for its cured hams. These are often served with a cream sauce, as in the following recipe. Virginia ham is more readily available here and makes a delicious substitute.

PREPARATION TIME: *15 min*
COOKING TIME: *45 min*
INGREDIENTS *(for 6)*:
12 slices cooked ham, about 1½
*   pounds*
¼ pound button mushrooms
2 tablespoons butter
1 onion
3 shallots
½ cup dry white wine
1 cup canned tomatoes
1¼ cups heavy cream
Salt* and black pepper
¼ cup grated Parmesan cheese

Arrange the slices of ham, overlapping each other, in a large, shallow flameproof dish.

Trim the mushrooms and slice them thinly. Melt the butter in a small frying pan and cook the mushrooms for about 8 minutes over low heat. Spoon them, with the butter, over the ham. Peel and finely chop the onion and shallots and put them in a small pan with the wine. Bring to the boil and continue boiling over high heat until the wine has reduced to about 1½ tablespoons.

Chop the tomatoes roughly and add to the onions. Cover the pan with a lid and simmer over low heat for 10 minutes. Rub the onion and tomato mixture through a fine sieve, and put the resulting purée in a clean pan.

Blend the cream into the purée and bring this sauce to the boil. Season to taste with salt and freshly ground pepper. Pour the sauce over the ham and mushrooms and sprinkle the cheese on top. Bake the ham gratin near the top of the oven, pre-heated to 450°F (230°C, mark 8) for 10 minutes or until brown on top.

Serve the gratin while still bubbling, with boiled and buttered rice and a green salad.

PORK AND SPINACH PÂTÉ

This light, colorful pâté can be served hot or cold.

PREPARATION TIME: *20 min*
COOKING TIME: *1 hour 20 min*
INGREDIENTS *(for 8–10)*:
2 pounds spinach
2 pounds ground shoulder of pork
1 tablespoon salt*
1 teaspoon freshly ground black
*   pepper*
1 bay leaf
¼ teaspoon ground cloves
¼ teaspoon mace

Wash the spinach well. Bring 2½ cups of water to a boil in a large pot. Add the spinach, return to a boil, and cook only until the spinach has wilted, about 5 minutes. Drain and chop the spinach coarsely. Squeeze a small amount of spinach at a time in your hands to extract as much water as possible. Add the ground pork and all seasonings and stir until well blended.

Put this mixture into a 6–8 cup terrine or bread pan, cover with a piece of buttered wax paper, and bake at 375°F (190°C, mark 5) for 1¼ hours. Do not overcook, or it will become dry. Slice and serve hot or cold.

HAM WITH APRICOT STUFFING

Baked stuffed hams and gammons are often credited to American cookery, but this recipe originated in the Cotswolds centuries ago. The American glazed crust is a great improvement on the English flour and water crust.

PREPARATION TIME: *15–20 min*
COOKING TIME: *2¼ hours*
INGREDIENTS *(for 10–12)*:
6 pound piece of ham (boned)
1 cup red wine
2 bay leaves
½ pound apricots
½ teaspoon arrowroot (optional)
Cloves
2–3 heaping tablespoons light
*   brown sugar*

Ask the butcher to bone the ham, leaving plenty of room for the stuffing. Put the meat in a large basin, add the wine and bay leaves and leave to marinate for at least 6 hours; turn the meat frequently.

Wash and dry the apricots, cut them in half and remove the pits. Lift the meat from the marinade, and put the wine and bay leaves in a saucepan. Add the apricots and bring to the boil over low heat. Simmer for about 10 minutes or until the apricots are soft and the wine has been absorbed. Remove the bay leaves, and let the apricots cool slightly.

Pat the ham thoroughly dry. Stuff as much of the apricot purée as possible into the ham (any surplus can be made into a purée boiled up with extra wine and thickened with a little arrowroot to make a sauce). Wrap the stuffed ham tightly in a double layer of foil, and make a slit in the center of the foil for the

GRATIN OF HAM

GLUTEN-FREE
TOTAL CALORIES: ABOUT 5350

The high **salt** level, as in the previous recipes, is inherent in the ham.
The **fat** and **cholesterol** levels can be reduced to low by the following steps: choose lean ham and trim away the visible fat; cook the mushrooms in a pan lightly brushed with oil, omitting the butter; replace the cream with the same amount of low-fat thick yogurt, or low-fat imitation sour cream, making sure that the dish does not then boil again but only heats through; halve the amount of added Parmesan cheese (this will also reduce the salt a little). (Calories lost: up to 1000.)

Microwave: ☑

PORK AND SPINACH PÂTÉ

GLUTEN-FREE   WHOLEFOOD
TOTAL CALORIES: ABOUT 3000

The **fat** is given as medium, but in fact the level depends very much on the meat chosen. Ground meat often has a surprisingly high fat level, especially as pork is so pale that pale fat fails to show up clearly. For a low level, buy lean pork as a whole piece, checking that it has no visible fat, and grind it yourself. The **cholesterol** level cannot be reduced below medium.
To retain more vitamins and minerals in the spinach, cook it

briefly, tightly covered, in just the water that clings to the leaves after it has been washed.

Food processor: ✓

HAM WITH APRICOT STUFFING

SALT	SUGAR	FAT	CHOL	FIBER

GLUTEN-FREE
TOTAL CALORIES: ABOUT 8950

As with the ham recipes on the previous pages, the **salt** level is inherently high and cannot be reduced except by eating smaller helpings.

The **fat** and **cholesterol** levels can be reduced to low if you choose lean ham and remove both skin and fat before wrapping it in foil to cook; this method stops the meat from drying out. It also loses the crisp crust many people like, but if the cloves are inserted and the surface glazed as in the recipe, the flavor will be good. (Calories lost: up to 500.)

steam to escape. Place on a baking sheet and cook the ham in the center of the oven pre-heated to 350°F (180°C, mark 4) for 2 hours.

Remove the ham from the oven, unwrap the foil and let the ham cool slightly. With a sharp knife, slit the skin lengthwise and remove it entirely, leaving a layer of fat no more than $\frac{1}{8}$ in

thick over the meat. Make shallow diagonal cuts, $\frac{3}{4}$ in apart, through the fat to form a pattern of diamond shapes, and insert a whole clove at each intersection. Pat the brown sugar firmly over the ham and transfer it to a roasting pan.

Bake the ham in the oven, pre-heated to 425°F (220°C, mark 7), for about 15 minutes or until the

sugar has melted and set to a golden brown glaze.

Serve the ham hot or cold, cut into thin slices. Creamed spinach and buttered potatoes would be suitable for a hot roast, and salads for the cold meat.

Pork

CROWN ROAST OF PORK

This is an impressive and colorful main course for a large dinner party. The crown, which should be ordered in advance, is cut from a loin of pork and cannot be constructed from less than 12 chops. The crown should have the fat carefully trimmed off by the butcher, as it cannot crisp when filled with a stuffing.

PREPARATION TIME: *35 min*
COOKING TIME: *2½ hours*
INGREDIENTS *(for 10–12):*

1 crown roast of pork (12 chops)
Lard
1 bouillon cube
STUFFING:
1 large onion
2 stalks celery
2 medium carrots
6 canned pineapple rings
2 tablespoons corn oil
½ cup cooked rice
3 tablespoons chopped fresh
  parsley
1 teaspoon dried savory
1–2 teaspoons paprika
½ cup golden raisins
Salt* and black pepper
Lemon juice
GARNISH:
6 canned pineapple rings
Watercress

Prepare the stuffing first. Peel and finely chop the onion, celery and carrots. Finely chop six pineapple rings and set the juice aside.

Heat the oil in a pan over moderate heat and fry the onion and celery until just turning color. Add the rice, carrots and parsley, together with the savory, paprika, pineapple and raisins. Mix all the ingredients thoroughly and heat through. Season to taste with salt, freshly ground pepper and lemon juice. Set the stuffing aside to cool.

Stand the crown roast in a greased roasting pan and cover the meat thoroughly with melted lard. Spoon the stuffing into the center of the crown and cover it with a piece of foil. Wrap foil around each chop bone to prevent it charring. Roast the crown in the center of a pre-heated oven, at 375°F (190°C, mark 5) for 2¼ hours or until amber-colored juice runs out when a skewer is inserted in the meat. Lift out the crown and keep it warm on a serving dish in the oven.

Fry the pineapple rings for garnishing in the hot fat in the roasting pan for 4 minutes or until golden brown on both sides. Slit through one side of each ring and arrange in a curling twist around the crown of pork.

Pour the fat carefully from the roasting pan and add the pineapple juice to the residue in the pan. Crumble the bouillon cube into the juices and bring the gravy to boiling point. Cook over high heat until the gravy is brown and has reduced slightly. Pour into a warm sauce boat.

Remove the foil from the tips of the chops and replace with paper frills. Garnish with small sprigs of watercress between the pineapple twists. Serve the crown with roast or sauté potatoes and with green beans.

PORK WITH LEMON

In Portugal, where this recipe comes from, pork is generally of inferior quality to the dairy-fed pigs here. The Portuguese housewife cooks lean pork tenderloin in a spicy wine sauce.

PREPARATION TIME: *20 min*
COOKING TIME: *25–30 min*
INGREDIENTS *(for 4–6):*
2 pounds pork tenderloin
2 tablespoons lard
1¼ cups dry white wine
4 teaspoons ground cumin
2 cloves garlic
Salt* and black pepper
6 slices lemon
2 teaspoons ground coriander

Trim away any excess fat and the thin outer skin from the pork tenderloin, cut the meat into 1 in cubes and pat dry on kitchen paper towels. Heat the lard in a large sauté pan and brown the meat, turning it continuously to prevent it sticking to the pan. Stir in just over half of the wine and add the cumin. Peel the garlic and crush it over the meat; season to taste with salt and freshly ground pepper. Bring the mixture to the boil, lower the heat and simmer for about 25 minutes or until tender. Add the remaining wine, cut the lemon slices into quarters and add them to the pan. Continue cooking, stirring, until the sauce thickens slightly. Stir in the coriander.

Spoon the meat and the sauce on to a dish. Plain boiled rice is traditional with the pork.

PORK TENDERLOIN WITH MUSHROOMS

| SALT | SUGAR | FAT | CHOL | FIBER |

GLUTEN-FREE   WHOLEFOOD
TOTAL CALORIES: ABOUT 2415

For low **fat** and **cholesterol**, check that the tenderloin, usually a lean cut, is in fact particularly so. Omit the oil from the marinade (for low fat only – it will not affect the cholesterol); soften the onion in a pan lightly brushed with oil, omitting the butter; when adding the pork, add also a few tablespoons of unsalted stock to moisten it instead of the butter; and replace the cream with low-fat imitation sour cream, thick low-fat yogurt or cultured buttermilk. Do not let the sauce boil after adding these. (Calories lost: up to 1270.)

Freezing: ☑ up to 2 months.

PORK TENDERLOIN WITH MUSHROOMS

The lean tenderloin of pork usually needs marinating or stuffing to give the meat extra flavor. It can be cooked whole, or cut into thick slices for a quick main course.

PREPARATION TIME: *30 min*
COOKING TIME: *15 min*
INGREDIENTS *(for 6):*
1½ pounds pork tenderloin
2 tablespoons oil
1 tablespoon lemon juice
Black pepper
1 small clove garlic (optional)
SAUCE:
6 ounces button mushrooms
1 onion
¼ cup unsalted butter
2 tablespoons dry sherry
½ cup heavy cream

Trim away the thin skin, or sinew, and fat from the pork. Cut the meat crosswise into 2 in thick slices. Lay the slices between two sheets of wet wax paper and beat them flat with a rolling pin. Arrange the slices in a shallow dish. Measure the oil and lemon juice into a basin and season with black pepper. Skin and crush the garlic, and mix it into the oil and lemon juice. Spoon this marinade over the pork and leave for about 30 minutes.

Meanwhile, trim and thinly slice the mushrooms. Peel the onion and chop it finely. Melt the butter in a frying pan and gently fry the onion for 5 minutes until it is soft, but not brown. Add the mushrooms and fry for a few

minutes. Lift the vegetables from the pan and keep them hot. Drain the pork pieces from the marinade and fry gently in the hot butter for 3–4 minutes, turning once. Transfer the pork to a hot serving dish and keep it warm.

Measure the sherry into the frying pan and heat briskly, stirring until it has reduced to 1 tablespoon. Return the onion and mushrooms to the pan and season with salt and freshly ground pepper. Stir in the cream. Heat gently, stirring, until the sauce is almost boiling. Remove from the heat and pour the sauce over the pork.

Serve the pork surrounded by boiled or fried rice.

Pork

PORK NOISETTES WITH PRUNES

This is a specialty from Tours in the Loire district, where some of the finest French pork and wine are produced. It is an easily prepared dish, but the prunes – large Californian ones – should be soaked overnight.

PREPARATION TIME: *15 min*
COOKING TIME: *1 hour*
INGREDIENTS *(for 6):*
6 slices pork tenderloin, each 1 in thick, or 6 boned loin chops
1 pound large prunes
1½ cups dry white wine
Seasoned flour (page 184)
¼ cup unsalted butter
1 heaping tablespoon red currant jelly
2 cups heavy cream
Salt★ and black pepper
Lemon juice

Leave the prunes in a bowl to soak in the wine overnight. Put the prunes and the wine in a pan and simmer, covered, for 20–30 minutes or until tender.

Trim any excess fat off the slices or chops. Coat them with seasoned flour, shaking off any surplus. Melt the butter in a heavy-based pan and brown the meat lightly over gentle heat, turning it once only. Cover the pan with a lid and simmer the pork for 30 minutes.

When the meat is nearly done, pour the prune liquid into the pan. Increase the heat and boil rapidly for a few minutes until the liquid has reduced slightly. Lift the meat on to a warm serving dish and arrange the prunes around it. Keep the meat and prunes warm in the oven while making the sauce.

Stir the red currant jelly into the juices in the pan, and boil this sauce over high heat until it has the consistency of syrup. Gradually blend in the cream, stirring continuously until the sauce is smooth and thick. Season with salt, pepper and lemon juice.

Pour the sauce over the meat and serve at once. Traditionally, the noisettes are served with boiled potatoes only.

PORK COOKED IN MILK

The Italians frequently pot-roast meat and chicken in milk. For this recipe, choose boned leg of pork or, more economically, pork shoulder. It can be served hot or cold.

PREPARATION TIME: *10 min*
COOKING TIME: *2 hours*
INGREDIENTS *(for 6):*
2½-pound boned rolled pork
Salt★ and black pepper
1 clove garlic
12 coriander seeds
2 onions
2 slices cooked ham
1 tablespoon olive oil
4 cups milk

Ask the butcher to bone the meat and to take part of the fat off the pork before rolling it. Wipe the meat with a clean damp cloth and rub it all over with salt and freshly ground pepper. Peel the garlic and cut it lengthwise into small strips. Make small incisions in the meat with the point of a knife and push in the garlic strips and coriander seeds.

Peel and finely chop the onions; dice the ham. Heat the oil in a heavy-based pan or flame-proof dish into which the meat will fit closely. Fry the onions and

ham in the oil for a few minutes until they begin to color. Put in the meat and brown it lightly all over. In a separate pan, bring the milk to boiling point, then pour it over the pork so that it reaches ½ in over the meat.

Cook the pork, uncovered, over low heat (set the pan on an asbestos mat), for about 1 hour. The milk should be kept barely at simmering point during cooking and will form a cobwebby skin which gradually turns pale golden brown. After 1 hour break the milk skin and turn the meat over, scraping all the skin from the sides into the bottom of the pan.

Continue cooking the meat slowly for a further 45 minutes, or until the milk has reduced to a cupful of thick sauce.

Lift the meat on to a serving dish and pour the sauce with the bits of onion and ham over it.

Serve the pork hot or cold, with boiled potatoes and a crisp green side salad.

PORK NOISETTES WITH PRUNES

SALT SUGAR FAT CHOL FIBER

GLUTEN-FREE* WHOLEFOOD*
TOTAL CALORIES: ABOUT 6570

Assuming that the pork tenderloin is quite lean, to reduce **fat** and **cholesterol** to low depends on browning the chops in a non-stick pan brushed lightly with oil instead of butter, and replacing the cream with the same amount of thick low-fat plain yogurt, cultured buttermilk or low-fat small curd cottage cheese. Take care the mixture does not boil after adding any of these or it will curdle: just warm through gently, stirring. If you want a thicker consistency, allow the sauce to cool a little so that any fat can be skimmed off, then add 1 tablespoon arrowroot which has been mixed to a smooth paste with a little water and continue with the recipe. (Calories lost: up to 1680.)

Freezing: ☑ up to 2 months.
Microwave: ☑

PORK COOKED IN MILK

SALT SUGAR FAT CHOL FIBER

GLUTEN-FREE WHOLEFOOD
TOTAL CALORIES: ABOUT 4265

No one ingredient in this recipe is high in **salt** (apart from the ham, but the amount per person is small), but the contributions made by the pork, ham and milk add up to a moderate level. Serving smaller portions, say 4–5 ounces of meat, combined with halving the amount of ham, will reduce this level to low.

It is not easy to find lean pork, but if you can, it will be low in fat. If you trim off all visible fat, use only 2 teaspoons of oil for preparing the filling and substitute skim milk, the total **fat** and **cholesterol** content will be low. However, skim milk tends to burn easily when boiled, and great care must be taken to ensure that it simmers very gently indeed, heating it slowly and stirring constantly while heating. The heavy pan and asbestos mat specified will be of help. (Calories lost: up to 300.)

Slow cooker: ☑

ROAST PORK WITH APPLE AND NUT STUFFING

SALT	SUGAR	FAT	CHOL	FIBER

GLUTEN-FREE *
WHOLEFOOD *
TOTAL CALORIES: ABOUT 6000

For very low **salt**, use bread made without salt for the cubes. For low **fat** and **cholesterol** levels, choose a lean piece of pork and trim it thoroughly of visible fat. Halve the amount of nuts (you could substitute lightly roasted hazelnuts, which have less fat); color the onions in a pan brushed lightly with oil, omitting the butter; and do not brush the meat with oil (this last step does not affect the cholesterol level). As there will be no fat to moisten the meat, cover the roasting dish in foil during the cooking. (Calories lost: up to 400.)

ROAST PORK WITH APPLE AND NUT STUFFING

Shoulder of pork is a good cut for roasting, as the meat is tender. When boned and stuffed it is easily carved even by the unskilled.

PREPARATION TIME: *20 min*
COOKING TIME: *2 hours*
INGREDIENTS *(for 6):*
3½-pound pork shoulder, boned
1 small onion
½ cup cashew nuts or peanuts
2 thick slices crustless bread
1 tart apple
1 stalk celery
2 teaspoons chopped parsley
2 tablespoons butter
Salt★ and black pepper
½ teaspoon dried summer savory
Lemon juice
2–3 tablespoons vegetable oil
½ cup dry hard cider

Peel and finely chop the onion and roughly chop the nuts. Dice the bread; peel, core and dice the apple. Wash and finely chop the celery and parsley.

Melt the butter in a small pan over moderate heat and fry the onion and nuts until they are just turning color. Add the bread, apple, celery, and parsley to the onion and nuts and continue cooking until the apple has softened. Season to taste with salt, pepper, summer savory and lemon juice.

Open up the pocket in the pork and spread the stuffing evenly. Roll up the meat and tie securely with string at regular intervals.

Place the pork in an oiled roasting pan; brush with oil and sprinkle generously with salt. Roast above the center of an oven pre-heated to 400°F (200°C, mark 6) for 20–30 minutes. Move the pan to a shelf just below the center and reduce the temperature to 350°F (180°C, mark 4). Cook for a further 1½ hours or until the juice comes out amber-colored when a skewer is pushed into the meat.

Put the roast on a serving plate and keep it warm. Leave the residue in the roasting pan to settle, then carefully skim or pour off the fat. Add the cider to the pan juices and bring to the boil over moderate heat, scraping in all the residue. When the gravy has colored, season to taste and pour it into a warm sauce boat.

Creamed potatoes and buttered cabbage or green beans are ideal with this tasty roast.

Pork

PORK CHOPS WITH APPLE

Tart apples are traditionally served with pork to counteract the fattiness of the meat. They appear as stuffings and sauces with roasts, and can also, as here, be used with oven-cooked chops.

PREPARATION TIME: *15 min*
COOKING TIME: *1 hour 10 min*
INGREDIENTS *(for 4):*
4 thick pork chops
2–4 tablespoons unsalted butter
Salt* and black pepper
3–4 large tart apples
Juice of a lemon

Trim any excess fat from the chops, wipe them dry with a damp cloth, and put them in a buttered ovenproof dish. Season to taste with salt and freshly ground pepper. Peel, core and thinly slice the apples and arrange over the chops to cover them completely. Melt the remaining butter and brush some of it over the apple slices. Sprinkle with lemon juice and cover the dish closely with a lid or foil.

Cook the chops in the center of a pre-heated oven, at 325°F (170°C, mark 3) for 1 hour. Remove the foil, brush the apples with the remaining butter and cook for a further 10 minutes, or until the apples are lightly browned but not dry, and the chops are tender.

Serve the chops from the cooking dish or on a warmed serving plate. Small new potatoes and braised endive go well with the sharp apple taste.

FLAMED PORK TENDERLOIN WITH APRICOTS

This quick and easy dish is suitable for cooking in a chafing dish at the table, once all the ingredients have been prepared. Prunes may be used instead of apricots; both should be soaked in water for 3–4 hours.

PREPARATION TIME: *25 min*
COOKING TIME: *15 min*
INGREDIENTS *(for 4):*
1¼ pounds pork tenderloin
Seasoned flour (page 184)
2 tablespoons dry sherry
⅔ cup dried apricots
2 tablespoons unsalted butter
2 tablespoons brandy
5 tablespoons sour cream
Salt* and black pepper
Lemon juice

Put the apricots and the water in which they were soaking into a saucepan, add the sherry and cook over low heat for 15 minutes. Trim any fat off the pork tenderloin and remove the outer skin. Cut it into 1½ in thick slices or round medallions and toss them in the seasoned flour.

Heat the butter in a frying pan or chafing dish over medium heat and fry the pork on both sides until golden and tender, turning once only. Pour off any surplus fat. Heat the brandy, set it alight and pour it over the pork. Add the drained apricots and stir until the brandy flames have burnt out.

Mix the sour cream with the apricot liquid and pour it into the pan. Simmer for a few minutes, then season to taste with salt, freshly ground pepper and lemon juice. Serve with fluffy boiled rice.

PORK CHOPS WITH ALMONDS AND SHERRY

When a special main course is required at short notice, this dish may provide the solution. Choose large, thick pork chops, preferably with the kidneys still attached.

PREPARATION TIME: *10 min*
COOKING TIME: *20 min*
INGREDIENTS *(for 4):*
4 pork chops
1 clove garlic
1 teaspoon crushed dill seeds
1 tablespoon olive oil
3 tablespoons unsalted butter
1 cup sliced almonds
½ cup dry sherry

Trim any excess fat off the chops, leaving ¼ in round the edge. Peel and crush the garlic and rub this and the dill seeds into both sides of each chop. Brush the chops all over with oil and put them under a pre-heated broiler, for 8 minutes to each side. Brush the chops again with oil when they are turned.

Meanwhile, melt the butter in a small pan and cook the almonds over low heat until they are straw-colored. Pour in the sherry, boil until bubbling, and then reduce the heat to simmering point and continue cooking until the almonds turn a caramel color.

Arrange the chops on a serving dish, with the sherry sauce and almonds poured over them. Creamed potatoes and Brussels sprouts with sour cream would be suitable vegetables.

PORK CHOPS WITH APPLE

| SALT | SUGAR | FAT | CHOL | FIBER |

GLUTEN-FREE   WHOLEFOOD
TOTAL CALORIES: ABOUT 2930

To restrict **fat** and **cholesterol** levels to low, grease the ovenproof dish by brushing it lightly with oil and omit the butter here and for brushing the apples. Make sure the pork is carefully trimmed of fat and the portions are not too large. You may still find that the juices at the bottom of the dish look fatty. If possible, skim them off, using a fat-separating gravy boat or a fat-skimming brush, before serving. (Calories lost: up to 400.)

Microwave: ✓ but may need final browning under broiler.

FLAMED PORK TENDERLOIN WITH APRICOTS

| SALT | SUGAR | FAT | CHOL | FIBER |

GLUTEN-FREE*   WHOLEFOOD*
TOTAL CALORIES: ABOUT 2500

For low **fat** and **cholesterol** levels, choose very lean pork, trimming off any visible fat; brown the pork in a heavy or non-stick pan brushed lightly with oil, omitting the butter; and replace the sour cream with imitation low-fat sour cream or cultured buttermilk. (Calories lost: up to 300.)

PORK CHOPS WITH ALMONDS AND SHERRY

SALT	SUGAR	FAT	CHOL	FIBER

GLUTEN-FREE   WHOLEFOOD
TOTAL CALORIES: ABOUT 3340

For low **fat** and **cholesterol** levels choose lean pork; trim off all visible fat; broil the chops without brushing with oil (this step affects the fat level only); and color the almonds in only 1 teaspoon of oil in a heavy pan, omitting the butter. As almonds are roughly half oil (though do not contain cholesterol), the amount can be reduced to half or even a quarter, reducing the amount of sherry to match. (Calories lost: up to 240.)

STUFFED PORK TENDERLOIN

SALT	SUGAR	FAT	CHOL	FIBER

GLUTEN-FREE*   WHOLEFOOD*
TOTAL CALORIES: ABOUT 4175

For low **fat** and **cholesterol** levels, choose very lean tenderloin and brown the stuffed meat in a heavy or non-stick pan brushed lightly with oil, omitting the butter; omit the melted butter added to the stuffing. For even lower levels, use only white of egg to bind the stuffing, or leave out the egg altogether and substitute a small apple, peeled and grated. If you are concerned that the meat may be dry, add a little stock to the cooking pan. (Calories lost: up to 1000.)

Food processor: ☑ for the stuffing.

STUFFED PORK TENDERLOIN

The tenderloin of pork is a lean, economical cut of meat. A tenderloin weighs about 12–16 ounces and should be stuffed, marinated or larded to prevent the meat drying out.

PREPARATION TIME: *30 min*
COOKING TIME: *1½ hours*
INGREDIENTS *(for 6)*:
1½–2 pounds pork tenderloin
¼ cup unsalted butter
1 clove garlic
STUFFING:
2 cups fine soft breadcrumbs
⅓ cup mixed dried fruits
1 tablespoon finely chopped parsley
1 heaping tablespoon finely chopped onion
1 clove garlic (optional)
½ tablespoon chopped tarragon
¼ cup melted butter
1 orange
1 egg
Salt★ and black pepper
SAUCE:
1 pound fresh apricots
1 tablespoon water
1 tablespoon dark brown sugar
Juice of a lemon
½ teaspoon curry powder
1 tablespoon Kümmel

Prepare the stuffing first: mix the breadcrumbs, the cut-up fruits, parsley, onion, crushed garlic and tarragon in a bowl. Stir in the melted butter. Add the grated rind of the orange, remove pith and membrane from the flesh, cut this up and mix into the stuffing. Beat the egg lightly and use to bind the mixture. Season with salt and freshly ground pepper.

Trim all the fat off each tenderloin and remove the transparent skin. Slit the meat lengthwise through half its thickness, open it out and flatten with the fist or the edge of a cleaver.

Spread the stuffing over the tenderloins, roll them up tightly from the bottom and tie with string. Melt the butter in a flame-proof dish on the stove. Peel and slice the garlic and fry until brown, then remove. Fry the pork for a few minutes in the butter until evenly browned. Cover the pan with the lid and roast for 1 hour 20 minutes or 40 minutes to the pound on the center shelf of an oven pre-heated to 325°F (170°C, mark 3). Remove the lid for the last 10 minutes for the meat to brown.

To make the sauce, halve and pit the apricots, tie up the pits in a piece of cheesecloth and put them with the apricots in a saucepan. Add the water and stew until the apricots are tender, stirring constantly. Mix in the sugar, lemon juice and curry powder and cook for 5 minutes or until thick. Remove the pits; beat the apricots to a paste or liquidize in a blender before stirring in the Kümmel.

Before serving, remove the string and carve the meat into slices. Arrange on a serving dish and spoon over a little of the sauce. Offer the remaining sauce separately with, for example, sauté potatoes and broccoli.

KIDNEYS IN CREOLE SAUCE

Creole sauce, the classic sauce of the West Indies, is composed mainly of sweet peppers, tomatoes and fiery Tabasco sauce – which is hotter than sweet chili sauce. It is often served as a garnish with noodles or rice.

PREPARATION TIME: *15 min*
COOKING TIME: *15–20 min*
INGREDIENTS *(for 4–6):*
1¼ pounds veal or pork kidneys
1 small onion
16-ounce can tomatoes
1 clove garlic
1 small green pepper
2 teaspoons capers
¼ cup or 2 tablespoons olive oil
1 teaspoon dark brown sugar
1 tablespoon tomato chutney
Salt★
Tabasco or chili sauce
Lemon juice
6–8 ripe olives

Skin the kidneys and cut them into thin slices. Snip out the white cores with scissors. Peel and thinly slice the onion. Peel the garlic. Wash the pepper, remove the stalk and the seeds and chop the flesh. Chop the capers.

Heat the butter, or oil, in a heavy-based pan and cook the onion over moderate heat until soft and transparent. Turn up the heat, add the sliced kidneys and fry them for 3–4 minutes or until browned, stirring frequently.

Crush the garlic into the pan and add the chopped tomatoes with their juices, the pepper and capers. Stir in the sugar and tomato chutney, and season to taste with salt, Tabasco or chili sauce and lemon juice.

Cover the pan with a lid or foil and simmer over low heat for 10–15 minutes. Meanwhile, halve and pit the olives and add them to the kidneys.

Spoon the kidneys and the sauce over ribbon noodles tossed in butter. A crisp green salad could be served as a side dish.

BRAISED OXTAIL

Oxtail is an inexpensive, nourishing but fatty meat. This stew is best cooked the day before so that the fat can settle and be lifted from the top before the stew is re-heated.

PREPARATION TIME: *40min*
COOKING TIME: *4¾ hours*
INGREDIENTS *(for 6):*
2 oxtails
Seasoned flour (page 184)
3 tablespoons beef drippings
2 onions
1 bottle red wine or 4 cups beef stock
Bouquet garni (page 183)
Salt★ and black pepper
2 bay leaves
1 tablespoon red currant jelly
Peel of half lemon and half orange
¾ pound carrots
2 small turnips
1 tablespoon lemon juice
1 tablespoon tomato paste
6 ounces mushrooms
GARNISH:
3 tablespoons chopped parsley
2 teaspoons grated lemon rind

Chop the oxtails into 2 in lengths and coat lightly with the seasoned flour. Peel and slice the onions.

Melt the drippings in a large sauté pan and fry the oxtails in the hot fat for 5 minutes until they glisten, then transfer to a large fireproof cooking pot. Fry the onions in the residue of the fat, and as soon as they begin to take color add them to the oxtail. Pour the wine or beef stock over the oxtail and onions, put the pot over the heat and bring the wine to the boil. Add the bouquet garni, salt, pepper, bay leaves, jelly and peel, and simmer on top of the stove for 2 hours. Strain off the liquid into a wide bowl and leave to cool.

Peel and slice the carrots and turnips and add to the oxtail. Spoon as much fat as possible from the cooled liquid (if it is thoroughly cold, the fat will have settled in a layer on top and can easily be lifted off). Pour the liquid over the oxtail. Add the lemon juice and tomato paste, bring to the boil and immediately place on the lowest shelf of the oven, heated to 275°F (140°C, mark 1); cook for 2½ hours. Add the trimmed and sliced mushrooms to the dish for the last 10 minutes.

Serve sprinkled with parsley mixed with the lemon peel; rice with leeks would also be suitable.

KIDNEYS IN CREOLE SAUCE

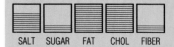

SALT SUGAR FAT CHOL FIBER

GLUTEN-FREE★ WHOLEFOOD★
TOTAL CALORIES: ABOUT 1470

To reduce the **salt** level use fewer kidneys and olives, and add more onions. For a low-salt dish, replace the olives with grapes. Check the tomatoes are canned without added salt. The kidneys, although fairly low in **fat**, are quite high in **cholesterol**. However, the remaining cholesterol from the butter can be avoided by cooking the kidneys in oil; this gives an overall moderate level of cholesterol. The fat content can be reduced to low at the same time by using only 1 tablespoon of oil. (Calories lost: up to 300.)
Use **gluten-free** chutney.

Freezing: ✓ up to 2 months.
Microwave: ✓

BRAISED OXTAIL

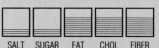

SALT SUGAR FAT CHOL FIBER

GLUTEN-FREE★ WHOLEFOOD★
TOTAL CALORIES: ABOUT 2500

For a low **fat** and **cholesterol** level trim the meat carefully, and let the dish chill so that fat settling on the top can be removed; brown the oxtails in a heavy pan brushed lightly with oil. (Calories lost: up to 350.)

Pressure cooker: ✓
Slow cooker: ✓
Freezing: ✓ up to 2 months.

ROGNONS TURBIGO

SALT	SUGAR	FAT	CHOL	FIBER

GLUTEN-FREE*
TOTAL CALORIES: ABOUT 1950

The raised **salt** level comes from the sausages and kidneys; using only 1 sausage will reduce it to medium.

To reduce the amount of **fat**, again use only 1 sausage (or omit the sausages completely and treble the amount of onion), as it is the sausages, with a typical fat level of at least 25%, which make this dish high in both fat and cholesterol.

The **cholesterol** level of this dish can be reduced by cooking the kidneys in 1 tablespoon of oil, omitting the butter, but will remain high, as organ meats have a much greater amount than other meats. However, this recipe does not use a large amount of kidney. Without the butter, with fewer sausages and if the sauce is made as suggested below, both fat and cholesterol will be medium. To make the sauce, substitute cornstarch for the flour, blend with water to make a smooth paste, and work in the liquid when cold. Then heat gently together, stirring steadily, until boiling. Simmer for a few minutes before stirring in the tomato paste and sherry. (Calories lost: up to 850.)

Gluten-free sausages can often be produced on request by small butchers, and a cornstarch sauce will be gluten-free.

The dish is not really **wholefood**, as sausages generally contain additives.

Freezing: ✓ up to 2 months.
Microwave: ✓

ROGNONS TURBIGO

This French family meal consists of halved fried kidneys, supplemented with pearl onions and small sausages.

PREPARATION TIME: *25 min*
COOKING TIME: *20–25 min*
INGREDIENTS *(for 4):*
6 lamb kidneys
4 small pork sausages
¼ cup unsalted butter
8 pearl onions
1 tablespoon flour
1¼ cups chicken or beef stock
½ cup dry white wine
1 heaping teaspoon tomato paste
2 tablespoons dry sherry
Salt★ and black pepper
1 bay leaf
GARNISH:
Chopped parsley and bread
  croûtons (page 178)

Skin the kidneys, cut them in half and snip out the white core with scissors. Separate the sausages and twist each in opposite directions so that they can be snipped in half.

Melt the butter in a large heavy-based pan. Gently fry the kidneys and sausages until brown, then remove from the pan and keep them hot.

Meanwhile, peel the onions, leaving them whole; put them in a saucepan and cover with cold water. Bring to the boil, simmer for 3–5 minutes, then drain.

Stir the flour into the hot fat remaining in the sauté pan, until well blended; cook gently for a few minutes. Gradually add the stock and wine, stirring well until the sauce is smooth. Bring to the boil, stir in the tomato paste and sherry; season to taste with salt and freshly ground pepper.

Put the kidneys, sausages and onions back into the pan; add the bay leaf, cover tightly with a lid and simmer gently for 20–25 minutes.

Transfer the sausages, kidneys and onions to a hot serving dish. Remove the bay leaf, check seasoning and strain the sauce over the meat. Garnish with crisp bread croûtons and sprinkle with chopped parsley.

Spiced rice or creamed potatoes and broccoli go well with this dish

LIVER WITH DUBONNET AND ORANGE

Lamb – or the more expensive calf – liver is most suitable for this recipe. The fruity, sweet-wine sauce blends surprisingly well with juicy, slightly undercooked liver.

PREPARATION TIME: *15 min*
COOKING TIME: *10–15 min*
INGREDIENTS *(for 6)*:
1 pound lamb liver
2 small onions
1 clove garlic
1 tablespoon olive oil
3 tablespoons butter
Seasoned flour (page 184)
SAUCE:
1 tablespoon orange juice
½ cup red Dubonnet
2 heaping tablespoons fresh chopped parsley
Rind of an orange, coarsely grated
1 teaspoon finely grated lemon rind

Wash the liver, trim off any tough and discolored parts and dry it thoroughly. Cut the liver into slices, ½ in thick, and coat them with seasoned flour.

Peel and finely chop the onions and garlic. Heat the oil and butter in a large, heavy-based pan over moderate heat and cook the onion and garlic, covered, until soft and beginning to color.

Add the liver slices to the onions, in a single layer, and cook over low heat. As soon as the blood begins to run, turn the liver over and cook the other side for a slightly shorter time.

When cooked, arrange the liver on a warm serving dish. Cover with the onion, lifted from the pan with a slotted spoon. Keep the dish hot.

To make the sauce, stir the orange juice and Dubonnet into the pan juices. Boil rapidly until the liquid has reduced by half. Take the pan off the heat and stir in most of the chopped parsley, grated orange and lemon rind, reserving a little for garnish.

Pour the sauce over the liver, sprinkle with the parsley and orange and lemon rind. Serve at once, with creamed potatoes and a green vegetable.

FRIED LIVER WITH ONION GRAVY

Liver, whether from lamb, veal or pork, is one of the most nourishing and digestible meats. The flavor is best preserved by steeping the liver in milk before frying.

PREPARATION TIME: *20 min*
COOKING TIME: *25 min*
INGREDIENTS *(for 4)*:
1 pound lamb liver
Seasoned flour (page 184)
1 pound onions
⅔ cup unsalted butter
1 tablespoon flour
½ cup beef stock
1 teaspoon vinegar
Salt★ and black pepper

Cut away any skin and gristle from the liver and cut it into ¼ in slices. Soak the liver slices in milk for 1 hour. Drain the liver well, pat it dry on kitchen paper towels, then coat each slice with seasoned flour, making sure both sides are evenly coated.

Prepare the gravy before frying the liver: peel and thinly slice the onions. Melt ¼ cup of the butter in a large frying pan, add the onions and fry over low heat for about 20 minutes or until soft and golden brown. Turn frequently to prevent the onion

LIVER WITH DUBONNET AND ORANGE

SALT SUGAR FAT CHOL FIBER

GLUTEN-FREE★   WHOLEFOOD★
TOTAL CALORIES: ABOUT 1815

Liver is high in **cholesterol** although fairly low in **fat**. For low fat, cook the onion and liver in a heavy-based pan brushed lightly with oil. (Calories lost: up to 350.)

FRIED LIVER WITH ONION GRAVY

SALT SUGAR FAT CHOL FIBER

GLUTEN-FREE★   WHOLEFOOD★
TOTAL CALORIES: ABOUT 2120

For a low **fat** (but still high **cholesterol**) dish, cook the onions in only 2 teaspoons of fat (butter, oil or vegetable margarine), adding a few tablespoons of the stock to prevent sticking, and cooking tightly covered so that the juices do not evaporate. To make the onions into gravy, thicken with cornstarch, made into a smooth paste with a little cold stock or water, then mixed into the remaining stock. Heat gently, stirring, and simmer for 1–2 minutes. Do not add extra butter.
The liver itself can be broiled on a baking sheet lightly brushed with oil, for about 4 minutes each side. (Calories lost: up to 1000.)

DANISH LIVER PÂTÉ

SALT	SUGAR	FAT	CHOL	FIBER

GLUTEN-FREE* WHOLEFOOD*
TOTAL CALORIES: ABOUT 3680

To reduce the **salt** and **fat** to low and **cholesterol** to medium, line the pâté dish with a double layer of spinach leaves which have been softened by dipping in simmering water for about 40 seconds, and omit the bacon and anchovies; replace the fresh pork fat in the pâté with ½ pound chopped mushrooms; use skim milk and make the binding sauce by mixing a little of this with the flour, then working in the warm infused milk, and continuing with the recipe. Omit the butter. (Calories lost: up to 2600.)

Food processor: ☑
Freezing: ☑ up to 2 months.

BRAINS IN BLACK BUTTER

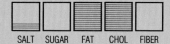

SALT	SUGAR	FAT	CHOL	FIBER

GLUTEN-FREE WHOLEFOOD
TOTAL CALORIES: ABOUT 2000

Although brains are high in **cholesterol**, the total fat content of the dish can be kept low if the brains are served with a non-buttery sauce. This can be a Chinese-style sweet-sour sauce, made by mixing 1 tablespoon each of soy sauce, brown sugar, wine vinegar, dry sherry and tomato paste with about 2 teaspoons cornstarch worked to a paste with water. Heat gently until it thickens. (Calories lost: up to 1000.)

sticking to the bottom of the pan. A pinch of sugar may help the onions to brown more quickly.

Blend 2 tablespoons of butter with the flour and add in bits to the hot onions. Stir until melted and blended, then gradually stir in the hot stock. Bring the gravy to the boil, simmer for a moment, then stir in the vinegar and season to taste with salt and freshly ground pepper.

Melt the remaining butter in a heavy-based pan, add the liver slices and fry them quickly for about 5 minutes, turning once. Lift them out on to a hot serving dish and pour over the onion gravy. Creamed or boiled potatoes go well with the liver.

DANISH LIVER PÂTÉ

The inexpensive pork liver is not much used for broiling or frying, but is ideal when made into a pâté. This pâté should be left until completely cool under a heavy weight before being served. It will keep for up to a week in the refrigerator.

PREPARATION TIME: *35 min*
COOKING TIME: *2 hours*
INGREDIENTS *(for 6–8):*
1 pound pork liver
1¼ cups milk
1 onion
1 bay leaf
6 ounces fresh pork fat from the pork loin
6 anchovy fillets
Salt★ and black pepper
¼ teaspoon each of ground nutmeg, cloves and allspice
2 tablespoons unsalted butter
2 tablespoons flour
1 egg
½ pound bacon slices

Measure the milk into a saucepan. Peel the onion and cut in half; add it, with the bay leaf, to the milk and bring to the boil over gentle heat. Remove the saucepan from the heat and allow the milk to infuse for 15 minutes. Strain through a sieve and set the milk aside.

Remove any skin and gristle from the liver. Grind the pork fat, the liver and anchovy fillets twice through the fine disk. Blend the mixture thoroughly and season to taste with salt, freshly ground pepper and the spices.

Melt the butter in a saucepan, add the flour and cook over low heat for 1 minute; gradually stir in the milk, beating continuously. Bring the mixture to the boil and cook for 2–3 minutes. Draw off the heat and blend in the liver mixture. Bind with the lightly beaten egg.

Line a 1-pound loaf pan with the bacon slices, leaving the slices to hang over the edges. Alternatively, bake the pâté in two smaller loaf pans and store one in the freezer. Spoon the pâté mixture into the pan and fold the bacon slices over the top.

Cover the pan with a piece of buttered wax paper and place in a large roasting pan holding 1 in of cold water. Place in the center of a pre-heated oven and bake for 2 hours at 325°F (170°C, mark 3). The pâté is baked when a stainless steel skewer comes away clean.

Remove the pâté from the oven, cover with freshly buttered wax paper and place a heavy weight on top. Leave the pâté until quite cold, preferably overnight, before turning it out. Serve the pâté, cut into thick slices, with hot toast and butter.

BRAINS IN BLACK BUTTER

Veal brains are traditionally used in this classic French recipe. But they are often difficult to obtain, and lamb brains are also good.

PREPARATION TIME: *30 min*
COOKING TIME: *35 min*
INGREDIENTS *(for 4):*
1 pound brains
1 bay leaf
Salt★ and black pepper
¾ cup unsalted butter
½ tablespoon caper vinegar
1 tablespoon capers

Soak the brains in a bowl of cold, lightly salted water for at least 30 minutes to remove all blood. Drain the brains, remove any bone fragments and peel off the outer transparent skin. Rinse the brains again in cold water and divide each brain into two (if using the larger veal brains, each brain should be cut into thick slices).

Put the brains in a saucepan and cover with cold, lightly salted water. Bring to the boil over moderate heat, and carefully remove any scum. Lower the heat, add the bay leaf, and cover the pan with a lid; cook the brains gently for 20 minutes. Drain well and transfer the brains to a warm serving dish. Sprinkle with salt and freshly ground pepper.

Melt the butter in a small pan over moderate heat and let the butter brown without burning it. Stir in the vinegar and capers, and pour this sauce over the brains immediately.

Serve the brains with crusty bread to mop up the butter.

Variety Meats

BRAINS IN CURRY SAUCE

Brains, like any other variety meat, require careful cleaning, and soaking for at least 1 hour. But they are so tasty, nourishing and inexpensive that they are worth a little trouble.

PREPARATION TIME: *15 min*
COOKING TIME: *30–35 min*
INGREDIENTS *(for 4–6):*
2 pounds veal brains
2½ cups milk
1 onion
1 clove garlic
¼ cup butter
1 heaping tablespoon flour
1 heaping teaspoon curry powder
1¼ cups chicken stock
½–¾ pound green or purple grapes
½ cup heavy cream (optional)
Salt★ and black pepper

Cover the brains with cold water, add 2 tablespoons of salt and leave to soak for 1 hour. Rinse them thoroughly under cold running water and remove the fine skin that covers the brains. Cut away any fibers and discolored parts and remove any bone splinters.

Put the brains in a pan with enough milk to cover. Bring to the boil and simmer for 10 minutes or until the brains are firm. Drain and set the milk aside. Cut the brains in ½ in thick slices. Arrange them on a dish, cover with foil and keep warm.

Peel and finely chop the onion and garlic. Melt the butter in a saucepan and cook the onion and garlic over gentle heat for 5 minutes. Stir in the flour and curry powder, mixing well. Gradually add the chicken stock and ½ cup of the milk in which the brains were cooked; blend thoroughly. Simmer this sauce until it has reduced to the consistency of thick cream.

While the sauce is cooking peel the grapes and remove the seeds if necessary (page 178). Add the grapes to the sauce and simmer for a further 5 minutes. Stir in the cream and season to taste with salt and freshly ground pepper.

Pour the sauce over the brains and serve with plain boiled rice and with triangles of toast.

SWEETBREADS WITH BEURRE NOISETTE

Ideally, this lunch or supper dish should be made with veal sweetbreads. These are often difficult to come by, and lamb sweetbreads make a good and inexpensive alternative. Both types of sweetbreads should be soaked for several hours before cooking.

PREPARATION TIME: *30 min*
COOKING TIME: *40 min*
INGREDIENTS *(for 4–6):*
1¼ pounds veal or lamb sweetbreads
¼ cup white wine vinegar
1 carrot
1 stalk celery
2 cups chicken or veal stock
½ bay leaf
1 sprig thyme
6 peppercorns
¾ cup clarified butter (page 182)
Salt★ and black pepper
Seasoned flour (page 184)
3 tablespoons unsalted butter
1 tablespoon olive oil
GARNISH:
Chopped fresh parsley
Lemon wedges

Soak the sweetbreads for at least 3 hours in several changes of cold water to remove all traces of blood. For the last 1½ hours, soak the sweetbreads in fresh cold water with 1 tablespoon of vinegar. Put them in a pan with fresh cold water and bring slowly to the boil. Take the pan off the heat, drain the sweetbreads and cool under running water. Remove the black veins and pull off as much as possible of the thin skin around them, without tearing the sweetbreads. Wrap them in a clean cloth and let them cool between two weighted plates or

BRAINS IN CURRY SAUCE

| SALT | SUGAR | FAT | CHOL | FIBER |

GLUTEN-FREE★   WHOLEFOOD★
TOTAL CALORIES: ABOUT 3080

For notes on the **fat** and **cholesterol** content of brains, see the preceding recipe.
To give this dish a low overall fat content, use skim milk for cooking; cook the onion in a pan lightly brushed with oil, not in butter; do not add extra fat before stirring in flour and curry powder to make the sauce, but stir over lowest heat; replace the cream, if wished, with the same amount of low-fat imitation sour cream or thick low-fat yogurt into which you have stirred a teaspoon of cornstarch. (Calories lost: up to 1000.) This will be **gluten-free** if cornstarch or potato starch is used for the sauce and there is no gluten in the curry powder – check the label.

Microwave: ☑

SWEETBREADS WITH BEURRE NOISETTE

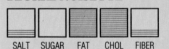

| SALT | SUGAR | FAT | CHOL | FIBER |

GLUTEN-FREE★   WHOLEFOOD★
TOTAL CALORIES: ABOUT 2780

Like liver and kidneys, sweetbreads are high in **cholesterol**, on a par with eggs, though much lower than brains. The cholesterol content of these cannot be reduced (except by using smaller portions), but although the remaining **fat** content is fairly low, reductions are possible here. If the meat is cooked in oil or vegetable fat rather than butter, the cholesterol level will be medium to high. To reduce the fat content to low, either sauté in a heavy pan brushed lightly with oil or broil on a baking sheet brushed with oil. The butter sauce can be replaced by a Chinese-style sauce (see the notes on Brains in Black Butter on the previous page), or by a purée of boiled beets, flavored with a little lemon juice or vinegar. (Calories lost: up to 1550.)

COEUR CORIANDRE

| SALT | SUGAR | FAT | CHOL | FIBER |

GLUTEN-FREE*   WHOLEFOOD*
TOTAL CALORIES: ABOUT 1650

Like kidney and liver, heart is higher in **cholesterol** than it is in **fat**; it has less than the two other organ meats, but more than most meats. As this cannot be reduced, avoid the remaining fat in this dish (from the butter) by browning the meat in a non-stick or heavy pan brushed lightly with oil, rather than in butter. After adding the onion, add a few tablespoons of stock and cover tightly to avoid drying out. This gives a low-fat dish, although the cholesterol remains medium to high. (Calories lost: up to 300.)

Pressure cooker: ☑
Slow cooker: ☑
Freezing: ☑ up to 2 months.

wooden boards to flatten them. Meanwhile, scrape, wash and slice the carrot and celery.

Put the sweetbreads in a pan, cover with the stock by about 1 in and add the carrot, celery, bay leaf, thyme and peppercorns. Put the pan over low heat and bring slowly to simmering point; cook for 10 minutes, uncovered. Remove the sweetbreads, strain the stock through a fine sieve and leave the sweetbreads in the stock until they are cool enough to handle.

Remove the sweetbreads from the stock and dry them on a clean cloth. Heat the remaining vinegar in a small pan and boil until it has reduced by two-thirds. In a separate pan, heat the clarified butter gently and, when light brown, stir in the vinegar. Season to taste with salt and freshly ground pepper.

Cut the sweetbreads into thick slices and coat lightly with seasoned flour. Melt the unsalted butter and oil together over moderate heat and cook the sweetbreads in it for about 3 minutes on each side, or until lightly browned. Remove the sweetbread slices to a heated serving dish and pour the brown butter over them.

Sprinkle with chopped parsley and serve at once garnished with wedges of lemon. They go well with boiled rice and cucumber au gratin.

COEUR CORIANDRE

Hearts are usually stuffed and braised slowly for several hours as they tend to be dry. In this French farmhouse recipe they are marinated in lemon juice before being braised in an apple and cider sauce, with an unusual spicing of coriander.

PREPARATION TIME: *20 min*
COOKING TIME: *1–1½ hours*
INGREDIENTS *(for 4):*
4 lamb or 2 veal hearts
Juice of a lemon
½ pound onions
2 medium-size tart apples
2–3 tablespoons flour
3 tablespoons butter
Salt* and black pepper
2 bay leaves
½ cup hard cider
1 teaspoon crushed coriander seeds
1 teaspoon sugar
2 thin slices unpeeled lemon

Cut the hearts in slices, about ½ in thick, and remove all fat, gristle and blood vessels. Put the slices in a basin with the lemon juice and leave to marinate for 30 minutes. Meanwhile, peel and slice the onions and the cored apples.

Dry the heart slices and coat them with flour, then fry them in the butter in a flameproof casserole over high heat. Add the onion and continue frying until pale golden. Season well with salt and freshly ground pepper. Add the bay leaves and the cider. Cover the heart slices with the apple and sprinkle them with coriander seed and sugar. Lay the lemon slices on top of the apples.

Put the lid on the casserole and cook over low heat on top of the stove or in a pre-heated oven, at 300°F (160°C, mark 2), for about 1 hour or until tender. When cooked, remove the lemon slices and bay leaves and stir the apple slices into the sauce.

Serve the casseroled hearts with creamed potatoes and green beans or snow peas.

Variety Meats

TRIPE PROVENÇALE

Tripe, which is a much-neglected food in this country, has a long history in Europe. The Normans introduced it as a food to Britain; the following recipe comes from southern France.

PREPARATION TIME: *20 min*
COOKING TIME: *2½ hours*
INGREDIENTS *(for 6)*:
2 pounds honeycomb tripe
2½ cups chicken stock
Salt* and black pepper
1 onion
1 clove garlic
2 tablespoons unsalted butter
1 pound tomatoes
Dried thyme
¼ cup dry white wine
1 tablespoon chopped parsley

Wash the tripe thoroughly. Put it in a saucepan and cover with cold water. Bring to the boil. Remove from the heat, drain the tripe and rinse under cold running water. Cut into 2 in cubes and return them to the saucepan. Pour over the boiling stock and add a pinch of salt. As soon as the stock is boiling again, reduce the heat. Cover the pan with a lid and simmer the tripe for 2 hours.

Meanwhile, peel and roughly chop the onion, and skin and crush the garlic. Melt the butter in a frying pan and gently fry the onion and garlic for about 5 minutes until transparent. Skin the tomatoes (page 179) and chop them roughly; add them, with a pinch of dried thyme, the wine and parsley, to the frying pan. Bring this mixture to the boil over gentle heat, cover with a lid and simmer for 30 minutes. Season to taste with salt and freshly ground pepper. If the sauce is still thin,

remove the lid and boil the sauce over high heat for 5 minutes until it has reduced and thickened.

When the tripe has finished cooking, drain it and stir it into the tomato mixture. Cook over low heat for a further 10 minutes. Arrange the tripe on a hot serving dish and surround it with plain boiled rice.

TRIPE WITH ONIONS

Fresh, ready-to-cook tripe usually needs only about 2 hours' cooking time, but it is best to check with the butcher.

PREPARATION TIME: *10 min*
COOKING TIME: *approx. 2¼ hours*
INGREDIENTS *(for 4)*:
1 pound honeycomb tripe
3 large onions
2½ cups milk
2 tablespoons butter
2 tablespoons flour
Salt* and black pepper
*1 heaping tablespoon finely
   chopped parsley*

Cut the tripe into ¾ in pieces, and peel and roughly chop the onions. Place these ingredients in a heavy-based pan; pour over the milk to cover (if necessary, top up with water). Cover the pan and cook over gentle heat for about 2 hours or until the tripe is tender. Strain through a coarse sieve and set aside about 2½ cups of the liquid.

Make a roux (page 154) from the butter and flour and gradually blend in the liquid. Bring to the boil and season to taste with salt and ground pepper. Re-heat the tripe and onions in the sauce, add the parsley and serve.

BRAWN WITH SPICED PRUNES

Brawn – similar to our head cheese – is a traditional English dish made from pork trimmings and pig's head. It dates from the 15th century and is always served cold, usually as a first course. However, it also makes an attractive main course for lunch or supper. Preparations should begin at least 2 days in advance.

PREPARATION TIME: *1¼ hours*
COOKING TIME: *4 hours*
INGREDIENTS *(for 8)*:
½ pig's head
⅔ cup sea salt
2 onions
4 shallots
2 carrots
2 turnips
12 whole allspice
Bouquet garni (page 183)
4 cloves
2 blades mace
6 peppercorns
Juice of a lemon
Oil
Salt* and black pepper
SPICED PRUNES:
1 pound prunes
2½ cups cold tea
2 cups white wine vinegar
1⅓ cups firmly packed brown sugar
1 level teaspoon pickling spices
GARNISH:
Cucumber and tomato slices

Make the spiced prunes first, as they have to steep in pickling liquid for 24 hours. Soak the prunes in the cold tea for 8 hours or overnight. Cook the prunes, with the cold tea, over low heat for 20 minutes or until tender.

Meanwhile, put the vinegar into a separate pan and stir in the sugar. Add the pickling spices,

TRIPE PROVENÇALE

SALT SUGAR FAT CHOL FIBER

GLUTEN-FREE WHOLEFOOD
TOTAL CALORIES: ABOUT 1400

Tripe is lower in both **salt** and **fat** than most kinds of meat. If you wish to reduce the **cholesterol** and fat level of this recipe further, substitute vegetable fat or oil for the butter, and use only half as much of it. (Calories lost: up to 100.)

Pressure cooker: ☑
Freezing: ☑ up to 1 month.

TRIPE WITH ONIONS

SALT SUGAR FAT CHOL FIBER

GLUTEN-FREE* WHOLEFOOD*
TOTAL CALORIES: ABOUT 1280

As tripe is naturally lower in **salt** and in **fat** than most meats, the fat and **cholesterol** content of this dish can both be low if skim milk is used, and the sauce made either with vegetable margarine (lowering cholesterol only), or with half the amount of fat (lowering fat). (Calories lost: up to 300.)

Pressure cooker: ☑
Freezing: ☑ up to 1 month.

BRAWN WITH SPICED PRUNES

SALT	SUGAR	FAT	CHOL	FIBER

GLUTEN-FREE   WHOLEFOOD
TOTAL CALORIES: ABOUT 4725

The **salt** content is difficult to judge, as it depends how much salt the meat picks up from the brine. If wished, omit this step, giving a low salt level.

The high **sugar** content can simply be reduced (to medium-low) by not adding more than a few tablespoons of sugar to the vinegar. Prunes are quite sweet by themselves.

The dish will be fairly fatty. Even if the fat that solidifies on top of the meat is carefully removed, the **fat** level is still likely to be medium.

The **cholesterol** level will also be high, because brains are extraordinarily high in this sterol. However, only those on strict low-cholesterol regimes need avoid occasional use of this recipe.

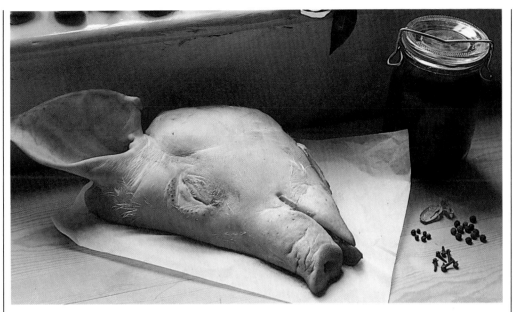

wrapped in cheesecloth. Bring to the boil and simmer briskly for 5 minutes. Remove the pan from the heat and stir in half the cooking liquid from the prunes. Drain the prunes and pack them into a preserving jar, pour over the spiced vinegar and seal immediately. The prunes are ready for use 24 hours later.

Ask the butcher to cut the half pig's head in two and to remove the eye. Scrub the portions under cold running water until thoroughly clean. Leave them to soak for 12 hours in a bowl of cold water to which the salt has been added.

Remove the pig's head, rinse it thoroughly in fresh water and put it in a large saucepan. Cover with fresh cold water. Bring to the boil, and cook the pig's head at near-boiling point for 2 hours or until the flesh leaves the bones easily Remove the meat from the pan. Strip all the flesh, including the ear, tongue and brain, from

the bones – it should yield approximately 2 pounds of meat. Return the bones to the pan with the cooking liquid and bring back to the boil.

Meanwhile, peel and roughly slice the onions, shallots, carrots and turnips. Add the vegetables to the boiling liquid, together with the allspice, bouquet garni, cloves, mace, peppercorns and lemon juice. Continue boiling this stock, uncovered, for about 1 hour until the liquid has reduced to just over $1\frac{1}{4}$ cups. Remove from the heat, strain and set the liquid aside until cold.

Skin the tongue and dice that and all the meat finely. Put the meat in a large bowl and work it through the fingers until thoroughly mixed, discarding any pieces of gristle. Remove the solidified fat from the surface of the cold stock, and strain the liquid through two thicknesses of

cheesecloth into a clean pan. Season with salt and freshly ground pepper and bring to the boil. Remove the pan from the heat immediately and stir in the chopped meat.

Clean and thinly slice the cucumber and the tomato. Brush a 5-cup metal mold with oil and decorate the bottom with thin slices of cucumber and tomato, and a few cut-up prunes. Spoon the brawn carefully into the mold, without disturbing the decorative pattern. Firm the top of the brawn and set it aside for 1 hour.

Cover the brawn with a wooden board, with a heavy weight on top, and chill in the refrigerator for at least 24 hours.

To serve, turn the brawn out of the mold. Arrange the spiced prunes around the brawn, garnished with a few tomato slices for added color.

Beef

Wholesale cuts of beef graded by the United States Department of Agriculture (USDA) are marked with a purple shield-shaped imprint containing the letters USDA and the name of the grade–prime, choice, good, standard, and commercial. This stamp is found along the entire length of the carcass on all meat sold in interstate commerce. Prime is the highest grade and the most expensive. It is juicy, fine-textured, well marbled (streaked with fat), flavorful, and the most tender of all grades. Choice is also good. It is the grade in greatest supply and the one most commonly sold in retail stores. The lean is usually bright red but slightly less marbled than prime lean. The covering of fat is firm, thick, and white or creamy white. Good is less juicy, less flavorful, less marbled, and is usually lean. The outer fat is yellowish and thin. This grade is still relatively tender. Standard has a high proportion of lean meat and very little fat. It is usually cut from young animals and lacks flavor. Commercial is cut from mature animals and has good marbling and flavor, but it will require long, slow cooking, since it is less tender. Other grades of beef are sold only to wholesalers, and neither standard nor commercial grades can be found in most markets.

Cheap cuts of beef are as nutritious as the expensive ones; the only difference is that more time is required to prepare and cook them. Another point to remember is that price is controlled by supply and demand. Because only a given number of steaks can be cut from one animal, steaks are always expensive. In summer, cuts for stewing and braising are not popular, and so should be relatively inexpensive. They are ideal for use in dishes that can be stored in the freezer.

The cuts of meats illustrated on the following pages may not always be available at supermarkets that specialize in prepacked meats, but a good butcher will supply any cut of meat if he is given a few days' advance notice.

CUTS FOR ROASTING

Allow $\frac{3}{4}$–1 pound of rib roast per serving and $\frac{1}{2}$–$\frac{3}{4}$ pound of boneless beef per serving.

From the rib: a **rib roast**, the most tender of all the beef roasts, is a perfect cut for a dinner party. The best section, called the first cut or front cut, is taken from the first three ribs nearest the loin. It is priced slightly higher than the other ribs, but it has less fat and less waste. The center cut, from the two middle ribs, has more fat and waste. The end cut, from the last two ribs closest to the chuck, is likely to be the least tender. Buy a roast with at least 2 ribs.

The **rolled rib roast** is a rib roast that has been boned, rolled, and tied. Buy at least a 4-pound roast. The **rib eye roast** is the boneless rib eye. Buy at least a 4-pound roast.

From the short loin: the **tenderloin**, although expensive, is excellent company fare. It is always tender, cooks in a short time, and carves easily. A lower grade of tenderloin will have less fat covering and will brown better than a higher grade of meat.

From the round: the **rump roast** must be of high quality to roast. It is triangular in shape and may be boneless or have the bone in. The rump is juicy and tender and has an excellent flavor. The **eye of round** should be of high quality for roasting, and fat should be wrapped around it to make it juicy.

From the tip: the **tip roast**, cut from the end of the sirloin, should be of high quality for roasting.

STEAKS

Allow $\frac{1}{3}$–$\frac{1}{2}$ pound of boned steak per serving and $\frac{1}{3}$–$\frac{3}{4}$ pound bone-in steak per serving.

From the rib: the fine-flavored **rib steak** is not as tender as the top loin from the short loin but it has more fat and should be less expensive. The best rib steaks come from the section nearest the short loin. A 1-inch-thick steak weighs approximately 12–14 ounces and serves 1–2. A rib steak can also be purchased without the bone. The **rib eye steak** (Delmonico), cut from the eye of the rib roast, is boneless, weighs approximately 8–10 ounces, and serves 1.

From the short loin: the **top loin** (club) **steak** is cut from the loin next to the rib end and has no tenderloin. This small steak, averaging about $\frac{1}{2}$–$\frac{3}{4}$ pound, serves 1–2. The **T-bone steak** from the center section of the short loin is easily identified by the T-shaped bone. It is similar to the porterhouse but smaller in size, and it has less tenderloin. The average T-bone weighs about $1\frac{1}{2}$–2 pounds and serves 2–3.

The **porterhouse steak** from the larger end of the short loin is one of the most popular steaks because it has a good portion of tenderloin. The tail can be ground for making beef patties. The average cut is about 3 pounds and serves 3–4. The **boneless top loin steak** is not widely available in retail stores. A 1-inch-thick steak weighs about 8–10 ounces and serves 1.

The tenderest steak in the entire carcass is the small, expensive **filet mignon**, cut from the tenderloin. The sizes of the steaks vary because the tenderloin tapers at one end. A 4–6 ounce steak serves 1.

From the sirloin: these steaks can be identified by the shape of the bones that give them their names. They vary in weight from 3–$4\frac{1}{2}$ pounds and make 4–5 servings. The smallest, called the **pinbone**, is cut from the end of the sirloin nearest the short loin. This steak has a good portion of tenderloin, but a great deal of bone, and is the most wasteful of the sirloins. The largest, called the **wedge bone**, has the least waste of all the sirloins. It is the least tender because it is closest to the bone. The **flat bone** is the most desirable of all the sirloins. The cut of beef nearest the rump of the round is usually sold as **boneless sirloin**.

From the round: **top round**, if of high quality, can be broiled. A $1\frac{1}{2}$–$2\frac{1}{2}$ pound steak serves 4.

From the flank: the tasty **flank steak**, the true London broil, is a thin, boneless, coarse-grained cut about 12–14 inches long, 4–6 inches wide, and 1 inch thick. A 1–2 pound flank steak serves 4. Top-quality steak can be broiled.

CUTS FOR BRAISING

Count on $\frac{1}{4}$–$\frac{1}{3}$ pound of boned meat per serving.

From the chuck: a **blade steak** from the shoulder has a blade bone or a round bone (arm), or it may be boneless. A $\frac{1}{2}$-inch-thick piece weighs 8–12 ounces. The **boneless shoulder** from the chuck and the **short ribs** from the end of the rib roast are good for braising.

From the round: the **rump steak**, usually boned, is about $\frac{1}{2}$ inch thick and weighs 5–6 ounces. The popular **round steak**, from the leg, may be cut into top or bottom round. A better quality of **top round** steak will have a good layer of fat and streaks of fat in the lean. A 1-inch thick steak weighs 2–3 pounds. **Bottom round steak**, less tender than the top round, is usually cut $\frac{1}{2}$ inch thick, but it is available as **cubed steak** and as smaller steaks. Average weight is about 12 ounces.

From the flank: **flank steak** is normally broiled, but when it is lean and of low quality, it is better braised to make it tender.

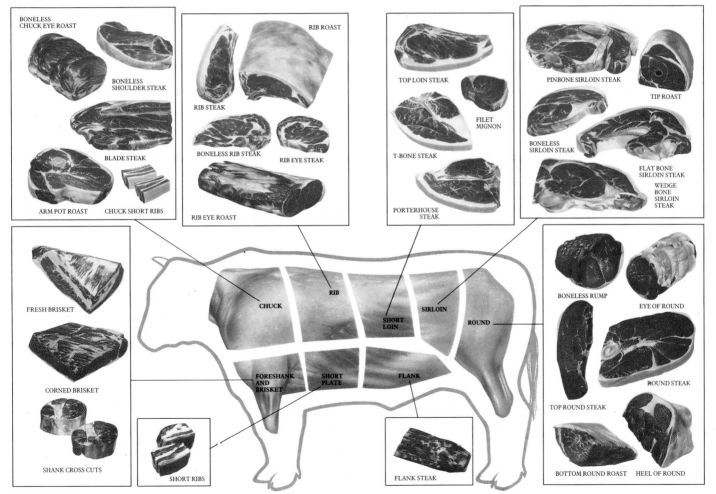

145

BUYING FOR QUALITY

From the tip: the **tip steak**, from the tip roast, is lean and boneless. A ½-inch-thick steak weighs about 6 ounces.

CUTS FOR POT-ROASTING

Count on ⅓ pound bone-in meat per serving and about ¼ pound boned meat per serving.

Boneless chuck eye roast has the blade bone removed, and it is tied. The **blade roast**, from the chuck, is usually moderately priced but contains 2 or 3 small bones and a larger blade bone. The **arm pot roast** or **steak** is an ideal cut because its uniform shape cooks evenly throughout.

The **boneless rump** is a fine meaty pot roast from the round. It contains some fat and a good deal of connective tissue. A **tip roast**, from the side of the round, makes a good, meaty pot roast, but it lacks fat. It should be boned, rolled, and tied.

Top round, **bottom round**, and **eye of round**, from the leg, can be pot-roasted. **Brisket** makes a good pot roast, but it needs long, slow cooking to make it tender. Make sure it is well trimmed of fat.

CUTS FOR STEWING

Boneless chuck makes a fine stew with good texture and a rich flavor, but it costs more than other cuts. **Neck**, sold boned or bone-in, requires long, slow cooking. The lean, flavorful **shank** and **shank cross cuts** have plenty of connective tissue and must be cooked slowly and for a long time to ensure tenderness.

The **bottom round** is well flavored, lean, and boneless. The **heel of round**, cut from the extreme end of the round, does not have the fine flavor of chuck, but it is tenderer. The choice grade is best for stewing.

The **plate** and **fresh brisket** should be boned; avoid fatty pieces. **Flank steak** makes a savory stew, but because it is thinner it takes less time to cook than the other cuts.

GROUND BEEF

Top round is the highest in price of the ground meats, but it lacks the fine flavor of chuck. **Ground chuck** has slightly more fat than top round and many believe it has the best flavor of all ground beef. It is ideal for hamburgers, meat loaves, and meatballs. **Ground meat loaf blend** is a mixture of ground beef, veal, and pork. It may also be used for other dishes, such as meatballs.

Tip sirloin, from the end of the sirloin or sides of the round, is lean and has more flavor than the round. The **flank** is not often sold ground, but it has a delicate taste and is different from any of the other kinds of ground beef.

Ground beef or **hamburger**, made up of trimmings from the plate, flank, and brisket, is sold at the lowest price per pound; but it has more fat than ground chuck and shrinks during cooking.

CORNED BEEF

Corned beef is the rump, plate, or brisket that has been cured in brine. About 4 pounds of corned beef will serve 8 people.

Veal

Veal tends to be dry, with little fat, and therefore requires careful cooking. Its flavor is delicate and somewhat bland, so that sauces, stuffings, and seasonings are often used to provide additional flavor.

Veal is often in short supply, except in larger towns and cities. When buying veal, look for soft, finely grained, moist flesh that varies in color from off-white to palest pink. Avoid flabby and wet veal, and also meat that is dry and brown or has a blue tinge or mottling. The lean should have a fine texture with a thin outside layer of firm, creamy-white fat without any yellow discoloration. Bones should be soft and almost translucent, with a reddish tinge.

Vealers that yield the best veal are usually slaughtered by the age of 3 months and weigh about 150 pounds. They are raised on milk, which helps to produce the white flesh. Much of the high-quality veal from these calves is sold to hotels and restaurants. However, it can be purchased from specialty butchers.

Old vealers, called calves, are from 14 weeks to 1 year old and weigh about 250 pounds. They provide most of the veal on the market; it is less expensive than milk-fed.

CUTS FOR ROASTING

Choose a roast that is at least 3–4 pounds. Allow ½–¾ pound bone-in veal per serving and ⅓–½ pound boned veal per serving.

From the shoulder: the **shoulder roast** is boned, rolled, and tied to make carving easier. Extra fat should be added to the exterior of the roast to make it tenderer and juicier. It weighs 4–7 pounds.

From the rib and loin: the **rib** and **loin roasts** make excellent roasts but are rarely available because they are cut into chops. A **crown roast** of veal is 2 or more rib sections that have been tied together to form a circle, which can then be filled with a stuffing or vegetables.

From the sirloin: a **sirloin roast** of 3–4 pounds is a very tender cut, sometimes sold boned.

From the leg: the **rump roast**, a good roast for a small family, is a wedge-shaped cut from the upper leg. It weighs 3–5 pounds. It can be boned, rolled, and tied to make the carving easier.

A **leg roast** is a meaty cut with a small bone. A center cut or **round roast** is especially fine. The size of a roast can be 4–6 pounds or larger. This roast may be cut into steaks or cutlets. A **rolled leg** of veal is a center leg roast that has been boned, rolled, and tied for easier carving.

CHOPS AND STEAKS

Allow ⅓–½ pound bone-in veal per serving and ¼–⅓ pound boned veal per serving. These cuts are tenderer and more succulent if braised.

From the shoulder: the meaty **arm steak** with a round bone has little fat. It is not as tender and is usually less expensive than the rib, loin, or leg cuts of veal. The arm steak can be left whole or cut into pieces before cooking. A ¾- to 1-inch-thick slice serves 2.

The **blade steak** has more bone and less meat than the arm steak. It is usually less expensive than the rib, loin, or leg cuts. A $\frac{3}{4}$-inch-thick slice serves 2. If the steak is cut into cubes and made into a stew, it will serve 3.

From the rib: the **rib chop** with a rib bone is less meaty than the loin chop and contains no tenderloin. The chops nearest the loin are the best. Those nearest the shoulder have more fat and bone. A $\frac{1}{2}$-inch chop weighs about 4 ounces. Rib chops are also boned.

From the loin: the T-shaped **loin chop** contains part of the tenderloin. It is the best of the chops and the most expensive, although it contains a good deal of bone. A $\frac{3}{4}$-inch-thick chop weighs 6–8 ounces and serves 1. A loin chop containing a portion of the kidney is called a **kidney chop**.

From the sirloin: **cubed steak** and the **sirloin chop** are cheaper than loin chops. They should be braised to make them tender.

From the leg: **round steak** looks like an arm steak, but it is larger. It is perhaps the most widely available of all the cuts of veal. It has no fat, no waste, and little bone. Cook whole or in serving pieces. A $\frac{1}{2}$-inch-thick steak weighs 1–1$\frac{1}{2}$ pounds.

Cutlets, boneless slices taken from the leg, are often flattened for veal scaloppine. A $\frac{1}{4}$-inch-thick slice weighs 3–4 ounces.

CUTS FOR BRAISING
Allow about $\frac{1}{3}$ pound bone-in veal per serving and about $\frac{1}{4}$ pound boneless veal per serving.

From the shoulder: the **arm roast** (4–5 pounds), **blade roast** (4–5 pounds), and a **boneless rolled shoulder** (4–7 pounds) are moderately priced and are ideal for braising.

From the breast: the breast of veal can be purchased with or without the bone. It is delicious stuffed. Other veal cuts for braising are the **neck, shank, shank cross cuts**, and **riblets**.

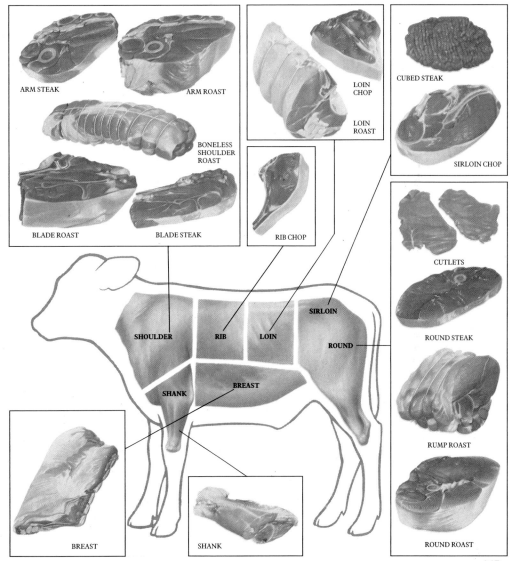

ARM STEAK

ARM ROAST

BONELESS SHOULDER ROAST

BLADE ROAST

BLADE STEAK

LOIN CHOP

LOIN ROAST

RIB CHOP

CUBED STEAK

SIRLOIN CHOP

CUTLETS

ROUND STEAK

RUMP ROAST

ROUND ROAST

SHOULDER

RIB

LOIN

SIRLOIN

ROUND

SHANK

BREAST

BREAST

SHANK

Lamb

The grades of lamb are prime, choice, and good. Prime is the highest quality grade and the most expensive, but it is not widely available in retail markets. It is flavorful, tender, and juicy, with considerable marbling (flecks or streaks of fat within the lean). The choice grade is more widely available and is also of high quality.

Lamb varies in color according to the age and breed of the animal. Meat from a young lamb is usually bright pink; red meat comes from an older animal. The fat should be creamy white, not oily or yellow – a yellowish tinge shows excessive age. Lamb roasts should have a good depth of lean meat covered by a moderate layer of fat. The skin should be pliable to the touch, not hard or wrinkled. Legs and shoulder roasts should have a plump, not a flat appearance. A blue tinge in the knuckle and rib bones indicates that the animal is young.

Frozen lamb has a less delicate flavor than fresh, and the lean is paler and does not have the bloom of fresh meat. The fat is whiter and crumbles more easily. If the fat looks very brittle, it is a sign that the lamb has been frozen for a long time; it will generally shrink during cooking and some of the flavor will be lost.

Although the choicest cuts of lamb for roasting and broiling come from the rib, loin, leg, and shoulder, do not ignore the cheaper cuts. They may take more time to prepare, but they can be as delicious and are as nourishing as the expensive cuts of lamb.

CUTS FOR ROASTING

Buy $\frac{1}{2}$–$\frac{3}{4}$ pound lamb with bone in per serving and $\frac{1}{4}$–$\frac{1}{2}$ pound boned lamb per serving.

From the shoulder: the flavorful **boneless shoulder** is rolled and tied and weighs 3–5 pounds. This tender, juicy roast is easy to carve, but contains more fat than the leg. The **square shoulder** is difficult to carve because of its complicated bone structure, but it is usually inexpensive. Allow a pound of shoulder per serving. The **cushion shoulder** – a square, flat roast – is boned and tied to make carving easier. One side can be left open for stuffing. It weighs $2\frac{1}{2}$–4 pounds.

From the rib: the **rib roast**, or rack of lamb, is unsurpassed for tenderness and flavor. It contains very little meat and is expensive. A 3-pound rack will serve only 3. When two racks are tied together in a circle, it is called a **crown roast**. Allow 2 ribs per serving. Make sure the chine bone is cracked for easy carving.

From the loin: the expensive **loin roast**, also boned, is not often available in the markets because it is usually cut into loin chops.

From the sirloin: the **sirloin roast** from the upper end of the leg will make a small roast weighing 2–$2\frac{1}{2}$ pounds.

From the leg: the **whole leg** of lamb, weighing 5–9 pounds, contains the sirloin and the short leg. This cut is a good buy for a large family and has little waste. The **French-style leg** has the meat around the end of the leg bone removed. This cut serves 6–8. (An easy method of carving a whole leg of lamb is to cut the meat parallel to the bone rather than perpendicular to the bone.)

The **round roast**, or short leg, is the full leg after the sirloin chops or roast have been removed. When the meat around the end of the leg bone has been removed, it is called the **French-style leg, sirloin off**. When the shank bone is removed and the meat is skewered to the thicker part of the leg, this cut is called an **American leg**.

The **sirloin half of the leg**, weighing 3–5 pounds, comes from the upper end of the full leg and is usually cheaper than the shank half. It is a good buy, although it is bony and has less meat than the shank. Ask the butcher to crack the bones to make the carving easier. Allow 1 pound per serving. The **shank half of the leg**, weighing 3–5 pounds, has more meat than the sirloin half and is easier to carve. A $2\frac{1}{2}$–$4\frac{1}{2}$ pound roast serves 3–4.

The **boneless leg** (rolled) is a full leg of lamb that has been boned, rolled, and tied. It weighs 3–6 pounds and serves 5–8.

CHOPS AND STEAKS

Chops and steaks 1–2 inches thick should be broiled. Those cut less than 1 inch thick should be pan-broiled or braised. Count on $\frac{1}{3}$–$\frac{3}{4}$ pound per serving.

From the shoulder: the **blade chop**, boned or bone-in, contains the blade bone and is larger than the loin or rib, but cheaper. It is not as tender as the rib chop. The chops nearest the rib are tenderer. A $\frac{3}{4}$-inch, 5–8 ounce chop serves 1. The **arm chop** has an arm bone and a cross section of the rib. It is not as delicately flavored as the blade chop, but it is less expensive.

From the rib: the **rib chop** is smaller than the loin chop and contains the rib bone and no tenderloin. The best and leanest chops are cut nearest the loin. Those cut nearest the shoulder are larger but have less meat and more fat. A 1-inch-thick chop weighs 3–4 ounces. Provide 2 chops per serving. The **double rib chop** is like the rib chop but has 2 ribs and is twice as thick. A chop 2 inches thick weighs about 5–7 ounces and serves 1. The **Frenched rib chop** of lamb has the meat removed from the end of the bone.

From the loin: the meaty, T-shaped **loin chop** contains tenderloin and is the most expensive of the lamb chops. Be sure that the tough tail of the chop is well trimmed. A 1-inch-thick chop weighs 4–6 ounces. A **double loin chop** is available boned. In the 2-inch **English chop** from the unsplit loin, the backbone has been removed and the chop skewered together. The kidney may be secured to the center of the chop. It weighs 7–12 ounces.

From the sirloin: the **sirloin chop**, cut nearest the loin end, is the best. Cuts from the rump end have more bone and waste and less meat. A 1-inch-thick chop weighs 4–8 ounces and serves 1.

From the leg: the **leg chop** (steak) contains the round leg bone. It is the leanest and has the most meat of all the chops. A

1-inch-thick chop or steak weighs 5–8 ounces.

CUTS FOR BRAISING AND STEWING

Allow $\frac{1}{3}$ pound bone-in lamb or $\frac{1}{4}$–$\frac{1}{3}$ pound of boned lamb per serving.

From the shoulder: a 6-pound **boneless shoulder** will yield 4 pounds of lean cubes to serve 8.

From the neck: **neck slices**, inexpensive but flavorful, have a lot of bone and less meat than some other cuts. Three pounds will serve 3–4.

From the leg: the **leg chop**, cut from the center of the leg, provides solid meat with a small bone. One and a half pounds made into a stew will serve 4.

The **shank half of leg** from a mature animal is good for moist-cooking. A 5-pound shank half cut into cubes will serve 6–8.

From the shank: the inexpensive but flavorful **shank** contains a lot of bone. One shank will make only a single serving.

From the breast: the **breast** of lamb, weighing about 2 pounds, will serve 2. It is also available boned. The economical **lamb riblets**, 4–6 inches long and 1 inch wide, are thick strips with streaks of fat cut from the breast.

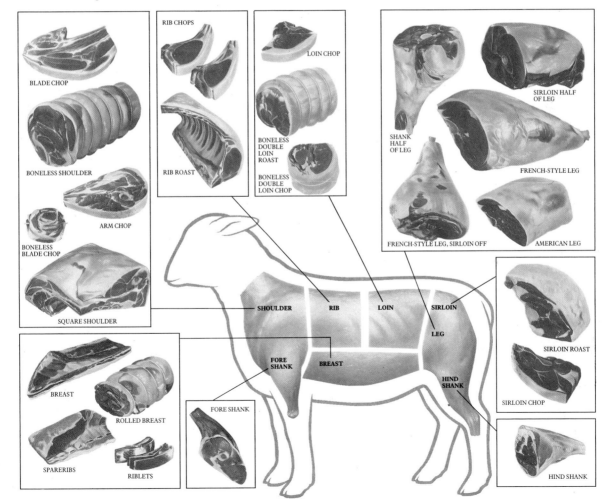

Pork

Prime pork should be well developed, with small bones and without excessive fat. The fat should be firm and a clear milk-white color. Avoid cuts with soft, gray, and oily fat, which leads to excessive weight loss in cooking.

Lean pork should be pale pink, firm, and smooth to the touch, with very little gristle. Freshly cut surfaces should look slightly moist, and the bones should be pinkish-blue.

Pork is highly nutritious. It contains more vitamin B_1, which prevents fatigue and stimulates the appetite, than any other meat, even lamb, which is very rich in vitamins of the B complex. It has more flavor if cooked on the bone, but many roasts are often sold boned and rolled ready for stuffing.

CUTS FOR ROASTING

Buy at least a 3-pound roast. One pound with the bone will serve 2 or 3 people, 3 or 4 if boned.

From the Boston shoulder: The **blade Boston roast** from the upper shoulder is available with the bone in or boned. It weighs 3–8 pounds.

From the loin: the **rib roast** is as tender as the center loin, but it has no tenderloin. A **crown roast**, an excellent party roast, is made by tying 2 or more center-cut rib sections together to form a circle. The **blade loin** is the most economical section of the loin. It is fatty, however, and may contain rib bones and part of the blade bone. The **center loin** is meaty from end to end and includes the tenderloin. The backbone should be cracked for easier carving. A **boneless top loin** roast can come from the blade center or sirloin section of the loin.

The **sirloin roast** contains tenderloin, but it is difficult to carve because of the bones. The **tenderloin** is a 9–12 inch boneless cut that is equivalent to the beef fillet and weighs $\frac{3}{4}$–$1\frac{1}{2}$ pounds. It is also cut into slices and flattened into fillets.

From the leg: because of the high ratio of lean meat to bone, the **whole fresh ham** makes an excellent choice for a large party or family gathering. It weighs 12–16 pounds and serves 18–20 or more. It is also available boned.

A fresh ham can also be cut into two smaller roasts: a full shank portion and a full rump (butt) portion. The full **rump (butt) portion** is perhaps the better buy because it is leaner and meatier. It is harder to carve than the shank end, however, but the hip (or aitchbone) can be removed. The full **shank portion** has less meat, but it is easier to carve.

From the picnic shoulder: a 5–8 pound **fresh arm picnic** is not as lean as the loin or fresh ham, but it has a great deal of flavor and is good value for the money. A picnic that is boned, rolled, and tied is more attractive and easier to carve. It will take almost a pound of bone-in roast for 1 serving, but a pound of boned pork will serve 2–3.

The **cushion shoulder roast** comes from the arm section of the picnic. It is boned but not rolled and has a pocket for stuffing. The **arm roast** is the top part of the picnic without the shank.

CHOPS AND STEAKS

Count on $\frac{1}{2}$–$\frac{3}{4}$ pound chops and steaks with bone per serving, and $\frac{1}{3}$–$\frac{1}{2}$ pound boned chops per serving.

From the shoulder: the **blade steak** contains a section of the blade bone and a good deal of fat and gristle, but its cost is low.

From the loin: the **blade chop** from the shoulder of the loin is a tender cut, but it contains a lot of fat. The **rib chop** differs little in flavor or quality from the loin chop, but it does not include the tenderloin. A **butterfly chop** is a boned, double-rib chop. The popular **loin chop**, containing part of the tenderloin, is the best chop of all because it has more lean meat and less bone and waste. A **top loin chop** has no tenderloin. The **sirloin chop** comes from the ham end of the loin. It has a lot of bone and less lean meat than the center loin.

From the leg: a fresh **ham steak** with its small, round bone is lean and tender. Cuts from the shank end are particularly attractive and uniform in size.

From the picnic shoulder: the **arm steak** with the round bone is an economical buy, but it is not as tender as a ham steak.

HAMS AND PICNICS

Hams are cut from the hind leg of the pig while picnics come from the shoulder, or fore leg.

For cooked bone-in hams, allow $\frac{1}{3}$ pound per serving and $\frac{1}{8}$–$\frac{1}{4}$ pound per serving if they are boned. For uncooked bone-in hams, allow $\frac{1}{2}$–$\frac{3}{4}$ pound per serving and $\frac{1}{3}$ pound if boned. The label on packaged hams should identify them as either fully cooked or cook-before-eating hams.

A **whole ham** with the bone is the least wasteful and the most prized for flavor of all the hams. For best quality, choose a plump ham with a stubby shank end. A 10–14 pound ham will serve 12–18. A full **rump (butt) portion** is a good size to buy for the average family. It is harder to carve than the shank portion, but it is meatier.

The full **shank portion** has as much flavor as the butt portion and is easier to carve, but it has less meat and is less expensive.

An 8–12 pound **boneless ham** can be purchased in many different shapes, in cans and in airtight wrappers. A boneless ham will not have as much flavor as a ham with the bone, and it will cost more per pound.

The **smoked half loin** is not readily available, but it is gaining popularity because of its fine flavor.

The **smoked arm picnic** is cheaper than other hams because it has more skin, fat, and bone in proportion to lean. It is also difficult to carve. A picnic weighs 5–8 pounds.

The **smoked shoulder roll** from the neck and shoulder is boneless. It makes a delicious, economical substitute for bacon.

HAM AND PICNIC SLICES

These are available as cook-before-eating slices or as fully cooked slices.

SPARERIBS

Country-style ribs from the shoulder end of the loin are delicious and contain more meat than the **back ribs** or the **spareribs**. One pound of 2 or 3 ribs makes 1 serving.

BACON, JOWL, AND SALT PORK

Slab bacon is cheaper than sliced bacon and will keep longer in the refrigerator than sliced bacon will. The **smoked jowl** can be used like bacon.

Salt pork is cured but not smoked and is used to flavor braised dishes and baked beans, or to bard the dry flesh of game birds like partridges, squab or pheasant, in the same way as bacon (see illustration on page 168).

HOCKS AND PIG'S FEET

Hocks, or **pig's knuckles**, available fresh or smoked, are good in soups or stews. Allow 1 pound per serving. **Pig's feet** may be bought fresh or pickled.

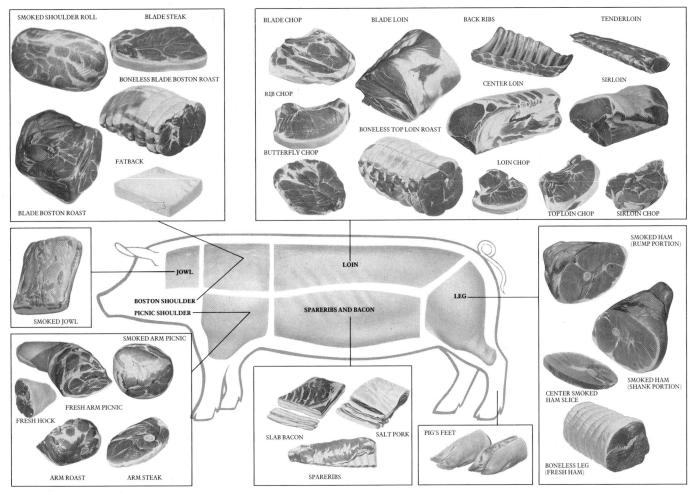

SMOKED SHOULDER ROLL

BLADE STEAK

BONELESS BLADE BOSTON ROAST

RIB CHOP

FATBACK

BUTTERFLY CHOP

BLADE BOSTON ROAST

BLADE CHOP

BLADE LOIN

BACK RIBS

TENDERLOIN

CENTER LOIN

SIRLOIN

BONELESS TOP LOIN ROAST

LOIN CHOP

TOP LOIN CHOP

SIRLOIN CHOP

JOWL

LOIN

BOSTON SHOULDER

PICNIC SHOULDER

SPARERIBS AND BACON

LEG

SMOKED JOWL

SMOKED ARM PICNIC

FRESH ARM PICNIC

FRESH HOCK

ARM ROAST

ARM STEAK

SLAB BACON

SALT PORK

SPARERIBS

PIG'S FEET

SMOKED HAM
(RUMP PORTION)

SMOKED HAM
(SHANK PORTION)

CENTER SMOKED
HAM SLICE

BONELESS LEG
(FRESH HAM)

Variety Meats

Variety meats are the parts of slaughtered pigs, cattle, or sheep that are left after the carcass has been cut up. Despite the fact that these meats include some of the most nourishing food available, they have been considered low-priority products by some consumers.

Some variety meats, such as liver, are excellent sources of the minerals and vitamins necessary for good health; however, most of them, particularly brains, kidney, and liver, are high in cholesterol.

Ironically, certain variety meats, such as brains, veal liver, and sweetbreads, are considered gourmet's delicacies and have become expensive for the average family; yet they still compare favorably with other meats in price. Most variety meats seldom require lengthy preparation and cooking. And because they contain no bones and little fat or gristle, waste is cut to a minimum.

Variety meats do not keep well. They should be stored in the refrigerator until ready to be used and should be cooked on the day of purchase. Liver, hearts, sweetbreads, and brains are available fresh and frozen.

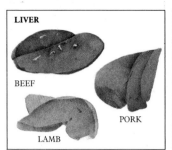

LIVER — BEEF, PORK, LAMB

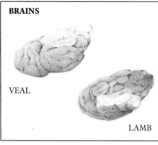

BRAINS — VEAL, LAMB

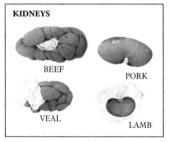

KIDNEYS — BEEF, PORK, VEAL, LAMB

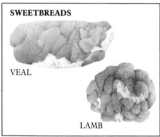

SWEETBREADS — VEAL, LAMB

LIVER

Veal liver is the most expensive, the tenderest, and the mildest-flavored of all the livers. The best quality is light reddish-brown. It is available fresh or frozen in slices. Sauté or broil. **Lamb liver** is less expensive than veal liver and an excellent substitute. Avoid any that is dark brown; it is from an older animal. **Pork liver** has a stronger flavor than either veal or lamb liver. It is best braised or used in pâtés. **Beef liver** is coarse and tough but inexpensive. It is not recommended for broiling or sautéing. Soak in milk or lightly salted water for a few hours to mellow the strong flavor. Stew or braise. Allow 1 pound of beef liver for 4 servings.

KIDNEYS

Lamb and **veal kidneys** are considered best because of their delicate flavor and tenderness. Broil or sauté. The stronger-flavored **pork** and **beef kidneys** are tougher and should be stewed or braised. Allow 2 lamb kidneys per serving, 1 veal or pork kidney per serving, and 1 beef kidney for 4 servings.

SWEETBREADS

This is the name given to the two portions of the thymus gland, one in the throat and one in the chest cavity. **Veal sweetbreads** are considered a delicacy and are the most readily available of all the sweetbreads. They can be purchased fresh or frozen. Broil, sauté, or braise. Allow 1 pound for 4 servings.

BRAINS

Veal brains have the mildest flavor and are the most popular but they are not always available. **Lamb brains** may be used in any recipe for veal brains. Both types must be soaked in cold water for a couple of hours to remove all blood. **Pork** and **beef kidneys** are not as delicate in texture and

have a stronger flavor. Allow 1 pound for 4 servings.

HEARTS

Hearts are flavorful and nutritious but need long, slow cooking. **Veal heart** is the most delicate-flavored, and **lamb heart** is the smallest and the tenderest. **Pork heart** is larger than lamb heart and may be stuffed and braised. Choose bright red, firm hearts and avoid any that are gray. **Beef heart** is best cut into cubes and used in stews and casseroles.

Veal heart makes 3 servings; lamb heart, 1 serving; pork heart, 2 servings; and beef heart, 8–10 servings.

TONGUE

Beef and veal tongue are the most readily available. **Beef tongue** is available fresh, pickled, corned, smoked, and in some areas, ready-to-serve. **Veal tongue** is usually sold fresh. **Lamb** and

pork tongues are usually precooked and ready to serve. Tongue requires long, slow cooking in liquids to make it tender. 1 pound serves 4–5.

TRIPE

Tripe comes from the inner lining of the stomach of beef. The choicest is **honeycomb tripe** from the second stomach. It should be thick, firm, and white. Avoid any that is slimy and gray or that looks flabby. Tripe can be stewed, broiled, or fried and is also sold pickled or canned. Allow 1 pound for 4–5 servings.

OXTAIL

Oxtails are the tails of beef cattle and have a great deal of bone and very little meat. The fat should be creamy white, and the meat deep red. Oxtails require long, slow cooking to make them tender and are excellent in casseroles, or as a base for soup. Allow 2–3 pounds for 4 servings.

Stocks and Soups

The basis for all soups is good fresh stock usually made from the bones and flesh of fish, meat and poultry, with added vegetables, herbs and spices. Fresh bones and meat are essential ingredients for brown and white stocks. Use marrow bone and shank of beef for brown stock and shank of veal for a white stock. Ask the butcher to chop the bones into manageable pieces. The chopped bones release gelatin while cooking, which gives body to the stock.

Vegetables give additional flavor, but avoid potatoes, which make the stock cloudy. Strong-flavored vegetables, such as turnips, rutabaga and parsnips, should be used sparingly.

STOCKS

Brown Stock
PREPARATION TIME: *15 min*
COOKING TIME: *5 hours*
INGREDIENTS (*for 3½ quarts*):
1 pound marrow bones
2–3 pounds shank of beef
3 tablespoons butter or drippings
1–2 leeks
1 large onion
1–2 celery stalks
½ pound carrots
2 bouquets garnis (page 183)
Salt★ and black peppercorns

Blanch the bones for 10 minutes in boiling water, then put them, with the chopped meat and butter or drippings, in a roasting pan. Brown the bones in the center of the oven for 30–40 minutes, at a temperature of 425°F (220°C, mark 7). Turn them over occasionally to brown them evenly.

Put the roasted bones in a large pan, add the cleaned and sliced vegetables, the bouquets garnis and peppercorns. Cover with cold water, to which ½ teaspoon of salt has been added.

Bring the contents slowly to boiling point, remove any scum from the surface and cover the pan with a tight-fitting lid. Simmer the stock over lowest possible heat for about 4 hours to extract all flavor from the bones. Top up with hot water if the level of the liquid should fall below the other ingredients.

Strain the stock through a fine sieve or cheesecloth into a large bowl. Leave the stock to settle for a few minutes, then remove the fat from the surface by drawing paper towels over it. If the stock is not required immediately, leave the fat to settle in a surface layer which can then be easily lifted off.

Once the fat has been removed from the stock, correct seasoning if necessary.

White Stock
This is made like brown stock, but the blanched veal bones are not browned. Place all the ingredients in a large pan of water and proceed in the same way as for brown stock.

Chicken, Turkey or Game Stock
The main ingredient for this is the carcass of a chicken. A turkey or game bird can also be used, together with the scalded feet of the bird, if available, and the cleaned giblets. Alternatively, a whole chicken, poached, produces very good stock: if the chicken itself is carved and served straight away, the bones may in this case be added back and simmered for another hour to give more flavor.

Fish Stock
The basis for this stock is bones and trimmings, such as the head and the skin. White fish such as cod, haddock, halibut, whiting and flounder can all be used. Sole is particularly good.

PREPARATION TIME: *5–10 min*
COOKING TIME: *30 min*
INGREDIENTS (*for 2½ cups*):
1 pound fish trimmings
Salt★
1 onion
Bouquet garni (page 183) or 1 large leek and 1 celery stalk

Wash the trimmings thoroughly in cold water and put them in a large pan, with 2½ cups lightly salted water. Bring to the boil over low heat and remove any surface scum. Meanwhile, peel and finely chop the onion and add to the stock with the bouquet garni or the cleaned and chopped leek and celery. Cover the pan with a lid and simmer over low heat for 30 minutes. Strain the stock through a fine sieve or cheesecloth.

SKIMMING STOCK

Lifting scum from boiling stock

Removing surface fat

Cooking stock in a pressure cooker
Place the stock ingredients, with lightly salted water, in the pressure cooker – it must not be more than two-thirds full. Bring to the boil and remove the scum from the surface before fixing the lid. Lower the heat and bring to 15

153

pounds pressure. Reduce the heat quickly and cook steadily for 1 hour. Strain the stock and remove the fat.

Storing stock

After the fat has been removed, pour the cooled stock into a container and cover with a lid. It will keep for three or four days in the refrigerator, but to ensure absolute freshness, boil the stock every two days. Fish and vegetable stocks spoil quickly and should ideally be made and used on the same day, but will keep for two days if they are refrigerated.

Freezing stocks

Stocks can be satisfactorily stored in a freezer, where they will keep for up to two months. Boil the prepared stock over high heat to reduce it by half. Pour it into ice cube trays, freeze quickly and transfer the stock cubes to plastic bags. Or, pour the stock into freezing containers, leaving a 1 in space at the top.

To use frozen stock, leave it to thaw at room temperature, or simply put it into a saucepan and heat over low heat, stirring occasionally. Add 2 tablespoons water to every cube of stock.

Ready-made stocks

Many ready-made stock preparations are available, usually in the form of canned broths, bouillon cubes, meat extracts, and meat-and-vegetable extracts. In an emergency, these preparations are acceptable replacements for home-made stocks, but they have a sameness of flavor and lack body and jelling qualities. As they are highly seasoned, be careful about extra flavorings until the soup has been tasted.

SOUPS

Consommés

Consommés are clear soups made from meat, poultry, fish or vegetables and clarified stock. They are particularly suitable for party menus and may be served hot or as a chilled jellied soup.

Beef Consommé

PREPARATION TIME: *15 min*
COOKING TIME: *2 hours*
INGREDIENTS *(for 6):*
½ pound boneless lean beef
1 small carrot
1 small onion or leek
7–8 cups brown stock
Bouquet garni (page 183)
1 egg white

Shred the meat finely, and peel and chop the vegetables. Put all the ingredients in a large pan, adding the egg white last. Heat gently, whisking continuously with a wire whisk, until a thick froth forms on the surface. Cease whisking, reduce the heat immediately and simmer the consommé very slowly for 1½–2 hours. Do not let the liquid reach boiling point, as the foam layer will break up and cloud the consommé.

Strain the consommé into a bowl through a double layer of cheesecloth, or a scalded jelly bag. Strain the consommé again through the egg foam in the cheesecloth – it should now be perfectly clear and sparkling.

Correct the seasoning if necessary, and serve hot or cold.

Broths

These semi-clear soups are easy to make and consist of uncleared brown or white stock with added meat, vegetables, rice or barley.

Sauces & Dressings

Sauces first came into widespread use in the Middle Ages, to disguise the flavor of long-stored meat that had been inadequately cured. Today, they are used to add flavor to bland food, color to simple meals and moisture to otherwise dry foods.

BASIC WHITE SAUCE

This is prepared by either the roux or the blending method:

Roux method

A roux is usually composed of equal amounts of butter and flour which are then combined with liquid (usually milk) to the required consistency. Melt the butter in a heavy-based pan, blend in the flour, and cook over low heat for 2–3 minutes, stirring constantly with a wooden spoon.

Gradually add the warm or cold liquid to the roux, which will at first thicken to a near solid mass. Beat vigorously until the mixture leaves the sides of the pan clean, then add a little more milk. Allow the mixture to thicken and boil between each addition of milk. Continuous beating is essential to obtain a smooth sauce. When all the milk has been added, bring the sauce to the boil; let it simmer for about 5 minutes and add the seasoning.

A basic white sauce can also be made by the one-stage method. Put the basic ingredients (fat, flour and liquid) into a pan. Cook over low heat, beating until the sauce has thickened. Boil for 3 minutes and season.

Blending method

For this method the thickening agent is mixed to a paste with a little cold milk. Mix 2 table-spoons flour with a few table-spoons taken from 1¼ cups of cold milk. Blend to a smooth paste in a bowl, and bring the remaining milk to the boil.

Pour the hot milk over the paste and return the mixture to the pan. Bring to the boil over low heat, stirring continuously with a wooden spoon. Simmer the sauce for 2–3 minutes, until thick. Add a pat of butter and seasoning and cook for 5 minutes.

A basic white sauce can be made into other savory sauces, such as béchamel and velouté.

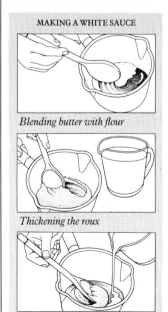

MAKING A WHITE SAUCE

Blending butter with flour

Thickening the roux

Adding the remaining milk

Béchamel Sauce

PREPARATION TIME: *20 min*
COOKING TIME: *5–10 min*
INGREDIENTS *(1 cup):*
1 cup milk
½ small bay leaf
Sprig of thyme
½ small onion
¼ teaspoon grated nutmeg
2 tablespoons butter
2 tablespoons flour
Salt★ and black pepper

Put the milk with the bay leaf, thyme, onion and nutmeg in a pan, and bring slowly to the boil. Remove from the heat, cover with a lid and leave the milk to infuse for 15 minutes. In a clean heavy-based pan, melt the butter, stir in the flour and cook the roux for 3 minutes.

Strain the milk through a fine sieve and gradually blend it into the roux. Bring to the boil, stirring, then simmer for 2–3 minutes. Adjust the seasoning.

Velouté Sauce

PREPARATION TIME: *5–10 min*
COOKING TIME: *1 hour*
INGREDIENTS *(1 cup):*
2 tablespoons butter
2 tablespoons flour
2 cups white stock
Salt★ and black pepper

Make the roux with the butter and flour. Gradually stir in the hot stock until the sauce is quite smooth. Bring to boiling point, lower the heat, and let the sauce simmer for about 1 hour until reduced by half. Stir the sauce occasionally. Strain through a sieve and season to taste.

BROWN SAUCES

A basic brown sauce is made by the roux method, using the same proportions of flour, fat and liquid (brown stock) as for a basic white sauce.

Melt the fat in a pan and stir in the flour. Cook the roux over low heat, stirring continuously with a wooden spoon, until the roux is light brown in color. Gradually stir in the brown stock and proceed as for a white sauce.

Espagnole Sauce

PREPARATION TIME: *10 min*
COOKING TIME: *1¼ hours*
INGREDIENTS *(approx. 1 cup):*
1 carrot
1 onion
2 ounces lean salt pork, blanched
2 tablespoons butter
2 tablespoons flour
2 cups brown stock
Bouquet garni (page 183)
2 tablespoons tomato paste
Salt★ and black pepper

Peel and dice the carrot and onion. Remove any rind from the salt pork and chop the pork. Melt the butter in a heavy-based pan, and cook the vegetables and pork over low heat for 10 minutes or until light brown.

Blend in the flour, stirring the roux until brown. Gradually blend in 1 cup stock, stirring constantly until the mixture has cooked through and has thickened. Add the bouquet garni, cover with a lid and set the pan on an asbestos mat. Simmer for 30 minutes. Add the remaining stock and the tomato paste.

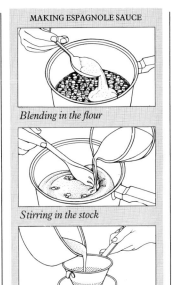

MAKING ESPAGNOLE SAUCE

Blending in the flour

Stirring in the stock

Straining the sauce

Cover the pan again, and continue cooking for 30 minutes, stirring frequently. Strain, skim off fat and adjust seasoning.

Gravies

The most frequently used brown sauce is gravy, made from the pan residues of a roast.

Thick gravy

Pour off most of the fat from the roasting pan, leaving about 2 tablespoons of the sediment. Stir in 1 tablespoon flour and blend thoroughly with the fat. Stir constantly with a wooden spoon, cooking until the gravy thickens and browns. Gradually blend in 1¼ cups hot brown stock or vegetable liquid. Bring to boiling point, and cook for 2–3

minutes. Season to taste, strain and serve hot with a roast.

Thin gravy

Pour all the fat from the pan, leaving only the pan residues. Add 1 cup hot vegetable liquid or brown stock. Stir well and boil for 2–3 minutes to reduce slightly.

Thickening agents for sauces

Basic white and brown sauces can be thickened or enriched with various other liaisons: cornstarch or arrowroot with water; beurre manié (kneaded butter and flour); egg yolks and cream.

Cornstarch and arrowroot

To thicken 1 cup of liquid to a sauce of coating consistency, stir 1 tablespoon cornstarch with 2 tablespoons cold water, and mix into a smooth paste. Blend a little of the hot liquid into the liaison, then return this to the sauce. Bring the sauce to the boil, stirring constantly for 2–3 minutes to allow the starch to cook through.

Arrowroot is best used to thicken clear sauces that are to be served at once. To thicken 1 cup sauce use 2 teaspoons arrowroot mixed to a paste with water. The sauce cannot be reheated and quickly loses its thickening qualities.

Beurre manié

This liaison is ideal for thickening sauces, casseroles and stews at the end of cooking. Knead an equal amount of butter and flour, about 2 tablespoons each, into a paste with a fork or the fingers.

Add small pieces of the beurre manié to the hot liquid. Stir or whisk continuously to dissolve the butter and disperse the flour. Simmer the sauce until it is thick and smooth and has lost the starchy taste of raw flour. Do not let it boil or the beurre manié will separate out.

EGG-BASED SAUCES

These rich sauces require care and practice to prevent them curdling. They are made from egg yolks and a high proportion of butter. Through continuous whisking, these two main ingredients are emulsified to a thick and creamy consistency.

Hollandaise Sauce
PREPARATION AND COOKING
 TIME: *20 min*
INGREDIENTS *(1 cup)*:
3 tablespoons white wine vinegar
1 tablespoon water
6 black peppercorns
1 bay leaf
3 egg yolks
¾ cup soft butter
Salt⋆ and black pepper

Boil the vinegar and water with the peppercorns and the bay leaf in a small pan, until reduced to 1 tablespoon. Leave to cool. Cream the egg yolks with 1 tablespoon butter and a pinch of salt. Strain the vinegar into the eggs, and set the bowl over a pan of boiling water. Turn off the heat. Whisk in the remaining butter, ½ tablespoon at a time, until the sauce is shiny and has the consistency of thick cream. Season with salt and pepper.
   Until the technique of egg-based sauces has been mastered, a Hollandaise sauce may some-

Whisking in pieces of butter to thicken Hollandaise sauce

times curdle during preparation. This is usually because the heat is too sudden or too high, or because the butter has been added too quickly. If the finished sauce separates, it can often be saved by removing from the heat and beating in 1 tablespoon of cold water.

Béarnaise Sauce
This sauce is similar to Hollandaise sauce, but has a sharper flavor. It is served with broiled meat and fish.

PREPARATION AND COOKING
 TIME: *20 min*
INGREDIENTS *(1 cup)*:
2 tablespoons tarragon vinegar
2 tablespoons white wine vinegar
½ small onion
2 egg yolks
6–8 tablespoons butter
Salt⋆ and black pepper

Put the vinegars and finely chopped onion in a small saucepan; boil steadily until reduced to 1 tablespoon. Strain and set aside to cool. Follow the method used for making Hollandaise sauce.

Mayonnaise
Mayonnaise and its variations are the most widely used of savory cold sauces. They are served with hors d'oeuvre, salads, cold meat,

poultry and vegetable dishes. Mayonnaise, like Hollandaise and Béarnaise sauce, is based on eggs and fat, but oil is used instead of butter.
   It is essential that all the ingredients and equipment are at room temperature.

PREPARATION TIME: *20 min*
INGREDIENTS *(½ cup)*:
1 egg yolk
¼ teaspoon salt⋆
½ teaspoon dry mustard
Pinch sugar
Black pepper
½ cup olive oil
1 tablespoon white wine vinegar
 or lemon juice

Beat the egg yolk in a bowl until thick. Beat in the salt, mustard, sugar and a few twists of freshly ground pepper. Add the oil, drop by drop, whisking vigorously between each addition of oil so that it is absorbed completely before the next drop. As the mayonnaise thickens and becomes shiny, the oil may be added in a thin stream. Finally, blend in the vinegar.
   A mayonnaise may curdle if the oil was cold or was added too quickly, or if the egg yolk was stale. To save a curdled mayonnaise, whisk a fresh yolk in a clean bowl, and gradually whisk in the curdled mayonnaise. Alternatively, whisk in a teaspoon of tepid water until the mayonnaise is thick and shiny.

Tartare sauce
This is made by combining ½ cup mayonnaise with 2 teaspoons capers, 3 finely-chopped cocktail gherkins, 1 teaspoon finely-chopped chives and 1 tablespoon heavy cream.

MISCELLANEOUS SAUCES

Horseradish Sauce
PREPARATION TIME: *10 min*
INGREDIENTS *(about 1 cup)*:
3 heaping tablespoons fresh grated
 horseradish
½ cup sour cream
Salt⋆ and black pepper
Pinch dry mustard

Fold the horseradish into the sour cream and season to taste. Serve with roast beef.

Mint Sauce
PREPARATION TIME: *10 min*
RESTING TIME: *30 min*
INGREDIENTS *(for 4–6)*:
Small handful mint leaves
1–2 teaspoons sugar
2 tablespoons vinegar

Wash and dry the mint leaves. Put them on a board, sprinkle with the sugar, and chop them finely. Put the chopped mint in a bowl and stir in 2 tablespoons boiling water. Add the vinegar and leave the sauce to stand for 30 minutes. Serve with roast lamb.

Applesauce
PREPARATION TIME: *10 min*
INGREDIENTS *(1 cup)*:
1 pound cooking apples
2 tablespoons unsalted butter
Sugar (optional)

Peel, core and slice the apples. Put them in a pan with 2–3 tablespoons of water and cook over low heat for about 10 minutes. Rub the cooked apples through a coarse sieve or purée them in the liquidizer. Stir in butter and season with sugar if necessary. Serve with roast pork, goose, or duck.

A good dressing is essential to a salad, but it must be varied to accord with the salad ingredients. A sharp vinaigrette sauce is probably best for a green salad, but egg, fish, meat and vegetable salads would nearly always need additional flavors.

Sauce Vinaigrette
PREPARATION TIME: *3 min*
INGREDIENTS (½ *cup*):
6 tablespoons oil
2 tablespoons vinegar
2 teaspoons finely chopped herbs such as basil, chives, parsley or tarragon; or ¼ teaspoon dried herbs (optional)
Salt★ and black pepper

Put the oil and vinegar in a bowl or in a screw-top jar. Whisk with a fork or shake vigorously before seasoning to taste with herbs, salt and freshly ground pepper.

French Dressing
PREPARATION TIME: *3 min*
INGREDIENTS (*1 cup*):
½ cup oil
4 tablespoons vinegar
2 teaspoons Dijon-style mustard
½ teaspoon each salt★ and black pepper
Sugar (optional)

Whisk or shake all the dressing ingredients together, seasoning with sugar (optional). Any of the following ingredients can be added to a basic French dressing: 1–2 crushed garlic cloves; 2 tablespoons chopped tarragon or chives; 1 tablespoon tomato paste and a pinch of paprika; 2 tablespoons each finely chopped parsley and onion; ¼–½ teaspoon anchovy paste (for cold fish).

Meat

Meat, especially beef, is the most popular food in the American diet. The average person eats 180 pounds of meat a year, of which beef represents about 110 pounds. Next comes pork, then lamb and veal.

Meat will keep for 2–3 days in the refrigerator. Remove the wrapping paper as soon as possible after purchase. Place the meat on a clean plate, wrap it loosely in plastic wrap, and, leaving the ends open to allow the air to circulate, store in the refrigerator.

Ground meat and variety meats do not keep well and should preferably be used on the day of purchase. Once meat has been cooked, it should be cooled as quickly as possibly before storing.

COOKING METHODS

There are no set rules for cooking meat, as each cut lends itself to preparation, cooking and presentation in several different ways. In general, however, the tender cuts are roasted or broiled, while the tougher cuts are more suitable for pot-roasting, boiling, braising, frying and stewing.

Roasting
This is the traditional method for cooking large cuts of meat. It can be done in several ways, oven roasting being the most common, and again there are two methods. With quick-roasting, the meat is cooked at a high temperature which quickly seals in the juices, thus preserving the full flavor. At the same time, however, the meat shrinks.

Slow-roasting is done at low temperature over a long period. This method reduces shrinkage of the meat and produces a roast that is usually more tender.

Whichever roasting method is used, the meat must first be weighed and the cooking time calculated. Put the meat, fat side up, on a wire rack in a shallow roasting pan. Rub a lean cut with drippings or lard first.

Place the pan in the center of the oven. During roasting the melting fat naturally bastes the meat; otherwise spoon the pan juices over it from time to time.

Roasting times and temperatures
The size and shape of a roast, and the way in which it has been prepared, influence cooking times. Large cuts require less roasting time for their weight than small ones, and cuts on the bone cook more quickly than boned roasts because bones are a conductor of heat. A roast on the bone is considered to have a better flavor. Roasts on the bone, especially from the loin and breast portions, usually have the chine bone removed by the butcher.

Boned roasts with a wide diameter take less cooking time than roasts with a narrow diameter although they may weigh the same. Roasts which weigh less than 3 pounds should always be slow-roasted for at least 1½ hours. Smaller roasts are unsatisfactory as they shrink and dry out.

Meat thermometer
A meat thermometer is useful for assessing roasting times. Before cooking, insert the thermometer into the thickest part of the meat, but make sure that it does not touch bone or fat. When the thermometer registers the required internal temperature, the roast will be cooked.

This type of thermometer is particularly useful for cooking beef, where there are wider margins of doneness dictated by personal preference.

A new, improved meat thermometer, more accurate than the kind that can be used in the oven, is inserted in the meat near the end of the roasting time and gives a fast temperature reading. As it registers from 0° to 220°F, the thermometer can also be used to determine the internal temperature before the meat is put in the oven.

Spit-roasting
This traditional roasting method has been revived by the invention of the electric rôtisserie. This device is attached to a grill or oven and consists of a horizontal revolving shaft or spit which can hold large roasts, whole game or poultry and kebabs.

Spit-roasting can be applied to prime cuts, but for even roasting the roast must have a uniform shape. Rolled and stuffed roasts must be tied firmly or skewered so as to keep their shape.

Thread the meat on the spit so that the weight is evenly distributed; place it on the rôtisserie and operate it according to the manufacturer's instructions. While the roast revolves, it is basted with its own juices.

157

Foil roasting

Roasting in foil is becoming more and more popular, mainly because it saves the oven from being spattered with the roasting juices. Wrap the meat loosely in foil, sealing the edges firmly; basting is unnecessary, but remove the foil for the last 20–30 minutes of cooking to brown the roast. Foil wrapping is particularly recommended for slightly tough cuts as the moist heat tenderizes the meat. The meat, however, steams rather than roasts and will have a different flavor and texture than meat roasted by dry heat. At the same time, foil deflects heat, and the oven temperature should consequently be raised.

Clear plastic roasting bags are now available which completely eliminate splashing of the oven, and the roast bastes and browns during roasting. Do not remove the bag until the meat has finished cooking.

Pot-roasting

This is particularly suitable for smaller and slightly tougher cuts, such as brisket, round and rump of beef. Melt enough fat to cover the bottom of a deep, heavy-based pan, put in the meat and brown it over moderately high heat. Lift out the meat, put a wire rack or a bed of chopped root vegetables in the bottom of the pan, and replace the meat.

Cover the pan with a tight-fitting lid and cook over low heat until the meat is tender; allow 45 minutes per pound. Turn the meat frequently.

Alternatively, put the browned meat in a deep baking dish, cover it tightly and cook in the center of a pre-heated oven, at 325°F (170°C, mark 3); allow 45 minutes per pound. Lift out the cooked meat, drain the fat from the juices and use them for gravy or sauce.

Braising

A cooking method used for smaller cuts of meat, such as less tender chops and steaks, and for large variety meats such as hearts. Coat the meat with seasoned flour (page 184) and brown it evenly in hot fat. Set the meat on a bed of diced, lightly fried root vegetables in a casserole or heavy-based saucepan. Pour over enough water or stock and tomato paste to cover the vegetables; add herbs and seasonings.

Cover the casserole with a tight-fitting lid and cook in the center of a pre-heated oven, at 325°F (170°C, mark 3), or on the stove until tender for 2–3 hours. Add more liquid if needed.

Stewing

This long, slow-cooking method is suitable for the tougher cuts of meat. Cut the meat into 1 in cubes, coat them evenly in seasoned flour (page 184) and brown them quickly, in a pan of very hot fat.

Lift the meat on to a plate and fry a few sliced carrots, onions and turnips in the fat until golden brown. Sprinkle in 1–2 tablespoons of flour, or enough to absorb all the fat; fry until the mixture is pale brown. Stir in sufficient warm stock or water to give a pouring consistency, season with salt, freshly ground black pepper and herbs and bring the sauce to the boil.

Put the meat in a flameproof casserole, pour over the sauce and vegetables and cover with a tight-

ROASTING TIMES FOR MEAT				
Cut	Weight in Pounds	Oven Temperature	Meat Thermometer Temperature	Approximate Minutes Per Pound
Beef				
Rib	6–8	300°–325°F	140°F (rare)	23–25
			160°F (medium)	27–30
			170°F (well)	32–35
	4–6	300°–325°F	140°F (rare)	26–32
			160°F (medium)	34–38
			170°F (well)	40–42
Rolled rib	5–7	300°–325°F	140°F (rare)	32
			160°F (medium)	38
			170°F (well)	48
Rib eye (Delmonico)	4–6	350°F	140°F (rare)	18–20
			160°F (medium)	20–22
			170°F (well)	22–24
Boneless rolled rump (high quality)	4–6	300°–325°F	150°–170°F	25–30
Tip (high quality)	3½–4	300°–325°F	140°–170°F	35–40
	4–6	300°–325°F	140°–170°F	30–35
Veal				
Leg	5–8	300°–325°F	170°F	25–35
Loin	4–6	300°–325°F	170°F	30–35
Boneless shoulder	4–6	300°–325°F	170°F	40–45
Lamb				
Leg	5–8	300°–325°F	165°F (well)	20–25
Shoulder	4–6	300°–325°F	165°F (well)	20–25
Boneless	3–5	300°–325°F	165°F (well)	30–35
Cushion	3–5	300°–325°F	165°F (well)	20–25
Pork, Fresh				
Loin				
Center	3–5	325°–350°F	170°F	30–35
Half	5–7	325°–350°F	170°F	35–40
Blade loin or sirloin	3–4	325°–350°F	170°F	40–45
Arm picnic shoulder	5–8	325°–350°F	170°F	30–35
Boneless	3–5	325°–350°F	170°F	35–40
Cushion	3–5	325°–350°F	170°F	30–35
Blade Boston shoulder	4–6	325°–350°F	170°F	40–45
Leg (fresh ham)				
Whole (bone in)	12–16	325°–350°F	170°F	22–26
Whole (boneless)	10–14	325°–350°F	170°F	24–28
Half (bone in)	5–8	325°–350°F	170°F	35–40
Spareribs		325°–350°F	170°F (well)	1½–2½ hours
Pork, Smoked				
Ham (cook-before-eating)				
Whole	10–14	300°–325°F	160°F	18–20
Half	5–7	300°–325°F	160°F	22–25
Shank or rump portion	3–4	300°–325°F	160°F	35–40
Ham (fully cooked)★				
Half	5–7	325°F	140°F	18–24
Arm picnic shoulder	5–8	300°–325°F	170°F	35
Shoulder roll	2–3	300°–325°F	170°F	35–40

★Allow approximately 15 minutes per pound
Adapted from the National Livestock and Meat Board chart

fitting lid. Simmer the stew on top of the stove or in an oven, at 325°F (170°C, mark 3), until tender, after 1½–3 hours.

Boiling

Suitable for tough cuts of beef, tongue and corned beef. Bring a pan of water, in which the meat will fit snugly, to the boil. Add 2 teaspoons of salt to each pound of meat, a bouquet garni (page 183), a large onion studded with cloves, and the meat. Bring the contents of the pan to the boil, remove any scum from the surface, then cover the pan with a tight-fitting lid and lower the heat.

Simmer the meat over very low heat until tender. Add a selection of chopped root vegetables to the pan for the last 45 minutes of cooking, if the meat is to be served hot. For cold, boiled meat, leave the meat to cool in the cooking liquid. Drain the meat thoroughly before serving.

Corned beef should be placed in cold water and brought quickly to the boil. Drain the meat and proceed as already described. A very salty piece should be soaked in water overnight or for several hours before being boiled. If possible, change the water at least once.

Broiling

This quick-cooking method is suitable for small tender cuts, such as prime steaks, chops and cutlets, and for sausages, liver, kidney, bacon and ham slices.

Brush the meat with oil or melted butter, and sprinkle with a little salt and pepper (omit salt on steaks as this draws out the juices, and on bacon and ham

slices). On pork chops, use sharp scissors to snip the outer layer of fat at 1 in intervals to prevent curling and shrinkage during broiling.

Grease the broiler rack with oil or butter to prevent the meat from sticking to it. Put the meat on the rack and set it under a pre-heated broiler. Turn the meat once only during cooking and baste with the pan juices if the meat begins to dry out.

Frying

Another quick-cooking method for the same types of meat as suggested for broiling. Frying times are the same as those for broiling.

Melt just enough butter or oil to cover the bottom of a frying pan (drippings may be used for beef and lard for pork), and heat it quickly. Put the meat in the pan and cook it on a high heat, turning once only. For thick cuts, lower the heat after the meat has browned and continue frying until tender.

Lift out and drain the fried meat and keep it warm while making the gravy. Pour the fat from the pan, and stir a little stock or wine into the pan juices. Bring to the boil, correct seasoning and pour the gravy into a warm sauce boat.

Bacon slices need little or no extra fat for frying. Set the slices so that the lean parts overlap the fat in a cool pan, then fry over moderate heat, turning once, until the slices are cooked.

Sausages are often pricked with a fork before they are fried, to prevent the skins bursting. This is unnecessary if they are fried over low heat for about 20 minutes.

BEEF

Allow ¾–1 pound per person from a roast on the bone, and ½–¾ pound per person from boned roasts. For average portions, allow an 8-ounce steak per person.

Roasting

The best beef cuts for roasting include sirloin, the rib roasts, and whole fillet. Rump, too, may be slow-roasted, but is usually more suitable for pot-roasting.

Sirloin and rib roasts are sold on the bone or as rolled roasts. Boning and rolling may also be done at home without a lot of trouble.

Boning and rolling (of sirloin)
Lay the meat, bones down, on a steady board. Using a sharp, broad knife, cut the meat across the grain at the thick bone at the top of the meat (chine bone). Insert the knife at the top where the meat has been loosened and move it downwards, following the bones carefully, in sawing movements until the meat comes away from the bones in one piece. Use the bones for stock or a soup.

Lay the boned meat on the board, skin side up, and roll it tightly from the thickest end. Tie it securely with a piece of string to hold its shape. Cut 2 in strips of pork fat and tie them, slightly overlapping, around the roast. A wider strip of fat may be tied over the top of the rolled roast to provide extra fat during roasting. Remove this piece of fat before carving.

Larding (fillet)

A whole piece of fillet is an excellent, if expensive, cut for

roasting. As it has no fat this must be added in some form to prevent the meat drying out while it is roasting.

First trim any skin or sinews from the fillet, then cut pork fatback into strips narrow enough to be threaded through the eye of a larding needle. Thread short lengths of the fat at intervals through the fillet, about ½ in deep and on all four sides. A fillet encased in pastry does not need larding.

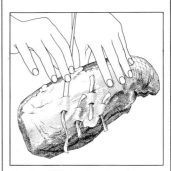

Lard beef fillet by threading short lengths of fat through the meat

Alternatively, wrap thin bacon slices, slightly overlapping, round the fillet and secure with thin string. Fillet should be quick-roasted, at 12–15 minutes per pound, or roasted on a spit, at 15–20 minutes per pound.

Pot-roasting and braising

Flank, brisket, top round, rump, chuck and bottom round are the best cuts for pot-roasting or braising; for cooking these cuts, follow the directions given under Meat.

Boiling

Plate, brisket and short ribs are ideal for slow boiling with vegetables. Plate and brisket can often

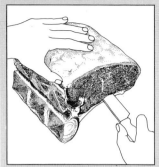

1. *Severing the meat from the bone*

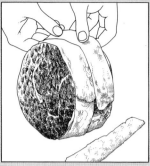

3. *Laying pork fat around the roast*

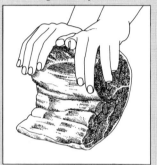

2. *Rolling up the boned meat*

4. *Rolled roast with fat tied on top*

be bought corned, or the curing may be done at home. See recipe for Spiced Brisket of Beef given on page 96.

Salting or pickling
(plate, brisket)
Put 1 gallon cold water with 1½ pounds salt, 1 ounce saltpeter and 1 cup brown sugar in a large pan. Bring to the boil and boil for 20 minutes. Strain the liquid through cheesecloth into a large earthenware bowl and leave to cool. Put the meat in the liquid, and keep it submerged by covering it with a weighted plate. Leave the meat in the liquid for 5–10 days, depending on thickness. Soak in cold water for about 1 hour before boiling.

Broiling and pan-broiling
These cooking methods are suit-able for all steaks – fillet, sirloin, rump, porterhouse and T-bone. Follow the general directions, but never sprinkle beef with salt as this draws out the juices.

Stewing
This slow-cooking method is ideal for all the tougher cuts of beef, such as round, chuck, arm and shank. Stews store well in a freezer. Many people consider them best if cooked a day in advance, but pre-cooked stew must be heated through thoroughly before being served.

The Hungarian stews, known as goulashes, are internationally famous and differ from the average stew in their piquant, sweet and spicy flavor. They are ideally made from chuck steak, but lean boned shoulder of lamb or pork may also be used.

VEAL

The flavor of veal is delicate, and the flesh tends to be dry unless carefully cooked. It does not keep well and should be used on the day of purchase. Allow ½–¾ pound per person from veal on the bone, and about ⅓–½ pound per person of boneless veal.

Roasting
This method is suitable for large cuts such as shoulder, rump, leg and loin. The shoulder is often boned and stuffed. As the meat is fairly dry, it must be basted frequently. Boned breast is the most economical veal roast. It is ideal for stuffing – allow 1 pound stuffing to a 6 pound breast. Use the slow-roasting method rather than the quick-roasting one.

Pot-roasting and braising
Boned and stuffed shoulder of veal can be pot-roasted or braised. Stuffed breast is also recommended for braising, allowing about 3 hours for a 6 pound stuffed roast.

Boiling and stewing
Veal sold for stews usually comes from the shoulder, breast, shank, and the neck. These contain a large amount of bone. If bought on the bone, allow at least ⅓ pound per serving.

Broiling and pan-broiling
Chops from the loin or rib of veal are suitable for sautéing and braising. Broiling, however, is usually less successful, since the meat tends to dry out and toughen when cooked this way.

For sautéing, the most popular veal cuts are scallops – thin slices, usually cut from the top of the leg.

Veal scallops should be thinned and tenderized by pounding before they are cooked. Purchase ¼-inch-thick slices from the butcher. Place them between sheets of waxed paper and beat them flat with a meat pounder or rolling pin. Before cooking, dip the scallops in beaten egg, then coat them with fresh bread crumbs. Sauté in a little hot butter and oil for 5 minutes, turning once.

LAMB

Lamb is a rather fatty meat, and the fat which rises to the surface from stewed, boiled or braised lamb should be skimmed off. Dust the basted skin of roast lamb with seasoned flour (page 184) to absorb excess fat and to crisp the surface.

Allow ½–¾ pound lamb on the bone per person, and ¼–½ pound of boned lamb per serving.

Roasting
The double loin, or saddle, with the kidneys attached, can be roasted whole.

Whole leg and shoulder of lamb are among the most popular cuts. They are usually sold on the bone, but may also be purchased boned for stuffing and rolling.

Rack of lamb, from the rib section, is probably the most versatile cut of all meats. It is quick-cooking and can be used in a number of ways. It is the basis of classic dishes – Lancashire hot pot, navarin of lamb, Scotch broth, to name but a few – but the cut is also excellent for roasting when prepared in classic roasts, such as crown roast and guard of honor.

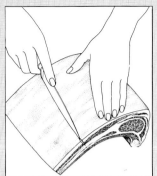

1. Trimming meat from bones

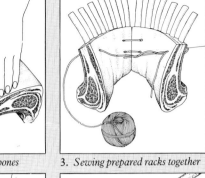

3. Sewing prepared racks together

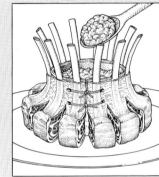

2. Scraping bone ends clean

4. Filling the crown with stuffing

1. Easing out rib bones

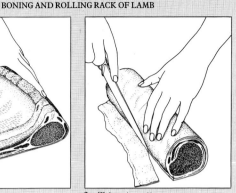

3. Trimming off excess fat

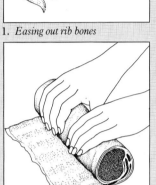

2. Rolling up the boned rack

4. Cutting meat into noisettes

Crown roast

Many butchers will prepare a crown roast if given a few days' notice, but if this is not possible, buy two matching racks of lamb, each containing seven to eight rib chops.

Trim the fat from the thick part of each rack, and with a sharp knife cut the top 1½–2 in layer of meat from the thin end of the bones. Scrape off all gristle and meat to leave the bone ends clean. When the two pieces of meat have been prepared, sew them together, with a trussing needle and fine string, having the thick ends of the meat as the base of the crown.

Slit the lower half of the formed crown between each bone, about two-thirds up from the base and, if necessary, tie a piece of string around the middle. Fill the cavity of the crown with stuffing and slow-roast.

Butchers who sell prepared crowns often put the trimmings into the hollow crown. Remove them before stuffing and roasting. The circle of fat covering the trimmings may be replaced on top of the stuffing as it bastes the meat during roasting, but it should be removed for the last 30 minutes.

Pot-roasting and braising

The best cuts for braising are the shoulder, breast, and shank. The shoulder or breast can be boned and rolled, but make sure most of the fat has been trimmed off by the butcher.

Guard of honor

This is also prepared from two racks, but the bones are trimmed clean to about 2½–3 in. The two pieces of meat are then joined and sewn together, skin side up, along the bottom meaty part of the racks. Fold the meat together, skin outside, so that the cleaned bones meet and criss-cross on top. Protect these with foil. Fill the cavity with a savory stuffing; tie the roast at intervals to keep its shape; roast at low temperature.

Stewing and boiling

Breast of lamb, shoulder and neck are the best and most economical cuts for stews and casseroles. Trim off as much fat as possible before cooking.

Broiling and pan-broiling

Lamb rib chops, which have a high proportion of bone, may be broiled or pan-broiled. Chops from the loin are meatier than rib chops. Shoulder chops are less expensive and also less tender, but can be very tasty when pan-broiled.

Noisettes

These are trimmed, round slices taken from the rack. Cut off the thick chine bone at the thick end of the rack and trim away all excess fat from the meat. Cut along either side of each rib bone and ease it out. Roll up the boned rack, trim it and tie with string at ½ in intervals. Cut the rolled rack into 2 in thick slices and fry or broil.

161

PORK

A good-quality pork roast should have a moderate amount of fat – lean pork is generally lacking in flavor, and fatty pork is wasteful. Allow $\frac{1}{2}$–$\frac{3}{4}$ pound of pork on the bone or $\frac{1}{3}$–$\frac{1}{2}$ pound of boned meat per serving.

Pork must be thoroughly cooked to be digestible, and underdone pork can be dangerous because of disease-producing organisms in the meat. It was formerly recommended that pork be cooked to an internal temperature of 185°F; research has now proved that pork is safe at a temperature of 170°F.

Roasting
The pork cuts considered most suitable for roasting, on or off the bone, are the leg, the loin, and the more economical pork shoulder. Leg and loin are often boned, stuffed, and rolled before roasting; shoulder of pork, which is an awkward cut to carve, should also be boned and rolled.

Pork Loin Stuffed with Prunes
A prune stuffing makes this pork roast an attractive and unusual main course for a dinner party.

MARINATING TIME: *24 hours*
PREPARATION TIME: *30 min*
COOKING TIME: *2½ hours*
INGREDIENTS *(for 6):*
1 box pitted prunes
¼ cup cognac
5–6 pounds pork loin roast
2 large yellow onions, sliced
2 stalks celery, sliced
2 carrots, sliced
5 bay leaves
8 peppercorns
2–3 cups dry red wine
⅓ cup butter
2 tablespoons flour
1 cup cream (optional)
Salt★ and pepper

Soak the prunes in the cognac for 24 hours, turning them occasionally. Ask the butcher to bone the roast but save the bones. Roast the bones in the same pan with the loin; they will make a tasty leftover for the cook and can also be used for making stock.

With a larding needle or a knife, make a small hole the entire length of the meat (or ask the butcher to do this). Stuff the hole with the prunes, pushing them in with the handle of a wooden spoon. Tie the roast securely with string in several places. Put the meat in a deep bowl and add the sliced onions, celery, carrots, bay leaves, peppercorns, and the red wine.

Marinate the meat in this mixture for 24 hours if possible. Drain, dry with paper towels, and brown the roast on all sides in butter. Put it on a rack in a roasting pan, baste well with the strained marinade, and roast in a preheated 450°F oven for 15 minutes. Reduce the heat to 350°F and cook until the roast is done, about 2 hours, basting from time to time with the marinade.

Make a gravy to accompany the roast by skimming the fat from the pan juices; add about 2 tablespoons of flour to the remaining juices. Then pour in the cream if you are using it and cook, stirring constantly with a wire whisk or wooden spoon, over low heat until thickened. Season to taste with salt and pepper. Let the roast stand for 15 minutes before carving. Serve the gravy separately.

Sautéing and broiling
Pork chops are better sautéed than broiled, as the lean meat may dry out and toughen while cooking. Large pork loin chops often have a thick strip of fat around the outer edge, which tends to curl during cooking. To prevent this, snip the fat with scissors or make cuts with a sharp knife at 1-inch intervals.

Pork spareribs, which are cut from the lower rib section of the belly, are usually roasted or broiled and are excellent when barbecued over charcoal.

Slices of lean pork tenderloin may be sautéed, but the whole tenderloin or fillet of pork is usually cooked by roasting or broiling.

HAM

Hams are sold whole, halved, or cut into thick slices. They are suitable for all cooking methods – boiling, baking, broiling, braising, and sautéing.

Cooking methods
Whole hams, unless they are the tenderized and ready-to-bake type, should be soaked in cold water to remove excess salt. They are then boiled or parboiled before being roasted, braised, or baked.

Put the ham in a large pan, cover with cold water, and bring slowly to a boil. Cover the pan with a lid and reduce the heat so that the meat is cooked at a slow simmer. Fast boiling hardens the tissue and causes shrinkage of the meat. Cook for 20 minutes per pound.

Lift out the ham, allow it to cool and set slightly, then peel off the skin with the fingers.

To roast or bake a ham, put in a roasting pan, fat side up, and brush with a glaze. Then wrap the ham in foil and bake in the center of a preheated oven at 300°F for 45 minutes–1 hour until well glazed and heated through.

If desired, score a diamond pattern in the exposed fat, insert whole cloves in the intersections, and pat brown sugar over the top of the ham to glaze it. Return the ham to the oven and roast at 425°F for the last 30 minutes. Honey can be used for glazing instead of brown sugar.

Aged and country hams are sold with cooking instructions printed on the package that vary according to the curing methods. Follow the manufacturer's instructions carefully.

PREPARING HAM

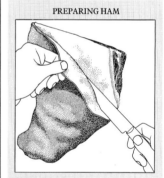

Skinning a ham

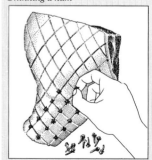

Studding the fat with cloves

Cooking a country ham

To prepare a country ham, soak the ham in cold water to cover for 24–36 hours. Drain. If mold remains, scrub well with a vegetable brush and a mild unscented soap. Rinse thoroughly, making sure that no trace of soap residue remains on the meat.

Place the ham in a large pot of simmering water to cover. Simmer over low heat, allowing 25–30 minutes per pound. Remove the ham from the pot. With the fingers, remove the skin from the ham while it is still warm.

If desired, score the fat as described opposite. An alternative glaze can be made as follows:

Mix 1 cup light brown sugar with 2 teaspoons dry or Dijon mustard and ½ teaspoon ground cloves. Add some of the rendered fat from the cooking liquid to make a stiff paste and brush this evenly over the ham.

Bake the ham at 425°F for 30 minutes. Serve it hot or cold, cut into very thin slices.

Broiling and frying

Bacon slices and ham slices are suitable for both broiling and frying. To prevent the fatty edges curling during cooking, snip them as for pork chops.

Bacon rolls

Bacon slices are used for barding and are also rolled up, broiled or baked, and used as a garnish with poultry. Before rolling bacon slices they should be stretched. Lay the slices on a board and run the blade of a knife over each one.

Bacon slices should also be stretched when they are used for Devils on Horseback (prunes wrapped in bacon, fastened with a wooden pick and broiled).

VARIETY MEATS

Some of the internal organs of beef, veal, lamb and pork, are edible. These organs include the hearts, kidneys, livers, brains, tongues and sweetbreads. Also classed as variety meats are beef and veal marrow bones, oxtail, and pigs' heads and feet, as well as pork sausages and blood sausages. Variety meat is highly nutritious, easily digestible and generally cheap.

Brains

Veal, lamb and pork brains may all be prepared and cooked in the same manner. Soak the brains in lightly salted cold water to remove all traces of blood. Remove the thin covering membrane. Put the brains in a pan of well-flavored stock, bring to the boil and simmer over low heat for about 20 minutes. Drain thoroughly, then leave the brains to cool and press under a weight.

Cut the cold brains into ½ in slices, coat them in beaten egg and breadcrumbs and fry in butter until golden brown. Alternatively, coat the slices in batter and deep fry them. Allow 2 sets of brains per person.

Hearts

Beef, veal and lamb hearts are used. They are usually stuffed and pot-roasted, braised or stewed. Beef heart, however, being very tough and muscular, is better chopped and used in casseroles. Veal and lamb hearts are more tender.

Rinse off all the blood under cold running water and snip out the stumps from the arteries and the tendons with scissors. Stuff the hearts with an onion or bread stuffing and sew up the opening. Pot-roast or braise the hearts for 1½–2 hours or until tender.

Kidneys

Beef kidneys are strongly flavored and are used, chopped, for braising, or in pies and puddings. Veal, lamb and pork kidneys are all suitable for broiling and frying, although pork kidneys are less tender than veal and lamb. Allow two or three per person.

Kidneys are sometimes sold in a thick layer of solid fat; this must be removed, and the thin transparent skin surrounding the kidneys must be peeled off. Cut the kidney in half lengthwise and snip out the central core.

Brush the kidneys with melted

TRIMMING KIDNEYS

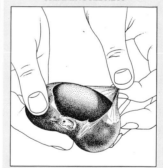

Removing kidney membranes

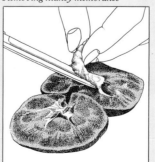

Snipping away the core

butter, sprinkle with salt and pepper, and broil or fry them for not more than 6 minutes, turning them once only.

Fat from lamb kidneys can be rendered down for frying and roasting; fat from beef kidneys is sold as suet and, after rendering down, is also suitable for deep-frying.

Liver

Beef liver, which is slightly coarse and tough, should be soaked for at least 1 hour in cold water to remove excess blood. It is best braised, although it can be sautéed like veal, lamb and pork liver.

Cut beef liver into ¼ in slices, coat with seasoned flour (page 184) and brown in butter together with thinly sliced onion and a few bacon slices. Put the liver in a casserole dish, with the onion and bacon, and cover with stock or tomato sauce. Put the lid on the dish and cook in the center of a pre-heated oven, at 350°F (180°C, mark 4), for 45 minutes.

For broiling and frying, veal and lamb liver are better. Cut off any gristly portions and remove, with a knife or scissors, any central cores. Wash and dry the liver thoroughly, then cut into ¼ in thick slices. Brush with melted butter and sprinkle with salt and pepper before broiling.

Alternatively, coat the slices in seasoned flour (page 184) and fry in butter over gentle heat. Avoid overcooking liver as this toughens it – as soon as blood begins to run, turn over the slices and cook the other side for a shorter time.

Pork liver may be prepared and cooked as veal and lamb liver, and is also used in pâtés, stews and casseroles.

Sweetbreads

Veal and lamb sweetbreads are prepared in the same way. One pair of sweetbreads will serve two people. Soak the sweetbreads in cold water for 1–2 hours to remove all blood. Drain and put in a pan with cold water.

Bring to the boil and drain off the liquid immediately; cover the sweetbreads with cold salted water and bring them to the boil again over low heat. As soon as boiling point is reached, lift out the sweetbreads and rinse under cold running water. Remove the black veins and as much as possible of the thin membranes which cover them.

Put the sweetbreads in a pan, barely cover with white stock and add a pat of butter and a squeeze of lemon juice. Bring to the boil, cover the pan with a lid and simmer gently for 15–20 minutes. Leave the sweetbreads to cool in the liquid, then drain. Coat with seasoned flour, beaten egg and breadcrumbs and fry in butter or bacon fat until golden.

Tongues

Beef tongue is the largest, weighing 4–6 pounds. It can be pickled, smoked, canned or fresh, and is cooked whole and usually served cold. Soak a pickled tongue overnight in cold water, drain and put in a large pan. Cover with cold water, bring to the boil, then drain thoroughly. Return the tongue to the pan, cover with fresh cold water and add 6 peppercorns, 1 bouquet garni (page 183) and a sliced onion. Bring to the boil, cover with a lid and simmer for 2–3 hours or until tender (cook a fresh tongue for 5–6 hours).

Plunge the cooked tongue into cold water, then peel off the skin, starting from the tip end. Remove bones and gristle from the root end; trim it off neatly. Arch the tongue into a round shape and press it into a deep, round cake pan, about 7 in wide. Spoon over a little of the strained stock, cover the tongue with a weighted board and leave to set.

Lamb tongues are much smaller, weighing only about ½ pound each. Soak them for 1–2 hours in lightly salted water. Boil the tongues, with 1 sliced onion, 1 bouquet garni (page 183), a few peppercorns and enough water to cover, for about 2 hours. Peel the tongues and serve them hot with parsley sauce made from the stock, or press the tongues in aspic as described for beef tongue and serve cold.

Tripe

This is sold blanched and partly cooked, and additional cooking time varies according to the pre-cooking. Always check with the butcher how much longer the tripe should be cooked.

Marrow bones

The marrow contained in the large beef thigh and shoulder bones is considered a delicacy.

Scoop cooked marrow from the bone, using a small, pointed teaspoon

Have the bones sawn into manageable lengths, scrape and wash them before sealing the ends with a flour and water paste. Tie each bone in a piece of cheesecloth, cover with water and simmer gently for 1½–2 hours. Drain, then extract the marrow with a teaspoon and spread on toast.

Veal bones

The bones of young calves contain a large quantity of gelatin which sets to jelly after boiling. Calf's head and feet are ideal for jellied stocks and head cheese; they are, however, scarce and pigs' feet, which also contain gelatin, may be used instead.

Oxtail

Although not strictly variety meat, this is often classed as such. It is sold skinned and cut into pieces about 2 in long and is ideal for rich stews. As oxtail has a high proportion of fat and bone, allow one oxtail for 3–4 servings.

PREPARATION TIME: *25 min*
COOKING TIME: *3–3½ hours*
INGREDIENTS *(for 4):*
1 oxtail
¼ cup seasoned flour (page 184)
¼ cup drippings or oil
2 onions
½ pound carrots
2 stalks celery
1½ cups brown stock (page 153)
Bouquet garni (page 183)

Trim as much fat as possible from the oxtail pieces and toss in seasoned flour. Heat the drippings in a heavy-based pan and brown the oxtail over high heat. Lift out the oxtail and put in a casserole.

Fry the sliced onions, carrots and celery in the fat until lightly brown, sprinkle in the remaining seasoned flour and cook until it has absorbed all the fat. Stir in the stock gradually, then pour this sauce over the oxtail. Add the bouquet garni, cover the casserole and cook on a low oven shelf, at 300°F (160°C, mark 2), for about 3 hours. Add more stock during cooking if it seems to be necessary.

Pig's head

This is often used for making head cheese. It must be soaked for at least 24 hours in cold salted water before being boiled. Calf's head, too, makes an excellent head cheese, but is now rarely obtainable.

Sausages

Pork sausages are easily made at home. They consist of equal amounts of lean ground meat and fat, seasoned with salt, pepper and herbs. This mixture is stuffed into the blanched intestines (obtainable from some butchers) with the aid of a sausage funnel attached to a meat grinder. Twist the filled intestines every 3–4 in.

Blood puddings or sausage

Blood puddings are made from seasoned pig's blood and suet, stuffed into blanched pig intestines and slowly poached before being marketed. Cut the puddings in half lengthwise or into thick slices and fry in hot butter. Serve with applesauce and mashed potatoes.

Trotters

Pig's feet or trotters contain a large amount of gelatin and are used, with pig's or calf's head, to produce head cheese or jellied stock.

Carving Meat

For many people, carving meat with the bone in can be a perplexing and messy task. Carving is made considerably easier when the carver knows the positions of the bones in the roasts.

When carving, it is essential to use a good sharp knife and a two-pronged carving fork with a thumb guard. Most meat – whether beef, pork, lamb, or veal – should be carved across the grain because this makes it tenderer. Beef blade roasts and rib roasts should be sliced thin; whole hams, rump and shank halves of ham, arm picnic shoulders, pork roasts, and veal roasts should be sliced slightly thicker than beef. A leg of lamb should be cut fairly thick; it can be carved with the grain into horizontal slices, but in this case the slices should be cut thin to ensure tenderness.

LEG OF LAMB

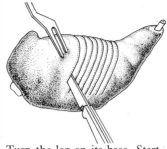 

With the lower leg bone to the right, remove 2 or 3 lengthwise slices from the thin side of the leg to form a steady base.

Turn the leg on its base. Start cutting a few inches in from the end of the shank bone, making perpendicular slices to the leg. Carve horizontally along the leg bone to enable the slices to be removed. Cut off the base in one piece, then slice across the grain.

PORK LOIN ROAST

If the backbone has not been removed by the butcher, cut it off before bringing the roast to the table. Steady the roast with a fork. Insert the tip of a knife between the backbone and the meat and cut away the backbone, leaving as little meat on the bone as possible.

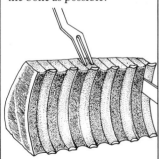

Set the meat on a platter on its broad end, the curved rib side facing you. Slice vertically between each rib, allowing 1 chop per serving. For thinner slices, cut as close as possible along each side of the rib bone. Alternate slices will thus be boneless.

BEEF RIB ROAST

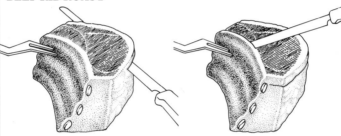

If necessary, remove a slice from the large end to form a steady base for the roast. Then slice the meat across the top of the roast.

To remove each slice from the bone, cut down vertically, following the edge of the rib bone, with the tip of a sharp knife.

Slide the knife under the slice, steady it with a fork, and lift the slice onto a serving platter. Slice thinly or as thick as ½ inch.

BEEF BLADE ROAST

 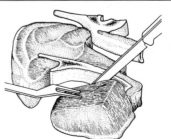 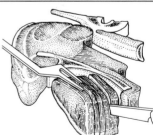

Steady the roast with a carving fork and cut between the meat and bones, removing one section of the roast at a time.

Turn each section of meat so that the meat fibers are parallel to the platter. This makes it possible to carve against the grain.

Steady the meat with a fork and cut across the grain of the meat in slices about ¼ inch thick. Lift the slices onto a serving platter.

WHOLE HAM

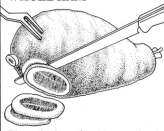  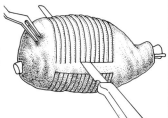

Place the ham fat side up, shank end to the right. Remove the first 2 or 3 slices from the thin side of the ham to form a steady base.

Set the ham on this base. Cut thin slices perpendicular to the leg bone, or lift off in one piece and slice as for picnic shoulder.

Remove all slices by cutting along leg bone. If more meat is needed, remove the base in one piece, then cut across the grain.

SHANK HALF OF HAM

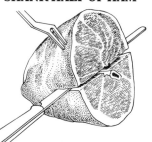 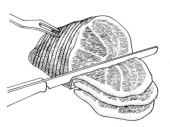 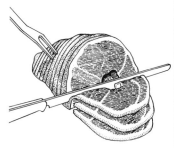

Place the shank end at the left; turn the ham so that the thickest portion is up. Steady shank with a fork and cut along the bone.

Place the section just removed, with the freshly cut side down, on a carving board and carve into thin, vertical slices.

To slice the lower part, remove the bone with the tip of the knife, turn the thickest part down, and slice as for the upper portion.

RUMP HALF OF HAM

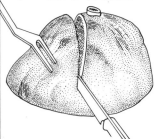 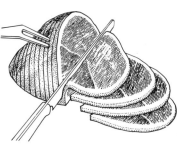 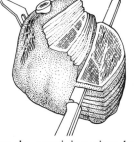

Place ham, cut side down, on a platter. Cut down the length of the interior bone and remove the boneless piece.

Place the boneless piece, with the freshly cut side down, on another platter. Carve into thin slices across the grain.

Carve the remaining piece by cutting horizontal slices to the bone. Remove each slice from the bone with the tip of the knife.

ARM PICNIC SHOULDER

Carving is the same for a roasted smoked picnic and a roasted fresh picnic. Remove a few lengthwise slices from the smaller side of the shoulder to form a steady base.

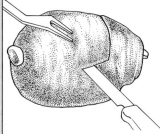

Turn the roast on its base. Starting on the left side of the elbow point, cut down to the bone, turn the knife, and cut along the bone to remove the upper portion.

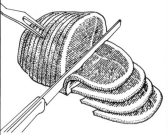

Steady this portion with a carving fork and cut the boneless portion into thin perpendicular slices, slicing across the grain of the meat with a very sharp knife.

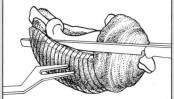

Remove the remaining meat of the shoulder from both sides of the arm bone and cut it into thin perpendicular slices across the grain, as for the upper portion.

166

Poultry and Game

As with many foods which were once seasonal, poultry and game are now available all the year round, because of the advent of freezing. Even so, freshly killed poultry is superior in taste to frozen birds, and game is at its best when it is in season, which generally lasts from early fall through the winter.

PREPARATION OF POULTRY

Most poultry is sold ready for cooking – that is hung, plucked, drawn and trussed. Oven-ready frozen poultry must be thawed slowly before cooking. It should be left in its wrapping and placed in a refrigerator for 24–48 hours, according to size, to thaw. It must never be thawed in hot water.

Stuffing

Before being trussed ready for cooking, poultry is usually stuffed. A stuffing improves the flavor of poultry, and it also makes the meat go further.

Stuffings are based on breadcrumbs – made from day-old bread – meat and rice to which butter is added together with herbs and seasonings. As a stuffing expands during cooking, stuff the bird loosely; 2 cups of stuffing or forcemeat mixture is sufficient for a $3\frac{1}{2}$ pound chicken.

Basic Forcemeat Stuffing

PREPARATION TIME: *15 min*
INGREDIENTS:
2 cups soft breadcrumbs
2 tablespoons butter (melted)
1 small onion
Salt★ and black pepper
1 egg
Stock or water

Put the breadcrumbs in a bowl and stir in the melted butter. Peel and finely chop the onion and blend into the breadcrumbs. Season with salt and pepper; beat the egg lightly and mix into the breadcrumbs. Add enough stock or water to give a moist but firm consistency.

Using a small spoon, fill the cavity of the bird with the stuffing. Chicken is stuffed from the neck end, duck and goose from either neck or vent end. Turkey is usually stuffed from both neck and vent ends.

The basic stuffing can be mixed with 2 tablespoons finely chopped parsley or 1 teaspoon sage.

Celery stuffing

Chop 3 stalks of celery finely and sauté them in a little butter for a few minutes. Add to the basic stuffing. This mixture may be flavored further by adding about $\frac{3}{4}$ cup finely chopped dried apricots.

Apple stuffing

Chop 2 medium-sized cooking apples finely. Replace the butter in the basic stuffing with 2 tablespoons bacon fat or finely chopped bacon and blend in the apples.

Mushroom stuffing

Trim and chop 4 ounces of mushrooms and sauté them in the melted butter for the basic stuffing. Mix with the breadcrumbs, onion, egg and seasonings to taste.

Sausage stuffing

For a large bird, a meaty stuffing helps to keep the flesh moist. Make up the basic stuffing and mix it with $\frac{1}{2}$ pound bulk sausage meat. Alternatively, melt 2–4 tablespoons of butter and lightly fry 1 finely chopped onion and 1 pound of sausage meat for 2–3 minutes. Turn the mixture into a bowl and add $\frac{1}{2}$ cup breadcrumbs, salt and pepper to taste, 1 beaten egg and water to bind. Leave the mixture to cool before stuffing the bird.

Cutting up

A chicken – or duck – can be cooked whole or cut into pieces. A small bird can be halved by placing it, back down, on a board and cutting lengthwise down and through the breastbone and then through the backbone.

Each half can be further divided into two. Tuck the blade of the knife underneath the leg joint and slice this away from the wing portion, holding the knife at an angle of 45 degrees.

To cut up a chicken, pull the chicken leg away from the body, and slice down to where the thigh joins the carcass. Break the bone and cut the whole leg away with a knife. A large leg piece can be cut into the drumstick and thigh. Next, cut down from the breast towards the wing joint, severing the wing from the body, and fold the breast meat over the wing pieces. Cut along the natural break in the rib cage to separate the top of the breast from the lower carcass. Divide the top. Divide this breast meat into two or three pieces. The remaining carcass can be used for making stock.

Trussing

Once stuffed, the bird should be trussed so as to keep it in shape during cooking, and to make it look attractive when it reaches the table. To tie up a bird, use a trussing needle, which has an eye large enough to take a piece of fine string.

If a trussing needle is not available, use poultry skewers and string to secure the bird.

Using a trussing needle

Place the chicken, breast down, on a board. Fold the loose neck skin over the back, closing the neck opening. Fold the wing tips over the body so as to hold the neck skin in position. Turn the chicken breast side up.

Make a slit in the skin above the opening at the vent of the body, and put the tail through this.

Thread the trussing needle with string. Insert the needle through the second joint of the right wing, push it through the body, and out through the corresponding joint on the left side. Insert the needle through the first joint, where the wing is attached to the body, on the left side. Pass the needle through the body again and out through the corresponding joint on the right side. Tie the ends of the string securely.

To truss the legs, press them close to the body; thread the needle again and pass it through the right side of the tail. Loop the string first around the right leg and then around the left leg. Pass the needle through the left side of the tail, pull the string tightly to draw the legs together and tie the ends securely.

Trussing with a skewer

Fold the neck skin and wing tips over the back of the bird and pull the tail through the slit above the vent.

Lay the bird on its back and, pushing the legs up towards the neck, insert a poultry skewer just below the thigh bone. Push the skewer through the body so that it comes out below the thigh bone on the other side.

Turn the bird on its breast. Pass a piece of string over the wing tips and beneath and up over the ends of the skewer. Cross the string over the back of the bird.

Turn the bird on to its back again, loop the string around the drumsticks and tail, then tie the string securely.

Barding

After trussing, the bird is ready for cooking. If it is to be roasted, the lean breast flesh should be protected to prevent it from drying out. This is known as barding and consists of covering the breast with bacon slices.

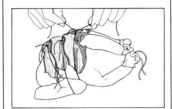

During cooking, the fat from the bacon melts and bastes the flesh. About 20 minutes before the end of cooking time, remove the bacon slices and return the bird to the oven.

COOKING METHODS

Roasting is the most popular method of cooking whole chicken, duck, goose, guinea hen and turkey. With the exception of duck and goose, which are fatty birds, all poultry should be barded or generously brushed with butter before roasting.

Boiling and steaming is suitable for older birds and pieces. The cooked flesh is mainly used in other dishes, such as fricassées and curries. Braising and casseroling are ideal, but slow, methods of cooking older birds or pieces.

Broiling or frying is reserved for whole small and young birds, and for chicken pieces.

CHICKEN

Boiling

Rub the surface of a whole chicken with lemon juice to preserve the color, and put it in a large pan. Add a bouquet garni (page 183), a peeled carrot and onion, and just enough water to cover the bird. Bring the water to the boil, and remove any scum from the surface. Reduce the heat to a gentle simmer, then cover with a lid and cook until the bird is tender, after 2–3 hours; chicken pieces need only 15–20 minutes. Lift the chicken from the pan and serve hot or cold with a white sauce (page 154).

Braising and casseroling

Lightly fry a whole bird or pieces in a little butter until golden. Remove the bird from the pan and fry about 1 pound of cleaned, roughly chopped vegetables, such as carrots, onions, celery and turnips, in the butter. Replace the poultry on the bed of vegetables, and cover the pan tightly with a lid. Cook over low heat on top of the stove or in the center of an oven, at 325°F (170°C, mark 3), until tender. Braising is a slow process, up to 3 hours, but cooking time depends on the size and age of the bird.

For a chicken casserole, fry the pieces in butter until golden, then put them in a flameproof casserole dish. Pour stock, wine or a mixture of both into the dish to a depth of 1 in. Add seasoning, chopped herbs or a bouquet garni, and cover the dish with a lid. Cook as for braising, on top of the stove or in the oven, for 1–1½ hours or until tender. A selection of lightly fried vegetables, such as pearl onions and mushrooms, baby carrots and small new potatoes, may be added halfway through cooking.

Broiling and frying

Tiny game hens, squabs, guinea hens and small broilers are excellent for broiling. One average bird (weight about 1½ pounds), will serve two persons. To prepare a whole bird for broiling, place it on its breast, cut through the backbone and open the bird out. Flatten the bird with a meat pounder, breaking the joints where necessary.

Brush the bird all over with melted butter, and season lightly with salt and pepper. Cook the bird on the broiler pan under

DISJOINTING A CHICKEN OR DUCK

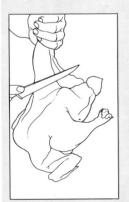
1. *Cut off legs*

2. *Break the leg joints*

3. *Slice toward wing joint*

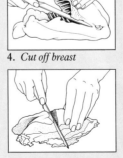
4. *Cut off breast*

5. *Cut breast in half*

moderate heat for 20–30 minutes, turning it over frequently.

Before frying chicken pieces, coat them with seasoned flour (page 184), or with beaten egg and breadcrumbs. Brown the pieces quickly in hot fat, then lower the heat and fry gently until the meat is tender, after 15–20 minutes.

Roasting

A roasting chicken weighing $3\frac{1}{2}$–4 pounds will serve 3–4 persons. Place the barded chicken in a roasting pan in the center of a pre-heated oven at 375°F (190°C, mark 5). Allow 20 minutes per pound, plus 20 minutes extra. A chicken weighing 4–6 pounds will give 4–6 servings. It should be roasted at 325°F (170°C, mark 3), allowing 25 minutes per pound, plus 25 minutes extra. A capon, with an average weight of 6–8 pounds, provides 8–10 portions; it should be roasted at 325°F (170°C, mark 3).

Alternatively, loosely wrap the chicken in foil and roast at 400–425°F (200–220°C, mark 6–7), allowing 20 minutes per pound, plus an extra 20 minutes. Open the foil 20 minutes before cooking is completed to allow the bird to brown. Use a skewer to test that the bird is cooked. Insert the skewer through the thickest part of the thigh; if clear juices run out, the bird is cooked.

Steaming

Place the trussed but unstuffed chicken on a wire rack or trivet over a deep pan of boiling water. Cover the chicken with foil and steam for 3–4 hours. Remove the skin from the cooked chicken and use the flesh in low-calorie diets and other dishes.

DUCK

Duck is prepared for roasting in the same way as chicken. Because duck is a fatty bird, it does not need barding or brushing with butter before cooking, but the skin should be pricked all over with a needle to allow the fat to run out of the bird during cooking. Season the duck with salt and pepper, and cook in a moderately hot oven, 400°F (200°C, mark 6), allowing some 20 minutes per pound.

Duck can also be cut up and braised for about 1 hour in the oven, at 350°F (180°C, mark 4).

Because the meat is very rich, duck is best served with sharply flavored sauces and fruit, such as oranges, peaches and cherries. When buying, allow 1 pound of duck per person.

GOOSE

Goose is more fatty than chicken, and therefore does not need to be brushed with melted butter before cooking. Before roasting a young bird, stuff it from the neck end, sprinkle with salt, and bard the bird with any fat taken from its inside. Loosely cover the bird with a piece of foil and roast at 400°F (200°C, mark 6), allowing 15 minutes per pound, plus an

extra 15 minutes. Or, slow-roast the goose, near the bottom of the oven, at 350°F (180°C, mark 4), allowing 25 minutes per pound. Serve with applesauce. When shopping, always allow $\frac{3}{4}$ pounds of goose for each person.

GUINEA HEN

All the methods of cooking chicken can be applied to guinea hen, particularly braising. When roasting the bird, bard the lean breast meat well.

TURKEY

A drawn turkey is usually filled with two different stuffings. The neck end can be stuffed with chestnut or veal forcemeat, and the body cavity filled with a sausage stuffing (page 90). An average 10–12 pound turkey will require a sausage stuffing made from at least 2 pounds of sausage meat.

Chestnut stuffing
PREPARATION TIME: *20 min*
INGREDIENTS:
Basic veal forcemeat stuffing (see below)
2 tablespoons chopped parsley
2 slices streaky bacon
$\frac{1}{2}$ pound canned chestnut purée
Grated rind of a lemon

Make up the basic veal forcemeat stuffing and blend in the finely chopped parsley. Chop the bacon finely; fry it without any extra fat for 2–3 minutes or until crisp. Mix the drained bacon thoroughly into the stuffing, together with the chestnut purée and finely grated lemon rind.

Veal Forcemeat
PREPARATION TIME: *20 min*
INGREDIENTS:
$1\frac{1}{2}$ cups soft breadcrumbs
2 tablespoons melted butter
1 small onion
$\frac{1}{4}$ pound boneless lean veal
2 slices lean bacon
Salt ★ *and black pepper*
1 egg
Stock or water

Mix the breadcrumbs with the butter and the finely chopped onion. Finely grind the veal and bacon and add to the breadcrumbs. Season with salt and pepper, then add the lightly beaten egg and enough stock or water to bind the stuffing.

Roasting

Before roasting the stuffed and trussed turkey, it should be coated with softened butter and barded with fat bacon strips. Roasting methods depend on the size of the bird and the time available. At low oven temperature, the turkey must be frequently basted. At the higher temperature, wrap the bird loosely in foil to prevent the flesh from drying out. About $\frac{1}{2}$ hour before cooking is complete, open the foil to allow the bird to brown.

When buying turkey, allow $\frac{3}{4}$ pounds oven-ready weight per person, and 1 pound if the bird is not drawn and trussed.

ROASTING TIMES FOR TURKEY		
Weight of bird	Method 1 (325°F, 170°C –mark 3)	Method 2 (450°F, 230°C –mark 8)
6–8 pounds	$3–3\frac{1}{2}$ hours	$2\frac{1}{4}–2\frac{1}{2}$ hours
8–10 pounds	$3\frac{1}{4}–3\frac{3}{4}$ hours	$2\frac{1}{2}–2\frac{3}{4}$ hours
10–14 pounds	$3\frac{3}{4}–4\frac{1}{4}$ hours	$2\frac{3}{4}–3$ hours
14–18 pounds	$4\frac{1}{4}–4\frac{3}{4}$ hours	$3–3\frac{1}{2}$ hours
18–20 pounds	$4\frac{3}{4}–5\frac{1}{4}$ hours	$3\frac{1}{2}–3\frac{3}{4}$ hours
20–24 pounds	$5\frac{1}{4}–6$ hours	$3\frac{3}{4}–4\frac{1}{4}$ hours

GAME BIRDS

All game birds should be hung before plucking and drawing to allow the flavor to develop and the flesh to become tender. Most game birds are bought already hung, plucked and trussed (and sometimes barded). Freshly killed birds should be hung by their heads in a cool, airy place. The period of hanging depends on the age of the bird, the weather and individual taste. Young game is hung for a shorter time than old, and warm, damp weather causes the flesh to decompose quicker than cold, dry weather. On average, hang game birds for 7–10 days or until the breast feathers can be easily plucked out.

After hanging, game birds are plucked, drawn and trussed in the same way as poultry, but the feet are left on. They are best cooked quite simply, and young birds are excellent for roasting; they do not require stuffing. Older and tougher birds are better braised or casseroled.

Braising
Older birds and those of uncertain age are best cooked by this method. Before cooking, cut the bird into pieces, coat with seasoned flour (page 184) and brown in hot fat in a pan. Remove the browned game from the pan and place in a casserole dish. Rinse the pan with $\frac{1}{2}$ cup dry red wine or game stock. Add the liquid to the casserole, cover tightly with a lid and cook in the center of a preheated oven, at 325°F (170°C, mark 3), for 1 hour, or until the meat is tender.

Broiling
Small, tender birds, such as

ROASTING TIMES FOR GAME BIRDS		
Bird	**Temperature**	**Time**
Grouse	400°F (200°C, mark 6)	30–45 minutes
Partridge	400°F (200°C, mark 6)	30–45 minutes
Pheasant and Pigeon	425°F (220°C, mark 7)	allow 20 minutes per pound
Plover	425°F (220°C, mark 7)	30–45 minutes
Quail	425°F (220°C, mark 7)	20 minutes
Snipe and Woodcock	425°C (220°C, mark 7)	20 minutes

grouse, partridge and quail, can be broiled. Split them through lengthwise along the breastbone and flatten the bird; brush generously with melted butter. Place under a hot broiler and cook for 25–30 minutes, basting continuously and turning frequently.

Roasting
Before roasting, game birds must be barded with strips of fat pork or bacon. Sprinkle the inside with salt and pepper and put a large pat of butter inside the bird to keep it moist. Place the prepared game bird on a piece of toast in the roasting pan. Baste frequently during cooking and remove the fat strips for the last 10–15 minutes. Sprinkle the breast lightly with flour and continue cooking until brown.

Serving roast game
Small birds, such as grouse, partridge, quail, snipe and woodcock, are served whole on their toast, and garnished with watercress. One bird should be allowed per person. Larger birds are split through lengthwise with a knife or poultry shears to give two portions. Matchstick potatoes are traditional with roast game and so too are fried breadcrumbs or bread sauce. A well-flavored brown gravy, a tossed green salad, buttered sprouts or braised celery are served separately.

WILD DUCK

These game birds, which include mallard, teal and canvasbacks, should be hung for only 2–3 days. After hanging, the birds are plucked, drawn and trussed as other game.

Wild duck should not be overcooked. Coat the bird with softened butter, and roast at 425°F (220°C, mark 7), allowing 20 minutes for teal, and 30 minutes for mallard and canvasback. For extra flavor, baste with a little orange juice or port.

Serve with wild rice and an orange and onion salad.

WILD GOOSE

This can be prepared and roasted in the same way as the domestic kind but, as the flesh is dry, it should be barded thoroughly.

FURRED GAME

This includes hare, which is a true game animal, and rabbit which is now specially bred for the table. A wild rabbit is cooked in the same way as one bred for the table. Hare is prepared for cooking by hanging, skinning and removing the internal organs.

Rabbit is eaten when $3–3\frac{1}{2}$ months old. Fresh or frozen prepared rabbits are sold cleaned and skinned. If necessary, rabbit can be prepared at home. It should not be hung, but skinned and cleaned as soon as killed.

Always wear rubber gloves when dressing rabbit or any wild meat. Although the danger of tularemia infection is not great, it can be transferred by hares, rabbits and other animals to man through cuts and scratches on the hands and arms. Take care to see that all wild meat is thoroughly cooked.

Cutting up
A hare or rabbit is more often stewed or braised rather than roasted whole. Cut the skinned and cleaned animal into eight serving pieces. First cut off, with a sharp knife, the skin flaps below the rib cage and discard them. Divide the carcass in half lengthwise along the backbone, then cut off the hind legs at the top of the thigh, breaking the bone. Cut off the forelegs around the shoulder bones, then cut each half of the carcass into two.

If the saddle of the rabbit – the section between the hind legs and forelegs – is to be roasted whole, cut off the skin flaps below the rib cage and the hind and forelegs as already described, but do not slit the rabbit through the backbone.

COOKING HARE AND RABBIT

Braising
This is a suitable cooking method for hare or rabbit pieces. Coat the pieces in seasoned flour and brown them in hot fat in a pan. Remove and place in a casserole. Rinse the pan with $1\frac{1}{4}$ cups red wine or game stock, scraping up the pan residues. Pour this

liquid over the pieces, cover tightly and cook at 325°F (170°C, mark 3) for about 2 hours, or until the meat is tender. Add a little more stock or wine, if necessary, and thicken the juices with a little of the reserved blood, or beurre manié (page 155).

Roasting

Fill the body cavity of the animal with forcemeat (page 169) and sew the flesh together. Lay slices of fat bacon over the back and add $\frac{1}{4}$ cup drippings to the pan. Roast at 350°F (180°C, mark 4) for 1½–2 hours. Baste frequently. Remove the bacon 15 minutes before cooking is completed to allow the hare to brown.

VENISON

This must be hung in a cool airy place for 2–3 weeks. Wipe away any moisture as it accumulates on the flesh during hanging.

Meat from a young deer is delicate and can be cooked without marinating, but the flesh of an older animal is tougher and is usually steeped in a marinade for 12–48 hours before cooking.

CARVING POULTRY AND GAME

The technique for carving poultry follows certain basic steps which consist of first removing the legs and wings and then carving the breast meat downward in thick or thin slices. When carving turkey, serve each person with both white meat – from the breast – and brown meat – from the body or legs.

Chicken and large game birds are carved in the same way as turkey. Small game birds are

either served whole, one per person, or may be cut in half.

To carve whole saddle of hare and venison, cut across the base of the loin and at a right angle down the center of the saddle, forming a T shape. The French method is to cut fairly thick even slices down the length of the saddle. The English way is to remove the meat completely before it is carved. Carve the loin end from each side in turn, slanting the knife towards the middle. Turn the roast over and slice the fillet lengthwise.

DUCK

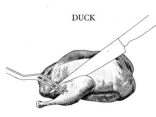

First cut off both legs.

Remove the wings on either side of the breast, and detach the wishbone from the neck end.

Slice down the center of the breast.

Holding the knife blade at an angle of 45 degrees to the breast, carve the meat in fairly thick, slightly wedge-shaped slices. Make them parallel to the first cut along the breast bone.

DUCKLING

Small duckling – and some larger game birds – are often split after cooking and half a bird is served to each person. Remove the trussing string or skewers from the roast duckling, then split the bird in half with a carving knife or with a pair of poultry shears or strong kitchen scissors. Insert the scissors in the neck end and cut along the center of the breastbone to the vent; split the bird in half by cutting through the backbone.

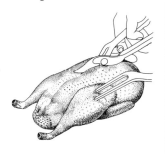

GOOSE

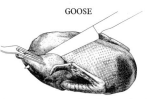

Begin by cutting the legs from the bird at the point where the thigh bones meet the body.

Remove the wings from either side of the breast.

If the goose has been stuffed from the neck end, first cut thick slices across the stuffing.

Fairly thick slices are then taken from both sides of the breast bone along the whole length of the bird. Carve downward with the knife blade held almost flat against the body of the bird.

TURKEY

Cut the large drumsticks from either side of the body.

Hold the knuckle end of the drumstick in one hand and slice the meat downward, following the direction of the bone. Rotate the drumstick and carve off all the meat. Next, carve thin slices from the thigh bones.

Cut off both wings and set them aside.

Carve the white breast meat in long thin downward slices, from either side of the breast bone.

Fish

Fish are sold fresh, frozen, salted from the barrel, smoked, pickled or canned. Flat fish, such as flounder and sole are sold whole or filleted. Whole round fish, such as cod and haddock, are also sold as steaks.

Many shellfish are sold already boiled and even prepared. The exceptions are mussels, clams and oysters which must always be bought live.

Cook fish on the day it is bought; for a main course allow ½ pound of dressed fish per person, or one good-sized fillet or steak.

PREPARATION OF FISH

Fish markets will usually clean and fillet fish ready for cooking. But if this has not been done, a few simple preparations are necessary. Unwrap the fish as soon as possible and if it has to be stored in the refrigerator, wrap it in plastic or foil to prevent its smell spreading to other food.

Scaling
Cover the wooden board with several sheets of newspaper. Lay the fish on the paper and, holding it by the tail, scrape away the scales from the tail towards the head, using the blunt edge of a knife. Rinse the scales off under cold water. Alternatively, cook the fish without removing the scales, and skin it before serving.

Cleaning
Once scaled, the fish must be cleaned, or gutted. This process is determined by the shape of the fish – in round fish the entrails lie in the belly, in flat fish in a cavity behind the head.

Round fish
(cod, bluefish, mackerel, trout, for example). Slit the fish, with a sharp knife, along the belly from behind the gills to just above the tail. Scrape out and discard the entrails. Rinse the fish under cold running water and, with a little salt, gently rub away any black skin inside the cavity.

The head and tail may be left on the fish if it is to be cooked whole, but the eyes should be taken out. Use a sharp knife or scissors to cut off the lower fins on either side of the body and the gills below the head. Or cut the head off below the gills and slice off the tail.

Small round fish such as smelt need less preparation. Wipe the fish with a damp cloth and cut off the heads just below the gills, leaving the tails intact. Squeeze out the entrails. Fresh eels are sold live; the fish man will cut off the heads and may also skin the fish. Otherwise, loosen the skin at the head with the tip of a knife. Grip the skin in a rough cloth and peel it down and over the tail. Cut the skinned eel into pieces and rinse in cold water to remove blood.

Flat fish
(sole, flounder, for example). Make a semi-circular slit just behind the head, on the dark skin side. This opens up the cavity which contains the entrails. Scrape these out, wash the fish and cut off the fins.

CLEANING FLAT FISH

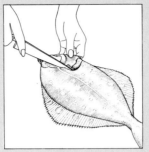

1. *Slitting behind the head*

2. *Cutting off the fins*

CLEANING ROUND FISH

1. *Slitting fish along the belly*

2. *Cutting off the gills*

SKINNING A FLAT FISH

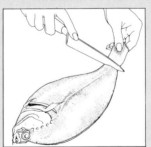

1. *Slitting skin above the tail*

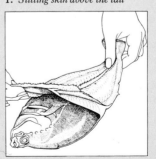

2. *Drawing the skin towards the head*

SKINNING A ROUND FISH

1. *Loosening skin below head*

2. *Drawing skin towards the tail*

172

1. *Cutting along the backbone*

2. *Freeing the first fillet*

3. *Removing the backbone*

4. *Cutting off the tail*

Skinning

Again, the method varies according to the type of fish.

Round fish

These are usually cooked with the skin on, but it is also possible to remove the skin before cooking. Using a sharp knife, loosen the skin around the head and then gently draw it down towards the tail. Cut it off. Repeat the process on the other side.

Flat fish

Lay the fish, dark skin uppermost, on the board. Make a slit across the skin just above the tail. Slip the thumb into the slit, and gently loosen the skin. Holding the fish firmly by the tail, pull the skin quickly towards the head (dip the fingers in a little salt to get a better grip), and cut it off. The white skin on the other side may be removed in the same way, but it is usually left on.

Filleting and boning

The fish can now be cut into serving portions. Fillets of both round and flat fish are popular as they provide a solid piece of fish without any bones.

Round fish

To fillet a large fish, such as haddock, cut the head off the cleaned fish, and then cut along the backbone, working towards the tail. Insert the knife blade at a slight angle to the bone and, keeping the sharp edge towards the tail, gently ease the flesh from the bone with slicing movements.

Continue cutting in line with the backbone, until the whole fillet is freed. Open out the fish and cut off the fillet at the tail. With the tip of the knife, ease off the backbone to reveal the other fillet, and cut off the tail. If the fish is large, the fillets can be cut into smaller portions of a size suitable for serving.

Boning large round fish

(salmon and lake trout)
Using a sharp knife or scissors, cut the fins and gills off the cleaned fish, and cut an inverted V into the tail. Wash the fish under cold water to remove all traces of blood, then place it in a fish cooker or large flameproof dish and poach in court bouillon (see page 175).

Lift the poached fish on to a board, and with a sharp knife or scissors snip the skin just below the head and above the tail. Carefully peel off the skin, leaving head and tail intact. Snip the backbone below the head and above the tail, then with the blade of a sharp knife split the fish along the backbone. Ease the bone out from the back without breaking the fish.

Boning small round fish

Smaller round fish such as trout and mackerel may be filleted as already described, but are more often boned and cooked whole or with a stuffing.

To bone a cleaned mackerel, cut off the head, tail and fins. Open out the split fish and spread it flat, skin side up. Press firmly along the center back of the fish to loosen the backbone, then turn the fish over. Starting at the head, ease away the backbone with the tip of the knife, removing at the same time as many of the small bones as possible. The mackerel can now be folded back into its original shape or cut into two long fillets.

Steaks

Large round fish are often sold in thick steaks, from the middle of the fish or from the tail end. These should be cleaned, but not skinned before cooking. The small central bone is best removed after cooking. If it is removed before cooking, the center should be stuffed.

Filleting flat fish

A large sole or flounder will yield four small fillets, two from each side. Lay the fish, dark skin up, on the board and with a sharp knife cut off the fins. Make the first cut along the backbone, working from the head towards the tail. Then make a semi-circular cut, just below the head, through half the thickness of the fish. Slant the knife against the backbone, and with short sharp strokes of the knife separate the left fillet from the bone. Make a thick cut just above the tail and remove the fillet. Turn the fish around and remove the right fillet in the same way. Turn the fish over and remove the fillets on the other side.

COOKING METHODS

A number of basic cooking methods are suitable for all fish whether they are whole, filleted or cut into steaks. But whatever cooking method is chosen, fish should be cooked for a short time only and at low heat. Prolonged cooking time and high heat toughens the flesh and destroys the flavor.

Baking

This method is suitable for small whole fish and for individual cuts, such as fillets and steaks.

173

Brush the prepared fish with melted butter and season with lemon juice, salt and freshly ground pepper. Make three or four diagonal score marks on each side of whole round fish so that they will keep their shape. Lay the fish in a well-buttered, ovenproof dish. Bake in the center of a pre-heated oven at 350°F (180°C, mark 4), allowing 25–30 minutes for whole fish and 10–20 minutes for fillets and steaks.

During baking, baste the fish frequently – this is particularly important with white fish.

Alternatively, lay bacon slices over the fish to provide basting during cooking.

Before baking, fish may be stuffed with a filling of fine breadcrumbs seasoned with salt, pepper, herbs or parsley and bound with a little melted butter. Spoon the filling loosely into the cavity, as it tends to swell during cooking. Close the opening on round fish with toothpicks.

Whole flat fish have only small cavities which must be opened up to allow room for stuffing. To do this make an incision down the center of the back. Ease the flesh from the backbone on either side, as far as the fins, with the knife blade to form a cavity and loosely stuff this. Leave the pocket open.

For individual stuffed fillets, spread the mixture over the fish, roll it up and secure with wooden skewers.

Baking can also be done in foil, which is excellent for sealing-in both flavor and aroma. It also cuts down on oven cleaning. Place the prepared fish on buttered foil and sprinkle with lemon juice, salt and pepper. Wrap the foil loosely over the fish, place in a baking pan, and cook in the center of a pre-heated oven at 350°F (180°C, mark 4). Allow 20 minutes for steaks, and about 8 minutes per pound for large fish plus 10 minutes extra in all.

Braising

Large flat fish, such as halibut and salmon, can be cooked by this method which adds flavor to their somewhat dry flesh. Peel and finely chop 2 carrots, 1 onion, 1 leek or parsnip. Sauté these vegetables in a little butter and spread them over the bottom of an ovenproof dish. Lay the prepared fish on top and sprinkle with salt and freshly ground pepper. Add a few sprigs of fresh herbs, such as parsley and thyme, or a bay leaf. Pour over enough fish stock or white wine to come just level with the fish.

Cover the dish and cook in the center of a pre-heated oven at 350°F (180°C, mark 4) until the fish flakes when tested with a fork. Lift out the fish carefully and strain the cooking liquid. This may be used as a sauce and can be thickened with egg yolks or cream, or by fast boiling until the sauce has reduced to the desired consistency.

Frying

This is one of the most popular cooking methods, and is suitable for steaks and fillets of cod, haddock, hake, flounder and eel and for small whole fish such as sardines, mackerel, smelt, catfish and trout. Coat the prepared fish in seasoned flour (page 184) or dip them first in lightly beaten egg, then in dry breadcrumbs, shaking off any surplus. Heat an equal amount of butter and cooking oil in a frying

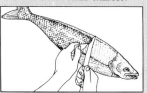

1. *Peeling skin towards the tail*

2. *Snipping the backbone*

3. *Easing backbone from the fish*

1. *Slitting fish along the belly*

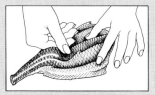

2. *Pressing along the backbone*

3. *Easing away the backbone*

REMOVING THE FOUR FILLETS FROM A FLAT FISH

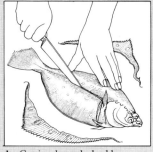

1. *Cutting down the backbone*

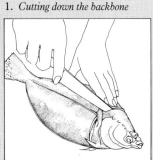

2. *Slitting just below the head*

3. *Separating fillet from the bone*

4. *Removing the fillet*

pan over moderate heat. Put in the fish and fry until brown on one side; turn it over with a fish slice or wide spatula. Allow approximately 10 minutes frying depending on the thickness of the fish. Remove from the pan and drain thoroughly on paper towels.

Broiling

This quick cooking method is suitable for small whole fish, either round or flat, and fillets and steaks. Whole fish should be scored with three or four diagonal cuts on each side of the body. This allows the heat to penetrate more evenly and prevents the fish splitting.

Brush white fish, such as flounder or sole, with melted butter or oil, and sprinkle with lemon juice or a little finely chopped onion. Baste two or three times during broiling to prevent the flesh from drying out. Oily fish need no brushing or basting.

Broil all fish under a preheated hot broiler. Allow 4–5 minutes for fillets, and 10–15 minutes for thick steaks and whole fish. The fish is cooked when the flesh separates into flakes when tested with a knife.

During broiling, whole fish and thick steaks should be turned over once to ensure that both sides are evenly cooked. Thin steaks and fillets need to be cooked on one side only.

Poaching

This is ideal for all types of fish, whether whole, filleted or cut into steaks. Poaching – slow simmering in liquid – can be done in a large saucepan or fish cooker on top of the stove, or in a shallow covered dish in the oven at 350°F (180°C, mark 4). For easy removal, tie the fish loosely in a piece of cheesecloth.

Cover the fish completely with lightly salted water (1½ teaspoons salt to 5 cups of water). Add to the pan a few parsley or mushroom stalks, a good squeeze of lemon juice, a slice of onion and carrot, together with a bay leaf and 6 peppercorns.

Bring the liquid to the boil over moderate heat, then cover the pan and lower the heat. Simmer the fish until it flakes when tested with a fork, allowing 8–10 minutes per pound. Lift out the cooked fish with a slotted spatula, and use the poaching liquid as the base for a sauce.

Whole fish, such as salmon, trout and striped bass, are usually poached in a classic preparation or fish stock known as court bouillon.

Court Bouillon

PREPARATION TIME: *10 min*
COOKING TIME: *20 min*
INGREDIENTS:
2 carrots
1 onion
2 stalks celery
2 shallots
1 bay leaf
3 parsley stalks
2 sprigs thyme
2 tablespoons lemon juice
1 cup dry white wine
Salt* and black pepper

Peel and finely chop the vegetables. Put them in a large saucepan with all the other ingredients and 1 quart of water. Bring to the boil, cover with a lid and simmer over low heat for 15 minutes. Leave the court bouillon to cool slightly, then strain it and pour it over the fish to be poached.

Steaming

Fillets and thin cuts of fish cooked in this manner are easily digestible and are ideal for invalids and young children.

Roll the fillets or lay them flat in a perforated steamer and sprinkle lightly with salt and freshly ground pepper. Set the steamer over a pan of boiling water and cook the fish for about 10–15 minutes.

If a steamer is not available, place the fish on a buttered deep plate and cover with a piece of buttered waxed paper. Alternatively, wrap the fish loosely in a piece of buttered aluminium foil. Set the plate over a pan of boiling water, cover with another plate or a lid from a saucepan, and steam for about 15 minutes.

SHELLFISH

Small shellfish are served as hors d'oeuvre, and in soups and sauces. Large shellfish, such as crabs and lobsters, can be served as either a first or a main course. If they are bought ready-prepared, they must be used on the day of purchase.

All fresh shellfish must be boiled before being served or used in a recipe. Oysters and clams, which are usually eaten raw, are the exception. Shellfish require little cooking time, and over-boiling causes the flesh to become tough and fibrous.

Most shellfish have indigestible or unwholesome parts, such as the beard of the mussel and the "dead men's fingers," or gills, in crabs and lobsters. These parts, together with the stomach sac and the intestinal tubes, must be removed during preparation. Shellfish are often served with a wedge of lemon, with mayonnaise or a sharp sauce.

Clams

Clams are of two types: hard-shell and soft-shell. Hard-shell clams are usually served raw, but can also be used for clam fritters and of course in clam chowder. Soft-shell clams are steamed. Allow 12 clams per person. Smoked and canned clams are also available.

Crab

This is often available cooked and prepared by the fish man. When buying a fresh crab, make certain that it has both claws and that it is heavy for its size. The edible parts of a crab are the white meat in the claws and in the body shell. Allow 8–10 ounces prepared crab per person.

Wash the crab and put it in a large saucepan with plenty of cold water seasoned with 1 tablespoon lemon juice, a few parsley stalks, 1 bay leaf, a little salt and a few peppercorns. Cover the pan with a lid and bring the water slowly to boiling point. Cooking time is short: a 2½–3 pound crab, measuring about 8 inches across the body shell, should be boiled for only 15–20 minutes. Leave the crab to cool in the cooking liquid.

Preparation

Place the cooked crab on a board and twist off the legs and two large claws. Twist off the pincers and crack each claw open with a nutcracker, a hammer or the handle of a heavy knife.

Empty the white meat into a bowl and use a skewer or the handle of a teaspoon to scrape all the white meat from the crevices in the claws. Set the small legs aside for decoration or, if they are large, crack them open with a hammer and extract the white meat with a skewer.

Remove the back and the spongy parts under the crab's shell. Then remove the apron from the underside of the body.

Using a spoon, gently scrape the meat from the shell and put it in another bowl until required.

Cut the body in two and pick out all the meat left in the leg sockets.

Lobsters

These are often sold ready-cooked, but ideally should be purchased alive. A 1½-pound lobster will serve two people.

If bought alive, rinse the lobster under cold running water. Grip it firmly around the body part and drop it into a large pan of boiling salted water. Cover with a lid and bring back to the boil. Simmer over low heat, allowing 5 minutes for a 1-pound lobster and 3 minutes for each additional pound.

Broiled lobster

To prepare a lobster for broiling, kill the lobster by inserting the point of a heavy knife between the head and the tail to sever the spinal cord. Turn the lobster over on its back and cut down through the entire length of the lobster, leaving the back shell intact.

Spread the lobster open and remove the dark intestinal vein that runs down the center and take out the stomach, or sac, about 2 inches below the head. The green liver, or tomalley, and the coral, only in the female lobster, is edible and need not be removed. Crack the large claws with a hammer or mallet.

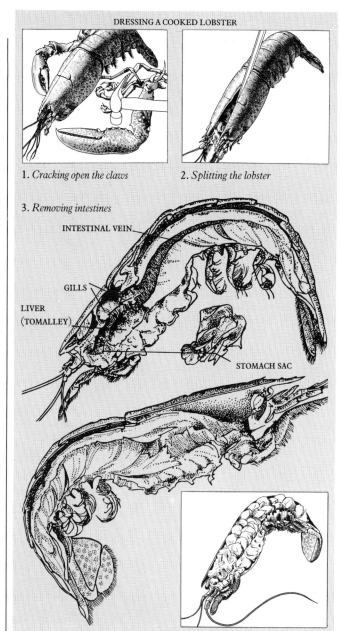

DRESSING A COOKED LOBSTER

1. *Cracking open the claws*

2. *Splitting the lobster*

3. *Removing intestines*

INTESTINAL VEIN

GILLS

LIVER (TOMALLEY)

STOMACH SAC

4. *Cleaned half lobster*

5. *Half lobster ready to serve*

Place the lobster on a broiler pan, shell side down, and brush generously with melted butter. Broil 3 inches from the heat for 15–20 minutes, depending on size, and baste occasionally with melted butter. Serve with melted butter and lemon wedges.

Cold lobster

Twist the claws off the boiled lobster. Using a hammer, or a special lobster cracker, crack open the large and small claws and carefully extract the meat. Remove the thin membrane from the center of each claw.

Place the lobster on a board, shell side up, and split in half lengthwise with a sharp knife. Open out the two halves and remove the gills, the dark intestinal vein which runs down the tail, and the small stomach sac which lies just below the head.

The green creamy liver, or tomalley, in the head is a delicacy and should not be discarded. The coral – or roe – in a female lobster should also be kept; it is bright coral red and contained in the tail. It is usually added to the accompanying sauce.

Extract the meat from the tail, and with a small lobster pick take out the meat from the feeler claws or set them aside for decoration. Wash and polish the empty half shells and put all the meat back in them. Garnish with the claws and serve with mayonnaise or a vinaigrette dressing (page 157).

Boiled lobster may also be served hot, in which case each person will remove the meat himself.

Mussels

These must always be bought alive and absolutely fresh. As soon as possible put them into a pail of cold salted water and throw away any mussels with open or broken shells. If time allows, sprinkle a little oatmeal or flour into the water. Add about ⅓ cup for every 2 quarts of water. Let the mussels soak an hour or more. The live mussels will feed on the

176

oatmeal and excrete their dirt. Throw away any mussels that float to the surface.

Scrub the shells with a stiff brush to remove all grit. With a sharp knife, scrape away the beard or seaweed-like strands protruding from each shell, and also scrape off the barnacles growing on the shells. Rinse the mussels in several changes of cold water to remove remaining grit.

Put the cleaned mussels in a large, heavy-based pan containing $\frac{1}{2}$ inch of water or white wine, chopped parsley and shallots or onions. Cover the pan with a lid and steam the mussels over low heat. As soon as the shells open, take the pan off the heat and remove a half shell from each mussel. Keep the mussels warm under a dry cloth, and strain the cooking liquid through cheese-cloth. Serve on a deep warmed platter, with the liquid poured over them.

Oysters

Until the 19th century, oysters were everyday fare, but they are now expensive and something of a luxury. Oysters are usually served raw as an hors d'oeuvre, when six oysters per person should be allowed.

Scrub the tightly closed shells with a stiff brush to remove all sand. Open the shells over a fine strainer, set in a bowl to catch the oyster juice. Hold the oyster in one hand, deep shell in the palm, and insert the tip of an oyster knife, or a knife with a short strong blade, into the hinge. Twist the knife to pry the hinge open and cut the two muscles which lie above and below the oyster. Run the knife blade between the shells to open them and discard the rounded shell. After opening the shell, cut away the oyster with a knife.

Serve the oysters lightly seasoned with salt and pepper in their flat shells, and on a bed of cracked ice. They are traditionally served with lemon wedges, often accompanied by a tomato-based cocktail sauce.

Scallops

Fresh bay scallops and the larger sea scallops are sold already cleaned and removed from their shells.

Put the scallops in a pan of cold water. Bring to a boil, remove any scum, and simmer the scallops for 5–10 minutes, being careful not to overcook them.

Scallops can be baked, sautéed, deep-fried, broiled, or served in a cheese or mushroom sauce.

Scallops Seviche

PREPARATION TIME: *10 min*
MARINATING TIME: *3 hours*
INGREDIENTS *(for 4):*
½ pound bay scallops
Juice of 4 limes
2 tablespoons finely chopped onion
¼ teaspoon minced garlic
2 tablespoons finely chopped green chili peppers or green bell peppers
1 tablespoon chopped parsley
3 tablespoons olive oil
Salt* and pepper

Put the scallops in a large bowl and cover them with the lime juice. Chill in the refrigerator for at least 3 hours. Drain well in a colander. Add the remaining ingredients, except the salt and pepper, and toss well. Season to taste with salt and pepper.

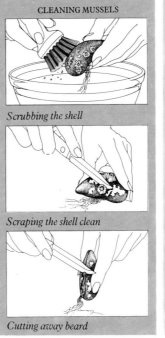

CLEANING MUSSELS

Scrubbing the shell

Scraping the shell clean

Cutting away beard

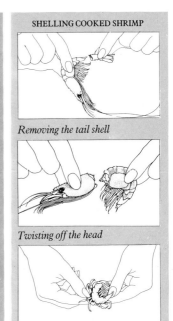

SHELLING COOKED SHRIMP

Removing the tail shell

Twisting off the head

Peeling off body shell

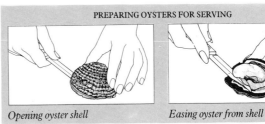

PREPARING OYSTERS FOR SERVING

Opening oyster shell

Easing oyster from shell

Shrimp

These shellfish are available all year round and are sold both raw and ready-cooked and often shelled. Live shrimp are gray, pink or brown, but turn bright red during cooking. Drop the raw shrimp into a pan of boiling water, cover with a lid and boil for 2–4 minutes, according to size.

To shell cooked shrimp, hold the fish between two fingers, then gently peel away the soft body shell, together with the small crawler claws.

These shellfish are served hot or cold, as hors d'oeuvre, in sea-food cocktails, salads, curries, soups and sauces. The large or jumbo shrimp may be broiled or coated in batter or in beaten egg and breadcrumbs and deep fried.

SMOKED FISH

Fish can be preserved by smoking. Cold-smoked fish, which include cod and haddock, require cooking, but hot-smoked fish are ready for the table because they have been cooked during smoking. They include mackerel, trout, salmon, eel, sturgeon, whitefish and buckling (herring).

Garnishes

A well-chosen garnish adds texture, color and flavor to a dish. It should be fresh and simple rather than cluttered, and if the dish is hidden by a sauce, the garnish should give a clue to what is in the sauce. For instance, a dish served *à la véronique* – that is, with a sauce containing white grapes – is always garnished with small bunches of grapes. Many garnishes are classic – lemon and parsley, for example, are traditional with fried fish.

Bread croûtons

Bread croûtons are a classic garnish with thick soups. Remove the crusts from $\frac{1}{2}$ in thick slices of bread; cut into cubes and toast or fry in a little butter until crisp and golden. Serve the croûtons in a separate dish or sprinkled over the soup.

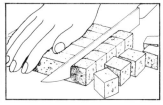

Cutting bread croûtons

Breadcrumbs

Fried crumbs are a traditional garnish for game and *au gratin* dishes. Melt 2 tablespoons butter or margarine in a frying pan, stir in 2 cups soft breadcrumbs and fry over moderate heat until the crumbs are evenly browned and golden. Turn frequently.

Celery tassels

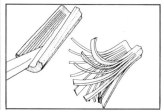

Edible garnish used with dips. Scrub the celery stalks, cut them in 2 in lengths, then cut down the lengths at narrow intervals almost to the base. Leave the stalks in a bowl of water to curl.

Cucumber

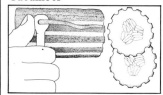

Sliced cucumber is a traditional garnish for a cold mousse or terrine. Scalloped or ridged cucumber makes a more unusual decoration: wipe but do not peel a piece of cucumber; score it along the length with a fork or canelle knife, so that it has a serrated edge when cut into slices.

Gherkin fans

Drain cocktail gherkins thoroughly, then slice each three or four times lengthwise almost to the stalk end. Ease the slices apart to open out like a fan.

Grapes

Most grapes are easily peeled, away from the stem end using the fingernails. If the skins are difficult to remove dip a few grapes at a time in boiling water for 30 seconds, then plunge them immediately into cold water.

Remove the seeds from whole grapes by digging the rounded end of a clean new hair pin into the stem end of the grape; scoop out the seeds. Alternatively, make a small cut down the length of the grape, being careful not to cut right through, and ease out the seeds with the tip of the knife.

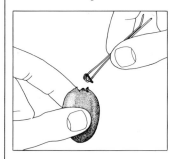

Mushrooms

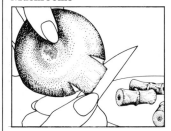

Trim by removing stalks, and peeling ragged skin

Fluted, these are a traditional garnish with broiled meat. Choose large button mushrooms, wipe with a damp cloth and trim the stem level with the cap. Peel off any ragged skin. With a sharp knife make a series of curving cuts, $\frac{1}{4}$ in apart, following the natural shape of the cap and from the top of the cap to the base. Take out a narrow strip along each indentation.

Nuts

Almonds are bought whole, halved, chopped or sliced and slivered. Whole almonds, bought with or without their skins, can be used whole, split in two along their natural seam, cut into slivers or chopped. For slivered almonds blanch whole unskinned almonds in boiling water for 2–3 minutes; rub off the skins and, while still soft, cut the almonds into strips. For toasted almonds, spread the nuts in a shallow pan and brown under a broiler.

Hazelnuts need to be toasted before the skins can be removed. Place the shelled nuts in a single layer on a shallow pan and toast under a pre-heated broiler until the skins are dry and the nuts begin to color. Cool slightly, then rub the nuts against each other in a bag to loosen the skins.

Onions

Diced onions can be scattered over salads and other dishes. Peel off the skin and trim the root. Cut the onion in half through the root, then cut downwards in slices. To chop, turn the onion and slice across the first cuts. To dice, chop again across these cuts.

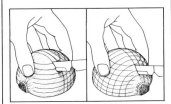

Parsley

Wash freshly picked parsley as soon as possible, shake well and remove long stems. Place in a jar of water reaching to the base of the leaves, or put in a plastic bag, tied at the neck. Parsley will then stay crisp and green for several days. Change the water in the container daily.

Scissors can be used for chopping parsley, but the result is coarser than when chopped with a knife. Gather the parsley into a tight bunch and with scissors snip off as much as is required straight on to the dish to be garnished.

To chop parsley, put the leaves on a chopping board. Hold the handle of a sharp straight-bladed knife firmly with one hand and the tip of the knife blade with the other; lift the handle in a see-saw action, gradually chopping the parsley finely or coarsely as required. Alternatively, bunch the parsley leaves in one hand on the chopping board and, using the knife, gradually shred the parsley, moving the fingers back to reveal more parsley.

Radish roses

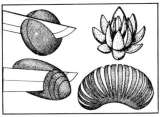

Used to garnish cold entrées, open sandwiches, hors d'oeuvre and salads. Make 6–8 cuts lengthwise through a radish from the base towards the stalk; put the radishes in a bowl of iced water until they open like flowers. Long radishes look attractive when cut at intervals along the length to open out accordian-fashion.

Tomatoes

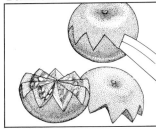

Serrated or vandyked tomatoes can be stuffed or used as tomato halves as a garnish for salads, quiches, fried or broiled fish and meat. Choose firm tomatoes of

TWO WAYS OF SKINNING FRESH TOMATOES

1. Put in hot water for 1 min

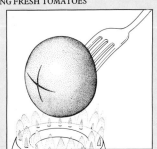

1. Hold tomato over open gas flame

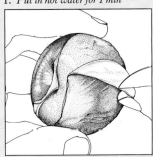

2. Peel soft skin from wet tomato

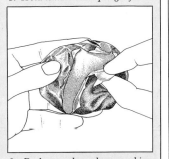

2. Peel away charred tomato skin

even size. Using a small sharp knife, make a series of small V-shaped incisions around the circumference of the tomato. Carefully pull the two tomato halves apart. Oranges, grapefruit and melons may also be separated in this way.

Twists and butterflies

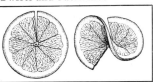

Tomatoes, cucumbers, beets, lemons and oranges make attractive garnishes to any number of dishes, both savory and sweet. Slice the vegetable or fruit thinly, though not wafer-thin. For twists, cut each slice through to the center, then twist the two halves in opposite directions and place in position. For butterflies, cut two deep V-shaped incisions to meet near the center of each round lemon slice. Remove the two wedges in order to leave a butterfly shape.

Watercress

Another favorite garnish for meat, poultry and fish dishes. Trim off the stems, and wash the watercress leaves in plenty of salted water. Lift out, rinse and shake well. Discard any ragged and yellow leaves; arrange the watercress in small bunches to be added as garnish just before the dish is served. Washed watercress, with part of the stem left on, will keep for 1 day in the refrigerator if stored in a polythene bag.

Freezing

The freezer is a time and money saver for anyone who cooks for a family. It enables a cook to plan well ahead, both in bulk-buying and in cooking. And, if the rules for the preparation, packaging and thawing of the raw materials are carefully followed, frozen food loses nothing in freshness and quality.

Being able to freeze pre-cooked dishes for later use also has numerous advantages. Leftovers can be stored for later use. Time can be spent in the kitchen when it is convenient. Quantities of recipes can be doubled to save time, energy and cooking expense, with one dish eaten at once and the other frozen. People who entertain frequently can do most of the cooking well in advance, and those with large families can stock up for the holidays.

GUIDE TO FREEZING PRE-COOKED FOOD

For successful freezing of pre-cooked food, it is important to follow these points carefully:
1. Working surroundings must be scrupulously clean, as freezing does not destroy germs in food.
2. Use top-quality ingredients and season lightly; more seasoning can always be added later.
3. Always slightly undercook dishes which are to be frozen, allowing for the time the food will be in the oven to heat up.
4. When recipes for soups, sauces and casseroles call for the addition of cream or egg yolks, omit these before freezing and add them when the dishes are being reheated. Do not freeze dishes with custard or mayonnaise.
5. Omit garlic before freezing (it can be added later) unless the food is going to remain in the freezer for only a short time.
6. Be generous with sauces, so that meat, chicken, fish and game will not dehydrate when frozen.
7. Cool all cooked and baked dishes thoroughly before packing and freezing them. An easy way to do this is by placing the dish, pan or casserole in a sink of cold water. Ice cubes added to the water will help to cool the dish even faster.
8. Garnish re-heated food before serving, not before freezing.
9. Pack and label all pre-cooked foods carefully and note the number of portions. Soups can be frozen in square containers, removed when solid and then packed in polyethylene bags; casseroles can be frozen in their cooking dishes, turned out and packed in polyethylene bags to be returned to their dishes for thawing and re-heating.

You can freeze small amounts of vegetable cooking water, broth, or stock in ice-cube trays, then empty the cubes into plastic bags and use them as and when they are needed in recipes for soups, stews, casseroles and sauces.
10. Do not freeze whole roasts, poultry or cold meat without a sauce, as the results are often apt to be disappointingly dry.

GUIDE TO FREEZING FRESH FOOD

Meat
Only good-quality fresh meat should be frozen. Cut the meat into convenient sizes, such as joints and chops. Remove as much bone as possible so that the meat will take up less space in the freezer. The bones can be used to make stock.

Meat to be used in stews and casseroles can be cut into cubes and packed in rigid containers.

Remove excess fat, as it can become rancid if exposed to oxygen. For the same reason, pack meat carefully in airtight wrappings. Pad sharp corners or bones with foil or thin self-adhesive plastic wrap, to prevent

FREEZING PREPARED AND PRE-COOKED DISHES

Meat dishes (2 months)	Cook for a slightly shorter time than usual to allow for re-heating. Do not season heavily. Make sure meat is completely immersed in gravy or sauce. It is better to add potatoes, rice, noodles, garlic and celery at time of serving. Pack in rigid foil containers; or freeze in foil-lined casserole, remove and pack in polyethylene bags	Turn frozen food out of container into saucepan to re-heat. Pre-formed foil-lined dishes may be re-heated in oven in original casserole for 1 hour at 400°F (200°C, mark 6), reducing heat if necessary to 350°F (180°C, mark 4) for last 40 minutes
Meat loaves, pâtés, terrines (1 month)	Make in usual way, taking care not to season or spice heavily. When cold, remove from pans or molds and wrap in plastic wrap before freezing	Thaw in wrapping for 6–8 hours, or overnight in refrigerator

FREEZING UNCOOKED MEAT

Meat (storage time in brackets)	Preparation and Packaging	Thawing
Roasts (beef 8 months; lamb, pork and veal 6 months)	Wrap in heavy-duty plastic bags, seal well and label. May be overwrapped with foil	Thaw thoroughly before cooking, preferably in the refrigerator. Allow 5 hours per pound in the refrigerator, 2 hours per pound at room temperature
Scallops, chops, hamburgers, steaks and cubed meat (3 months)	Pack in suitable quantities. Separate scallops, chops, hamburgers and steaks with waxed paper. Pack in plastic bags or rigid containers	These small cuts can be cooked frozen over gentle heat
Ground meat and sausage meat (3 months)	Pack in small quantities in bags or rigid containers	Thaw in a cool place for 1½ hours or in the refrigerator for 3 hours
Variety meats and sausages (1–3 months)	Clean and trim variety meats. Pack in small quantities in plastic bags	Thaw in a cool place for 1½ hours or in the refrigerator for 3 hours

them from perforating the packaging. Wrap in foil first, then overwrap with heavy-duty freezer wrap, excluding as much air as possible.

Weigh the meat before freezing, and label it with weight, description and date. Chops, steaks and hamburgers should be interleaved with waxed paper or plastic wrap, so that they can be easily separated.

Allow meat to thaw slowly in its wrapping in a cool place or in the refrigerator. If it is needed in a hurry, the thawing can be speeded up by placing the meat, in its wrapping, in cold water; part of the flavor is, however, lost. Small cuts of meat such as chops and steaks can be cooked from the frozen state, but it is advisable to cook them over lower heat than usual.

Fish
Fish should be frozen fresh and within 12 hours of being caught. It is not advisable to freeze even fresh shellfish at home, but you can buy frozen crab, clams and shrimp. These may be stored in the home freezer for about one month.

Small round fish may be frozen whole after scaling and gutting. Larger round fish should be scaled and gutted and have heads and tails removed. Flat fish is best frozen in fillets, interleaved with waxed paper. To preserve moisture in the prepared fish rub with a little olive oil. Wrap in heavy-duty plastic wrap, freezer wrap or foil, or pack in rigid containers; label as usual.

The delicate flavor of whole salmon and trout can be maintained by freezing these fish in a sheet of ice. Dip the fish in cold salted water several times (placing it on a tray in the freezer between immersions) so that a layer of ice forms round the fish and seals it from the air. Then pack carefully in heavy-duty polythene, as for other fish. Salmon and other fatty fish should not be frozen for longer than 2 months.

Thaw whole fish slowly, preferably in the refrigerator and in the original wrappings. Allow about 8 hours per pound if thawing on the refrigerator shelf, 4 hours per pound at room temperature. If the fish is placed in front of an electric fan, it will take about 2½ hours per pound to thaw out. Cook as soon as the fish is thawed. Cutlets, steaks and fillets may be cooked from the frozen state, if you are short of time.

Poultry and game
Only young plump birds should be frozen fresh, whole or cut up. Older birds, whether poultry or game, are best cooked as casseroles before freezing.

Remove giblets and clean and freeze separately as they have a shorter storage life. Clean the birds thoroughly; do not stuff them, but truss ready for cooking. Pad the legs with foil, before wrapping the whole bird in heavy-duty plastic wrap. Label with weight, description and date. Pack cut-up birds interspersed with waxed paper, in portions.

Stuffings should be frozen separately, as they store only for one month. Pack livers in plastic bags and freeze for use in pâtés and risottos.

Poultry and game birds should ideally be thawed slowly, in their wrappings in the refrigerator. In an emergency a frozen bird can be thawed, wrapped, in cold water.

Young game birds, well-hung, are frozen as poultry. Hare must be hung, skinned and cleaned; it is best frozen in pieces ready for cooking. Rabbit is frozen like hare, but is not hung first. Venison should be hung before being cut up and frozen.

FREEZING UNCOOKED FISH

Fish (storage time in brackets)	Packaging	Thawing
Whole fish (6 months)	Pack tightly in heavy-duty polyethylene	Thaw large fish in wrapping in the refrigerator for about 6 hours. Small whole fish may be cooked frozen over low heat
Fillets, steaks (6 months)	Wrap each piece in waxed paper, then pack in suitable portions in heavy-duty polyethylene	Thaw in wrapping in the refrigerator for about 3 hours

FREEZING UNCOOKED POULTRY AND GAME

Poultry	Preparation and Packaging	Thawing
(Chicken 12 months; duck 4–6 months; goose 4–6 months; turkey 6 months; giblets 3 months; livers 3 months)	Wrap whole birds in heavy-duty polyethylene. Trim bones from joints and wrap individually before packing in heavy-duty polyethylene. Pieces for pies and casseroles may be packed in rigid containers. Pack giblets and livers separately in plastic bags	Thaw in wrapping in the refrigerator, a whole bird for 8 hours, parts and pieces for 2–3 hours. Thaw livers and giblets in wrapping in the refrigerator for 2 hours
Game birds (6–8 months)	as poultry	as poultry
Hare, rabbit (6 months)	Wrap each piece in plastic wrap and pack several portions in heavy-duty polyethylene	Thaw in wrapping in the refrigerator for 2–3 hours
Venison (up to 12 months)	Freeze well-hung meat in roasts or chops. Wrap roasts in plastic wrap and polyethylene bags; overwrap with foil. Pack chops individually	Thaw in wrapping in the refrigerator for 5 hours

Fats and Oils

Fats and oils play an important part in cooking, as they contribute to or sometimes alter the flavor of food, especially when frying. The term "fat" can be taken generally to include all fatty substances, but it can also mean those which are solid at room temperature, those which are liquid being called "oils." Conveniently, this division more or less coincides with the division into saturated and unsaturated fats.

FATS

These are mainly derived from animal foods, such as meat and dairy products, but can also be produced from oily fish, nuts and vegetables.

Butter
Butter is made from the fatty substances skimmed from full cream milk. It is churned and then pressed to squeeze out water, and sometimes salt is added. It is used as the cooking medium for egg dishes and for sautéing and shallow frying over moderate heat. It is not suitable for frying at high temperatures as it burns easily, but a mixture of oil and butter will withstand quite a high heat without turning black.

Clarified butter
This can be heated to a much higher temperature than ordinary butter without burning, and is therefore more suitable for frying and also for brushing food, for example fish, that is to be broiled. It is an expensive cooking medium, as 1 pound of butter produces only about 10 ounces of clarified butter. To make it, melt the butter in a small pan over gentle heat and cook without stirring until the butter begins to foam. Continue to cook without letting it brown until the foaming stops. Remove the pan from the heat and let it stand until the milky deposits have sunk to the bottom, leaving a clear yellow liquid. Pour this carefully through cheesecloth into a bowl. Clarified butter can be used in liquid or solid form and will keep for several weeks in the refrigerator.

Maître d'hôtel butter
A popular garnish for broiled meat or fish. Blend a tablespoon of finely chopped parsley with $\frac{1}{2}$ cup of softened butter and season to taste with salt, freshly ground pepper and a few drops of lemon juice. Other herbs, such as tarragon, chervil or chives, can also be used.

Drippings
This is the rendered fat from beef, bacon, pork or poultry. A roast or bird will usually yield quite a lot, or it can be bought already rendered down. As it has a fairly high water content, it tends to splatter and is better used for roasting and shallow-frying than for deep-frying.

Lard
This is processed from pure pork fat and is excellent for frying. It is also used in baking some pastries and cakes.

Margarine
Made from vegetable oils blended with milk and vitamins, and sometimes with butter, margarine is interchangeable with butter for baking purposes and for sautéing.

Shortening
That sold under various brand names in cans is usually composed of oils, such as soybean, corn or peanut, made solid by incorporating hydrogen into them, which also improves the keeping qualities. Some shortening is a combination of vegetable and animal or dairy fats. Use for sautéing, deep-frying and for baking.

Suet
Suet is the fat deposit from the loins and around the kidneys of beef or sheep. It is sold fresh for grating or already shredded and packed; it can be used in pastries, puddings and stuffings.

OILS

Edible oils are derived from fish, vegetables, cereals, fruit, nuts and seeds. They vary in color and flavor, and choice is a matter of individual taste. Cold-pressed oil is the most natural (and most expensive) form, smelling and tasting strongly of its origin. Refined oil (often misleadingly called "pure") has had most of the vitamins and virtue bleached out or otherwise chemically removed, although some vitamins may be added back.

Corn oil
Fairly inexpensive and a good all-purpose oil with a mild taste.

Olive oil
Valued for its distinctive fruity taste and its affinity with certain foods. Suitable for frying and also for salad dressings: for these the best, but alas expensive, is the first pressing, also known as virgin oil.

Peanut oil
Also known as groundnut or arachide oil, this is a pleasant-tasting oil which will withstand quite high heat without burning.

Safflower oil
Expensive, but often recommended for a cholesterol-lowering diet as it is extremely high in polyunsaturated fats and in particular linoleic acid, the one essential fatty acid which cannot be manufactured by the body.

Sesame oil
Made from sesame seeds, this has a distinctive taste. It is much used in the Middle East for baking and also makes a good salad dressing.

Soy oil
A neutral-tasting oil, this is high in polyunsaturates and not too expensive.

Sunflower oil
An excellent all-round oil: can be used for frying and for salad dressings, high in polyunsaturates but cheaper than safflower oil.

Walnut oil
Very expensive; its strong nutty taste is much appreciated in salad dressings.

A to Z of Cooking Terms

A

antipasti Cold or hot Italian hors d'oeuvre

arrowroot Starch made by grinding the root of a plant of the same name. Used for thickening sauces

aspic Clear jelly made from the cooked juices of meat, chicken or fish

au bleu Blue; fish, especially trout, cooked immediately after being caught in a court bouillon with vinegar will turn blue

au gratin Cooked food, covered with a sauce, sprinkled with crumbs or grated cheese, dotted with butter and browned under the broiler

B

barding Covering lean meat, game and poultry with thin slices of pork fat or bacon to prevent the flesh drying out during roasting

basting Moistening meat or poultry with pan juices during roasting by using a spoon or bulb baster

beating Mixing food to introduce air, to make it lighter and fluffier, using a wooden spoon, wire whisk or electric mixer

binding Adding eggs, cream or melted fat to a dry mixture to hold it together

blanching Boiling briefly 1. To loosen the skin from nuts, fruit and vegetables. 2. To set the color of food and to kill enzymes prior to freezing. 3. To remove strong or bitter flavors

blanquette Veal, poultry or rabbit stew in a creamy sauce

blending Combining ingredients with a spoon, beater or liquidizer to achieve a uniform mixture

boiling Cooking in liquid at a temperature of 212°F (100°C)

bouquet garni A bunch of herbs, including parsley, thyme, marjoram, bay, etc., tied with string; or a ready-made mixture of herbs in a cheese-cloth bag. Used for flavoring soups and stews

bourguignonne In the style of Burgundy, e.g. cooked with red wine

braising Browning in hot fat and then cooking slowly, in a covered pot, with vegetables and a little liquid

brine Salt and water solution used for pickling and preserving

browning Searing the outer surface of meat to seal in the juices

C

carbonnade Beef stewed with beer

casserole 1. Cooking pot, complete with lid, made of ovenproof or flame-proof earthenware, glass or metal. 2. Also, a slow-cooked stew of meat, fish or vegetables

cassoulet Stew of dried white beans, pork, lamb, goose or duck, sausage, vegetables and herbs

chasseur Cooked with mushrooms, shallots and white wine

chaud-froid Elaborate dish of meat, poultry, game or fish, masked with a creamy sauce, decorated and glazed with aspic. Served cold

chilling Cooling food, without freezing it, in the refrigerator

chining Separating the backbone from the ribs in a joint of meat to make carving easier

chorizo Smoked pork sausage

chowder Fish dish, half-way between a soup and stew

clarified butter Butter cleared of water and impurities by slow melting and filtering

cocotte Small ovenproof, earthenware, porcelain or metal dish, used for baking individual dishes, mousses or soufflés

colander Perforated metal or plastic basket used for draining away liquids

cornstarch Finely ground flour from corn, which is used for thickening sauces, puddings, etc.

creole Style of cooking using bell peppers, tomatoes, okra, rice and spicy sauces

crêpe Thin pancake

curdle To cause fresh milk or a sauce to separate into solids and liquids by overheating or by adding acid

cure To preserve fish or meat by drying, salting or smoking

cut up To divide poultry or game into individual pieces

D

dariole Small, cup-shaped mold used for making puddings, sweet and savory gelatins, and creams

darne Thick slice cut from round fish

daube Stew of braised meat and vegetables

déglacer To dilute pan juices by adding wine, stock or cream to make gravy

deviling Preparing meat, poultry or fish with highly seasoned ingredients, for broiling or roasting

dice To cut into small cubes

dough Mixture of flour, water, milk and/or egg, sometimes enriched with fat, which is firm enough to knead, roll and shape

dress 1. To pluck, draw and truss poultry or game. 2. To arrange or garnish a cooked dish

dressing 1. Sauce for a salad. 2. Stuffing for meat or poultry

drippings Fat which drips from meat, poultry or game during roasting

dumplings Small balls made of dough, forcemeat or potato mixture, which are steamed or poached. Used to garnish soups and stews.

E

en croûte Encased in pastry

entrée 1. Third course in a formal meal, following the fish course. 2. The main course

F

fines herbes Mixture of finely chopped fresh parsley, chervil, tarragon and chives

flake 1. To separate cooked fish into individual flaky silvers. 2. To grate chocolate or cheese into small slivers

flambé Flamed; e.g. food tossed in a pan to which burning brandy or other alcohol has been added

florentine Of fish and eggs; served on a bed of buttered spinach and coated with cheese sauce.

folding in Enveloping one ingredient or mixture in another, using a large metal spoon or spatula

freezing Solidifying or preserving food by chilling and storing it at 32°F (0°C) or lower

fricadelles Meatballs, made with ground pork and veal, spices, breadcrumbs, cream and egg; poached in stock or sautéed

fricassée White stew of chicken, rabbit or veal first fried in butter, then cooked in stock and finished with cream and egg yolks

fumet Concentrated broth or stock obtained from fish, meat or vegetables

G

galantine Dish of boned and stuffed poultry, game or meat glazed with aspic and served cold

garnishing Enhancing a dish with edible decorations

gelatin Transparent protein, made from animal bones and tissue, which melts in hot liquid and forms a jelly when cold

ghee Clarified butter made from the milk of the water buffalo

giblets Edible internal organs and trimmings of poultry and game, which include the liver, heart, gizzard, neck and pinions

glace de viande Meat glaze or residue in the bottom of a pan after roasting or frying meat; also, concentrated meat stock

glaze A glossy finish given to food by brushing with beaten egg, milk, sugar syrup or jelly after cooking

goujons 1. Gudgeons – small fish fried and served as a garnish. 2. Small strips of fried fish such as sole

goulash Meat and onion stew flavored with paprika

gratiné See au gratin

gravy 1. Juices exuded by roasted meat and poultry. 2. A sauce made from these juices by boiling with stock or wine, and sometimes thickened with flour

A to Z of Cooking Terms

H

hanging Suspending meat or game in a cool, dry place until it is tender

hash Dish of leftover chopped meat, potatoes or other vegetables, which are fried together

herbs Plants without a woody stem. Culinary herbs, which are available in fresh or dried form, include basil, bay leaf, chervil, marjoram, mint, oregano, parsley, rosemary, sage, savory, tarragon and thyme. Used for their aromatic properties

hors d'oeuvre Hot or cold appetizers served at the start of a meal

J

jardinière, à la Garnish of fresh, diced and cooked vegetables, arranged in separate groups

jugged Of dishes, such as jugged hare, stewed in a covered pot

jus Juices from roasting meat used as gravy

K

kebab Meat cubes marinated and broiled on a skewer

kedgeree Breakfast or lunch dish of cooked fish or meat, rice and eggs

L

lard Natural or refined pork fat

larding Threading strips of fat through lean meat, using a special needle. This prevents the meat becoming dry during roasting

M

marinade Blend of oil, wine or vinegar, herbs and spices. Used to tenderize and flavor meat or fish

marinate To steep in marinade

marinière 1. Of mussels; cooked in white wine and herbs, and served in half shells. 2. Of fish; cooked in white wine and garnished with mussels

matelote In the sailor's style; e.g. fish stew made with wine or cider

meunière In the style of a miller's wife; e.g. fish cooked in butter, seasoned, and sprinkled with parsley and lemon juice

moussaka Middle Eastern dish of ground meat, egg plant and tomatoes, which is topped with cheese sauce

mousse 1. Light sweet or savory cold dish made with cream, whipped egg white and gelatin. 2. A light hot or cold savory dish made with meat, poultry, game, fish or shellfish

N

navarin Stew of lamb and small onions and potatoes

normande, à la In the Normandy style, e.g. cooked with cider and cream

O

osso buco Dish of braised veal marrow bones prepared with tomatoes and wine

P

paella Dish of saffron rice, chicken and shellfish, which is named after the large shallow pan in which it is traditionally cooked

paprika Ground, sweet red pepper

par-boiling Boiling for a short time to cook food partially

pastry Dough made with flour, butter and water and baked or deep-fried until crisp

pâté 1. Savory mixture which is baked in a casserole or terrine, and served cold. 2. Savory mixture baked in a pastry case and served hot or cold

paupiette Thin slice of meat rolled round a savory filling

pickle To preserve meat or vegetables in brine or vinegar solution

pilaf, pilau Middle Eastern dish of cooked rice mixed with spiced, cooked meat, chicken or fish

pimiento Green or red bell pepper

pizzaiola Of meat or chicken: cooked in red wine and tomato sauce and flavored with garlic

poaching Cooking food in simmering liquid, just below boiling point

provençale In the Provence style, i.e. cooked with garlic and tomatoes

purée 1. Sieved raw or cooked food. 2. Thick vegetable soup which is passed through a sieve or an electric liquidizer

Q

quiche Open-face pastry case filled with a savory mixture

R

ragoût Stew of meat and vegetables

reducing Concentrating a liquid by boiling and evaporation

rendering 1. Slowly cooking meat tissues and trimmings to obtain fat. 2. Clearing frying fat by heating it

roasting Cooking in the oven with radiant heat, or on a spit over or under an open flame

roe 1. Milt of the male fish, called soft roe. 2. Eggs of the female fish, called hard roe. 3. Shellfish roe, called coral because of its color

roux Mixture of fat and flour which, when cooked, is used as a base for savory sauces

S

saignant Of meat; underdone

salmi Stew made by first roasting game and then cooking it in wine sauce

sauté To fry food rapidly in shallow, hot fat, tossing and turning it until evenly browned

scallop 1. Edible mollusk with white flesh. The deep fluted shell is used for serving the scallops and other foods. 2. Thin slice of meat that is beaten flat and sautéed.

scaloppine Small scallops of veal

schnitzel Veal slice; see scallop

scoring Cutting gashes or narrow grooves in the surface of food, e.g. in pork rind to produce crackling

searing Browning meat rapidly with fierce heat to seal in the juices

seasoned flour Flour flavored with salt and pepper. To 1 cup of flour, add 1 teaspoon salt and either $\frac{1}{4}$ teaspoon black pepper or $\frac{1}{2}$ teaspoon paprika

seasoning Salt, pepper, spices or herbs, which are added to food to improve flavor

simmering Cooking in liquid which is heated to just below boiling point

skimming Removing floating matter such as fat or scum from the surface of broth, jam or other liquid

smoking Curing food, such as bacon or fish, by exposing it to wood smoke for a considerable period of time

S (cont.)

soufflé Baked dish consisting of a sauce or purée, which is thickened with egg yolks into which stiffly beaten egg whites are then folded

soufflé dish Straight-sided circular dish for cooking and serving soufflés

spit Revolving skewer or metal rod on which meat, poultry or game is roasted over a fire or under a broiler

starch Carbohydrate obtained from cereal and potatoes

steaming Cooking food in the steam rising from boiling water

stewing Simmering food slowly in a covered pan or casserole

stuffing Savory mixture of bread or rice, herbs, fruit or ground meat, used to fill poultry, fish, meat and vegetables

suet Fat around beef or lamb kidneys

T

terrine 1. Earthenware pot used for cooking and serving pâté. 2. Food cooked in a terrine

timbale 1. Cup-shaped earthenware or metal mold. 2. Dish prepared in such a mold

trussing Tying a bird or roast of meat in a neat shape with skewers and/or string before cooking

V

variety meats Edible internal organs of meat, poultry and game, such as liver, kidneys, sweetbreads, brains, tripe, tongue and heart

velouté 1. Basic white sauce made with chicken, veal or fish stock 2. Soup of creamy consistency

vinaigrette Mixture of oil, vinegar, salt and pepper, which is sometimes flavored with herbs

W

whisk Looped wire utensil used to beat air into eggs, cream or batters

wiener schnitzel Veal slice cooked in the Viennese style, i.e. coated in egg and breadcrumbs, sautéed in butter and garnished with anchovies and capers

Y

yogurt Curdled milk which has been treated with harmless bacteria

Index

The Good Health Cookbooks

The Publishers wish to express their gratitude for major contributions by the following people:

Editor: URSULA WHYTE   Art Director: MICHAEL McGUINNESS   Designer: SANDRA DEON-CARDYN

Diet Consultant: MIRIAM POLUNIN   Home Economist: VALERIE BARRETT   Additional Photography: PHILIP DOWELL

Editorial Adviser: NORMA MACMILLAN

The Publishers also wish to acknowledge the help of the following:

Gilly Abrahams for editorial help; Fred and Kathie Gill for proof reading; Mary-Anne Joy for help with calorie counting;
Terri Lamb and Carol Perks for design assistance; Vicki Robinson for indexing; and Michelle Thompson for food preparation.
Additional photographic props were supplied by Graham and Green.

The Good Health Cookbooks are based on CREATIVE COOKING, **to which the following made major contributions:**

Chief Editorial Advisers: JAMES A. BEARD, ELIZABETH POMEROY, JOSÉ WILSON
Photographers: PHILIP DOWELL, ALBERT GOMMI
Home Economists: HELEN FEINGOLD, JOY MACHELL
Stylist: KATHY IMMERMAN

Writers:

Ena Bruinsma
Margaret Coombes
Derek Cooper
Margaret Costa
Denis Curtis
Theodora FitzGibbon
Nina Froud
Jane Grigson
Nesta Hollis

Kenneth H. C. Lo
Elizabeth Pomeroy
Zena Skinner
Katie Stewart
Marika Hanbury Tenison
Silvino S. Trompetto, MBE
Suzanne Wakelin
Kathie Webber
Harold Wilshaw

Artists:

Color:
Roy Coombs
Pauline Ellison
Hargrave Hands
Denys Ovenden
Charles Pickard
Josephine Ranken
Charles Raymond
Rodney Shackell
Faith Shannon, MBE
John Wilson

Black and white:
David Baird
Brian Delf
Gary Hincks
Richard Jacobs
Rodney Shackell
Michael Woods
Sidney Woods
Black and white photography:
Michael Newton

Typesetting: Tradespools Ltd, Frome   **Printing and Binding:** W. S. Cowell Ltd, Ipswich